THE SOCIAL LIVES
OF LAND

A volume in the

Cornell Series on Land: New Perspectives on Territory, Development, and Environment

Edited by Wendy Wolford, Nancy Lee Peluso, and Michael Goldman

A list of titles in this series is available at cornellpress.cornell.edu.

THE SOCIAL LIVES OF LAND

Edited by Michael Goldman,
Nancy Lee Peluso, and Wendy Wolford

CORNELL UNIVERSITY PRESS   ITHACA AND LONDON

First published 2024 by Cornell University Press

Library of Congress Cataloging-in-Publication Data

Names: Goldman, Michael, editor. | Peluso, Nancy Lee, editor. | Wolford, Wendy, editor.
Title: The social lives of land / edited by Michael Goldman, Nancy Lee Peluso, and Wendy Wolford.
Description: Ithaca : Cornell University Press, 2024. | Series: Cornell series on land: new perspectives on territory, development, and environment | Includes bibliographical references and index.
Identifiers: LCCN 2023057230 (print) | LCCN 2023057231 (ebook) | ISBN 9781501771231 (hardcover) | ISBN 9781501771248 (paperback) | ISBN 9781501771811 (epub) | ISBN 9781501771828 (pdf)
Subjects: LCSH: Land use—Social aspects. | Land tenure—Social aspects.
Classification: LCC HD111 .S635 2024 (print) | LCC HD111 (ebook) | DDC 333.73—dc23/eng/20240104
LC record available at https://lccn.loc.gov/2023057230
LC ebook record available at https://lccn.loc.gov/2023057231

Contents

Acknowledgments

The chapters in this book were first presented at a workshop on "The Social Life of Land" held at Cornell University in April 2018. We invited an eclectic group of scholars to share whatever struck them as most relevant about the diverse ways in which people lived and worked on the land. We wanted this book to offer new perspectives on how the social lives of land—with all of the energies, resources, meanings, and qualities we attribute to and utilize from the land—has historically shaped, and continues to shape, human societies.

The contributions collected here tell stories of the ways that land is experienced through a rich variety of actors, places, ideas, and relationships. This variety is a defining feature of our series, as is our commitment to focusing on land through historical, contemporary, small- and large-scale analytic lenses. We are grateful to the collection's authors for their unique contributions as well as for their patience and collaborative spirits.

We feel the result represents significant breadth and depth. Every author brings new and distinctive perspectives, which seems appropriate, given the multiplicities and inherent messiness of land's social lives. As in the series' monographs, we privilege empirically and theoretically rich work grounded in cases that have local significance and are broadly relevant. We are proud of this book and the series we have been building.

As long-time contributors of work on the social lives of land, we three editors share an interest in understanding and analyzing land's centrality to social-class formations, socioenvironmental transformations, political economies and cultural politics, nation-state building, and other colonialities. We share commitments to progressive politics of land as part of multiple understandings of commons, accessible to humans and non-humans alike. Each of us owes a debt of gratitude to an impossibly long list of scholars and colleagues on whose work we have built and continue to expand critically. We hope those authors, teachers, and mentors will recognize, forgive, and embrace our contributions to the conversations they started. It has been a privilege and a joy to work on this book, as it has been to work with every one of our manuscript authors.

We are grateful to Cornell University Press for taking a chance when we approached them with the idea of a series "on land." We worked for many years with editor Jim Lance, whose enthusiasm was infectious and helped us get the series established. We enjoyed the transition to editor Clare Jones, whose patience and calm demeanor would boost any editorial team. We would like to acknowledge and appreciate the Cornell faculty members who serve on the Cornell University Press Faculty Advisory Board. These faculty go above and beyond reading manuscripts and reviews, embracing the work with a love of knowledge production and publishing. We would also like to thank Andrew Ofstehage for his tireless work over the last few years helping to shepherd authors, editors, and this manuscript to publication. Finally, we want to express our deep gratitude to the vast community of generous and welcoming scholars and activists around the world who dedicate their lives to studying, understanding, and changing agrarian relations.

Introduction

THE SOCIAL LIVES OF LAND

Michael Goldman, Nancy Lee Peluso, and Wendy Wolford

Land is foundational to life. It is both generative of and embedded in cultural and environmental politics and political economies. The word *land* invokes landscapes, fields, forests, and mines but is also physical and philosophical—both as a whole entity and as divisible into parts, from its material components of soil particulates and microorganisms to its multiscaled territorial and commodity regimes and to other modes of claiming based on cultural politics, practices, and emotional attachments. Land is symbolic and affective whether or not it has been commodified. Land invokes strong opinions about its material nature and capacities. From some perspectives, land is sentient and agential; from others, it is objectifiable and transferable, backed by government policies that justify its transactions and transformation. Scholars past and present have researched land in all its complexities, and it remains a never-ending source of fascination and teaching. Just as stories of life often begin with land, those stories finish with the recognition that a return to the land lies at the end of human, animal, or plant lives. Land is always part of life's many possible rebirths. Land has many social lives.

Multidimensional perspectives on land have taken center stage since the turn of the twenty-first century, generating scholarly and general interest in land-related topics. Land took a back seat for several decades, while not entirely disappearing, as social theorists and practitioners chose to examine the politics and practices around natural and agrarian resources, commodifications, climate change, urban-rural relations, and food security. Yet land and its myriad social lives have come back into focus as key battlegrounds, where critical contests over access and control, natural and human crises, and extraction and production are in play. Whole journals are devoted to land. Whereas early theories about the political economy of land depended on practices, experiences, and ideas formulated in the countries and capitals of today's Europe, the majority of cases presented in this book have emerged from contributors' deep archival and field research conducted outside of Europe. Nevertheless, the effects of European interventions through colonialism, the rise and constant changes in global markets, and institutional forms of land control remain visible through their interactions with local power relations, their attempts to control, or material qualities of the land.

Much of the writing on land today is inspired by political organizing among those whose claims to the land have been violently erased or challenged. Development models originating in the West favored industrial, urban, capitalist-based economies and societies, a privilege that made rural life and livelihoods "always already" counterhegemonic and marginalized or, as commentators have noted, "awkward" (Shanin 1972), reactionary (Rostow 1960; Marx 1977), subaltern (Gramsci 1971; Guha 1983), and inefficient (Lewis 1964).

Contemporary inequalities and injustices on and over land articulate with long histories of expropriation, exclusion, and extraction (Marx 1977; Harvey 2003), giving rise to agrarian, Indigenous, and urban movements all over the world. Land-based and other concerned movements organized since the early 1990s strengthened their reach after the 1997 Asian Economic Crisis (AEC) and the 2008 global financial crisis. The AEC led to considerable economic restructuring, affecting access to land across Asia and increasing structural violence in Southeast Asian forests, rural communities, and cities. These reforms destroyed many sustainable land use practices, favored extractive regimes in rural areas, and displaced working-class communities with retractable rights to the city and its commons (Hall 2011; Rigg and Vandergeest 2012; White and Boomgaard 2017). Centers of global North capitalism, such as New York, Barcelona, Berlin, and Tokyo, are also home to the Rights to the City, Occupy, and Black Lives Matter movements. These have caused urban and rural planners to analyze the ways in which urban land arrangements (settlement, ownership, use) are shaped by past racializations, the policing of public spaces, and other consequences of changes in policy, law, and governance practices (Safransky 2017, 2020). The contradictions manifested in the tensions between movement and fixity generate fierce struggles over land.

In the three countries where the authors of this introduction work, resistance to state and corporate land occupations is longstanding. For instance, in India, for the past twenty-five years, the National Alliance of People's Movements has mobilized against large corporate and government land grabs of forests, farms, and pastures from the lowest castes, Dalits, and Indigenous (Adivasi) communities living in these resource-rich landscapes (Alka 2018). In Indonesia, activists and activist scholars, silenced under the Suharto regime (1966–1998), have since engaged agrarian actors in public, internet-friendly, and on-the-ground agrarian, urban, and labor movements (Lucas and Warren 2003; Peluso, Afiff, and Rachman 2008; McCarthy and Robinson 2016). And in Brazil, the thirty-seven-year-old Movement of Landless Workers continues to fight for access to land, collective production, food sovereignty, agroecology, and gender equality (Stronzake and Wolford 2016). During the COVID-19 pandemic, movement members distributed food baskets to the rural and urban underserved people whose access had been negatively affected by disruptions in the long supply chains characterizing the global food system (Wolford 2021). Movements and movement organizing in these countries continue to inspire the authors and illuminate the political stakes of working on the social lives of land.

Other Indigenous, peasant, smallholder, and communal lands have been caught up in new forms of class struggle that include concerns over racialized, gendered, and generational differences. Glen Coulthard, author of *Red Skin, White Masks: Rejecting the Colonial Politics of Recognition* (2014) and member of the Dene tribe of Canada, explained his approach: "I'm situating class struggle alongside, in a more thorough way, the anticolonial efforts of Indigenous peoples that are often grounded in a defense of land and a way of life" (Coulthard 2015). He is speaking of a North American-wide movement, Idle No More, that, since 2012, has been "led by women and with a call for refounded nation-to-nation relations based on mutual respect. Idle No More rapidly grew into an inclusive, continent-wide network of urban and rural Indigenous people working hand-in-hand with non-Indigenous allies to build a movement for Indigenous rights and the protection of land, water, and sky" (Idle No More 2021). The challenge he posits reflects movements globally, some of which include women leaders, as in Bangladesh, Myanmar, Indonesia, Kenya, Tanzania, Guatemala, and Hawaii.

Our book engages with these new articulations of land politics as our authors rethink conventional wisdom on social-land-environment-commodity connections. The book's twenty contributors come to the topic of land from a variety of disciplines and interdisciplinary fields across the social sciences and humanities. All demonstrate the importance of historical perspectives for understanding the crises of land in the contemporary moment, wherever in the world they work. Insights gained from their experiences as researchers and scholars help them to explore the material conditions, philosophies, historical geographies, and socioenvironmental contexts that shape and are shaped by the land. The book starts with Robert Nichols' discussion of British and Scottish philosophers who were forced to take account of land questions as their kings and queens engaged them in settler colonial projects in the Americas. It closes with Kirsteen Shields' narrative on a contemporary movement in Scotland striving to transform private property land tracts into new sorts of commonly held property. Along the way, chapter authors focus on the social lives of land playing out through practices, institutions, and ideas of property, territory, environment, and development, as they are forged in practice in Liberia, Tanzania, the Ecuadorian Amazon, Transylvania, First Nations territories of Canada, the Cherokee Nation, Indonesia, India, Mozambique, Cambodia, Singapore, Brazil, and the US Midwest. Although many different themes crosscut our collection, we highlight three below: unsettled territories, materialities and mobilities, and speculative transformations. Each of these themes reflects some of the most pressing debates and conflicts concerning land as we write in 2021.

Unsettled Territories

Territory-making and human settlement are partly tied together by the contestations the two localized but broad processes generate (Winichakul 1994; Sassen 2008; Elden 2013). Territories are claimed spaces emerging from not only spatialized power relations imposed by governing authorities (e.g., Vandergeest and Peluso 1995) but also from on-the-ground practices, formalized and informal property relations, and conflicts over access to land, which Hall, Hirsch, and Li (2011) call "powers of exclusion" (e.g., Dwyer 2015). The politicization of territory as both a concept and a means of control has long led to the transformation of settlements. This is true whether we are referring to urban, rural, or unincorporated areas where people live and work or to created resource or socionatural territories defined as forests, riparian areas, air spaces, and oceans where human presence has been rendered minimal by restrictive policies and surveillance. Many colonial contests have been sites of conflict over different conceptions of territory and opposing land claims (e.g., Li 1999; Sikor and Lund 2009; Peluso and Lund 2011; Carroll 2015).

Settler colonialism has recently reemerged as an important analytical tool and strategy for understanding modern global transformations, including the losses of Indigenous territories to new settlements around the world. From the fifteenth century at least, the colonial conquest of territory led to extensive and permanent European settlement in many regions and concurrent resource, labor, and energy extraction in those settlement areas or elsewhere (Wolf 1982). Not all new colonists were elite settlers holding land grants overseen by resident governing authorities; some was accomplished through the cooptation of local leaders.

Further, colonial exploitation and territorial "improvements" often involved the forced movement of slave, indentured, and other coerced or contracted laborers. Mahmood Mamdani (1996) famously interpreted varied forms of colonial rule as "centralized and decentralized despotism," also connecting the varied ways that commodifying production on and of land was brutal for all but the few. Settler colonialism became one of the more complicated manifestations of long-distance European rule, as it rapaciously extracted with one hand while enabling foreign settlers to claim land and make new homes with the other. The chapters in this section highlight the ways in which Indigenous and other settlements shaped and were shaped by their colonial experiences, past and present, as life on the land changed demonstrably around the world.

In "Colonization and the Recoding of Land in Classical Political Economy," Robert Nichols deepens our understanding of settler colonialism by asking what the designers and promoters of colonization desired from making land into territory and property and how they constructed the rationale and logic for territorial acquisition and transformation. He notes that leading eighteenth- and nineteenth-century philosophers pondering questions of land, value, and wealth production and accumulation did not originally see the value of land acquisition for the making of a robust national economy. On the contrary, it was not the land itself but what was produced on the land that mattered. The concept of land as territory underwent a significant recoding by English writers from 1776 to 1848, from Adam Smith to John Stuart Mill, reflecting the shifting fortunes and ambitions of settler colonization. Colonial conquest in North America, Australia, and New Zealand inspired the perspective that capitalism and colonization as a means of claiming and controlling land were commensurable and mutually reinforcing—the job of political economy, therefore, was to unite them. Nichols vividly demonstrates how this "intellectual and political pivot" helps to explain "the mercurial history of colonization in its imbrications with the social life of land."

Here starts a global journey derived from a seventeenth-century English ideology that privileged small-scale landholdings based on the logic of land as property to be acquired and improved (see also Williams 1973) alongside a stream of utopian egalitarian thought that challenged the prevailing forces of feudalism while doubling as a justification for foreign land conquest. Nichols demonstrates how the intellectual, political, and social lives of land were actively remade by processes of colonization and discursive validation. This moment provides a useful point of departure for this section on unsettled territories, the gateway into other contemporary themes on the social lives of land.

Clint Carroll picks up on these same themes in his chapter on the layered history of the Cherokee Nation's relations with land within the context of violent

US settler colonialism. Carroll's chapter, "Shaping New Homelands: Colonial Politics of Land Relations and Management in the Cherokee Nation," highlights the variety of ways in which Cherokee tribes managed the bounty of their lands before the arrival of bureaucratic rule by the US state. Carroll shows how a land management system without fences but with the careful use of fire to make boundaries and territorial claims was disrupted by formal mandates. These included, for example, those spelled out in political treaties and imposed by newly designated US government oversight agencies, as well as by Cherokee practices, such as theft. These formal and informal mandates and practices stripped Indigenous nations of their land and stripped the land of its biodiversity, undermining Cherokee livelihoods based on hunting and gathering as well as medicinal practices rooted in a once-rich botanical landscape. In his overview of these historical relations between Indigenous peoples and their land, Carroll highlights the relevance of internal differences within the Cherokee nation and argues for seeing Indigenous communities holistically, in all of their complexity. Based on the collective expertise of tribal elders and Cherokee knowledge holders, Carroll describes the tribe's recent accomplishments in reorienting land use and management. These efforts are galvanizing the Cherokee Nation to take back control of their land and revitalize fragmented Cherokee communities.

In "'I am Waorani': Between Indigenous and Settler Land Ontologies in the Ecuadorian Amazon," coauthors Kati Álvarez, Ciara Wirth, Gabriela Valdivia, and Flora Lu challenge the settler colonialism analytics of foreign settler/Indigenous displaced. Recurring yet altered practices of settler colonialism in the Americas are at the heart of this chapter. Amazonian land settlement has a volatile and sordid history that does not strictly align with the common binary of the noble forest dweller and the foreign colonizer. In the late 1800s, forest dwellers all over the Amazon were chased out, often enslaved, if not killed, by industrial rubber extractors. In the twentieth century, the Ecuadorian state appropriated large blocks of land from original communities and gave these as concessions to oil companies and to Catholic and evangelical Protestant missions practicing occupation for conversion, leading to evictions of Indigenous peoples. More recently, agricultural settlement has been led by displaced Indigenous Andean peoples and other Ecuadorians seeking land and better futures in the "emptied" space that constitutes the Amazon River Basin.

The authors focus on the Waorani in the Ecuadorian Amazon to demonstrate that settler logic and practices "have redrawn not only how Waorani live on the land, but also how they self-identify and recognize family members separated by settlement practices." Mainstream media reproduce the settler-Indigenous binary via narratives that depict the Waorani as a culturally violent people, depicting an ongoing feud between "settled Waorani"—those who consented to settlement and recognize themselves as Ecuadorians—and "Waorani in voluntary isolation"—those who have not. In contrast to these simplified and ahistorical representations of the Waorani, this chapter presents the voices of the settled (Ecuadorian) Waorani as they encounter the Waorani in voluntary isolation. They trace the nuanced ways in which those who reject settler logic are increasingly pushed into more fragmented and deforested landscapes. This then throws into question the humanity and epistemic positionalities of settled Waorani. At the same time, the existence and presence of Waorani in voluntary isolation are misrepresented, even negated, by the Ecuadorian state, which sees them as potential challenges to the legitimacy of state investments in oil extraction.

Building on the theme of indigeneity and land dynamics, in "What is Land? Ontology, Practice, and Indeterminacy," Paul Nadasdy presents a nuanced appreciation of the representations by others of Indigenous communities and their relations with land. He sees land's social lives as articulated through culturally varied human relations, including the ways they engage with other-than-human actors on the land. As Nadasdy argues, "land can be a powerful actor in its own right. It can enter into social relations with humans, including relations of kinship. Like humans, land can provide care, demand respect, and mete out punishment. From such a perspective, it is even possible to view land itself as an owning subject, reversing the usual relations of ownership." Drawing on his research with Indigenous people in Canada's Yukon, he asks readers to reconsider dominant theorizations of land by acknowledging the multiple alternative meanings and experiences of Indigenous and non-Indigenous peoples living among hybrid socionatures. He accomplishes this without homogenizing perspectives on these animate worlds or imposing universal claims upon them, instead offering a compelling perspective on the idea of indeterminacy in the social lives of land.

In the last chapter of this section, "The Autobiography of a Transylvanian Land Parcel: From Late Feudalism to Postsocialism," Katherine Verdery transports us into the social lives of a single parcel of land through the telling of its history of settlement and its territorializations under colonizing feudal, communist, and capitalist occupations. By letting a parcel tell its own life story, Verdery foregrounds the experiences of land under different overseers, owners, laborers, and property regimes. With artistry and humor, she uses her indepth, decades-long fieldwork experience and historical research to demonstrate how new economic and political formations and new arrangements of people/settlements on the land have affected the sociality and territorialities emergent through the uses of a single parcel of land.

According to the parcel through which she speaks, land has been a vehicle for people to connect with others within and across different time periods, each governed under different political economic regimes and affected by myriad land use and control practices. Verdery illustrates how the land changes and its social lives adapt, as lives and land-based livelihoods transform under disparate political economies. From communitarianism to feudalism to communism and capitalism, the land parcel contributes to different beneficiaries of wealth production and social reproduction. At times, human practices cause the land to suffer from exhaustion, depletion, neglect, and indifference. In other moments, land enables humans' survival and conviviality. As neoliberal capitalism marches forward, the value of land in society shifts: people strive to become liberated from the onus of protecting "their" land through its conversion into an alienable commodity. In light of the parcel's historical socialities, Verdery and her introspective and worldly land parcel subsequently ask us to wonder about the deeper implications of such forms of liberation and freedom.

Materialities of Life on the Land

The second section addresses a theme that runs through all of the chapters in the book but is particularly clear in the chapters included here: the materialities of life on the land and the ways in which land and its uses are both fixed (or located) and yet always in motion. We define materiality in its most expansive sense to mean a focus on the tangible conditions of everyday life, particularly oriented to production and social reproduction on and of the land. Quoting Laura Schoenberger from this book, land in this sense is "both form and process." She shows that land is fixed in place, except when it is sand that is relocated to other countries as building material. Land is also in movement even when it "sits in place," being constituted by the movement of millions of particles, plants, pests, and people. All work furiously to stake claims to the land and, in so doing, move over and through it in ways that question land's apparent fixity.

In thinking through the importance of materiality in relation to land, one contemporary process of clear relevance is the rise of large-scale land acquisitions across the globe in the first decade of the twenty-first century. Dubbed the "Global Land Grab," these were not new for students of colonial history. Rather, they were newly enacted by a host of actors who assembled millions of hectares of land for investment. Most of these land deals were associated directly or indirectly with national states' policies and practices, mimicking classic colonial modes of grabbing; others engaged in corporate financing and alliances with states in completely different sorts of governing and extractive arrangements. They drew on discourses of productivity, sustainability, and do-gooding (feeding the world) that recalled the worst of extractive colonial conquests and territorial occupations across the

Americas and South and Southeast Asia in the eighteenth and nineteenth centuries and the "scramble for Africa" of a century ago (Wolf 1982; Moyo, Jha, and Yeros 2019). Verifiable estimates are difficult to obtain, but, by all accounts, corporations, sovereign wealth and private equity funds, and nation-states grabbed tens of millions of hectares of farmland in the first two decades of the twenty-first century to corporatize food, fodder, and fuel production (Chung 2019) and much more land was appropriated in the name of biodiversity conservation, climate mitigation, watershed protection, and urbanization (Yang and He 2021). Entirely new markets sprang up dedicated to producing, investing in, and trading this land, as Madeleine Fairbairn illustrates in her Cornell Series on Land book, *Fields of Gold: Financing the Global Land Rush* (2020).

The material processes of claiming land are implicated in broader dynamics of state formation and social, economic, and ecological configuration (Borras Jr. et al. 2011; Hall 2011; Wolford et al. 2013). The territorializing dimensions of state land grabbing are often hidden in its acquisition of land for environmental protection, forestry, and resettlement programs (Vandergeest and Peluso 2006a, 2006b). Formalization of private property rights, the growth of state authority through territorial expansion, and the sedentarization (or "villagization") of mobile peoples are often part of these efforts, bringing together processes of land enclosure, labor force formation, and inequitable land management (Makki 2014, 2018; Kelly and Peluso 2015).

For some, the drive to acquire and aggregate land today reflects a dominant characteristic of the modern era: life on the land for the past five centuries has been shaped by plantation, with its racialized regimes of forced labor, extraction, and lived experiences. Scholars see these land-based agrofactories generating export crop booms characterized by single-crop expanses of land controlled by multinational behemoths (often vertically integrated with grocery store chains) or national state authorities (Hall 2013). Rob Cramb and James McCarthy (2016) have written about the extensive corporate and state plantation territories straddling the Malaysian-Indonesian borderlands as the "Oil Palm Complex," a moniker that references land use, land cover, and the nature of land claims, all highly complex. Some call this five-century epoch the Plantationocene to capture the spatial, temporal, and violent social lives of the land that plantations and concessions have wrought throughout: a territorialized aspect of extraction that began with the so-called Age of Exploration and continues to the present age of speculation, colonizing science and natures along the way (Wolford 2021). Plantations figure prominently in the chapters by Gregg Mitman, Wendy Wolford, Nancy Peluso, and Andrew Ofstehage, and the ideology of plantations as the ideal expression of rational, productive nature runs throughout the collection.

The materialities of land and its social relations change, shaped by values, meanings, and the practices of extraction, production, and preservation that have preceded land located in specific times and places. In this section, then, authors contend that the materialities of land—its substance, ecologies, and production relations—matter. Contributors explore the mutual constitution of meanings and materialities necessary to understanding the social and environmental lives of land. They highlight the importance of studying how power and hierarchical social relations infuse access to the land, from laboring to landscape making. In unpacking land's materialities, as we describe below, they provide insight into the relationships between the biophysicality of land and its social lives.

The first chapter in this section, by Laura Schoenberger, focuses on sand that is dredged and excavated from Cambodia and physically carted off to Singapore, where it undergoes a series of highly industrialized transformations in order to become solid land. She argues that an emphasis on land's materialities enables us to see the "multiple ontologies of sand," with its shifting temporalities and forms—from the desiccated materials making a riverbed in Cambodia to a cement boardwalk in Singapore. Schoenberger's focus is on "modified landscapes"— landscapes that are reclaimed, constructed, and rebuilt from one location to another. The focus here is on the knowledge that brings these different ontologies to life, as well as the assemblage of technologies required to enact these varied sand-based landscapes. Schoenberger embeds her analysis within critical historical materialism, paying close attention to the unequal production of values within Cambodia and between countries. She highlights the techniques that sand grabbers use to cart their substance away without notice, evocative of Marshall Berman's suggestion that "all that is solid melts into air." When social movement activists finally realize that their land—in small, water-bound fragments—is being taken from under their feet, they begin to mobilize by situating the sand-land grabbing in a longer history of elite dealmaking in Cambodia and Singapore.

Andrew Ofstehage's chapter focuses on a similarly effervescent materiality in another region of the world and with different implications. He outlines the discursive power that presents land as waste, showing how such a definition affects land's value and valuation when matched with the masculinist discourse of agricultural yield growth that circulates across national boundaries. US Midwest farmers migrate to Brazil's Cerrado to take advantage of cheap land to re-create the dying art of large-scale soy production; by cutting down the low-growth forest, they produce the category of wasteland necessary for new forms of value accumulation. While Ofstehage focuses on the social relations and narratives of waste that enable the farmers' access to extensive tracts of Brazil's land, he also considers relations between biological and physical natures that make

Cerrado land unique: their "nematodes, rhizomes, and earthworms on the one hand and water, soil, and chemical reactions on the other." Young, white capitalist farmers transform this land into something they see as more productive by creating monocultures for export, augmenting or replacing the local soils, and imagining themselves as pioneers. They see their efforts as improvement, mobilizing the age-old trope of colonialists (Williams 1973). In Ofstehage's ethnographic analysis, soil is as multiple as the sand in Schoenberger's analysis, simultaneously material, mobile, and meaningful, carrying with it the hopes of a new generation of settler colonists, even as it sweeps the region clear of other alternative forms of agriculture and society.

In "Mobile Labor, Shifting Land Regimes, and Social Reproduction in East Java, Indonesia," Nancy Peluso brings mobility together with materiality, focusing on landless mobile laborers, their search for work, and their class positions as dependents in relation to landholders at the center of upland Java's agrarian history. The paper begins and ends with the stories of two low-income, proletarian women's transnational labor experiences whose mobile work has changed the fates of their plantation-based families. Remittances these women sent from their work sites in Hong Kong have enabled both their natal and nuclear families to move off the plantations where more than three generations of their extended families have worked, buy land off the plantations for housing, and invest small amounts of capital in livestock and the forest where they now grow elephant grass to feed them. They have transformed this montane agrarian environment through labor conducted abroad. Using oral histories and in-depth interviews collected during extensive fieldwork, in concert with archival and secondary sources, Peluso then demonstrates how mobile labor and land relations have been locally reproduced through a class-like relationship common to three land regimes in East Java's mobile uplands: peasant/smallholder agriculture, private coffee and tea plantations, and a state-run forest plantation. Each of these grew out of migrations into the uplands over two centuries. The contemporary moment, characterized by transnational and transinsular circular labor migration, is thus understood as part of a longer trajectory of land-mobile labor-class relations. The focus on dependent laborers and their social reproduction in the uplands adds a new dimension—labor mobilities—to classic understandings of Java's rural populace as settled and tied to place. It also recognizes the ways laborers and smallholders have made territory under varied agrarian regimes and forms of colonial and postcolonial control. The study thus addresses the agrarian question of labor raised by Bernstein (2004), specifically in the uplands of Java.

Wendy Wolford's chapter, "'Incompatible with a Progressive Agriculture': The Role of Manioc in Colonial and Postcolonial Visions for Land and Labor in Mozambique," focuses on the materiality of a crop that played an outsized but underappreciated role in the history of colonial and postcolonial Mozambique. In their search for tropical export commodities throughout the twentieth century, the Portuguese neglected manioc, seeing it as a "native" crop, one whose properties echoed the material nature of the natives themselves: fast propagating, widespread, and lacking essential forms of value. Although it provided sustenance for laborers, manioc was given little attention by the colonial research office, where agronomists and bureaucrats alike concentrated instead on their most important export crop, cotton. Ultimately, Wolford writes, "the history of manioc in the country is thus a history of empire itself." It is a story "of naturalizing and neglecting local crops and people in an attempt to bend both to the service of tropical commodities for the global market." In the past decade, new plans for manioc in the postcolony have developed, marrying manioc to the market through new, standardized cultivation practices and new markets for manioc-derived beer. Wolford argues that these plans turn on a new naturalization of the Mozambican farmer as entrepreneur and landowner and manioc as a market commodity. In both colonial and postcolonial times, the materialities of land, crops, and humans disrupt the official narrative and intended plans.

In the final chapter of this section, "'Sitting on Old Mats to Plait New': The Gendered Struggle over Land and Livelihood in Liberia," Gregg Mitman and Emmanuel King Urey interweave past with present to articulate ongoing struggles over land in Liberia. They historicize the context in which a surge of land grabs by foreign investors has taken place across sub-Saharan Africa, which they describe as the latest form of colonialism. Settler colonialism manifested in Liberia in an unusual way, as freed slaves escaping from the racisms of a settler colonial grip of a young United States traveled to West Africa to found a new colony. No longer enslaved, these settlers arrived by ship and founded the new nation of Liberia in the nineteenth century. Mitman and Urey traverse the historical political economies of colonial land use, settlement, and claiming—first in plantations producing coffee and tree stocks for export, then through the plantation production of industrial rubber in Liberia for tires back in the United States. Illuminated by voices and memories of contemporary Liberians enduring waves of state and corporate land grabs and dispossessions, the chapter asks what is new and what persists from earlier eras of troubled settlement. By emphasizing the enduring racialized and gendered logics of these settler colonialism waves, Mitman and Urey uncover the multiple materialities of history and society in Liberian land. Even while the government offers new land-based mineral concessions to multinational firms for timber, agriculture, and mining, the vibrant post-Civil War politics have produced a new Land Rights Law and call for reparations and protection of customary rights to devolve authority over land rights to villages, intending to reinvigorate rural life and livelihoods.

To say that land is material calls up images of sifting through the soil with your hands or seeing giant excavators tear into the land. Throughout the book, we call attention to the materiality of land as a way of liberating the land from a fixation on the ground. We trace the materiality of land through different substances, meanings, and values as well as through that which land allows: settlement, property, identity, territory, progress, and more. This material life of land is infinitely more mobile than we tend to think. Land is not fixed in place or time. Rather, land is always becoming something new, emerging, and giving shape to our aspirations even as it is stamped with the legacies and memories of a thousand generations. Attention to both materiality and mobility results in an appreciation of sedimented as well as chaotic multiplicities.

Speculative Transformations

Part III highlights the idea of speculative transformation, utilizing two connotations of the word *speculative*. One involves speculation by partaking in high-risk ventures to sell rather than own land—and watch one's investment depreciate over time. The other engages speculation by creating future imaginaries, as is true in speculative (utopian/radical) politics. The first two chapters here emphasize two trends in the global economy today: the conversion of land into tradeable assets (i.e., its assetization) and the global impetus to make cities attractive to finance capital through the discursive practices of "speculative urbanism." Pursuing an alternative notion of speculative transformation, the latter two chapters shift from the economic to the political. One features historical tensions between the speculative politics of emancipation and land redistribution, and the other challenges the unequal and often violent processes of liberalization and elite class control with a speculative form of radically democratic land use.

Although finance has always played a pivotal role in the *longue durée* of colonial-capitalist expansion, the 1990s mark a palpable resurgence of finance's power in the accumulation process. As larger percentages of corporate profits accumulate through financial institutions rather than from trade and commodity production, the power of finance—and financialization—increases within the economy and society (Krippner 2005, 174; Moreno 2018). Land has become a form of currency used as collateral by governments in order to borrow capital, for instance, to modernize urban infrastructure and housing or, in many cases, just to maintain the basic public provisions for urban living.

Hence, capital tends to switch from the more tangible economy of goods and service production to a land-assetization economy in which financial actors worldwide participate in land transactions globally. Swyngedouw and Ward's and Goldman's chapters (this book) explain how David Harvey's thesis of accumulation by dispossession can be nuanced to better interpret these volatile land practices, specifically in "the mobilization of land as a financial asset" (Kaika and Ruggiero 2015). Though materiality and territoriality certainly play a role in the speculative translation of land's value, land becomes a financial asset in much more different ways than as noted in the book's first section on territorial expansion.

When governments embrace the prevailing discourse of global urbanism based on high-risk borrowing of finance capital for state-of-the-art infrastructure, they put a new spin on the idea of urbanization as a development policy to solve worsening problems of social inequity and environmental vulnerability. In practice, building major infrastructure for global cities requires large land gifts from nation-states as incentives for capitalists to invest (Roy and Ong 2011; Goldman 2020). This global policy shift, backed by international financial institutions, aims to increase land's value as well as the value of a city's assets to global financiers (Zoomers et al. 2017). In many of the rural peripheries of expanding cities of the global South, this policy effectively expels nonelites from rural lands, a cruel commitment that Indigenous land activists call the recolonization of land (Estes 2019; Goldman, this book). These rural land relations have become achievable through brutal, structural, and epistemic violence (Peluso and Watts 2001; Nixon 2011; Guardiola-Rivera 2017).

In the section's first chapter, "Producing Assets: The Social Strife of Land," Erik Swyngedouw and Callum Ward argue that speculation is crucial to understanding the social lives—and strife—of land today. They analyze how land is assetized so that its future value can travel far in financial portfolios while concurrently remaining in place, often as a debt burden to the landholder. This mysterious process of land transformation, a phenomenon of the twenty-first century, generates what they call an "asset-class struggle" that can only thrive with the help of political and state-class actors who creatively realign laws, regulations, and social power to support such inventive but dangerous class-based, liquid-asset market opportunities.

The puzzle is partially revealed by their attention to the interscalar or what occurs beyond the single plot of land and its captured rent. Classical political economists such as Ricardo and Smith once explained rent in terms of supply and demand as valued by a specific parcel of land's unique characteristics. By contrast, Swyngedouw and Ward argue that under twenty-first-century financial capitalism, land can be mobilized as a financial asset beyond its common use for reproduction (e.g., housing) or exploitation (e.g., mining). It becomes assetized when landlords—as a class—engage in political and social struggles to remake the institutional order to satisfy the needs of finance capital. Thus, they argue rent should be understood not as a pure artifact of a parcel of land but as a result of the parcelization of land across boundaries and the ability of the landlord class and those in charge of finance capital to convert land into a liquid asset according to their own contrived rules and regulations. In this way, the top 1 percent has replaced the kings and queens who financed colonial voyages in search of new land hundreds of years ago.

In "The Financialized and Dispossessed: Transforming Land and Lives into Speculative Assets," Michael Goldman elaborates upon Swyngedouw and Ward's argument with questions about the ongoing transformation of the midsized city of Bengaluru (once known as Bangalore) into a global city. For example, he asks (this book): "How does fertile farmland purchased for global-city dreams become so profitable for investors (including Wall Street's) even though much of it remains vacant or unfinished—neither a site of world-class infrastructure nor the once-vibrant agrarian economy it displaced?" This chapter highlights the relational and interscalar dimensions of land transformation, noting that international finance institutions and consultants, such as the World Bank and McKinsey Global, play key roles in promoting policies for states to borrow from international capital markets for urban infrastructure. This requires working closely with national-level officials to support these expectations that cities will borrow internationally and shoulder the full burden of risk. Liberalized, cash-scarce cities fall into the difficult position of borrowing expensive capital to build speculatively in hopes that the deal pays off and will stimulate the local economy and fill the city coffers. Often written into the contract to build new airports, IT-BioTech campuses, light-rail systems, luxury apartment complexes, and shopping malls, however, is the obligation of governments to acquire land with which investors can speculate (and offset their risk of investing). These deals have triggered displacement and ill-compensation for many small landholders. In India, over the past few decades, rural dispossession has become the basis for urban financialization. Rather than land becoming generative based on its own characteristics (e.g., soil vitality, ecosystemic location, knowledge, and labor inputs), urban and rural lands alike become wealth-generating financial tools for elites.

The next two chapters pivot to the important question of how land can be rearticulated as a sociocultural and community-based source for life and livelihood. In "People, Livelihoods, and Contested Meanings of Land in Tanzania," Emmanuel Sulle and Richard Mbunda start with the aspirations of President Nyerere's 1960s vision of *Ujamaa* (which means "familyhood" in Swahili) for newly independent Tanzania. This vision outlined a postcolonial focus on land as the source of human life and an essential source of national wealth that should not be left to an elite class to control. The idea that forming a classless society is the most appropriate social relation to nurture and utilize land's wealth became the basis for an ambitious and empowering postcolonial land agenda. Sulle and Mbunda trace the evolution of official land policy and unofficial land practices, from colonialism to Ujamaa to neoliberalism, to help explain how the social relations of land might return from highly speculative and expropriative to the Nyerere's vision of land as sustenance for all. In tracing Tanzania's land policies across these different regimes, they conclude that the overlapping attempts to create a universal land tenure regime for individual ownership and exploitation have left crippling scars on the ecological and social lives of land. Starting with British rule, in which the Ministry of Lands had full authority to limit customary rights for local communities, to today's Land (1999), Forest (2002), and Wildlife Conservation (2009) Acts, these state practices consistently fail to recognize and strengthen community land rights and instead encourage large-scale land acquisition and exploitation. Most recently, the 2008 Mortgage Financing Act legalized the use of land as collateral, a key enticement for foreign investors to set speculative norms and financialized practices, further alienating communities from their land-protective practices.

Sulle and Mbunda also demonstrate how the largest and most recent land grabs—supported by major international banks and development agencies— have not succeeded in producing the wealth anticipated by investors but rather greater volatility in the region. As the major Southern Agricultural Growth Corridor of Tanzania corridor encompasses one-third of the country's land mass, these land grabs have sparked nationwide protest, critique, and alternative politics around land use and tenure.

The final chapter, "Dances with Lairds: Lessons from Scottish Land Reform" by Kirsteen Shields, highlights a dramatic change in land governance in parts of Scotland, the birthplace of the seventeenth-century politics of enclosing the commons. Amidst deepening political turmoil around the idea of the nation-state in the twenty-first century, specifically Brexit and Scottish, Welsh, and Irish movements to secede from the UK, land lies at the heart of a rising political consciousness among the Scots. More than half the country's rural land is owned by a small group of families, the most concentrated pattern of land ownership in Europe. Shields traces the emergence of a radical "community land vision" from a diverse set of actors to rethink the variety of community land projects surfacing around the world. She notes that some of these visions, however, fail to consider the racialized history of property law, how community land trusts mitigate rather than reverse land consolidation and exclusion, and how some alternatives fail to confront head-on the power asymmetries embedded in land distribution and redistribution.

Shields concludes that in sharp contrast to property advocates who rely on the rights of the individual, this radical discourse of collective ownership taps into a newly angled human rights perspective that promotes economic, social, and cultural rights as collective rights. Land activists and human rights activists are aligning, she argues, to "topple hierarchies" and to challenge the notion of property rights as understood within the rule of law of the nation-state. Shields shows how movements in Scotland—and beyond—work with smallholders and food-sovereignty movements to rearticulate social relations to land and to each other in efforts to create a more ecological and just vision of the social lives of land.

A Final Word: This Collection and Beyond

This collection speaks to the gendered, racialized, classed, caste, and generational dynamics of land across changing territories and environments; it thus speaks to the core interests of the Cornell Series on Land. Monographs in the series have built on decades of research on agrarian and urban questions and extending these questions into new spaces and politics. This series has published books examining the reasons communal Indigenous land titles have not been able to reverse centuries of land dispossession in Bolivia (Anthias 2018), land's role in violent state formation in Colombia (Ballvé 2020), financialization and control of land in Brazilian fields and New York boardrooms (Fairbairn 2020), spotty land reform attempts in the midst of rampant land speculation in Cambodia (Beban 2021), gendered reclaiming politics in rural commons in Morocco (Rignall 2021), the commodification of city and country as interpreted through the Polanyian notion of land fictions (Ghertner and Lake 2021), and climate crisis and speculative modes of its mitigation in Bangladesh (Paprocki 2021).

The present edited collection can be read as a challenge to expand further our understandings of land through its many social and socionatural lives. Our contributing authors have demonstrated that questions related to the meaning and future of land have taken on new urgency in the current historical moment, shaped by their place-specific and broader global social histories. Land has become a central component in most new policies to intensify the production of energy, food, and other natural resources; it also remains a primary and contested object of globalized and national speculation, expropriation, and territory-making.

We hope this book will stimulate further interest in examining the massive changes in our perceptions, speculations, and analyses of land beyond where we have tread here. Land's social lives are profoundly affected by ongoing changes in both political and biophysical climates. Though the manifestations and impacts vary, sea-level rise submerging Pacific Islands and coastal shores, warm winter days in Minnesota, the burning of thousand-year-old sequoias, and floods or pandemics with hundred-year cycles also unsettle territorial claims, remake land's materialities and workers' mobilities, and confound capital and governing authorities' capacities to speculate on what lies ahead for lands' myriad social lives. It is these and other large- and small-scale changes to which we hope readers will contribute, demonstrating that land's social lives are tied to environmental and nonhuman worlds in ever-expanding ways.

REFERENCES

Alka, P. 2018. "'Wither the People's Movements in India?' The Case of National Alliance of People's Movement." *International Journal of Research in Social Sciences* 8 (3): 835–853.

Anthias, P. 2018. *Limits to Decolonization: Indigeneity, Territory, and Hydrocarbon Politics in the Bolivian Chaco*. Ithaca: Cornell University Press.

Ballvé, T. 2020. *The Frontier Effect: State Formation and Violence in Colombia*. Ithaca: Cornell University Press.

Beban, A. 2021. *Unwritten Rule: State-Making through Land Reform in Cambodia*. Ithaca: Cornell University Press.

Bernstein, H. 2004. "'Changing Before Our Very Eyes': Agrarian Questions and the Politics of Land in Capitalism Today." *Journal of Agrarian Change* 4 (1–2): 190–225.

Borras Jr., S. M., R. Hall, I. Scoones, B. White, and W. Wolford. 2011. "Towards a Better Understanding of Global Land Grabbing: An Editorial Introduction." *Journal of Peasant Studies* 38 (2): 209–216.

Carroll, C. 2015. *Roots of Our Renewal: Ethnobotany and Cherokee Environmental Governance*. Minneapolis: University of Minnesota Press.

Chung, Y. B. 2019. "The Grass Beneath: Conservation, Agro-Industrialization, and Land-Water Enclosures in Postcolonial Tanzania." *Annals of the American Association of Geographers* 109 (1): 1–17.

Coulthard, G. S. 2014. *Red Skin, White Masks: Rejecting the Colonial Politics of Recognition*. Minneapolis: University of Minnesota Press.

Coulthard, G. S. 2015. "The Colonialism of the Present: An Interview with Glen Coulthard." By A. B. Epstein. *Jacobin*. https://www.jacobinmag.com/2015/01/indigenous-left-glen-coulthard-interview/

Cramb, R., and J. F. McCarthy, eds. 2016. *The Oil Palm Complex: Smallholders, Agribusiness and the State in Indonesia and Malaysia*. Singapore: NUS Press.

Dwyer, M. 2015. "The Formalization Fix? Land Titling, Land Concessions, and the Politics of Spatial Transparency in Cambodia." *The Journal of Peasant Studies* 42 (5): 903–928.

Elden, S. 2013. *The Birth of Territory*. Chicago: University of Chicago Press.

Estes, N. 2019. *Our History Is the Future: Standing Rock Versus the Dakota Access Pipeline, and the Long Tradition of Indigenous Resistance*. London: Verso Books.

Fairbairn, M. 2020. *Fields of Gold: Financing the Global Land Rush*. Ithaca: Cornell University Press.

Ghertner, D. A., and R. W. Lake. 2021. *Land Fictions: The Commodification of Land in City and Country*. Ithaca: Cornell University Press.

Goldman, M. 2020. "Dispossession by Financialization: The Making of a Land Market and the End(s) of Rurality." *The Journal of Peasant Studies* 47 (6): 1251–1277.

Gramsci, A. 1971. *Prison Notebooks: Selected Writings*. London: Lawrence and Wishart.

Guardiola-Rivera, O. 2017. "Concerning Violence, Part II: Fanon and the Intelligent Machine: Reflections from a Conversation with Gayatri Chakravorty Spivak." *Discourse* 39(2): 177–194.

Guha, R. 1983. *Elementary Aspects of Peasant Insurgency in Colonial India*. Durham, NC: Duke University Press

Hall, D. 2011. "Where the Streets Are Paved with Prawns: Crop Booms and Migration in Southeast Asia." *Critical Asian Studies* 43 (4): 507–530.

Hall, D. 2013. *Land*. Cambridge, UK: Polity Press.

Hall, D., P. Hirsch, and T. Li. 2011. *Powers of Exclusion: Land Dilemmas in Southeast Asia*. Singapore: National University of Singapore Press.

Harvey, D. 2003. *The New Imperialism: Accumulation by Dispossession*. Clarendon Lectures in Geography and Environmental Studies. Oxford, UK: Oxford University Press.

Idle No More. 2021. "About the Movement." *Idle No More*. https://idlenomore.ca/about-the-movement/.

Kaika, M., and L. Ruggiero. 2015. "Class Meets Land: The Social Mobilization of Land as Catalyst for Urban Change." *Antipode* 47 (3): 708–729.

Kelly, A. B., and N. L. Peluso. 2015. "Frontiers of Commodification: State Lands and Their Formalization." *Society & Natural Resources* 28(5): 473–495.

Krippner, G. R. 2005. "The Financialization of the American Economy." *Socio-Economic Review* 3 (2): 173–208.

Lewis, O. 1964. *Pedro Martinez, a Peasant and His Family*. New York: Random House.

Li, T. 1999. *Transforming the Indonesian Uplands*. London: Routledge.

Lucas, A., and C. Warren. 2003. "The State, the People, and Their Mediators: The Struggle over Agrarian Law Reform in Post-New Order Indonesia." *Indonesia* 76 (October): 87–126.

Makki, F. 2014. "Development by Dispossession: Terra Nullius and the Social-Ecology of New Enclosures in Ethiopia." *Rural Sociology* 79(1): 79–103.

Makki, F. 2018. "The Political Ecology of Land Grabs in Ethiopia." In *From Biocultural Homogenization to Biocultural Conservation*. Edited by Rozzi, R et al., 83–95. Vol. 3 of *Ecology and Ethics*. Edinburgh: Springer, Cham.

Mamdani, M. 1996. *Citizens and Subjects*. Princeton: Princeton University Press.

Marx, K. 1977. *Capital: A Critique of Political Economy*. New York: Vintage Books.

McCarthy, J. F., and K. Robinson, eds. 2016. *Land and Development in Indonesia: Searching for the People's Sovereignty*. Singapore: ISEAS-Yusof Ishak Institute.

Moreno, L. 2018. "Always Crashing in the Same City." *City* 22 (1): 152–168.

Moyo, S., P. Jha, and P. Yeros, eds. 2019. *Reclaiming Africa: Scramble and Resistance in the 21st Century*. Singapore: Singer.

Nixon, R. 2011. *Slow Violence and the Environmentalism of the Poor*. Cambridge, MA: Harvard University Press.

Paprocki, K. 2021. *Threatening Dystopias: The Global Politics of Climate Change Adaptation in Bangladesh*. Ithaca: Cornell University Press.

Peluso, N. L., S. Afiff, and N. F. Rachman. 2008. "Claiming the Grounds for Reform: Agrarian and Environmental Movements in Indonesia." *Journal of Agrarian Change* 8 (2–3): 377–407.

Peluso, N. L., and C. Lund. 2011. "New Frontiers of Land Control: Introduction." *Journal of Peasant Studies* 38 (4): 667–681.

Peluso, N. L., and M. Watts. 2001. *Violent Environments*. Ithaca: Cornell University Press.

Rigg, J., and P. Vandergeest. 2012. *Revisiting Rural Places*. Honolulu: University of Hawai'i Press.

Rignall, K. 2021. *An Elusive Common: Land, Politics, and Agrarian Rurality in a Moroccan Oasis*. Ithaca: Cornell University Press.

Rostow, W. 1960. *The Stages of Economic Growth: A Non-communist Manifesto*. Cambridge, UK: Cambridge University Press.

Roy, A., and A. Ong, eds. 2011. *Worlding Cities: Asian Experiments and the Art of Being Global*. Hoboken: John Wiley & Sons.

Safransky, S. 2017. "Rethinking Land Struggle in the Postindustrial City." *Antipode* 49 (4): 1079–1100.

Safransky, S. 2020. "Geographies of Algorithmic Violence: Redlining the Smart City." *International Journal of Urban and Regional Research*. 44 (2): 200–218.

Sassen, S. 2008. *Territory, Authority, Rights*. Princeton: Princeton University Press.

Shanin, T. 1972. *The Awkward Class: Political Sociology of Peasantry in a Developing Society: Russia 1910–1925*. London: Better World Books.

Sikor, T., and C. Lund. 2009. "Access and Property: A Question of Power and Authority." *Development and Change* 40 (1): 1–22.

Stronzake, J., and W. Wolford. 2016. "Brazil's Landless Workers Rise Up." *Dissent*, Spring 2016. https://www.dissentmagazine.org/article/brazils-landless-workers -rise-mst-land-occupation.

Vandergeest, P., and N. L. Peluso. 1995. "Territorialization and State Power in Thailand." *Theory and Society* 24 (3): 385–426.

Vandergeest, P., and N. L. Peluso. 2006a. "Empires of Forestry: Professional Forestry and State Power in Southeast Asia, Part 1." *Environment and History* 12 (1): 31–64.

Vandergeest, P., and N. L. Peluso. 2006b. "Empires of Forestry: Professional Forestry and State Power in Southeast Asia, Part 2." *Environment and History* 12 (4): 359–393.

White, B., and P. Boomgaard. 2017. *Dari krisis ke krisis: Masyarakat Indonesia menghadapi resesi ekonomi selama abad 20*. Yogyakarta: Gadjah Mada University Press.

Williams, R. 1973. *The Country and the City*. Oxford: Oxford University Press.

Winichakul, T. 1994. *Siam Mapped: A History of the Geo-Body of a Nation*. Honolulu: University of Hawai'i Press.

Wolf, E. 1982. *Europe and the People without History*. Berkeley: University of California Press.

Wolford, W. 2021. "The Plantationocene: A Lusotropical Contribution to the Theory." *Annals of the American Association of Geographers*. 111 (6): 1622–1639.

Wolford, W., S. M. Borras Jr., R. Hall, I. Scoones, and B. White. 2013. "Governing Global Land Deals: The Role of the State in the Rush for Land." *Development and Change* 44 (2): 189–210.

Yang, B., and J. He. 2021. "Global Land Grabbing: A Critical Review of Case Studies across the World." *Land* 10 (3): 324.

Zoomers, A., F. van Noorloos, K. Otsuki, H. Steel, and G. van Westen. 2017. "The Rush for Land in an Urbanizing World: From Land Grabbing toward Developing Safe, Resilient, and Sustainable Cities and Landscapes." *World Development* 92: 242–252.

Part I

UNSETTLED TERRITORIES

1

COLONIZATION AND THE RECODING OF LAND IN CLASSICAL POLITICAL ECONOMY

Robert Nichols

This book constitutes a collective inquiry into the forms of governance that have been historically linked to the appropriation, delineation, production, and management of land. There is perhaps no model more intimately linked to this question than that of settler colonialism. Indeed, the recent emergence of settler colonialism as a distinct research analytic has pivoted centrally upon arguments regarding the role that land plays in this configuration of power (e.g., Veracini 2010, 2012). As a transnational and transhistorical mode of governance, settler colonialism—from seventeenth-century New England to twenty-first-century Israel—is frequently said to be characterized by a specific territorial acquisition logic to notwithstanding other differences between its various iterations. As Patrick Wolfe put it in his groundbreaking intervention: "Whatever settlers may say [. . .] the primary motive for elimination is not race (or religion, ethnicity, grade of civilization, etc.) but access to territory. Territoriality is settler colonialism's specific, irreducible element" (Wolfe 2006, 388).

While attractive in the abstract, such claims remain underspecified. One cannot deduce from an analytic claim about the relationship between settler colonialism and territorial acquisition, very much about the *content* of the processes under description. Put differently, if it is axiomatic that settlers seek territory, we still will not know much about why this is the case until we can recover the meaning of *territory* in any specific case. The key term may cover a multitude of distinct denotations. Why, after all, would anyone want more land? Are they in pursuit of agriculturally productive soil? A commodity (i.e., real estate)? A space to call home? Specifying the precise parameters of this is no mere semantic game. Instead, it implies important consequences for understanding the scope, scale, motivations, and limitations of settler colonialism, historically and in the present.

The premise of this chapter is that such questions can only be studied historically, not analytically. This means investigating the concrete meanings and practices attached to notions of land in any given time and place. It requires unpacking the "social life" of land—as this book as a whole attests—but also, perhaps more precisely, the political economies of its production. The difficulty attending this, however, is that, as an intellectual tradition, "political economy" is already imbricated in the long history of territorial acquisition and transformation. So, to specify the content and context of territory, we must draw upon a tradition of thought that is at least in part an effect of the very processes under examination.

This chapter contributes to these debates by historicizing the relationship between land, colonization, and political economy at one particularly important historical juncture. The period from 1776 to 1848 saw the proliferation of major works in the emergent field of classical political economy by such luminaries as Adam Smith, David Ricardo, Thomas Malthus, and John Stuart Mill. Curiously, it was also during this era that classical political economy pivoted rather abruptly in its relationship to settler colonization. Whereas early contributors, such as Smith and Ricardo, were generally skeptical as to the benefits of new territorial acquisition and resettlement projects, later thinkers saw it as integral to the development of a modern economy. In what follows, I explain the shifting fortunes of settler colonization during the abovementioned period by tracing how the very concept of *land* underwent a significant recoding. Rather than serving as a stable empirical referent, I seek to demonstrate that *land* actually functioned as a rather protean term in these debates, one that underwent significant reformulation. In other words, late eighteenth-century Anglophone intellectuals and policy makers could be skeptical about the benefits of land appropriation, while their counterparts forty to fifty years later were enthusiastically in favor, because these two groups were operating with distinct notions of *land*. Focusing on only one small slice of this complex process, the chapter tracks the recoding of land in major works of classical political economy. A targeted reading of work by Smith, Ricardo, Malthus, and Mill—as well as a host of their lesser-known interlocutors—reveals several different conceptualizations of land that function to undergird the case for colonial capitalism (see Ince 2019). Here, I discuss various lineages of land—including republican, Lockean, Physiocratic, Malthusian, and industrial-capitalist—arguing that, although they coexisted and intertwined, we can observe a general shift in emphasis from the former to the latter. The increasingly abstract conceptualization of land (as both commodity and spatial field) that emerges from this period generated a renewed sense that colonization and capitalism were commensurable—indeed mutually reinforcing—and that it was the task of political economy to unite them.

British imperial administrators began to slow the pace of territorial expansion in North America through the imposition of the Royal Proclamation in 1763, a major catalyst to the American Revolutionary War. Ironically, the newly independent republic birthed by that revolution faced similar obstacles to curtailing settler expansion in the decades that followed. In 1785, the US Congress issued a proclamation forbidding unlawful settlement and authorizing the secretary of war to remove those in the breach (Ford 1910, 117–118). In 1806, the term *squatter* was used for the first time in congressional debates to refer to the growing problem of claims obtained outside of the formally recognized and legally sanctioned process. Formal, legislative prohibition peaked in the form of the Intrusion Act of 1807, which forbids US citizens not only from unlawfully taking possession or making settlements but also from surveying, designating boundaries, or even marking trees in such a way as to facilitate a future claim. It moreover reauthorized the president and his officials "to employ such military force as he may judge necessary and proper" to remove offenders (US Congress 1848, 445). In July 1827, federal troops were sent into Indigenous land in Alabama, where they forcibly removed squatters, burning their homes and crops. Repeated periodically throughout the 1830s and 1840s, this came to be known as the Intruders' War (Dick 1970, 51–53).

Uncertainty regarding the benefits of colonial land annexation was just as pronounced elsewhere in the British Empire. Many important and influential intellectuals came out against the policy of establishing new, neo-European settlements through territorial acquisition abroad. In particular, contributors to the nascent field of political economy, such as Adam Smith and David Ricardo, were notably opposed. At the turn of the nineteenth century, both of their respective branches of classical political economy tended to view settler colonization as unnecessary at best and disastrous at worst. The economic benefits to Britain were either nonexistent or insignificant compared to what might be reaped through similar capital investment at home, especially when combined with liberal trade policies between free, independent states. Adding more land to the nation was not necessary for a modern, capitalist, "free trade" society but an outdated throwback to earlier visions of empire. In this way, these schools of political economy also reflected a general skepticism about the benefits of colonization in the wake of the US Revolutionary War. The general atmosphere in the Anglosphere from the early 1780s to the mid-1820s was thus one of reticence and uncertainty with regard to the colonial question.[1]

In the latter half of the 1820s, however, the tide began to turn back once more; enthusiasm for land annexation was rekindled. In 1830, the US Congress passed its first properly titled "Preemption Act," which included a general pardon for all inhabitants of illegally settled lands. Initially intended to be a temporary measure, it set a new precedent. By that point, settlers recognized that they could effectively disregard the previous Intrusion Act since there was a high degree of probability they would simply be exonerated by later preemption legislation (Dick 1970, 56; Lester 1860, 64–65). By the 1840s, Congress did not even consider settlement before purchase as trespass per se (Robbins 1976, 89–90). New legislation not only removed restrictions on (illegal) land appropriation by "homesteaders" (as they were now more positively known), it actively encouraged it. This coincided with the founding of a host of new British societies and corporations whose purpose was to coordinate land appropriation efforts abroad with lobbying over allocation schemes at home, including the National Colonization Society (1830), the South Australian Association (1834), the New Zealand Association (1839), the New Zealand Land Company (1841), and the Colonial Reform Society (1850). A wave of new emigration schemes soon followed, with the express aim of populating extant or newly-founded colonies from western Canada to eastern Australia. The Colonial Reform movement, as it came to be generally known, grew in size and influence and built a new consensus on the viability of settler colonization. Curiously, in their renewed enthusiasm for land annexation, politicians and policy makers across the Anglophone world increasingly drew resources from classical political economy to explain and justify their aims. Major contributors to the discipline in this later period not only advocated for new colonial land acquisition, they did so in the name of the most modern economic theories of the day. As Mill put it in his 1848 work *Principles of Political Economy,* political economy supported the notion that colonization is "the best affair of business, in which the capital of an old and wealthy country can engage" (Mill 1994, 358).

How and why did the career of colonial land annexation wax and wane so dramatically at the turn of the nineteenth century? More precisely, how could colonial expansion through land appropriation move from being viewed as generally contrary to the foundations of classical political economy to centrally commensurate with it and in such a short time? Finally, what can the study of this intellectual and political pivot teach us more generally about the mutating, mercurial history of colonization in its imbrications with the social life of land? These are the questions with which this chapter is preoccupied.

Late eighteenth-century imperial visions of land in the Anglophone world were informed by a complex and contradictory mixture of intellectual traditions, which included republican, Lockean, and Physiocratic elements. While analytically distinct, these traditions overlapped and intermixed. Each provided conceptual resources to explain and justify the acquisition of new land.

In eighteenth-century republicanism, we see thinkers reach back to a rich Greco-Roman tradition, which placed great emphasis on the virtues of fixed agricultural property, not only for landholders but also for the political community as a whole. Fixed agricultural holdings, especially when held in small units by independent farmers, were considered the fount of republican excellence. Such farmers were relatively autonomous in a material and ethical sense: their unmediated access to land could provide them not only basic subsistence but also a medium for virtuous labor, rendering them less dependent upon others. Recalling this tradition, modern republicans oftentimes criticized feudalism for perverting this relationship, arguing that the majority of landholders were no longer independent farmers but proprietors of large estates funded by rent. We can find traces of this in the English republicanism of the Diggers and Levellers, but it is also quite evident in later writers, such as Rousseau, who was most critical of the kind of large landholdings that formed the foundation of the European nobility. As Alan Ryan summarizes this view: "Large property leads to corruption as the rich man tries to buy his fellow citizens; moveable property leads to corruption as it allows men to take their wealth wherever they choose, and it allows them to escape the censorship of their fellow citizens; the rise of money and commerce leads to corruption as it exacerbates these tendencies by creating a dependent urban mob who will follow the bidding of their corrupters" (Ryan 1984, 49).

In this way, modern republicanism could use arguments regarding the qualitatively unique nature of property in land (real estate) as a force for a certain form of (antifeudal) egalitarianism.

This can only be the basis of a "certain form" of egalitarianism, however, because such arguments have often had trouble overcoming a certain propensity to produce and justify other forms of inequality. Emphasis on land ownership as the fount of autonomy and virtue sits in fundamental tension with a more liberal commitment to formal, individual equality since it is based upon access to a scarce and limited resource. This was not a problem for earlier iterations of the tradition in the classical world because proponents were not then also committed to the formal equality of persons. But for republicans of, say, seventeenth-century England, it was difficult to ignore the fact that universalizing an egalitarian commitment to small-scale, independent agrarian holdings was not possible. There was simply not enough arable land to permit everyone to have their own piece. Thus, it is not difficult to see how this view of landholding could generate colonial ambitions. The acquisition of new lands—particularly those suitable for agrarian cultivation by small farmers—functions to ease the basic contradiction at the heart of "egalitarian landholding republicanism." Jefferson's vision of America as a vast nation of yeoman farmers is perhaps the purest expression of this ideal (Rana 2010).

It is worth highlighting one salient component of this conceptualization of land that will become important as a point of contrast with later formulations. In this republican lineage, the distinctive, positive feature of land ownership is precisely that it *differs* from other property forms. What commends ownership in land here is specifically that it is less alienable and fungible than chattel property. The immobility of real estate is what anchors the landholder to the earth and the community. If there is a connection between theories of republican landholding and colonization, then that connection resides in the qualitatively distinct and normatively elevated status of real estate.

In this context, a related but conceptually distinct Lockean lineage of land provides a powerful alternative formulation. Locke provided arguments that helped square a commitment to land ownership with liberal egalitarianism. The price, however, was relinquishing the qualitative distinctiveness of land ownership in favor of an increasingly abstract conception of "landed property."

Locke's original dilemma was to resolve how humans might come to have property in parts of what God gave to mankind in common "without any express Compact of all the Commoners" (Locke 1988, 286). His way out of this dilemma was to posit labor as an exclusive property in each person, the expenditure of which on the natural common removes a portion of it from the State of Nature and inscribes that person's private property in it (19, 22). This is subject to a "sufficiency limitation"—which dictates that "enough and as good" should be left in common for others—and a "spoilage limitation"—which prohibits one from engrossing more than one can mix one's labor with and making use of before it perishes. Together, these restrict the amount of private property in the state of nature to a "very moderate proportion" (22). For Locke, the invention of money effectively overcomes these limitations. Money permits unlimited accumulation because it does not spoil, but, importantly, this also enables Locke to square the equality of natural liberty with the facts of inequality in the "disproportionate and unequal Possession of the Earth" (29). My appropriation of a portion of our common inheritance cannot be justifiably considered a violation of your right to the same—even after all the earth has been apportioned and future generations have no opportunity to directly acquire property in land—if this process is the condition of possibility for the maximum productive use of our inheritance such that the "common stock of mankind" has been infinitely increased and all are better off.

Famously, one tradition of Lockean interpretation has held up (or assailed) his philosophy of property as a paradigmatic expression of a general culture of "possessive individualism" (Macpherson 1975, 2011). This interpretation held that Locke (explicitly or implicitly) justified private property as a means of capitalist accumulation. The contextualist rejoinder was that this approach conflated intent with effect. Locke does not build a defense of private property in order to advance the cause of capital accumulation but, rather, as a mechanism for withstanding the abuse of governmental authority (Tully 1980). He does this by couching a theory of entitlement in a natural law comprised of a series of fundamental rights and obligations. Self-preservation, for instance, combines both. My right to self-preservation must be respected by the state (thus providing a bulwark against royal absolutism), but it must just as equally be respected by me in relation to myself. For I do not so much have full *ownership* over my person (at least not in the modern sense of powers of control, exclusion, and alienation) as *use* of it, and even then only in accordance with God's purposes for it.

The same can be said for the earth. God did not merely give the earth to mankind in common; he also imbued us with reason such that we might divine his purposes behind doing so. One of these purposes is self-preservation, but even this should not be taken in a strictly narrow or negative sense. Preservation does not merely entail avoidance of death but, more positively, requires that we "Increase and Multiply" (Locke 1988, 25–26). This gives theological significance to our laboring activity. As Jeremy Waldron puts it: "Laboring is not just something we happen to do to resources, it is the appropriate mode of helping oneself to the resources given what resources are *for*" (Waldron 2002, 160).

As Waldon indicates here, the divine element of labor expresses itself in a further obligation: the subjection and improvement of the earth. In its original condition, nature is the common inheritance of all and, as such, exists undifferentiated and without boundary (which it would need if it were to be called property to the exclusion of another). Moreover, it is essentially without value; it is "waste." Nature only gains value through being subjected to one's dominion. This framework was not original to Locke, but it was adopted by him to furnish one of the major foundations for understanding the way that nature was to be "tamed." Nor is this peripheral to an understanding of what property is. But it marked the distinct worldview of what it meant to be a human being at the time: to be one who exists apart from nature. Stewardship represented a role not of working with nature to fulfil its mandates but rather to subject it to the will of the human. It is human labor that "puts the greatest part of Value upon Land," without which "Nature and the Earth" would remain "worthless Materials" (Locke 1988, 26–7). Land thus conceived is an originally valueless apparatus or medium of laboring activity. It acquires value only through a process of separation from nature (enclosure) and subsequent transformation to serve human ends.

A whole generation of scholars has unpacked the connections between this view of land and the processes of English colonization in the so-called new world (e.g., Tully 1993; Arneil 1996; Armitage 2004). In particular, foundational work in the "colonial turn" in Locke's scholarship has decisively demonstrated that he was personally invested in the English colonization of the Americas, that the colonial horizon informed his intellectual formation more generally, and that his contributions to legal and political thought had a major impact on the actual practices of colonization well beyond his own time. In so doing, these thinkers have provided a compelling explanatory account of Anglo-settler colonization in the seventeenth and eighteenth centuries. Driven to subdue the (supposed) vast wastelands of the Americas, mixing labor with nature by bringing new land under the till simultaneously fulfills the Biblical injunction to make productive use of the earth (God's gift, given to mankind in common), establishes the basis of civil society through the protection of private property, and develops the individual through virtuous (agrarian) labor. Gesturing ahead to the discussion of classical political economy to come, it is important to highlight one feature of the connection between colonization and land acquisition in the Lockean tradition, namely, that it does not operate through a strictly utilitarian logic. In this lineage, one is driven to enclose and subject the "natural waste" regions of the world not merely because the process of improvement better furnishes mankind with the conveniences of life (although this may also be true) but rather because this is the underlying purpose of nature. This is what nature is for, so not to use it in this way (to permit it to remain fallow) is more than a lost opportunity; it is immoral. However, to speak of fulfilling a natural purpose (connected in Locke to God's divine will) is to link land acquisition to a moral theory of collective human improvement. As we shall see, this component of the argument is largely abandoned by later thinkers, such as Mill, who advanced a more strictly utilitarian (or at least instrumental) defense of colonization.

Later developments in the eighteenth century did not so much negate these earlier republican and Lockean arguments as incorporate and reformulate them, drawing upon them for a more robust and direct defense of capital accumulation. In particular, the Lockean natural law theory of property was inserted into theories of capitalist economic development. This transition involved pivoting off the basic conceptual stance adopted by the thinkers in question from that of the individual laboring agent to a state-economic perspective. Whereas Lockeanism was generated by an interest in defending the natural right of individuals to private property against state authority, emergent forms of classical economics sought to reconcile these opposing forces by restructuring the state as a vehicle of private interests and capitalist accumulation.

With respect to the role that land appropriation plays in this process, the emergence of the Physiocrat school marks a key transition. The dominant approach to political economy in the eighteenth century, Physiocracy was developed predominantly in France by the *économistes* François Quesnay (1694–1774), Anne-Robert-Jacques Turgot (1727–1781), and Guillaume François Le Trosne (1712–1780) (see Winch 1996, 2009; Rothschild 2002; Vardi 2014). Derived from a Greek word meaning "power of nature," Physiocracy was a form of agrarian economics that emphasized the natural productivity of the earth. Physiocrats thus believed that agriculture was the fount of national power. They considered manufacturing labor to be ultimately unproductive and parasitic, in as much as it merely transformed one set of goods into another. Trade and finance were equally viewed as ultimately unproductive fields of industry, circulating goods and wealth but contributing no true value to the national economy. Only the agricultural sector could create value since labor invested in the earth produced new goods rather than merely transforming them. Rent from land use was one of the few sources of genuine wealth for the state since it reflected the value-added contributions of agriculture. In this way, the Physiocrat theory of natural productivity translated into state policies that favored the agricultural sector in general, the landed aristocracy in particular, and resisted both urbanization and industrialization.

Physiocratic and Lockean visions of land are not mutually exclusive. Locke certainly emphasized the wealth-generating function of agricultural labor and engaged in some comparative evaluation of different societies' productive capacities in relation to their land use practices, famously comparing the cultivated soil of Devonshire to the "wild woods and uncultivated waste of America," deeming the former more productive by ten times (Locke 1988, 294; see also Weaver 2005). If the Physiocrats seem to express a similar preference for agrarianism, however, their underlying rationale for doing so is quite different. Whereas Locke develops a philosophy of property that emphasizes enclosures and agricultural labor in order to construct a bulwark against unlimited, authoritarian government, the intention behind Physiocratic thought is precisely to place into state hands the tools required to govern. And whereas Locke views land as inert and barren without human intervention, the Physiocrats view it as a generative, even mysterious force. Tapping into "the era's romanticization of nature," the Physiocrats developed creative (if now somewhat perplexing) theories that emphasized the unpredictability of nature's reproductive capacities (Vardi 2014, 6, 63). The goal was to study, harness, and direct "nature's capacity to multiply itself" (3). Armed with the new science of life, the Physiocrats sought to amplify the natural productive tendencies of the earth for state purposes.

The best-known work of the Physiocrat school was Quesnay's *Tableau économique,* a complex diagram that purports to represent graphically the system of economic exchanges (themselves reflections of nature's currents). This work has historically attracted commentary by major thinkers, from Tocqueville to Marx to Foucault, who often emphasize its visual inventiveness (Foucault 1970; Marx 1989, 289–290; also Gherke and Kurz 1995). Instead of focusing on *Tableau,* however, the relevant shift tracked here is perhaps more easily expressed via an exemplary passage from one of Quesnay's famous *Encyclopedia* entries. In a passage simply titled "Farmers," Quesnay writes: "Agriculture is the inheritance of the sovereign: all its products are visible; one can properly subject them to taxation; financial wealth can evade its share of subsidies; the government can take them only through means which are onerous to the state" (Quesnay 1958, vol. 2, 455; also cited in McNally 1990, 103).

As the above makes clear, the Physiocrat case for agrarian labor rests not primarily on a Lockean theory of entitlement, nor even solely on the natural productivity of the land, but also on its visibility to power. Agrarianism does not merely generate new wealth; it circulates this wealth in highly legible and conspicuous forms. (In both respects, its opposite is finance capital.) The approach taken by the Physiocrats is thus still dependent on the qualitative distinctiveness of wealth in land but links this much more directly to the problem of governance over national territory. As Tocqueville observed: "According to the Economists, the State's role was not just to govern the nation, but to fashion it in a specific direction [. . .]. For the Economists, this power does not come from God, it is not bound by tradition, it is impersonal, it no longer refers to the King, but the State" (Tocqueville 2004, 190–94).

More recently, David McNally has extended Tocqueville's observation, noting that in as much as Quesnay's conceptual outlook adopts the "standpoint of the state," it "demonstrates that his is an exercise in political economy in the traditional sense" (McNally 1990, 102–03). We are already some distance from Locke's original concerns then, both with respect to the underlying conceptualization of the earth and the purposes for which it is set. A natural law theory of property in the context of a conflict with governmental authority has given way to an expressly state-centered economic theory based upon the natural vitality of the land itself.[2]

In sum, by the late eighteenth century, the case for land acquisition in the Anglophone colonial world was made through a strange mixture of arguments that drew from republican, Lockean, and Physiocrat sources. Land was a desired object of appropriation because it provided a medium of virtuous laboring activity, a distinct form of immobile real estate, and the (agrarian) basis for a robust national economy. How and why did this picture change?

The doyens of emergent classical political economy were initially skeptical of the benefits accrued through territorial expansion. These included Adam Smith and David Ricardo, both of whom thought that emphasis on the increase in landholdings was based on outdated economic theories linked to the Physiocrats. Accordingly, instead of pushing for the acquisition of more land, classical political economists emphasized the efficient use of existing holdings (a shift in focus from quantitative holdings to qualitative use). In this way, classical political economy fed a more general "anticolonial moment" in the Anglosphere of the 1780s to 1830s.

The locus classicus of this tradition remains *The Wealth of Nations* (Smith 1999). Among its many contributions, Smith's opus undermines the Physiocratic claim that agriculture is the sole source of true wealth. The accumulation of capital had many faces, including industrial manufacturing, trade, and finance. There is, therefore, no reason to favor agriculture universally at the expense of other sectors of the economy. However, Smith still holds that capital invested in the agricultural sector generates more new wealth than investment in any other domain. Although the Physiocrats erred in "representing the class of artificers, manufacturers, and merchants as altogether barren and unproductive," it is nevertheless true that the "labour of farmers and country labourers is certainly more productive than that of merchants, artificers, and manufacturers. The superior produce of the one class, however, does not render the other barren or unproductive" (Smith 1999, 260–261). Hence, we find in *Wealth of Nations* a ranking of relative capital return in various sectors, with agriculture still at the pinnacle but now followed by such fields as manufacturing, domestic distributive trade, and foreign exchange (346–355). Only the labor of "menial servants" is considered by Smith to be wholly unproductive (261). This new ordering already partially demoted the settler colonial fixation on land acquisition and bolstered the case for an oceanic empire of commerce and trade.

David Ricardo's *The Principles of Political Economy and Taxation* reaffirms the land, labor, and capital structure found in *Wealth of Nations* but places more emphasis on the tensions between their different corresponding classes. In particular, Ricardo locates in the struggle between workers and the landholding class a key to understanding the organization of society as a whole (not, as Marx would later find, between labor and capital). Hence, the pride of place given to an analysis of rent in Ricardo's work. This theme shall be touched upon in a moment in relation to the competing theories of Thomas Malthus. For the moment, at least, we can observe that Ricardo considered the efficient exploitation of land to be central to economic growth. A fixed supply of land would ultimately result in lower productivity. The resulting decline in the rate of profit within the agricultural industry would shift the terms of trade against industry and cool the accumulation process as a whole. Ricardo's solution was to develop systems of taxation (especially on rent) that might encourage efficient land use and improvement. However, as we shall see, others following in his wake, such as Mill, denied that the supply of land was indeed fixed at all and instead sought reprieve in colonial expansion.

Ricardo worked out his theory of rent and land use in a multiyear public conversation with Thomas Robert Malthus. The well-known core of Malthus's *An Essay on the Principle of Population* is the claim that food production increases arithmetically while population increases geometrically. Malthus is thus commonly associated with introducing a calculative and quantitative dimension to emergent modern biopolitics, and not without good reason. Malthus's quantitative formulas mask, however, a more profoundly qualitative innovation. In the seventeenth and eighteenth centuries, widespread common understanding had it that a large population corresponded more or less directly to economic well-being and national clout. This doctrine found its way into a number of fields of social life, from penology to marital relations. On the former, Bentham was fond of citing Étienne Dumont's argument against capital punishment, namely, that death was to be avoided at all costs since "la force et la richesse d'une nation, [c'est] le nombre des hommes" (Dumont 1840, 235).[3] On the latter issue, the Encyclopaedia Britannica of the period confidently declared, "As the strength and glory of a kingdom or state consist in the multitude of its subjects, celibacy above all things should be discouraged" (Ensor 1967, 9–10).[4] In short, before the turn of the nineteenth century, population was power. In the emergent world of industrial capitalism, however, the focus was no longer on large populations but on their efficient use and mobilization, another shift from quantity to quality. Malthus pushed this one step further in arguing that larger populations were more likely to threaten national well-being than secure it. The qualitative management of population growth thereby entered the science of governance.

Malthus's work overlaps considerably with the Physiocrats and classical political economists, such as Smith and Ricardo. With respect to the question of land, his approach might be considered merely another example of the Physio-cratic approach insofar as his primary focus is the agricultural sector, still un-derstood as the primary site of wealth production in the form of food and rent. The emphasis on food production is most notable and, given his context, understandable. While Malthus was working on revisions to the first edition of *Principle of Population*, the first of Britain's decennial censuses was released, re-vealing the extent of the population boom in the late eighteenth century (see Wrigley and Schofield 1989). Near continuous war with France between 1803 and 1815 saw Britain emerge as the dominant economic and political power in Europe but also generated massive national debt and spikes in food prices. The enclosure process (popularly associated with the seventeenth century as a result of Marx's periodization from volume one of *Capital*) actually accelerated and expanded during the period when Malthus was writing, reaching a peak in the Napoleonic war years when roughly 9 percent of the total land area of England came under parliamentary enclosure (Thompson 1991, 288). It was in the era of postwar stagnation that Britain became a net importer of food, a shift that in-fluenced Malthus and his concern for national self-sufficiency in agricultural production.

While briefly influential, it was not long before Malthus's views on agricul-tural production were challenged by rival economists. Through their longstand-ing public debates, Ricardo came to eventually displace Malthus as the key figure on these issues, often by either outright rejecting the claims of the latter or by subordinating them to his own system. Of paramount importance was Ri-cardo's contention that food production was, in fact, not fixed and could be boosted relative to demand. Malthus argued that, once land had been maximally distributed and productively used, it would reach a natural limit and, from this period on, food production could only advance arithmetically (thus producing a situation of diminishing returns). Ricardo rejected this, maintaining that there was no natural fixity of agricultural production and that periods of scarcity were a spur to growth (Ricardo 2004, chap. 33). Even when he partially agreed with Malthus, Ricardo often derived alternative policy conclusions from the basic the-oretical system. The most dramatic case was Ricardo's rejection of the Corn Laws, which Malthus publicly supported for some time.

Finally, there is the matter of rent. As we have seen, the Physiocratic influ-ence on classical political economy meant that many otherwise opposing think-ers were in agreement that rent from landed estates was a main source of national income, alongside wages and profits. For the Physiocrats, rent was de-fined as the cost incurred for access to the most important natural resource and instrument of labor: land. By contrast, in *The Wealth of Nations*, Smith treated land primarily as a mode of profit that accrues to the holders of a monopoly over a scarce and naturally limited resource. Malthus held the more strictly Physio-cratic view, defining rent as "the return to landowners after other costs of pro-duction had been met, which meant that the proximate cause of rent was the excess of food prices over production" (Winch 2013, 70). Land yielded more pro-ductive value than was necessary to support those living and working on it. The wealth generated by land was not limited to rent as payment for access to the means of production. Rather, since land also directly contributed to the national econ-omy in the form of a "bountiful gift of Providence," the theory of rent should rightly reflect this distinctive value-added quality. As a result of this providence, Malthus conjectured that any attempt to reduce food prices as a vehicle for con-trolling rent would have the opposite effect: it would make agricultural produc-tion less profitable, cause more land to be removed from production, and eventually upset the balance between food production and population growth.

Malthus's definition of rent as the above-cost value of food had the added political benefit of further ingratiating him to the landed aristocracy. His defini-tion shifted focus to the natural productivity of land and correspondingly de-flected from the alternative view, namely, that rent was the expression of a class monopoly over a natural resource and thus came at the expense of actual agricul-tural producers (not to mention consumers, in the form of food prices). In this regard, Malthus's view was on the outs. Whereas an earlier generation (not only the Physiocrats but also noticeably Smith) held that the interests of large landhold-ers were ultimately commensurate with the nation as a whole, most major thinkers of early to mid-nineteenth-century political economy shared the view, expressed in the new theory of rent, that the large landholders gained profits pri-marily by driving up food prices. Rent paid to large landholders was a drain on agricultural production rather than an honest reflection of it. Ricardo's work is something of a watershed in the transition between the two understandings. Since he did not accept Malthus's views on either rent or food production, Ricardo also did not share Malthus's fears of a general shift away from the agricultural sector and toward manufacturing. Instead, he argued that Britain could rely on the prof-its from its manufacturing industry to acquire cheap raw materials from abroad and, moreover, that problems with acquiring a stable supply were best resolved through an increasingly liberalized trade policy that opened up access to as many markets as possible, driving down prices and making restrictions less likely. His position eventually won out (e.g., the Corn Laws were repealed in 1846).

If Malthus may be grouped in with a broadly Physiocratic tradition, there is nevertheless an additional element to his work that justifies setting it apart as a distinct lineage of land. Malthus not only viewed land from the standpoint of its productive capacity relative to the national economy but also as a factor in the regulation of political density. By this phrase, I intend not merely the quantitative measure of a population's size but its politically significant, qualitative attributes, such as health and education, and their relationship to space. In his concern for the normal, healthy development of society viewed as an entire "population," Malthus exhibits elements of what Michel Foucault would later theorize as biopolitics (Foucault 2007, 70–77). However, Malthus was also concerned with class stratification and, vitally for our purposes here, geospatial concentration. The concern then was not merely with the biopolitical health of the population considered as a mass but also its vertical organization (stratification and class composition) and its horizontal distribution. A relatively small but highly stratified and densely packed population is a breeding ground (for Malthus, quite literally) for all manner of individual and social pathology. A densely populated underclass constitutes what Malthus terms an "overcharged population" (1993, 62), ripe for political upheaval and/or culling by a variety of natural checks, such as plague and famine.

In his concern with density, concentration, and biopolitical management, Malthus contributed to the recoding of land as abstract space. Malthus viewed the amount of land held by a country not only in terms of its productive capacity but also as a determining factor in population density. To anticipate the discussion to come, this has important implications for the distinctiveness of colonization.[5] Once one adopts a Malthusian concern with the spatial distribution of populations, it becomes possible to imagine colonial expansion and land acquisition as a political technology in the management of growth and the dispersal of various "redundant populations" (the kinds of "surplus laborers" or "industrial reserve army" that Marx later theorizes, drawing explicitly upon Malthus) (Marx 1990, 782–798). Colonization of those supposedly empty and underutilized territorial expanses of the earth thus becomes a viable extension of the new political economy.

In sum, the first wave of classical political economy was generally opposed to settler colonial land annexation projects abroad because its major adherents thought that such schemes were based on antiquated moral theories of land as a medium of virtuous agrarian labor or disproven Physiocratic theories of agriculture as uniquely productive (in the form of food and rent). Since they wished to resituate agriculture as but one field of productive industry, break the monopolistic hold of feudal tenure systems, and promote theories of statecraft based upon economic efficiency over national virtue, they viewed settler colonialism as it was practiced and conceptualized at the time with considerable skepticism.

Of course, this was always a very narrow and peculiar form of "anticolonialism." Notably, it was almost never a result of concern for Indigenous peoples in

newly acquired lands. No major work in political economy attempts to recon-
struct the perspective of Indigenous peoples in Australia, Canada, New Zealand,
or the United States and/or analyze colonization from their standpoint. Rather,
the debate pivots upon the economic and political benefits of dependency relations between settlers and the metropole. The prevalence of anticolonial sentiment during these decades derives from the growing sense that colonization is
costly and inefficient and that Great Britain can achieve global supremacy more
effectively by other means (e.g., "free trade imperialism") (Simmel 1970). For instance, Smith's extended analysis of colonialism in book 4 of *Wealth of Nations*
focuses largely on the deleterious effects of artificially enforced trade monopolies, which he views as "necessarily hurtful" to all parties. Liberal trade between
the metropole and a "natural and free" colony is, by contrast, viewed as "always
and necessarily beneficial" (Smith 1999, 190, 590). Although Ricardo took a
somewhat different route in his reasoning, he reached many of the same conclusions. Ricardo also reduces the polarity of the "colonial relation" to the settler-
metropole dyad (ignoring any distinct Indigenous interests altogether) and
focuses almost exclusively on the matter of free trade between them. While he
concurs with Smith that colonial trade restrictions are a hindrance to economic
liberty and long-term growth, unlike Smith, he at least concedes that politically
(and militarily) enforced trade monopolies are beneficial to dominant parties
in the immediate term (Ricardo 2004, 227–233). In general, classical political
economy at the turn of the nineteenth century was primarily anticolonial,
although only in a very narrow sense. As Donald Winch summarizes: "Colonial trade restrictions stood condemned on free-trade grounds; colonial markets
were held to have no effect, beneficial or otherwise, on profits; nor were they
necessary for the employment of the surplus capital of the mother country"
(Winch 1965, 44). However, to the extent that major thinkers of classical
political economy in this period can be said to have adopted an "anticolonial"
position, this tended to translate into a plea for "responsible government" and
independent home rule for already existing white settler societies. In this way,
this brand of "anticolonialism" was likely just as unsatisfactory to the Indigenous peoples trying to defend their lands from Anglo settler predation (a fact
that is similarly glossed in the secondary literature in this field).[6]

Beginning in the 1820s, enthusiasm for colonization began to rise once more as
the works of the classical economists, particularly with respect to land, came to
directly inform and buttress new colonization schemes.[7] A series of new societies and corporations were founded, whose purpose was to coordinate land appropriation efforts abroad with lobbying over allocation schemes at home. In

both the United States and within the British Empire, a host of new legislation was passed to encourage settler land annexation schemes. The Colonial Reform movement, as it came to be generally known, grew in size and influence and built a new consensus on the viability of colonization, often drawing resources from the classical political economists.

How and why did the "anticolonialism" at the turn of the nineteenth century reverse course? In particular, why did classical political economy move from providing resources for a critique of colonial land acquisition to become its handmaiden? To understand this, we must first note that the initial wave of debates concerning colonization from within classical political economy had already transposed the issue into a more fully instrumental register. This serves as a point of contrast to the republican and even Lockean thinkers that preceded them, who tended to view the matter of land acquisition in moral terms. By contrast, emergent analysis in classical political economy focused on the relative material benefits of colonization, not on Britain's underlying moral entitlement to engage in the practice. This provides the first clue to understanding the reversal. Since the "anticolonialism" of turn-of-the-century classical political economy was largely based upon an instrumental calculation of benefit, it could be relatively easily turned about by its own reasoning.

Perhaps more so than any other single figure, Robert Wilmot-Horton (1784–1841) serves to demonstrate how Physiocrat and Malthusian conceptions of land came to be rearticulated through colonial practice. In addition to being a prolific writer on the topic, Wilmot-Horton was able to implement his vision of colonization directly, serving as Undersecretary of State for War and the Colonies (1821–1828) and then as Governor of Ceylon (1831–1837). In this way, he articulates the relation between the classical political economists and Anglo-settler colonization in the field.

Wilmot-Horton is best known as an enthusiastic agent of colonial emigration schemes, which sought to move thousands of underserved and underemployed workers to "empty" lands in the "true colonies," focusing particularly on the transplanting of Irish families—themselves recently displaced from various rounds of enclosures—to Canada. Wilmot-Horton developed his case for colonial emigration on a theory of wages adapted from the classical political economists. He argued that if the working population grew too fast, then wages would fall, and poverty would increase. This matter was made all the more pressing by the simultaneous consolidation of agricultural landholdings into larger estates, which was intended to increase productivity in the long run but, in the short term, exacerbated problems associated with rapid urbanization and pauperism and led to a dip in food production. To enable landowners and parishes to take advantage of the benefits of emigration, Wilmot-Horton argued that the government should make loans to parishes on the security of a mortgage on the poor rates (Mills 1915, chap. 2; Winch 1965). He was opposed to what he called "desultory emigration" and proposed a more coordinated effort, for instance, suggesting emigrants be given land (especially in Canada) together with agricultural implements and provisions for a year (Wilmot-Horton 1831a, 20–21).

In the early 1820s, there were a series of organized political disturbances in southern Ireland. As chairman of the Select Committee of Emigration at the time, Wilmot-Horton was quick to attribute these to the existence of a large body of unemployed and dissatisfied persons and connect the matter to his own plans for colonial emigration. He believed that a plan to dispose of this surplus population through mass emigration would restore political "tranquility" (see Strachan 1827). Wilmot-Horton argued that the current state of the United Kingdom (especially vis-à-vis Ireland) meant that any plan for increasing the rate of capital accumulation or the flow of capital could be taken up successfully only "after the absorption of part of the redundant population, by the means of a well-regulated emigration" (Wilmot-Horton 1831a, 15–17; see also Ghosh 1964, 385–400). Wilmot-Horton referred to this process as the "abstraction" of labor, holding that the excess supply of labor could be resolved in punctuated acts of colonial displacement without influencing the mortality or fertility rates of the population; however, arguing this required some conceptual innovation. As Wilmot-Horton insisted, classical economists would need to view the local labor market as part of a global whole, taking means to shift populations across huge expanses, even continents, when necessary (Wilmot-Horton 1831a, 1831b).

Ensuing summary reports on Wilmot-Horton's Committee give us a clear picture of the conceptualization of "redundant" (or, in Malthus's phrasing, "overcharged") populations and demonstrate the circuit that connected these displaced European workers to settler colonization schemes abroad. In his summary of the Committee's findings, then Anglican Bishop of Toronto John Strachan made these linkages explicit and usefully clarified the terminology of the period. He relates that by "redundancy of population," the Committee does not mean to suggest that there is "absolutely an excess of population in the United Kingdom." Rather, "the redundancy here meant that the demand is not equal to the supply of labour" (Strachan 1827, 6–7). The greatest part of this redundancy, Strachan reports, is the result of the British "plan of consolidating farms" in Ireland. The resulting "disturbances" risk engulfing the whole of the United Kingdom in a "scene of anarchy, rapine, and misery." The only solution is to export these populations to the colonies, which, with their ample, fertile lands, are "well adapted to their reception, offering good neighbourhood, health, independence, and even opulence" (Strachan 1827, 12, 19).

Through such argumentation, Wilmot-Horton's efforts during the 1820s and 1830s to promote colonial emigration slowly paid off. In 1823 and 1825, the government supported emigration from Ireland to Canada along the lines suggested by his plan, enabling some 2,500 emigrants to leave Ireland at a cost to the taxpayer of over £56,000. Although doubts were expressed as to the success of these ventures, especially as they proved to be so expensive, Wilmot-Horton succeeded in obtaining parliamentary consent for the appointment of two Select Committees, in 1826 and 1827, to examine the whole question of emigration in the light of these experiments (Winch 1965, 54).

Several key British intellectuals were recruited to lend credence to this colonial emigration scheme. Malthus proved especially pivotal to its eventual success. Despite confessing privately his doubts as to the long-term viability of the plan, Malthus publicly supported Wilmot-Horton on numerous occasions, including serving as a "star witness" at the 1826 Parliamentary Committee on Emigration. There, Malthus testified that the empirical evidence and "general reasoning and scientific principles" alike supported the case for colonial emigration (Winch 1965, 57).

Part of Malthus's interest in colonial emigration policies of this sort must have derived from the widespread sense that they were a natural extension of his own version of political economy. Mill—a disciple of Ricardo and otherwise frequent critic of Malthus—directly connected Wilmot-Horton's vision to the Malthusian framework, calling it a natural working out of the "practical consequences of the *Principle of Population*" (Winch 1965, 62). Mill, along with Ricardo himself, publicly supported the emigration schemes, even while qualifying his enthusiasm. For his part, Malthus was slowly brought into the Colonial Reform camp by Wilmot-Horton. In the late 1820s and early 1830s, Wilmot-Horton and Malthus exchanged numerous letters on the issue, in which Malthus confessed his ambivalence. While acknowledging its temporary need, Malthus had difficulty accepting Wilmot-Horton's reassurance that large-scale assistance to emigration would not constitute a stimulus to population growth. In *Principle of Population,* Malthus had already acknowledged that the settler colonies appeared not to suffer from the same "want of room and food" (Malthus 1993, 49) plaguing Great Britain. The colonization of new lands appeared then as an ideal scenario for the resolution of European woes since, in these spaces, "the knowledge and industry of an old state operate on the fertile unappropriated land of a new one" (60). This claim appeared to sit in some tension with Malthus's generally pessimistic view, however, since it seemed to show that barriers to growth were, in fact, temporary and artificial and had been largely overcome in America.[8] To ward off this potential criticism, Malthus countered with a different narrative of colonial expansion. Although it was true that the American colonies had achieved enormous population growth—having been "found to double itself in twenty-five years" (16)—this miraculous combination of growth and well-being was only temporary because it was ultimately founded upon a limited and exceptional basis: access to enormous amounts of land. As Malthus argued, "the happiness of the Americans depended much less upon their peculiar degree of civilization than upon the peculiarity of their situation as new colonies, upon their having a great plenty of fertile uncultivated land" (138). What his more optimistic critics failed to see was that even a society founded under such ideal conditions would eventually go awry.[9] The natural good fortune of the American colonies could only delay the inevitable because limits to perfectibility are intrinsic to human sociality itself, not merely a function of technical incapacity or lack of resources.[10] Human institutions can guide and correct the natural passions but only in a relatively superficial manner—like "mere feathers that float on the surface" (75). More specifically, "[w]hen these two fundamental laws of society, the security of property and the institution of marriage, were once established, inequality of conditions must necessarily follow [. . .]. It has appeared that, from the inevitable laws of our nature, some human beings must suffer from want" (85).

Reference here to marriage points to further Malthusian concern. From Malthus's standpoint, one weakness of Wilmot-Horton's scheme was that, in order for it to address overpopulation and pauperism at home, it would need to promote emigration amongst the least "civilized" classes. The uneducated, dislocated, impoverished, and displaced Irish were the paradigmatic face of colonial emigration in the minds of both Wilmot-Horton and Malthus. However, as Malthus continually pointed out to his colleague, these were precisely the sort of people who ignored his other recommendations for population control. They showed little concern for delaying marriage, birth control, and small families. Thus, displacing them might provide England some temporary relief, but, in the long run, this was unlikely to satisfy Malthusian anxieties about overpopulation on a larger scale.

Partially in response to these concerns, Wilmot-Horton began to couple his arguments for colonial emigration with forms of "home colonization" (see Arneil 2017). In the latter case, surplus laborers would be confined to work camps in England and given state-facilitated labor to keep them occupied and productive. These "domestic colonies" still had a distinctly agrarian bent, often emphasizing the moral benefits of farm labor (recalling the Lockean framework), as well as being oriented towards the reclamation of wastelands. (Wilmot-Horton thought the paradigmatic case for such home colonization was camps focused on the reclamation of bog lands in Ireland.) Thus, he conceded that colonial emigration abroad ought to be viewed as one weapon in a larger arsenal aimed at diminishing and dispersing the "redundant populations." As he put it: "Colonization abroad, as a remedy for the evils of a relatively redundant population is, and has been, with me, only a subordinate object of enquiry. I consider it only as the best and cheapest mode of disposing of that superfluous labouring population from the general labour market, which I contend to be the main remedy for the distressed condition of the labouring classes in the United Kingdom, inasmuch as it is that superfluous labour which is not wanted by any party as a means of production, which deteriorates the condition of the whole labouring classes collectively."

He goes on to suggest that if it could be shown that "the superfluous population so abstracted can be disposed of more economically and more advantageously at home than abroad," he would "never be found to press for a moment the remedy of Colonial Emigration." However, since such an alternative method of abstraction had not been found, the latter was the only true and viable solution (Wilmot-Horton 1831a, 22–24).

By the 1830s, Malthus's rather tepid support for colonial emigration began to drive a wedge between him and its more enthusiastic supporters. An example of this can be found in the writings of Nassau Senior, whose *Two Lectures on Population* and *Outline of the Science of Political Economy* both distance themselves from Malthusian population theory precisely because it does not provide sufficient justification for colonization (see Winch 1965, 66). The Scottish economist and Ricardo disciple, J. R. McCulloch, provides another example. Rejecting strict Malthusianism as too pessimistic, McCulloch took the lead among economists in supporting Wilmot-Horton more directly (Chalmers 1995). Those more aligned with Malthus, such as Mill, thought that stricter birth control measures and public education could better control the population than emigration could (although most Malthusians still saw colonial emigration as an important tool, even if only a palliative one). Those who took a more critical view of Malthus were even more favorably disposed toward colonial emigration schemes. Unfortunately for Wilmot-Horton, many of them eventually became convinced that even his emigration schemes did not go far enough. As a result, men such as Nassau Senior and Robert Torrens eventually went over to Wakefield's position, believing a more robust and systematic project of colonization was required (see Ghosh 1964).

In short, by the 1830s, the general view was that colonization and classical political economy were complementary, not competing projects. This was a surprising turn, given that the two "founding fathers" of the latter field (Smith and

Ricardo) had themselves never shown much enthusiasm for the former. The renewed case for capitalist colonization was at least in part a function of the recoding of land itself in this period. Colonial advocates drew less and less upon expressly republican or Lockean idioms—with their emphasis on the virtuousness of agrarian landholding and/or improvement. Instead, they emphasized the unique, wealth-generating properties of arable land and the need for spatial redistribution of redundant populations. Land had simultaneously become a site of productive industry and a field of abstract space.

Mill's 1848 work *Principles of Political Economy* functions as a marker in the decisive victory over the "anticolonial" moment in classical political economy. Among its various arguments and themes, *Principles* sets out to demonstrate that settler colonization can be commensurate with modern forms of an industrial, commercial society and need not depend on outdated forms of mercantile agrarian economics. In his words, colonization is "the best affair of business, in which the capital of an old and wealthy country can engage" (Mill 1994, 358). We can perhaps now better see how the renewed interest in colonial expansion and annexation within Mill's work pivots centrally upon a recoded conception of "land." In Mill's work, land plays a distinct and central role in both the economic development and growth of capitalist societies and, secondly, in the normative theory of private property rights that undergirds and justifies this economic system. Land functions here as both an independent source of value and a spatial field upon which human societies are situated, playing an important role in both the analysis of wealth production and the regulation of population density. But it also functions as a unique form of property, access to which structures much of society as a whole. Finally, land plays a crucial role in limiting or enabling population growth for two reasons. It is the most important element in food production. The productivity of the soil sets out agricultural yields, which has a direct bearing on population growth (a theme borrowed from the Physiocrats). It is combined, however, with another conception. Land is also spoken of here as a metaphor for space, so access to it determines the effect that growth has on population density. Population density is, of course, related to a host of other important socioeconomic factors, everything from transportation to sanitation. In this regard, Mill's political economy adopts and reflects the general Malthusian influence on the field in his time. From this broadly Malthusian source, Mill adopts the view that increases in population (which naturally accompany civilizational development) produce new contradictions and tensions that need to be managed. Specifically, they can create what Wilmot-Horton termed the "redundant population," disturbing the balance between the three classes of laborer, capitalist, and landowner. Citing Malthus directly, Mill concludes that "even in a progressive state of capital, in old countries, a conscientious or prudential restraint on population is indispensable, to prevent the increase of numbers from outstripping the increase of capital, and the condition of the classes who are at the bottom of society from being deteriorated" (Mill 1994, 125).

In an ideal "stationary state," of course, the balance between labor, land, and capital could be maintained through market calibrations. In such a utopia, the system would be relatively self-sustained and would not tend toward the kinds of extremes envisioned here. However, Mill recognizes that the Western European countries of his era have not reached such a point. Although closer to achieving this telos, Europeans have not yet grasped the idea of dynamic equilibrium, let alone found a way to implement it in practice. While the "*density of population* necessary to enable mankind to obtain [. . .] all the advantages both of cooperation and of social intercourse had been attained in these *advanced* societies, Europeans have not yet learned to *be content to be stationary*" (Mill 1994, 129; emphasis added). As such, they continue to pursue an "ultimate increase of wealth and population" for its own sake, which threatens achievement of the truer object: the pleasant "art of living" (128–129). All actually existing capitalist societies have a tendency to *overreach*. They are growing faster than their societies can reasonably manage and thus cannot completely control the contradictions that arise from rapid development (e.g., "overcapitalization"; see 115). Again, this is very biopolitical: it is most clearly expressed for Mill by population growth (e.g., 73).

In this view, colonialization is crucial to human civilizational development because it is the means by which the most advanced (European) societies can manage the rapid population growth that accompanies material prosperity, especially during the intermediate period before those leading societies transition to "stationary states." Otherwise, the contradictions of capitalist development would continue to plague these leading societies, their material success would begin to reverse as the rate of profit falls, and capitalism would prematurely reach its boundary. In such societies, "the rate of profit is habitually within, as it were, a hand's breadth of the minimum, and the country therefore on the very verge of the stationary state [. . .]. [I]t would require but a short time to reduce profits to the minimum, if capital continued to increase at its present rate, and no circumstances having a tendency to raise the rate of profit occurred in the meantime. *The expansion of capital would soon reach its ultimate boundary, if the boundary itself did not continually open and leave more space*" (Mill 1994, 106–107; emphasis added).

We can see more clearly now why Mill commends colonization in particular. Territorial acquisition is the key element to surviving this transitional phase of capitalist development. Hence, land acquisition has nothing to do with an early modern romance with agriculture, small-holding farmers, or the like. Instead, it is connected to *industrialization*. For it is only in the so-called uninhabited regions of the world where agricultural development can keep pace with global population growth and where there is sufficient space to manage the distribution of populations (but especially the "redundant" underclass) that industrial capitalist development is required. Once again, then, land plays multiple roles, functioning both as an active, productive agent, a commodity, and a spatial horizon. Hence, the future management of the most industrialized and developed societies hinges to a considerable extent upon their ability to return to a previous period, a "natural state of a country," when "the land is highly productive, and food obtained in great abundance by little labour," and by Mill's own time, this was "only true of unoccupied countries colonized by a civilized people" (96).[11] The unique status of these "unoccupied lands"— paradoxically gesturing simultaneously toward Europe's past and its future—means that Mill dismisses altogether the criticisms of settler colonization that had arisen a generation earlier. In short, colonialism has been reformulated such that the enormous expenditures of capital and state power required for new land annexation schemes can now be viewed not as a violation of the principles of free trade and classical political economy but as their natural extension. Colonization benefits capital and labour at home, but more than this, it is in the "collective economic interests of the human race" (358).[12]

Historicizing the connections between land and settler colonialism enables us to grasp the variegated content of both terms, as well as the relations between them. Taking up only one small slice of this complex history, this chapter has focused on the period between 1776 and 1848—book-ended by two major works of classical political economy, Smith's *Wealth of Nations* and Mill's *Principles*— as a particularly dense moment of transition and change during which land underwent significant recoding. Through this close reading, I have attempted to demonstrate that, while settler colonialism may always be about land, this is not because colonial elites have sought to acquire some object of interest that preceded their investment in it. Rather, it is because land has been actively made and remade by processes of colonization. Close examination of the specific content of this at key periods retrains attention to the constitutive, rather than contingent, relation between settler colonialism, political economy, and land.

NOTES

1. The period from 1780 to 1830 saw a general rise in anti-imperial sentiment across major intellectuals in Britain and France (Pitts 2005).

2. Another indication of the difference between Locke and the later political economists is hinted at in the former's use of the term *industry* as nearly synonymous with agricultural cultivation, whereas the latter group would use them in opposition. In a clear demonstration of the Lockean frame at work as a tool of colonial legitimation, William Cronon has documented the manner in which seventeenth-century English colonial commentaries drew precisely the conclusion that Indigenous Americans lacked "industry" because they lacked settled agriculture (see Cronon 1983).

3. "1. La peine capitale n'est pas convertible en profit; elle ne donne point de dédommagement à la partie lésée: elle en détruit même la source ; le délinquant par son travail pourrait réparer une partie du mal qu'il a fait: sa mort ne répare rien. 2. Loin d'être convertible en profit, cette peine est une *perte,* une *dépense* dans ce qui fait la force et la richesse d'une nation, le nombre des hommes" (Dumont 1840, 235).

4. Cited by George Ensor in his polemic against Malthusianism (Ensor 1967, 9–10). Ensor was an Irish political writer and associate of J. S. Mill. He accompanied the young Mill on his trip to France in 1820.

5. Malthus had little direct influence on colonial policy in his time. It is possible he had a more indirect one, however: his main employment was as Professor of History and Political Economy at the East India Company's College in Hertfordshire, where he taught young boys intending to enter the imperial company's civil service.

6. One figure who stands somewhat outside the mainstream here is Jeremy Bentham. A prominent voice of anti-imperial and anticolonial sentiment at the turn of the nineteenth century, Bentham was approached by Wakefield in 1831 and was evidently able to change the utilitarian philosopher's mind on colonization. Bentham gave Wakefield his support in a scheme for the colonization of South Australia and, in so doing, drew arguments from the classical political economists (Winch 1965, 35).

7. As the historian John Waever (2005, 82) puts it, "by the late 1820s and early 1830s, the writings of classical economists about land's intrinsic value to its owners informed land allocation discussions in London and settlement colonies, stimulating new land allocation regulations for Australia and leading to the East India Company's reforms of land tenure and taxation."

8. Malthus and his critics shared a common adherence to a "stages of civilization" view of historical development in which humanity was progressing from lower/savage forms to higher/civilized, a view indebted to—inter alia—Adam Ferguson (1723–1816) and his influential 1767 text *Essay on the History of Civil Society* (1767). See Malthus (1993, chaps. 3–4).

9. As he puts it: "[I]t appears that a society constituted according to the most beautiful form that imagination can conceive, with benevolence for its moving principle instead of self-love, and with every disposition in all its members corrected by reason and not force, would, from the inevitable laws of nature, and not from any original depravity of man, in a very short period degenerate into a society constructed upon a plan not essentially different from that which prevails in every known state at present; I mean, a society divided into a class of proprietors and a class of labourers, and with self-love for the main-spring of the great machine" (Malthus 1993, 86). It is interesting and perhaps surprising to find in Malthus such a clear statement regarding the centrality of class division to modernization. As Marx would later point out, this is nevertheless still a rather conservative analysis, since Malthus views this division as natural, inevitable, and insurmountable. Still, from a Physiocratic vantage, he does provide some limited tools

for a critique of the emergent bourgeois industrial capitalists. For instance, Malthus agrees with Smith and Ricardo (contra the traditional Physiocrats) that manufacturing may be productive. However, he argues that, unlike agriculture, it is only productive for a certain segment of the population—the proprietors of the manufacturing industry— while nonproductive for the society as a whole. In effect, he is recognizing that the value created in manufacturing is really just a transfer of wealth from the laborers to the capitalists (chap. 18, 134–136)

10. Famously, Malthus generally viewed the idea of human perfectibility with great suspicion. The *Principle of Population* is offered as a "conclusive" argument "against the perfectibility of the mass of mankind" (Malthus 1993, 14), directly opposed to the Enlightenment vision of unlimited progress through the use of reason. Malthus's melancholic outlook on perfectibility meshed rather well with Anglican orthodoxy, which viewed life as a state of trial in which pain played an equally important role as pleasure in motivating action and, in particular, avoiding evil. As he puts it: "Evil exists in the world not to create despair, but activity" (158).

11. Mill's immediate example here is the United States. Elsewhere, he refers to these spaces as "the backward countries of the world," arguing that only there is "increased production is still an important object: in those most advanced, what is economically needed is a better distribution, of which one indispensable means is a stricter restraint on population. Levelling institutions, either of a just or of an unjust kind, cannot alone accomplish it; they may lower the heights of society, but they cannot, of themselves, permanently raise the depths" (Mill 1994, 127).

12. Mill goes on to detail the ways in which the English laboring class will only benefit in the long run from emigration/colonialism; for example, "To appreciate the benefits of colonization, it should be considered in its relation, not to a single country, but to the collective economic interests of the human race" (Mill 1994, 358). See also Ellis (1826), which is cited by Mill as an important source.

REFERENCES

Armitage, D. 2004. "John Locke, Carolina, and The Two Treatises of Government." *Political Theory* 32 (5): 602–627.

Arneil, B. 1996. *Locke in America: The Defense of English Colonialism.* Oxford: Oxford University Press.

Arneil, B. 2017. *Domestic Colonies: The Turn Inward to Colony.* Oxford: Oxford University Press.

Chalmers, T. 1995. *On Political Economy (with McCulloch's Review in the Edinburgh Review, 1832): The Supreme Importance of a Right Moral to the Right Economical State of the Community.* London: Routledge.

Cronon, W. 1983. *Changes in the Land: Indians, Colonists, and the Ecology of New England.* New York: Hill and Wang.

Dick, E. 1970. *The Lure of the Land: A Social History of the Public Lands from the Articles of Confederation to the New Deal.* Lincoln: University of Nebraska Press.

Dumont, E. 1840. "Examen de la peine de mort." In *Théorie des Peines et des Récompenses.* Edited by J. Bentham. Bruxelles: Société Belge de Libraire.

Ellis, W. 1826. "Employment of Machinery." *Westminster Review* 5: 101–130.

Ensor, G. 1967. *An Inquiry Concerning the Population of Nations, Containing a Refutation of Mr. Malthus's Essay on Population.* New York: Augustus Kelley.

Ford, A. 1910. *Colonial Precedents of our National Land System as it Existed in 1800.* No. 352 of *Bulletin of the University of Wisconsin.* History Series, vol. 2, no. 2. Madison: University of Wisconsin.

Foucault, M. 1970. *The Order of Things*. London: Routledge.

Foucault, M. 2007. *Security, Territory, Population*. New York: Palgrave Macmillan.

Gherke, C., and H. Kurz. 1995. "Karl Marx on Physiocracy." *The European Journal of the History of Economic Thought* 2 (1): 53–90.

Ghosh, R. N. 1964. "The Colonization Controversy: R. J. Wilmot-Horton and the Classical Economists." *Economica* 31 (124): 385–400.

Ince, O. U. 2019. *Colonial Capitalism and the Dilemmas of Liberalism*. Oxford: Oxford University Press.

Lester, W. 1860. *Decisions of the Interior Department in Public Land Cases*. Philadelphia: H. P. and R. H. Small.

Locke, J. *The Second Treatise of Government*. 2nd ed. Cambridge: Cambridge University Press, 1988.

Macpherson, C. B. 1975. "Capitalism and the Changing Concept of Property." In *Feudalism, Capitalism, and Beyond*. Edited by E. Kamenka and R. S. Neale. London: Edward Arnold.

Macpherson, C. B. 2011. *The Political Theory of Possessive Individualism: Hobbes to Locke*. Oxford: Oxford University Press.

Malthus, T. R. 1993. *An Essay on the Principle of Population*. Oxford: Oxford University Press.

Marx, K. 1989. "Theories of Surplus Value." In *Economic Manuscripts of 1861–1863*. Vol.31 of *Marx & Engels Collected Works*. New York: Lawrence and Wishart.

Marx, K. 1990. *Capital, Vol.1: A Critique of Political Economy*. London: Penguin Books.

McNally, D. 1990. *Political Economy and the Rise of Capitalism*. Berkeley: University of California Press.

Mill, J. S. 1994. *Principles of Political Economy, with Some of Their Applications to Social Philosophy*. Oxford: Oxford University Press.

Mills, R. C. 1915. *The Colonization of Australia: The Wakefield Experiment in Empire Building*. London: Sidgwick & Jackson.

Pitts, J. 2005. *A Turn to Empire: The Rise of Imperial Liberalism in Britain and France*. Princeton: Princeton University Press.

Quesnay, F. 1958. *Le Bicentenaire du Tableau Économique : François Quesnay et la Physiocratie*. Paris: Institut National d'Études Démographiques.

Rana, A. 2010. *The Two Faces of American Freedom*. Cambridge, MA: Harvard University Press.

Ricardo, D. 2004. *The Principles of Political Economy and Taxation*. Mineola, NY: Dover Publications.

Robbins, R. M. 1976. *Our Landed Heritage: The Public Domain, 1776–1970*. Lincoln: University of Nebraska Press.

Rothschild, E. 2002. *Economic Sentiments: Adam Smith, Condorcet, and the Enlightenment*. Cambridge, MA: Harvard University Press.

Ryan, A. 1984. *Property and Political Theory*. New York: Basil Blackwell.

Schumpeter, J. 1994. *History of Economic Analysis*. Oxford: Oxford University Press.

Simmel, B. 1970. *The Rise of Free Trade Imperialism: Classical Political Economy, the Empire of Free Trade and Imperialism, 1750–1850*. Cambridge: Cambridge University Press.

Smith, A. 1999. *The Wealth of Nations*. London: Penguin Classics.

Strachan, J. 1827. *Remarks on Emigration from the United Kingdom: Addressed to Robert Wilmot-Horton*. London: John Murray.

Thompson, E. P. 1991. *Customs in Common*. Pontypool: Merlin Press.

Tocqueville, A. de. 2004. "L'Ancien Régime et la Révolution." In *Oeuvres*. Edited by F. Furet and Fr. Mélonio, 190–194. Paris: Gallimard.

Tully, J. 1993. *An Approach to Political Philosophy: Locke in Contexts*. Cambridge: Cambridge University Press.

Tully, J. 1980. *A Discourse on Property: John Locke and his Adversaries*. Cambridge: Cambridge University Press.

US Congress. 1848. "An Act to Prevent Settlements Being Made on Lands Ceded to the United States, Until Authorized by Law." In *The Public Statues at Large of the United States of America*. Edited by R. Peters. Boston: Charles C. Little and James Brown.

Vardi, L. 2014. *The Physiocrats and the World of Enlightenment*. Cambridge: Cambridge University Press.

Veracini, L. 2010. *Settler Colonialism: A Theoretical Overview*. New York: Palgrave MacMillon.

Veracini, L. 2012. *The Settler Colonial Present*. New York: Palgrave MacMillon.

Waldron, J. 2002. *God, Locke, and Equality: Christian Foundations in Locke's Thought*. Cambridge: Cambridge University Press.

Weaver, J. 2005. "Concepts of Economic Improvement and the Social Construction of Property Rights: Highlights from the English-Speaking World." In *Despotic Dominion: Property Rights in British Settler Societies*. Edited by J. McLaren, A.R. Buck, and N. E. Wright, xx–xx. Vancouver: UBC Press.

Wilmot-Horton, R. *An Inquiry into the Causes and Remedies of Pauperism*. 2nd ed. London: Edmund Lloyd, 1831a.

Wilmot-Horton, R. 1831b. *Lectures on Statistics and Political Economy: As Affecting the Condition of the Operation and Labouring Classes*. n.p.

Winch, D. 1965. *Classical Political Economy and Colonies*. Cambridge, MA: Harvard University Press.

Winch, D. 1996. *Riches and Poverty: An Intellectual History of Political Economy in Britain, 1750–1834*. Cambridge: Cambridge University Press.

Winch, D. 2009. *Wealth and Life: Essays on the Intellectual History of Political Economy in Britain, 1848–1914*. Cambridge: Cambridge University Press.

Winch, D. 2013. *Malthus: An Introduction*. Oxford: Oxford University Press.

Wolfe, P. 2006. "Settler Colonialism and the Elimination of the Native." *Journal of Genocide Studies* 8 (4): 387–409.

Wrigley, E. A., and R. S. Schofield. 1989. *The Population History of England, 1541–1871*. Cambridge, MA: Harvard University Press.

2

SHAPING NEW HOMELANDS
Colonial Politics of Land Relations and
Management in the Cherokee Nation

Clint Carroll

The act of governing or bureaucratically managing land flattens the intricate relationships that constitute how people experience it. While scholars in political ecology and related fields have long centered this foundational premise in their work (see, e.g., Blaikie and Brookfield 1987, Peluso 1994, Fairhead and Leach 1996, Scott 1998), the complexities presented by historical and contemporary *Indigenous* land management institutions in settler colonial contexts like the United States have received much less attention. The political scales created by Indigenous nationhood, the treaties and governance structures that undergird and uphold this sovereign status, and the distinctive facets of settler colonialism as a "land-centred project [. . .] with a view to eliminating Indigenous societies" (Wolfe 2006, 393) all present unique formations and articulations of Indigenous land management and governance that complicate standard political-ecological analyses.

Further, as many scholars in critical Indigenous studies have expressed, Indigenous relationships to land entail mutual obligations of care that include but also exceed materiality (e.g., Deloria [1972] 2003; LaDuke 1999; Deloria and Wildcat 2001; Coulthard 2014). Land is widely understood as a network of relations, as well as a relative with whom human beings must maintain relationships of respect and reciprocity (Salmón 2000; McGregor 2005; Kimmerer 2013; Simpson 2017). This relationality with land has been obstructed by settler colonial forces, which not only seek to dispossess Indigenous peoples of their lands but, through assimilatory and other means, also seek to sever and alter the fundamental relationships that Indigenous peoples have to land. In this context,

Indigenous nations must navigate numerous arenas of "land management" that interface with present-day settler state polities, neighboring non-Indigenous communities, and the contemporary manifestations of centuries of settler colonial land policies. For those Indigenous nations that have developed bureaucratic forms of government—often as mechanisms to engage settler polities and thereby protect Indigenous land bases—land management programs carry historical and ontological baggage that impedes their ability to enact fully relational ways of knowing and interacting with the land that are integral to sustaining cultural lifeways.

The character and legal status of land for Indigenous nations in the United States is, of course, wrapped up in the same Euro-Western ontological baggage of defining land as a commodity that is subject to valuation on the capitalist market. And yet, despite this underpinning of land's character as alienable, "Indian land" in the United States is legally distinct, stemming from the trust relationship between Indigenous nations and the federal government codified in US Supreme Court decisions. Briefly, "trust lands" are tribally designated lands to which the US Interior Department holds legal title on the tribes' behalf, with the responsibility as trustee to manage them according to good-faith principles. Chief Justice John Marshall's decision in *Cherokee Nation v. Georgia* (1832) laid the foundation for the trust relationship, defining Indigenous nations as "domestic dependent" nations and attributing guardianship to the federal government. Such a colonial and paternalistic relationship continues to structure the ability of Indigenous nations to manage their lands according to their own principles and goals, as the Department of the Interior must approve any development activities or leases on them. Conversely, trust lands are not subject to the jurisdiction and related impositions from state governments (e.g., Oklahoma) due to their federal legal status. This status exempts trust lands from state taxation, affording Indigenous nations some legal entitlements, but nonetheless still within a colonial structure.

The US reservation system of the mid-1800s, although it varied widely in the experiences of each nation, was established to acquire land from Indigenous peoples and provide a permanent home and provisions from the federal government due to the tribes' "dependent" status. This was, by and large, accomplished through treaties—usually signed under duress—in which Indigenous representatives ceded portions of their homelands but often retained their rights to hunt, fish, and gather within the ceded areas. The reservations were assigned an agent who managed federal provisions of food and clothing, but who was often complicit in swindling Indian people out of mineral and timber resources obtained on reservation lands. In 1887, the General Allotment Act was passed by the US Congress to break up reservation land bases and encourage

Indian people to privatize and farm their lands according to yeoman ideals and principles. The result of this policy was the loss of millions of acres of Indian land over the course of the next four decades due to deception and fraud by white settlers, known as "land hawks" (Debo 1940).[1]

The experience of allotment also varied among tribal nations in time and effects, with some reservations like the Red Lake Ojibwe in Minnesota successfully resisting the policy entirely. In what was to become the state of Oklahoma, many nations, including the Cherokee Nation, temporarily managed to stave off allotment through political and spiritual movements that refused the ideology of land as a commodity (Holm 2005, 25–33). Before allotment, Cherokee lands were owned communally by the nation in fee simple. However, the federal government ultimately enforced the allotment policy on Cherokee people. As a result, of the original 4.42 million acres that formed the nation's territory, today only about 100,000 acres (under 2 percent) are tribal trust lands (fig. 2.1). The effects of this include exceedingly limited access to "checkerboarded" parcels of land, as well as complex jurisdictional authority and reduced authority to manage or caretake land within the reservation boundaries.[2]

This chapter considers these distinctive legal and political conditions in understanding Cherokee people's relationships to and management of land. I discuss the changing landscapes of the Cherokee Nation postremoval from their southeastern homelands in what was then known as the "Indian Territory" west of the Mississippi River.[3] I trace the development and adaptation of practices and laws that sought to manage and protect their new territory in the face of continued settler colonial encroachment and internal conflict. I view land itself as a player in the social lives that affect its character and health. In doing so, I evoke recent theorizations of relationality in the field of critical Indigenous studies, which center Indigenous ontologies of care and kinship among all beings (Yazzie and Baldy 2018). Such a framework assumes the validity of Indigenous knowledges and that from their associated land-based practices arise relational obligations that must be continually acknowledged, renewed, and acted on. Drawing from political ecology, I also follow Paul Robbins's (2004) emphasis on environmental production to stress the ongoing process of making and remaking landscapes dictated by both human and more-than-human forces, and the ever-present roles of power, politics, and time in shaping the outcomes. Land, in this sense, is both *relation* (kin) and a field on which relationships play out across political, material, philosophical, and spiritual registers.

My historical scope is admittedly wide. I divide the chapter into broadly defined eras, in which I illuminate specific forces and circumstances that greatly influenced Cherokee relationships to land. These eras include the decades following removal and encompassing the US Civil War and Reconstruction era

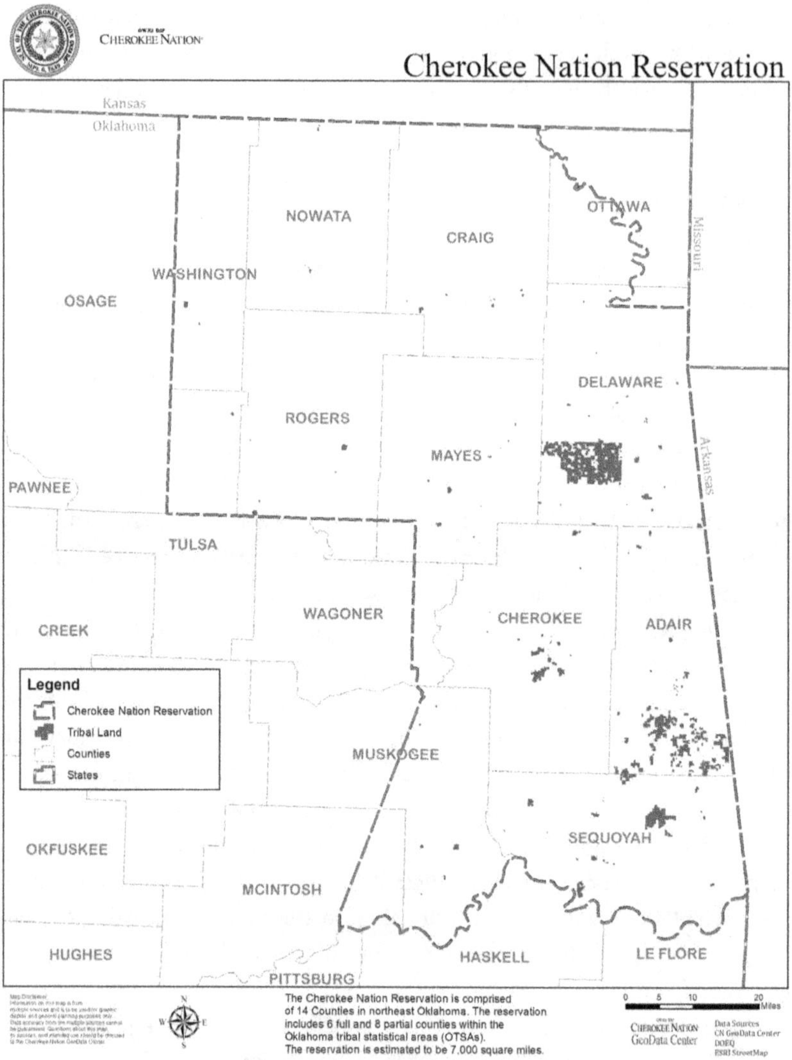

FIGURE 2.1. Cherokee Nation reservation with Oklahoma counties and the current extent of tribal trust land.

Courtesy of Cherokee Nation GeoData Center.

(ca. 1839–1880), allotment and Oklahoma statehood (1887–1934), and numerous Oklahoma rural development projects (1935–present). I conclude with a discussion of contemporary land management politics in the Cherokee Nation, drawing from interviews I conducted in 2015 with tribal Elders and knowledge holders and my ongoing ethnographic fieldwork. I approach this work from my position as a Cherokee Nation citizen who is invested in the well-being of our lands, culture, and communities, and from my long-standing relationships with tribal Elders and land managers. The chapter as a whole demonstrates how Indigenous land management in a settler colonial context must reconcile numerous overlapping and conflicting understandings of land, which manifest in both exogenous and endogenous articulations and practices.

The Produced Environment in the Early Cherokee Nation (Indian Territory)

Accounts of the environment in the Cherokee lands of the Indian Territory are scattered throughout the Indian-Pioneer Papers and the Doris Duke Collection, which contain interviews from the 1930s–1960s that capture entire generations of experience and memory.[4] Virtually every account on the environment in these collections tells of abundance in wild edibles and game. Even if one allows for a certain level of nostalgia reflected in these reminiscences, the consistent picture that emerges is significant. One account, given by E. F. Vann in 1938, asserts,

> The country of the Cherokee Nation was thinly populated [by humans] and wild game was abundant [. . .]. In the Flint District and in surrounding districts, except in the clearings which were being tilled, the country was still in its original condition, a hill country of forest with small areas of prairie scattered through it. It seemed the entire country abounded in wild game, deer, bear, opossum, raccoon, wild hogs, wild cattle, wild horses, bobcats, squirrels, rabbits, wild turkeys, quail, prairie chickens and wild pigeons [. . .]. All species of soft water fish were abundant in the creeks and rivers [. . .]. Each fall many nuts were gathered such as pecans, walnuts, hazelnuts, and chinquapins as well as hickory nuts [. . .]. Some orchards were planted but not many because there were plenty of wild fruits and berries such as plums, grapes, seedling peaches, dewberries, huckleberries and a number of others.[5]

The "wild hogs" and "wild cattle" were a result of free-range animal husbandry that was widely practiced at this time. Speaking more specifically of this, Elinor Meigs stated in 1937, "I can remember when there were dense canebrakes in the river lowlands which afforded wonderful winter range for cattle, also a shelter for the stock from the severe winter weather and a refuge for game [. . .]. The prairie grass in those days were [sic] as tall as a person's shoulder and grew in every nook that was not covered with trees, and it was free and open range for stock."[6]

Allowing stock to roam free throughout the woods was a practice afforded by the Cherokee land tenure system, in which all land was considered communally owned. This land tenure system modeled that which Cherokees had practiced in the eastern homelands and was backed by the Cherokee Nation constitutional government, reestablished in the new territory in 1839. Fences during this time were almost nonexistent, save for rudimentary "zigzag" rail fences that surrounded family plots of about twenty to twenty-five acres (Hewes 1978, 28). The accounts of dense canebrakes and shoulder-high prairie grass indicate an ample supply of wild fodder (which also included "mast," or wild nuts), eliminating the need for manufactured feed. Instrumental in creating this condition was the human use of fire.

In their inhabitation of the lands west of the Mississippi, Cherokees came across a lived environment. Quapaw, Osage, Wichita, and Caddo peoples had once inhabited parts of what would become the Cherokee Nation lands in the west (Baird and Goble 1994). Indigenous fire regimes had helped to define the character of the western Ozarks at that time: parklike old-growth forests with interspersed grassy meadows. As anthropologist Albert Wahrhaftig documented in the 1970s, "Cherokees say that, when they first came to the area, the Ozark forests had trees so big and so widely spaced that through them you could see a man on horseback a quarter-mile away" (1978, 421). In the eastern homelands, Cherokees had become very familiar with fire as a management tool; naturally, they would also find this practice useful in the western lands (Fowler and Konopik 2007, 168–170). In addition to documented evidence of Cherokee burning in the Ozarks (168–170), the above accounts—in their descriptions of abundant berries and game, and large meadows and canebrakes—suggest that a regime of controlled burning continued in the Indian Territory.[7]

Blackburn and Anderson assert that fire was used by Native Americans for "creating and sustaining vegetational mosaics" (1993, 19). The accounts of dense canebrakes, scattered prairies, and open forests in the Indian Territory indeed may describe examples of such mosaics, sustained by the Cherokee use of fire. Frequent light fires also stabilized forests by regularly burning off the "ladder fuels" that can carry fire into forest canopies, resulting in devastating "crown fires" (Huntsinger and McCaffrey 1995, 163). The time of year when one burned also factored into the efficacy of fire as a management tool. Oral accounts from my fieldwork say that burning the hills was an annual early fall activity. To this effect, the tribal government, as early as 1841, established a law that prohibited "any person or persons, to set the woods on fire, from the fifteenth of October to the first of March, in each year" (this implies that early spring was also an acceptable time to burn) (Cherokee Executive Committee 1969, 48–49). However, scientific research on river cane (*Arundinaria gigantea*) shows that longer burning intervals of seven to ten years would have been necessary to maintain large canebrakes (Platt and Brantley 1997; Brantley and Platt 2001), which suggests that Cherokees employed a nuanced application of fire for different vegetational zones.

Agriculture during this time was primarily subsistence based, and Cherokees also employed fire to clear their fields for planting. Large trees in a field plot were girdled, left to dry out, and then burned (Hewes 1978, 21). Among those in the eastern part of the Nation (the Ozark hill country), a community-based way of life was predominant, exemplified by another practice for clearing farm plots, called "rail maulings." Similar to the old *gadugi* work crews that Cherokee communities once formed to help families in need (see Fogelson and Kutsche 1961), rail maulings were social events designed to help neighbors and friends. To this effect, money was rarely needed or used. Yet class differences in the Cherokee Nation did constitute differences in agricultural production. Those affluent Cherokees who had assumed many practices of their white neighbors in the US South could farm the more expansive eastern prairies on a larger scale due to their enslavement of African Americans and the employment of white migrant workers. Despite these practices, which were viewed with contempt by many traditionalists, the early Cherokee Nation's agricultural economy consisted of minimal exports (Hewes 1978, 24–30).

The Cherokee communal land tenure system, couched in traditional values that condemned the alienation of land, required regulations and laws to protect and maintain it. For example, the tribal government strictly prohibited the sale of timber to US citizens and regulated the use of salt wells and salt springs by short-term leases limited to Cherokee citizens. Mineral resources such as coal and lead, although extracted on a very small scale, were also regulated and restricted to citizen use only. In 1841, the tribal government passed a law that prohibited the felling of pecan trees (a common way of harvesting the nuts had once been to cut down the entire tree) (Hewes 1978, 29). The same act regulated the burning of the woods, mentioned above. While these regulations were made, as geographer Leslie Hewes notes, "no doubt with popular approval [. . .] to preserve the resource for the general good," a subsistence economy undergirded by communal land tenure made it difficult for the Cherokee state to enforce these regulations for lack of a permanent source of funds normally obtained through the levying of property taxes (29, 31). This issue, along with increasing class divisions within the Cherokee Nation, would later result in serious problems for the Nation for which the US Civil War served as catalyst.

Threats to Cherokee Laws and Lands

The Civil War left the Cherokee Nation in a state of devastation; however, numerous accounts depict a rapid reconstruction. In as few as four years, most Cherokees had restored their farms and livestock (Hewes 1978, 33). Although Cherokees would once again enjoy a short time of prosperity, the Treaty of 1866—made with the United States following the Cherokee Nation's alliance with the Confederacy—contained harsh stipulations that would soon be set in motion.[8] The Treaty of 1866 opened up the Cherokee Nation to railroad companies, and with them came intensive resource exploitation and settler encroachment. In 1871, railroad tie cutting began in the northeastern part of the Nation. Mainly post oak was harvested for this purpose; however, the industry soon realized the abundance of quality timber for export and convinced local Cherokees to sell stands of old-growth black walnut (Bays 1998, 82). Although the Cherokee Nation passed laws to inhibit the sale of hardwood timber, Brad A. Bays notes that "the trade was a prime example of the ineffectiveness of Cherokee law and federal administration to control railroad exploitation and intruder spoliation in the Indian Territory" (82). It is unknown whether Cherokee lawmakers were operating from a traditional land ethic or from the need to protect tribal resources (or both), but it is clear that the forces of capitalism (through timber export) and colonialism (through settler and railroad encroachment) had created circumstances that were changing the land and Cherokees' relationship to it.

The railroad and timber industries, working in concert with each other, marked the onset of the Industrial Revolution in the Indian Territory. A different kind of fire emerged on the Cherokee landscape during this time. High-intensity, stand-replacing fires accompanied logging activity, as felled areas were often burned to prepare them for grazing livestock (Fowler and Konopik 2007, 170). Sparks from passing locomotives could also ignite exposed, dry, clear-cut areas (170). These activities changed the character and composition of the Cherokee forests by eliminating old-growth hardwoods and pines. Large fields eventually replaced many of the parklike expanses of forests that had once defined the Cherokee Ozarks. The disturbance also drastically affected important forest resources, such as huckleberry bushes. In 1969, the interviewer of Jake Whitmire gave the following account:

He recalls a long time ago when they looked forward to huckleberry time. Then families would go into the woods and gather the berries by the washtub full. The bushes would be so loaded they just set the tub under them and strip the berries off the limbs. But then came the whiteman and his timber cutting and burning of woods and another pleasure and suffice of the Indian went [. . .]. This at one time was a good timber country [Adair County], and many carloads of ties and lumber were shipped from Addielee [. . .]. When the railroad was taken out the town quickly died. He says the railroad was taken out because the whitemen mismanaged the cutting of timber. No reseeding or planting for the future was done and even today the once plentiful pine and hardwoods have not returned.[9]

The agricultural landscape in the Cherokee Nation was changing too, and this change primarily reflected culture and class differences that manifested in exploitative practices. An increasing population of noncitizen white tenant farmers, combined with increased agricultural activity among an elite Cherokee planter class and intermarried whites (who were considered citizens), resulted in the increase of illegal enclosures. Before 1875, the only legal fences in the Cherokee Nation were the previously mentioned zigzag rail fences—intended to enclose a small family plot (the legal amount was no more than fifty acres per family member). Regardless, by the early 1870s, numerous types of fences dotted the landscape, including board, barbed wire, hedge, and stone. In 1875, the Cherokee Nation government legalized board, hedge, and stone fences, among others (due to their benignity), but maintained the illegality of barbed wire. With barbed wire, one could cheaply enclose a vast amount of land, and this was the predominant practice on the larger Cherokee prairies among white and elite Cherokee farmers (Hewes 1978, 40).

The conservative faction of the Cherokee Nation, represented by smaller-scale and community-oriented Cherokee farmers (in contrast to the larger-scale and commercially oriented whites and elite Cherokee farmers), reacted strongly to these illegal enclosures. In 1875, a Cherokee man named Oochalata led a movement to protest the perversion of the traditional communal land tenure system. The actions of the whites and elite Cherokees (who were still in the minority in the Nation) were seen to lead to corruption and greed, which violated the core values of the traditionalist majority of the Nation. In 1876, Oochalata was elected principal chief. Soon thereafter, he passed strict labor permit laws in an effort to curtail the practices of the elite few and ensure the expulsion of laborers and tenants who remained illegally in the Cherokee Nation after the expiration of their leases (McLoughlin 1993, 349). The counterreaction to these laws by the small "progressive" group (i.e., citizen whites and elite Cherokees) was to circumvent the tribal government and petition the US federal government. Historian William G. McLoughlin aptly describes their situation: "They had become a small bourgeoisie without power" (313). Their petition, although very different from the ideas of US policy makers, called for the allotment of the tribal land base.

A foundational principle for the allotment of tribal lands in severalty was the characterization of the vast majority of Cherokee territory as "unused." The Cherokee citizens in favor of allotment proposed to allot the entire land base to citizens only. There would be no "surplus" land for outsider settlement, and "the [federal] government would not dare to take from individual property owners the land that these outsiders wanted" (McLoughlin 1993, 280). The problem with this proposal was that, while it might inhibit white encroachment, the land would become alienable. This struck the nerve center of the conservative faction. The tribal land base represented a sacred source of collective sustenance and prosperity, and the Cherokee Nation had already experienced the devastating effects of unauthorized land sales by losing the homelands in the east. The Cherokee Nation had initially avoided the allotment policy (enacted in 1887) because it held fee simple title to all tribal lands. But by undermining the process of handling internal affairs as a sovereign nation, the Cherokee "bourgeoisie" cut short any further deliberations when they took their case to the US government. Federal policy makers used this case of impeded "progress," in conjunction with contradictory reports of unchecked accumulation, as an excuse to intervene. By the time the Curtis Act asserted federal plenary power over the Five Tribes in 1898, the Dawes Commission was intent on creating a "surplus" of land for white settlement.

Whereas the railroads had opened up the Cherokee Nation for incorporation into the capitalist market economy, the implementation of allotment effectively territorialized tribal lands. Formerly, Cherokee farm plots, settlements, and towns had been seemingly scattered and nonuniform as a result of the Cherokee communal land tenure. Because land was not taxed or deeded to individuals, there was no need to uniformly map land claims. A look at pre- and postallotment US Geological Survey maps shows that boundaries to land claims and agricultural fields pre-allotment were determined more by natural features than by socially constructed, invisible lines (Hewes 1978, 58–59). With the imposition of allotment, surveyors needed to divide and map individual plots of land in order to assign them to tribal citizens. Thus, the postallotment map is a series of uniform square grids that transect natural boundaries. It represents former "experienced" space as imagined, "abstract" space (Vandergeest and Peluso 1995,

388–389). Doing so virtually erased established plots and facilitated land expropriation. By 1911, of the original 4.42 million acres of land once owned in fee by the Cherokee Nation, approximately 4.35 million acres were allotted to 40,196 Cherokee citizens, and 72,000 acres were sold, opened up to white settlement, or annexed for railroad right-of-way and townships (USDOI 1912, 389).

Colonial Forestry, Fire Suppression, and Land Restrictions

Around the turn of the twentieth century, resource conservation and scientific forestry were becoming the dominant frameworks for US land management policy. As a reaction to the destructive actions that accompanied railroad construction and industrial logging, the conservation movement advocated the professional management of natural resources to ensure sustained yields. In the absence of tribal governance institutions (a consequence of allotment), the Omnibus Bill of 1910 (36 Stat. 857) named the Bureau of Indian Affairs (BIA) the official managing body of Indian forests. In this capacity, the BIA oversaw trust property timber harvests, including the finances of these operations, which were also held "in trust." At this point, Indian forests became "part of a national, conservation-based forest management program that would assure a steady supply of timber and protection of watersheds" (Huntsinger and McCaffrey 1995, 171).

According to this new management regime, the key to ensuring the availability of timber was the suppression of fire. Whereas this position was aimed at eliminating catastrophic industrial fires, all forest fires were judged a threat to valuable national resources (Fowler and Konopik 2007, 171). The combination of clear-cut logging, catastrophic fires, and the elimination of controlled burns caused environmental changes in the western Ozarks that impeded Cherokee access to natural resources. The buildup of underbrush that accompanied the second-growth forests decreased the ease of hunting and gathering by obstructing formerly open forests and providing ample habitat for pests like ticks and chiggers. Wild game populations likely diminished as a result of fire suppression (combined with an increased human population), as Huntsinger and McCaffrey (1995, 175) have documented. After Oklahoma statehood in 1907, increased infiltration of the former tribal land base imposed new laws and jurisdiction on Cherokee people, including land use and hunting restrictions. "Hog-fencing laws" ended open range practices (Wahrhaftig 1978, 450), and non-Indians began to erect enclosures on former resource gathering areas. The

Great Depression in the 1930s, along with severe droughts in 1935 and 1936, made matters worse; while the restrictions on forest resources increased, so did Cherokees' reliance on them. During this time, Wahrhaftig notes, "Cherokees were increasingly blocked from their generalized utilization of the woods and streams, deprived of sufficient cash supplement to capitalize even a subsistence farm, and confined to the tiny island of their allotments. Cherokee self-sufficiency had seriously declined by the time World War II arrived" (450). The interviewer of Ross Bowlin gave another account in 1969: "For Ross much of the country has changed in his time. New roads and fences have been one of the big changes, which came with the white man who owns nearly all of the land now. He finds it hard to understand that the whitemen don't live here, but comes [sic] and fences up the land and refuses to let anyone hunt [. . .]. Over on a stretch of woodland Ross tells that it was once the finest huckleberry place in the country. But no one is allowed in there now."[10]

Cherokee distrust and bitterness toward the outsiders were heightened by the fact that many had directly deceived Cherokees and robbed them of their lands. "Grafters" and "land hawks" were terms for those who swindled Cherokees out of their allotment land—often with the help of the Indian agents (Wahrhaftig 1978, 424, 449). Many of the few white families with whom Cherokees had developed neighborly relations had moved elsewhere due to the Depression. Eventually many of these "abandoned" lands were consolidated into large ranches and bought by outsiders who rarely lived there, reflecting the above testimony (Wahrhaftig 1978, 420–421).

More restrictions came in the form of bureaucracy. The Dawes Commission tasked itself not only with allotting lands but with allotting blood quantum to individuals. Doing so tied the degree of "Indian blood" to a level of competency—the higher the quantum of Indian blood, the less competent an individual was to manage their land. "Restricted land" referred to land allotted to Cherokees of one-half or more Indian blood. Under this system, the land was exempted from property taxes, and the BIA held the title to the land in trust. A "restricted Indian" could not harvest timber on the land or "develop" it without prior approval from the BIA. Further, since the land was not alienable, individuals could not use the land as collateral for loans, thus restricting entry into the market. This system was notoriously manipulated and exploited by grafters and land hawks, who often "helped" individuals with the process of taking their lands out of restricted status. Once this was achieved, the land was easily stolen by manipulating the bureaucratic system that was unfamiliar to many non-English-speaking Cherokees. Much of the archaic policy and bureaucratic red tape surrounding allotments and restricted land continue to this day (see Leeds 2006).

Producing the "Green Country" of Oklahoma

As a reaction to the Dust Bowl and the Depression Era, the Oklahoma State Planning and Resource Board (formed in 1935) began the construction of dams throughout the state. With the help of the Army Corps of Engineers, the Bureau of Reclamation, and the Grand River Dam Authority, numerous lakes were formed throughout northeastern Oklahoma. The lakes were designed to provide flood control, a steady water supply, hydroelectric power, and opportunities for outdoor recreation (Johnson 1998, 4). As time went on, the area, with its large lakes and rolling green hills, became known among other Oklahomans and the surrounding states as a place for recreational tourism. In an effort to capitalize on the region's new image, northeastern Oklahoma was dubbed "Green Country." The establishment of a special organization in 1965—Green Country, Inc.—spearheaded this campaign and served to "coordinate [the] promotion and development of sixteen northeast Oklahoma counties" (Stauber, n.d.). Based on his ethnographic research with Cherokee people in Oklahoma that spanned the 1960s and 1970s, Wahrhaftig commented that the name Green Country

> evokes a new future for the region, as a paradise of woods, lakes, bass, legions of free-spending tourists and vacationers, second homes for Tulsans and Dallasites—the playground of Texas and Kansas [. . .]. The new image, and the national advertising that is merchandising it, has the timeless ring of God-created wilderness, revealing that Oklahomans are apparently oblivious to their impact on the environment. In less than a century it has been transformed, certainly to the disadvantage of the Cherokees and, perhaps, to that of everyone else. (1978, 421)

Also to the disadvantage of the Cherokees, as Wahrhaftig notes, was the flooding of numerous Cherokee settlements by the new lakes (421). Entire communities were relocated, and family and community cemeteries had to be excavated and moved. Speaking with animosity toward the rapid rate of "progress" throughout Cherokee country, Wahrhaftig notes, "The price Cherokees have paid for Green Country is scrub-choked, tick-infested, second-growth forests; fishing lakes that have drowned former Indian settlements; and a displaced Cherokee population which is either on welfare or in California" (421).

Whereas Oklahoma statehood had geopolitically subsumed the Cherokee Nation, the making of Green Country attempted to complete the incorporation of the Cherokee Nation into the state of Oklahoma through the superimposition of regional boundaries. Although the campaign was welcomed in some parts of the Cherokee Nation as a source of economic development, this proved to be for all the wrong reasons. Instead of promoting sustainable, locally based economic opportunities, white Oklahomans were more interested in resource exploitation (fish and game) and shallow cultural tourism that presented Cherokee people as remnants of the past (Wahrhaftig 1978, 430–432). The Oklahoma Office of Tourism and Recreation maintains the image and boundaries of Green Country today, along with five other tourism regions such as Kiamichi Country (i.e., the Choctaw Nation) and Arbuckle Country (i.e., the Chickasaw Nation). From the same entity comes the term "Oklacolor" to describe the geographical and cultural diversity of the state, and Green Country's tagline in a promotional video asserts, "Green Country: We've got all the Oklacolors of the rainbow waiting for you in northeast Oklahoma. Go for it."[11]

Although incorporation into the state of Oklahoma has resulted in a seemingly typical rural Oklahoma landscape throughout the Cherokee Nation's reservation (see fig. 2.1), the western Ozark Plateau remains the cultural and social heart of the Cherokee Nation. While Cherokees are still outnumbered by the local white population, cohesive Cherokee communities permeate the region— many of them, as Wahrhaftig (1968) documented, having persisted since Cherokee arrival in the Indian Territory. Wahrhaftig's (1966) work also documented the intense poverty of the region, and this by and large continues today. However, much has also changed since the time of Wahrhaftig's fieldwork, positively affecting Cherokees and their standing in the larger regional social milieu. Cherokees have been reasserting their presence and control in northeastern Oklahoma through the increasing sophistication of tribal governance structures. Many of these strides have been made in the realm of land management. At the time of Wahrhaftig's research, the Cherokee Nation had little to no authority over tribal lands; yet, in the 1980s and 1990s, the Cherokee Nation would regain this power by taking control of institutions designed to protect and manage them.

Environmental Self-Governance and the Reclamation of Land Control

In 1987, due to increasing frustrations with federal Indian bureaucracy, American Indian tribes throughout the United States began to question the efficacy of the then twelve-year-old Indian Self-Determination and Education Assistance Act and called for significant policy amendments. While the Self-Determination Act had promoted American Indian control over their own affairs, the BIA had been reluctant to step down from its paternalistic role. Many institutions, including Indian Health Service facilities and tribal forestry programs, were still operated by Department of Interior personnel. Along with pressure from the tribes, a BIA fiasco in Arizona that received wide media coverage prompted congressional action.[12] "Self-governance" became the new emphasis in federal Indian policy, and in 1988 new amendments to the Self-Determination Act created Self-Governance Compacts by which Indian tribes could "administer and manage programs, activities, functions and services previously managed by the BIA" (SGCEP 2006, 22). The legislation also acknowledged the authority of tribes to "redesign those programs and services to meet the needs of their communities, within the flexibility of allocating funds based on tribal priorities" (22).

On October 1, 1990, Chief Wilma Mankiller signed such an agreement on behalf of the Cherokee Nation and "put the Tahlequah BIA agency out of business."[13] At this time, the Cherokee Nation began to assume control over the former BIA trust programs, which included loblolly pine silviculture, cattle grazing leases, and noxious weed suppression on the forty-five thousand acres of Cherokee tribal trust land. The Cherokee Nation Department of Natural Resources (NRD) emerged as the new tribal entity for managing these activities. Yet while the Cherokee Nation worked to develop its own environmental programs, the BIA retained its authority in the form of "trust evaluations." Outlined in the Permanent Self-Governance Act of 1994 (P.L. 103-413, section 403[d]), the trust evaluation "allows the United States to exercise the necessary supervision or oversight relative to its obligations to the Tribe and to individual Indians. An escape clause is provided whereby the United States may assume direct management of the physical trust assets upon proper notice to the Tribe if the trust assets are in immediate jeopardy. Imminent jeopardy is defined as significant loss or devaluation of the physical Trust asset, caused by the Tribes' action or inaction" (SGCEP 2006, 45). By establishing regulations and normative "best practices" that are guided by the assumption that lands must be made profitable, trust evaluations have served to maintain BIA bureaucratic imperialism and land management hegemony.

Furthermore, the Cherokee Nation, although deemed "in control" of its own lands and resources, inherited a complex land management bureaucracy, which was also held under BIA supervision. In inheriting this bureaucracy, the Cherokee Nation essentially inherited the institutional legacy of allotment. "Checkerboarded" tribal lands and the red tape that accompanies them cause difficulties in jurisdiction and property maintenance. Messy land deeds and property lines tell the story of grafters and land hawks. Multiple heirs of individual allotments complicate ownership beyond comprehension and inhibit any effective use of the property through agreement. Before amendments to the federal Stigler Act in 2018, the rubric of blood quantum to determine "restricted" land status had continued to racialize property issues in the Cherokee Nation.[14]

The maintenance of BIA programs has often put undue strain on tribal land managers, who also have a professional duty to respond to Cherokee Nation citizen input (as they are tribal employees and, in most cases, tribal citizens themselves). Often, the two tasks are entirely at odds with each other. For instance, during my early fieldwork between 2004 and 2008, tribal citizens frequently complained to me that their land-based activities were jeopardized by the NRD silvicultural activities—programs that were carried out per BIA "best practices" guidelines. Of these, loblolly pine projects—although gradually phased out of practice since the mid-1990s due to economic impracticalities—were established through the clearcutting of oak and hickory forests in place of monocrop pine stands. In the early 2000s, these projects still entailed routine thinning, a practice that decreases species diversity in both flora and fauna and thus negatively affects hunting and gathering activities. There is also an intrinsic value to the hardwood forests that is compromised by these programs. In 2006, at a community meeting in Kenwood (located in Delaware County, where there is an abundance of tribal trust land—about 1,100 acres of which were being used for loblolly pine management), one participant expressed his regret about seeing the habitat for birds and other animals disappear along with the hardwood forests. With a tone of voice that conveyed a deep familiarity with and respect for the area's remaining hardwood stands, he said, "I would just hate to see them go."[15] With regard to leasing tribal lands for cattle grazing—a still-prevalent activity— important medicinal plants like milkweed (*Asclepias* L.) are becoming hard to find due to the fact that they cannot compete with the Bermuda and fescue grasses that are seeded on native prairies to achieve "improved" pastures.

Only recently have tribal land managers begun to deviate from BIA programs, and this stems largely from a response to the citizen input exemplified above. During my fieldwork in 2008, tribal land managers were reconsidering their use of harmful chemical herbicides on prairies in favor of brush hogging (clearing by mowing). While brush hogging would inevitably cut back some culturally significant prairie plants, land managers discussed with me their intent to reserve areas of important plant growth for cultural use. The reduction of BIA activities has been accompanied by the initiation of culturally inspired land management activities. In 1999, NRD staff launched numerous "cultural forestry" projects that prioritized the cultivation and reintroduction of culturally significant species. Most notable among these projects is the large-scale planting of shagbark hickory trees (*Carya ovata*), an important species for food, crafts, and medicine that has become increasingly scarce, and Osage orange trees (*Maclura pomifera*), which have long been used by Cherokees in the western lands for making strong bows. During this time, NRD staff also began to focus on nonwood forest products, which include the medicinal, edible, and crafts-based herbs, forbs, and grasses that have no significant "value" from the perspective of BIA forestry programs. Rivercane (*Arundinaria gigantea*), used for numerous traditional crafts, and ginseng (*Panax quinquefolius* L.), an extremely important medicinal herb, have been key species in these efforts.

These cultural forestry projects, although inspired by citizen input, also stemmed from a larger trend of cultural revitalization within the Cherokee Nation government (see Sturm 2002, 104). Such a political climate allowed tribal land managers to devote some of their time to the maintenance and protection of cultural resources and to explore alternative management practices. This ongoing work, although now housed in a different tribal department, directly informs a key policy initiative—the Cherokee Nation Integrated Resource Management Plan—with the goal of identifying and cataloging Cherokee knowledge of wild plants and animals in order to strategically conserve tribal lands for their protection.

Another component of this strategy has been a tribal ethnobotanical project that I helped to initiate in 2004, which seeks to revitalize Cherokee knowledge and land-based practices. My work on this project during the summers of 2004–2006 entailed conducting informal interviews with Elders and knowledge holders and led to the creation of an informal advisory council to the NRD. In October 2008, the NRD director and I decided to convene a small gathering of about ten women and men at the grounds of a Cherokee community nonprofit organization located in the woods of Sequoyah County. The purpose of the meeting was to bring together many of the Elders and experts whom I had consulted in the course of the ethnobotanical project. The meeting was informal in nature and took place outdoors and around a fire—not a typical meeting for a tribal government department. In this setting, the group openly discussed the issues and strategies regarding the preservation of Cherokee plant knowledge. Significantly, they noted that their generation is possibly the last one that carries a substantial amount of this knowledge. The meeting closed that day with the Elders' unanimous decision to work actively toward perpetuating land-based knowledge and practices through educational programs and lending their collective voice to advocate for tribal land conservation.

Continued work with this advisory council—now known as the Cherokee Medicine Keepers—has advanced a number of their goals in the form of a digital media photovoice production (see Carroll and the Cherokee Nation Medicine Keepers 2016), an 810-acre designated tribal conservation tract, and a pilot land education program for Cherokee youth. The Medicine Keepers' work earned the group a Cherokee Nation Community Leadership Award in 2017, and they now advise the Cherokee Nation secretary of natural resources—a cabinet position that maintains its own staff and programs, most of which were carried over from the previous NRD leadership after a change in tribal administration in 2011. As I have discussed elsewhere, the Medicine Keepers' direct influence on tribal land management policy and practice represents an important voice in Cherokee environmental governance that offers transformative potential for the form and function of constitutionally and bureaucratically organized Indigenous governments (Carroll 2015). In the next section, I discuss recent and emerging work that further shows the effects of their joint position on tribal land management.

Cowboys, Cattle, and Silver Bullets: Cherokee Contestations over Land

The Cherokee Nation's principal chief election in 2011 brought numerous changes to its governmental offices at the tribal complex in Tahlequah. Former principal chief Chad Smith had led the nation for over a decade since 1999. Shortly after his opponent, Bill John Baker, was sworn into office, many tribal staff members who had supported Smith found their jobs at risk. Higher-level administrators were especially targeted due to their hierarchical proximity to the chief's office and the drastic swing in politics represented by the Baker administration. The NRD was one of many departments that experienced a significant change in leadership during this time; however, the former director, a longtime employee of the tribe with a wide skill set, maintained his employment, albeit under a different office.

The newly appointed leadership of the NRD, who openly promoted cattle ranching and associated themselves with the "cowboy culture" of Oklahoma, quickly worked to revert the character of the department to the BIA programs that the previous director had sought to diminish in the interest of more culturally attuned land management practices. Not surprisingly, cattle grazing leases on tribal lands and the accompanying herbicide and range seeding programs continued in full force without regard for medicinal plant conservation. The new NRD director even pursued reinstating the loblolly pine monocropping programs that had been recently phased out due to citizen complaints and economic impracticalities. While the former director was able to transfer some of the cultural programs and their associated staff to his new office, he no longer conducted them with the land management authority of the NRD. Tensions with the new NRD director, who actively looked for ways to counteract the work of the previous director, further stalled their progress.

Yet the Medicine Keepers, because they are not formally wedded to any tribal department, continued working with the former NRD director and his project staff, who now made up the Administration Support Department. The Medicine Keepers thus were able to resume their influence on tribal land management issues as Elder knowledge holders.[16] In fact, the group discussed that their mission transcended tribal politics and that their work needed to continue despite any changes in administration. This stance was also an attempt to reconcile their own political differences, since some in the group had openly supported the Baker campaign. Nevertheless, their collective goals stood in stark contrast to the new NRD leadership's priorities. As part of the Medicine Keeper's mission, in 2011 (before the tribal election) they had identified a tract of tribal land in Sequoyah County for the establishment of a conservation and education site for their activities. Plans included the establishment of a greenhouse to cultivate threatened medicinal plants, as well as the conservation and maintenance of the existing flora. The plans aligned with one group member's long-standing vision to establish a Cherokee tribal national park that would promote cultural knowledge and land-based practices. However, not long after the NRD's transition to new leadership, this same tract of land was bulldozed for horse trails and converted to a "dude ranch" that featured "cowboy karaoke" nights. To add salt to the wound, the NRD named the site Cherokee Nation Park, emphasizing the land's recreational use for equine tourism and eschewing any focus on cultural knowledge and practices.[17]

In this context, in 2015, I facilitated a photovoice project with the Medicine Keepers as part of our ongoing work and with the support of the former NRD director and staff. Rooted in community-based participatory research methodology, photovoice is designed to provide a platform for social action through visual media (Wang and Burris 1997; Wang et al. 1998). Photovoice projects distribute cameras to individuals in a community for them to photographically document their perspectives on a defined topic or question. With participants' guidance, the facilitator compiles the photographs into a presentable format that conveys the community's voice in a visual form—a slideshow, collage, or still-image documentary. In our project, the Medicine Keepers centered their attention on the relationship between *land* and *health*. Their photographs represented their thoughts and perspectives on a wide range of topics, including tribal land use. Notably, tribal land leases for cattle grazing surfaced as a predominant point of concern for the Elders.

As facilitator, I interviewed the Elders individually to elicit their thoughts on selected photographs. Following the individual interviews, we met as a group to discuss the overall messages they wished to convey through the project. After transcribing and coding the interviews, I drafted a video with voiceovers from the interview recordings. I presented this video draft to the group for their review and, following minor revisions, the video was finalized as a thirty-minute still-image documentary titled *Cherokee Voices for the Land.*[18] The photovoice project was tied to a larger survey project, which sought to understand how the perspectives of the Medicine Keepers expressed in the video affected the views of ordinary tribal citizens on issues of land use, conservation, and community health. In fall 2015, I surveyed eighty-four tribal citizens at the annual Cherokee National Holiday before and after screening the video. The results of this survey found statistically significant changes in their opinions and priorities regarding tribal land use (Carroll et al. 2018). Both the video and the survey results amplified the perspectives of the Medicine Keepers and showed how their knowledge could guide tribal land use policy in the interest of cultural preservation and health promotion. In this regard, later that year, representatives from the Medicine Keepers and I met with tribal officials to discuss the project's implications, and the photovoice video was screened for the Cherokee Nation Tribal Council's culture committee.

Although the video touches on numerous themes ranging from the importance of traditional medicines to broader spiritual guidelines on the relationship of humans to the more-than-human world, numerous Elders explicitly called out the detrimental effects of cattle grazing on plants and places that are important to them.[19] This prominent critique coincided with their message to prioritize tribal land conservation in ways that protect plant and animal habitats and promote Cherokee relationships with them through sustainable use and caretaking. As Bonnie Kirk states in the video, "There's a lot of land clearing [. . .] for cattle—you know, cattle's got to have land—and people just go in and doze the place, never researching what is being destroyed by clearing land or making highways [. . .]. I mean where does it stop?" Another Elder, John Ross, remarks that

> the only way we can preserve [land] is we've got to protect it, and there's few areas that you can find all these medicinal plants. But, you know, there's a lot of farmers and ranchers, they'll just cut all, everything out to raise cattle [. . .] and the Cherokees didn't like that when I was growing up. That's where Cherokees used to hunt and now, they can't go in there. That's where they used to gather, even to go look for wild onions. You can't go into places anymore [. . .]. That's what was important to our people, and still is. We need to preserve our area somewhere and that's how important the plants are for us.

In our group meeting, when I asked the Elders whether my initial analysis of their interviews was accurate in identifying the theme of cattle grazing, they were adamant that this topic was important to include in the video. As Ross indicates above, their views reflect generations of disdain for this type of land use and its accompanying practices of clearing and herbicide spraying. Because the Elders expressed this position pointedly, along with their emphasis on land conservation and environmental protection as vital components of community health and cultural preservation, the former NRD director described the photovoice video as a "silver bullet" for advancing the Medicine Keepers' goals and consequentially providing a counterbalance to the activities and cowboy culture of the new leadership of the NRD.

If the happenings of the years since this time are any indication, the analogy of a "silver bullet" is fitting—at least in part due to the impact of the photovoice video, but also significantly due to the continued influence and work of the Medicine Keepers to advance their mission of protecting tribal lands and promoting land-based education. In 2022, a Cherokee Nation Executive Order designated an 810-acre tract of tribal land in Adair County as a cultural use site under a tribal conservation easement—distinct from the previously contested tract in Sequoyah County. The Adair County tract comprises an ideal mix of geological, topographical, hydrological, botanical, and biological characteristics that make it a "hotspot" for numerous plants and resources that are culturally significant for Cherokee people. Significantly, the Medicine Keepers have been using the site to conduct a pilot land education program with Cherokee youth, supported by grants from the National Science Foundation and the Indian Land Tenure Foundation, that the Elders, tribal staff, and I developed.[20] The program seeks to train a cohort of five Cherokee students in Indigenous and Western approaches to science, employing Cherokee knowledge and language, botany, biology, and tribal natural resource management strategies. The Medicine Keepers, in dialogue with the land education program students, renamed the tract of land from its formal tribal unit designation to *nvwatohiyadv nvwoti'i*—"the peaceful place of medicine"—expressing the character and significance of the land from their perspective (fig. 2.2).

Toward Indigenous Political Relationalities of Land

Although the contestations over land's meaning and value exhibited by the different perspectives and practices of the Medicine Keepers and the new NRD leadership are not novel when viewed in this chapter's historical scope, that such internal conflicts among Cherokees over their relationship to land are still prevalent today illuminates the ongoing complexities of Cherokee society, as

FIGURE 2.2. *Nvwatohiyadv nvwoti'i* ("the peaceful place of medicine").

Photo by author.

well as the structured and unceasing colonial politics that inform the parameters by which tribes are able to manage and govern land. And yet, the sustained arc of the Medicine Keepers' work since their formation in 2008 and the influence they continue to enact on Cherokee governing institutions are indicative of what I have termed "Indigenous state transformation" (Carroll 2015, 17–27), wherein constitutionally and bureaucratically organized Indigenous nations seek to reconcile the tensions between such structures and very different culturally held notions of relationality (with land, other humans, and other-than-humans), heterarchy, and nondomination in governance ideals.

The internal processes that Indigenous nations must navigate toward this end deserve much more attention, especially in political-ecological contexts. If, as many scholars have argued, the bureaucratic management of land and the governing of its use and access often reveal neoliberal motivations of accumulation by dispossession (e.g., Peluso and Lund 2011), then how can the employment of state forms by Indigenous nations inform understandings of the political possibilities of Indigenous environmental governance? For many Indigenous nations, including the Cherokee Nation, this is often expressed along a spectrum of practices and policies that demonstrate resource- and relationship-based approaches to environmental governance. Tribal land managers work along this spectrum—spanning everything from quotidian property valuations to the "cultural forestry" initiatives discussed above—toward reconciling the protection of territory (and the "flattening" management work this can entail) with the maintenance of relational obligations with land and other-than-human beings. Aligning with my past discussion of the Medicine Keepers' work in this regard (Carroll 2015), the designation of the tribal conservation tract in 2022 signals the persistence of a dialectical movement to center ancestral perspectives within Cherokee governance institutions and to influence accordingly how tribal policy makers, officials, and the Cherokee state relate to land.

These dynamics speak to recent calls for an Indigenous political ecology (Carroll 2014a, 2015; Middleton 2015), as well as other interventions in the field that question and complicate past preoccupations with property relations and peasant politics (Heynen and Ybarra 2021). Such calls also advocate for the decentering of Western epistemology to allow for alternative interpretations of land and its social lives. As Athabaskan scholar Dian Million writes,

> The difference between Western epistemological "land" as an environment and ecology and Indigenous place as relations with responsibility is a critical philosophical difference. Indigenous peoples' lifeways as ancient nations are different ontological and material interpretations of life that question and offer alternative imaginaries outside capitalism. The myriad Indigenous peoples who continue today practicing their heritage knowledge as daily, lived action, performed in ongoing relation with place, have ways of governing that perform what "ecology" implies. While none of these peoples are "outside" capitalism after hundreds of years of entanglement, they continue to act on principles and values that hold up different ideas about what might be lived. (2018, 26)

Centering issues of sovereignty, land, and relationality, a political ecology inflected and informed by critical Indigenous studies encourages analyses of environmental degradation *and* flourishing through critical understandings of coloniality and the philosophical and material conditions for decolonization (Middleton 2015). Incorporating Million's healthy critique of "ecology" above, such approaches may also prompt us to engage this space more fully as Indigenous political *relationalities*, and therefore to acknowledge that this "daily, lived action" of being in good relation radically exceeds previous frameworks (see also Yazzie and Baldy 2018).[21]

The Cherokee Nation landscape, when viewed diachronically and as a produced set of relationships between US state actors and agencies, Cherokee Nation state actors and agencies, Cherokee Nation citizens, and non-Indian intruders and landowners (to name but a few), emerges—as with most landscapes—as a complex and layered phenomenon of humans, more-than-humans, social and ecological processes, and politics. Land relations in the Indian Territory carried both political and relational meaning for Cherokee people, who needed to protect territory in the face of the devastating loss of the eastern homelands and ongoing colonial threats to their new land base, and who also needed to maintain their relationship to land as a communally held and sacred source of life and sustenance. Forces that compromised both of these meanings came from exogenous and endogenous sources, including colonial encroachment and impositions on the one hand, and elite Cherokee enclosures and exploitation of land and people on the other. In negotiating these meanings amid such forces, Cherokee people shaped and were shaped by land, which was experiencing its own changes in character and composition.

The recent resurgence of ethically and culturally informed approaches to land reflected in the work of the Medicine Keepers, coupled with a resurgence of tribal sovereignty since the mid-1970s, has presented opportunities for the Cherokee Nation to counteract colonial policies and practices of displacement, suppression, and domination. Simultaneously, the Cherokee Nation must come to terms with this strengthened sovereignty and the institutions that represent it by carefully considering the tradeoffs and traps that the adoption of state forms carries. And although the new "cowboy" leadership of the NRD represents a contemporary manifestation of long-standing conflicts in Cherokee society over land's meaning, they have Western colonial institutions in their favor toward this end. The Elders' ability to wield their cultural capital as traditional knowledge holders in order to influence lasting policies to counteract internal proposals for the exploitation of land is critical, as is their ability to impart their knowledge to future generations who can carry this work forward.

We cannot likely return fully to the landscapes described in the Indian-Pioneer Papers referenced above. Still, we can work toward this goal by continuing to build community-government relationships and expanding Cherokee Nation landholdings within and beyond our reservation boundaries to create the institutional and physical space necessary for the perpetuation of traditional knowledge and practices (see Carroll 2020). Yet, as one Elder reminded me, the purpose of this work is not just to contribute to our own cultural survival (as vital as this may be), but moreover "to honor the spirit of this land."[22] Our responsibility as Cherokees, displaced as we are from our original homelands, is to acknowledge our role as caretakers of the land we now inhabit, and to allow this responsibility—this *relationship*—to inform our understanding of land and how we purport to "manage" it into the future.

NOTES

Author's note: This chapter is a revised version of an article originally published as Carroll (2014b). The revisions entail substantial updates and additional material from my fieldwork and related projects since the original 2014 publication. Reprinted with permission of Duke University Press.

1. For foundational works on the history of US federal Indian policy, see Deloria and Lytle (1984), Prucha (1984), and Wilkins and Lomawaima (2001).

2. The US Supreme Court's *McGirt v. Oklahoma* decision in 2020 reaffirmed the "reservation" status of the Creek Nation, which neighbors the Cherokee Nation and was subject to similar Oklahoma state impositions and laws. Before *McGirt*, the boundary of the Cherokee Nation represented in figure 2.1 was referred to as the "Tribal Jurisdictional Service Area" to distinguish it from other Indian reservations that, in the eyes of the federal government (until recently), had maintained this status since their establishment. I use "reservation" here, in line with Cherokee Nation tribal officials, to refer to the Cherokee Nation territorial boundary today.

3. Cherokee people often refer to this forced removal from their homelands as "the Trail Where We Cried." It is often glossed by historians as "the Trail of Tears." Many other southeastern Indigenous nations experienced their own trail of tears in the 1830s under the removal policy of President Andrew Jackson. This period marks one of many genocidal events in US history in which Indigenous peoples were dispossessed of their homelands. In the Old Cherokee Nation, those who walked the trail began their march at gunpoint in October 1838, following weeks-long stays in guarded stockades where malnutrition was widespread and disease ran rampant. They were subsequently exposed to one of the harshest winters in years.

4. Both collections are housed in the University of Oklahoma's Western History Collection (available at http://digital.libraries.ou.edu/WHC).

5. "An Interview with Mr. E.F. Vann," March 10, 1938, Muskogee, Oklahoma, Interviewer: L.W. Wilson, Journalist, Volume 93, Interview ID 13177, Indian-Pioneer Papers, Western History Collections, University of Oklahoma, Norman, Oklahoma.

6. "Mrs. Elinor Boudinot Meigs, Informant," March 2–4, 1937, Fort Gibson, Oklahoma, Interviewer: Jas. S. Buchanan, Volume 62, Indian-Pioneer Papers, Western History Collections, University of Oklahoma, Norman, Oklahoma.

7. Additionally, the western lands were very similar to (although notably less biologically diverse than) the eastern Cherokee homelands (Hewes 1978, 15). Furthermore, Cherokees known as the Old Settlers had occupied parts of the Ozark Mountains since as early as 1721 (see Thornton 1990, 43), so the region was not completely unfamiliar to Cherokee people upon arrival after the Trail of Tears. For a detailed account of Cherokee environmental practices in the east, see Hill (1997).

8. In August 1861, the Cherokee Nation ended its neutrality in the US Civil War and sided with the Confederacy. The conditions leading up to this were complex. The nation had experienced deep internal divisions since the removal era, some of which manifested in the rise of a Confederate Cherokee faction. The nation also found itself geographically subsumed by the South, and the presence of Confederate forces was palpable and foreboding. John Ross, the principal chief at this time, who had held this position since 1828, acquiesced to this decision in the hope of preserving Cherokee nationhood.

He soon reneged on the decision with the support of the traditionalist majority, but by that time the Confederate Cherokees had taken hold of the Cherokee government. In February 1863, Cherokees who had maintained their alliance with the United States, and, by extension, their commitment to the treaties signed with the federal government, elected Ross as chief of the Cherokee National Council in the face of what they viewed as a coup by the Confederate Cherokees. In this forum, the National Council abrogated the Cherokee alliance with the South—noting that it had been made under duress—and abolished the practice of slavery in the nation. See Minges (2004, 95–158).

9. "Jake Whitmire, Cherokee," May 29, 1969, Interviewer: J. W. Tyner, Volume 22, Interview ID T-468-3, Doris Duke Collection, Western History Collections, University of Oklahoma, Norman, Oklahoma.

10. "Ross Bowlin, Cherokee," August 26, 1969, Interviewer: J. W. Tyner, Volume 11, Interview ID T-512-2, Doris Duke Collection, Western History Collections, University of Oklahoma, Norman, Oklahoma.

11. Travelok.com (accessed May 7, 2010). The video has been removed and is no longer accessible; however, the tourism regions are still viewable on this site. Note that Arbuckle Country has been changed to "Chickasaw Country," the only tourism region that bears the name of an existing tribal nation.

12. This fiasco involved numerous cases of blatant mismanagement of tribal development programs and funds by BIA personnel and was exposed through a series of articles published by the *Arizona Republic* in 1987 titled "Fraud in Indian Country: A Billion Dollar Betrayal."

13. Dr. Richard Allen, Cherokee Nation policy analyst, pers. comm.

14. "Congress Amends Stigler Act to Protect Tribally Restricted Land," *Cherokee Phoenix*, December 21, 2018, https://www.cherokeephoenix.org/news/congress-amends -stigler-act-to-protect-tribally-restricted-land/article_024eab2f-50e5-595d-9c53 -91d45dd85c3f.html.

15. Author's field notes, July 20, 2006.

16. It is important to note that, despite the change in tribal administration and the shift in NRD leadership, the Medicine Keepers still possessed substantial influence on tribal officials. This was displayed in 2017, when they learned of the new NRD leadership's intent to revert to the old BIA loblolly pine forestry program and issued a letter to the Cherokee Nation secretary of state and secretary of natural resources in disagreement. Soon after, the proposal was dismissed.

17. "Cherokee Nation Park Sees Continual Improvements," *Cherokee Phoenix*, March 3, 2016, https://www.cherokeephoenix.org/news/cherokee-nation-park-sees-continual -improvements/article_e56f7ec9-d4a9-50c8-87c8-b19e1b3fc3b8.html.

18. The Elders approved the release of this video on YouTube: https://youtu.be/B2h _CUF9scc.

19. The production of the photovoice video necessarily entailed the distillation of hours of interviews into a condensed format. Due to this limitation on time, more sustained conversations on tribal land management activities did not appear in the final product. For example, in my interview for this project with John Ross, I asked him what he thought was getting in the way of the goal of conserving tribal lands for cultural activities. His response raised the following concerns about tribal cattle grazing leases:

> My guess is just the economics of doing this. A lot of lands were leased to farmers, ranchers. [Then] they put cattle in there [. . .]. What I propose is, you know, setting [land] aside just for [conservation] and in the long run I think we could generate more funds doing this and then starting like, eco tourism [. . .]. If we

had that much acreage, we could do all this stuff we're talking about. We wouldn't have to worry about losing it. Somebody bulldozing the trees and plants and everything away and putting cattle in there, destroying the environment. We could protect that for our future generation[s].

In another interview, Roger Vann had this to say about ecological change and land use activities like spraying and cattle grazing:

I think there's come a day when we going to have to start back using that stuff [traditional medicines]. And we better know it. Because you know, just like—I've heard my grandpa and my dad say, if we're not using it, God's going to take it away. Man, I seen it. Dad and my grandpa both used to talk about hazelnut, being a bundle of it right behind my house. There's Sallisaw Creek that runs right by my house. Both sides of the bank, they said—they said in the fall, you could [. . .] go back over there and you'd go get it and you'd try to beat the squirrels and the birds. And instead, now, there's none because nobody don't use it no more. And you can't find no hazelnut no more. And so it's same thing to these kind of weeds. We're spraying them. We're killing them. And we don't really know the meaning of it. That's what's so sad. People don't know why, but they just want to get rid of it. And you know, just like they say, cattle is more important than this. I guarantee them cattle's going to go one of these days. Then what we gonna do?

20. NSF Award #1654217 (Cultural Anthropology Program); ILTF Grant # 2018-307-0601. "Tribal staff" include the former NRD director and many of the same staff members who have long assisted the work of the Medicine Keepers. In 2017, the former NRD director moved from the Administrative Support Department to the Office of the Secretary of Natural Resources, a cabinet office of the principal chief that is distinct from the NRD even though the name is similar.

21. I have been actively thinking with a group of scholars toward this notion of Indigenous political relationalities, and I credit the collective endeavor of articulating this concept and the intellectual work it entails. My gratitude for and acknowledgment of this community go out to my colleagues Dana Powell, Jessica Cattelino, Sarah Hunt, Kyle Whyte, Nicholas Brown, Andrew Curley, Michelle Daigle, Beth Rose Middleton Manning, and Jean Dennison.

22. Author's field notes, February 23, 2010.

REFERENCES

Baird, W. D., and D. Goble. 1994. *The Story of Oklahoma*. Norman: University of Oklahoma Press.

Bays, B. A. 1998. *Townsite Settlement and Dispossession in the Cherokee Nation, 1866–1907*. New York: Garland.

Blackburn, T. C., and M. K. Anderson, eds. 1993. *Before the Wilderness: Environmental Management by Native Californians*. Menlo Park, CA: Ballena.

Blaikie, P., and H. Brookfield, eds. 1987. *Land Degradation and Society*. London: Methuen.

Brantley, C. G., and S. G. Platt. 2001. "Canebrake Conservation in the Southeastern United States." *Wildlife Society Bulletin* 29 (4): 1175–1181.

Carroll, C. 2014a. "Native Enclosures: Tribal National Parks and the Progressive Politics of Environmental Stewardship in Indian Country." *Geoforum* 53: 31–40.

——. 2014b. "Shaping New Homelands: Environmental Production, Natural Resource Management, and the Dynamics of Indigenous State Practice in the Cherokee Nation." *Ethnohistory* 61 (1): 123–147.

——. 2015. *Roots of Our Renewal: Ethnobotany and Cherokee Environmental Governance*. Minneapolis: University of Minnesota Press.

——. 2020. "Cherokee Relationships to Land: Reflections on a Historic Plant Gathering Agreement between Buffalo National River and the Cherokee Nation." *Parks Stewardship Forum* 36 (1): 154–158.

Carroll, C., and the Cherokee Nation Medicine Keepers. 2016. "Cherokee Voices for the Land." *Langscape* 5 (2): 68–73.

Carroll, C., E. Garroutte, C. Noonan, and D. Buchwald. 2018. "Using PhotoVoice to Promote Land Conservation and Indigenous Well-Being in Oklahoma." *EcoHealth* 15: 450–461.

Cherokee Executive Committee. 1969. *Constitution and Laws of the Cherokee Nation: Passed at Tahlequah, Cherokee Nation, 1839–51*. Oklahoma City: Oklahoma Publishing. First published 1852.

Coulthard, G. S. 2014. *Red Skin, White Masks: Rejecting the Colonial Politics of Recognition*. Minneapolis: University of Minnesota Press.

Debo, A. 1940. *And Still the Waters Run: The Betrayal of the Five Civilized Tribes*. Princeton, NJ: Princeton University Press.

Deloria, V., Jr. (1972) 2003. *God Is Red: A Native View of Religion*. Golden, CO: Fulcrum.

Deloria, V., Jr., and C. M. Lytle. 1984. *The Nations Within: The Past and Future of American Indian Sovereignty*. New York: Pantheon Books.

Deloria, V., Jr., and D. R. Wildcat. 2001. *Power and Place: Indian Education in America*. Golden, CO: Fulcrum.

Fairhead, J., and M. Leach. 1996. *Misreading the African Landscape: Society and Ecology in a Forest-Savanna Mosaic*. Cambridge: Cambridge University Press.

Fogelson, R. D., and P. Kutsche. 1961. "Cherokee Economic Cooperatives: The Gadugi." In *Bureau of American Ethnology Bulletin 180: Symposium on Cherokee and Iroquois Culture*, 87–123. Washington, DC: Smithsonian Institution.

Fowler, C., and E. Konopik. 2007. "The History of Fire in the Southern United States." *Human Ecology Review* 14 (2): 165–176.

Hewes, L. 1978. *Occupying the Cherokee Country of Oklahoma*. Lincoln: University of Nebraska Press.

Heynen, N., and M. Ybarra. 2021. "On Abolition Ecologies and Making 'Freedom as a Place.'" *Antipode* 53 (1): 21–35.

Hill, S. H. 1997. *Weaving New Worlds: Southeastern Cherokee Women and Their Basketry*. Chapel Hill, NC: University of North Carolina Press.

Holm, T. 2005. *The Great Confusion in Indian Affairs: Native Americans and Whites in the Progressive Era*. Austin: University of Texas Press.

Huntsinger, L., and S. McCaffrey. 1995. "A Forest for the Trees: Forest Management and the Yurok Environment 1850 to 1994." *American Indian Culture and Research Journal* 19 (4): 155–192.

Johnson, K. S. 1998. *Mountains, Streams, and Lakes of Oklahoma*. Information Series No. 1. Norman: Oklahoma Geological Survey.

Kimmerer, R. W. 2013. *Braiding Sweetgrass: Indigenous Wisdom, Scientific Knowledge, and the Teachings of Plants*. Minneapolis: Milkweed Editions.

LaDuke, W. 1999. *All Our Relations: Native Struggles for Land and Life*. Cambridge, MA: South End.

Leeds, S. L. 2006. "Moving toward Exclusive Tribal Autonomy over Lands and Natural Resources." *Natural Resources Journal* 46: 439–461.

McGregor, D. 2005. "Coming Full Circle: Indigenous Knowledge, Environment, and Our Future." *American Indian Quarterly* 28 (3): 385–410.

McLoughlin, W. G. 1993. *After the Trail of Tears: The Cherokees' Struggle for Sovereignty, 1839–1880.* Chapel Hill: University of North Carolina Press.

Middleton, B. R. 2015. "Jahát Jatítotòdom: Toward an Indigenous Political Ecology." In *The International Handbook of Political Ecology,* edited by Raymond L. Bryant, 561–576. Northampton, MA: Edward Elgar.

Million, D. 2018. "We Are the Land, and the Land Is Us: Indigenous Land, Lives, and Embodied Ecologies in the Twenty-First Century." In *Racial Ecologies,* edited by Leilani Nishime and Kim D. Hester Williams, 19–33. Seattle: University of Washington Press.

Minges, P. N. 2004. *Slavery in the Cherokee Nation: The Keetoowah Society and the Defining of a People, 1855–1867.* New York: Routledge.

Peluso, N. L. 1994. *Rich Forests, Poor People: Resource Control and Resistance in Java.* Berkeley: University of California Press.

Peluso, N. L., and C. Lund. 2011. "New Frontiers of Land Control: Introduction." In "New Frontiers of Land Control." Special issue, *Journal of Peasant Studies* 38 (4): 667–681.

Platt, S. G., and C. G. Brantley. 1997. "Canebrakes: An Ecological and Historical Perspective." *Castanea* 612 (1): 8–21.

Prucha, F. P. 1984. *The Great Father: The United States Government and the American Indians.* Lincoln: University of Nebraska Press.

Robbins, P. 2004. *Political Ecology: A Critical Introduction.* Malden, MA: Blackwell.

Salmón, E. 2000. "Kincentric Ecology: Indigenous Perceptions of the Human–Nature Relationship." *Ecological Applications* 10 (5): 1327–1332.

Scott, J. C. 1998. *Seeing like a State: How Certain Schemes to Improve the Human Condition Have Failed.* New Haven, CT: Yale University Press.

Self-Governance Communication and Education Project (SGCEP). 2006. *Self-Governance: The Red Book.* Bellingham, WA: SGCEP.

Simpson, L. B. 2017. *As We Have Always Done: Indigenous Freedom through Radical Resistance.* Minneapolis: University of Minnesota Press.

Stauber, R. n.d. "Delaware County." In *Encyclopedia of Oklahoma History and Culture.* Oklahoma City: Oklahoma Historical Society. https://www.okhistory.org /publications/enc/entry?entry=DE010.

Sturm, C. 2002. *Blood Politics: Race, Culture, and Identity in the Cherokee Nation of Oklahoma.* Berkeley: University of California Press.

Thornton, R. 1990. *The Cherokees: A Population History.* Lincoln: University of Nebraska Press.

United States Department of the Interior (USDOI). 1912. *Reports of the Department of the Interior for the Fiscal Year Ended June 30, 1911.* Vol. 2, *Indian Affairs Territories.* Washington, DC: Government Printing Office.

Vandergeest, P., and N. L. Peluso. 1995. "Territorialization and State Power in Thailand." *Theory and Society* 24 (3): 385–426.

Wahrhaftig, A. L. 1966. "Community and the Caretakers." *New University Thought* 4 (4): 54–76.

——. 1968. "The Tribal Cherokee Population of Oklahoma." *Current Anthropology* 9 (5): 510–518.

——. 1978. "Making Do with the Dark Meat: A Report on the Cherokee Indians of
    Oklahoma." In *American Indian Economic Development,* edited by Sam Stanley,
    409–510. The Hague: Mouton.
Wang, C., and M. A. Burris. 1997. "Photovoice: Concept, Methodology, and Use for
    Participatory Needs Assessment." *Health Education and Behavior* 24 (3):
    369–387.
Wang, C., W. K. Yi, Z. W. Tao, and K. Carovano. 1998. "Photovoice As a Participatory
    Health Promotion Strategy." *Health Promotion International* 13 (1): 75–86.
Wilkins, D. E., and K. T. Lomawaima. 2001. *Uneven Ground: American Indian
    Sovereignty and Federal Law.* Norman: University of Oklahoma Press.
Wolfe, P. 2006. "Settler Colonialism and the Elimination of the Native." *Journal of
    Genocide Research* 8 (4): 387–409.
Yazzie, M. K., and C. R. Baldy. 2018. "Introduction: Indigenous Peoples and the
    Politics of Water." *Decolonization: Indigeneity, Education and Society* 7 (1): 1–18.

3

"I AM WAORANI"

Between Indigenous and Settler Land Ontologies in the Ecuadorian Amazon

Kati Álvarez, Ciara Wirth, Gabriela Valdivia, and Flora Lu

I was in my house all morning making a palm-fiber bag, and then I left it to one side. As it was now late, my husband said, "Let's go play soccer." I said, "You go first, I will meet you." And I stayed here. Without paying attention, I came down [from my house on stilts] and began to walk [towards the soccer field].

Without being noticed, without being seen, they grabbed my hair from behind [she gestures to indicate how]. I got scared, and I looked behind me, and there were many people. There were around eight tall women dressed *durani bai* [in ancestral clothing]. They had everything [she indicates, waving her hands across her body], and they carried many woven baskets. And one woman held me here [she holds her hair to the base of her nape], and she pulled me back and upwards.

Then, they asked me, "Are you an outsider, or are you Waorani?"

"I am not an outsider," I said, "I am Waorani. I am from here."

As she held me up, another woman came and wanted to take away my daughter. But the woman who held me said, "Leave her, leave her, let her carry her [daughter]." She is like us. Let her speak."

This excerpt is part of an emotionally gripping first-person account of a Waorani woman's encounter in September 2018 at her home in the community of Keweriono, an Indigenous community in the Ecuadorian Amazon (fig. 3.1). The "I" narrating the encounter is a twenty-three-year-old woman who was home alone with her one-year-old daughter. Her husband had just left to play soccer on the school field, a five-minute walk away. The day before, her nine-year-old niece, who was home alone, had also seen the unknown group approach her residence. She hid in fear they would kidnap her. When her family returned home, she told them she thought she saw the spirit of her deceased grandmother. The "they" in the account refers to people who are Waorani living in voluntary isolation (or WVI). WVI are Waorani who, unlike the woman relating the story or the young girl, refused to recognize the authority of the Ecuadorian State in their ancestral territory and were forced to leave and move deeper into the forest to protect themselves. The woman narrating this story estimated that she saw eight WVI women and fifteen WVI men.

Since 2014, settled Waorani, those who recognize the presence of the Ecuadorian State, have reported nondeadly encounters with WVI like the one described, though these reports are disregarded by official representatives and the media.[1] In fact, their veracity is routinely discounted. Nonetheless, they are significant to the current moment of Indigenous relations in the Ecuadorian Amazon. At the heart of these encounters is a struggle over how to lead a Waorani life when mobility across the landscape and reciprocity through landed relations are increasingly curtailed by governance schemes that settle land as an object of occupation and extraction. In this chapter, we work through the account of this particular encounter in Keweriono as a rich site for theorizing with Waorani ways of relating to land in the Ecuadorian Amazon.

Unsettling Settler Land Ontologies

The qualifier "settled" community is important for grasping the significance of this encounter (and similar ones) for both the Waorani and for current theorizations of life-land relations in the Amazon. In academic studies of Indigenous land relations, "to settle" is to establish a new society in the place of an Indigenous one by redefining the latter's rights to the land as belonging to the past (Deloria 1969; Wolfe 2006; Tuck and Yang 2012; Coulthard 2014; Manuel and Derrickson 2015; Simpson 2017). A settled community is a community colonized in space and time. Spatially, a settled community is a geographic area where individuals have consented (sometimes forcibly) to following the authority, governance logics, and social mores of an external and dominant society instead of Indigenous ones. The consensual bounds of colonized spaces are crafted over generations; settlement can operate through various channels and technologies of collective control, ranging from homicide and bioassimilation practices (e.g., child abduction) to religious conversion and resocialization (e.g., through missions or boarding schools), all of which break down existing bonds to land into individual and alienable freeholds that then become available for appropriation by others (Wolfe 2006, 388). In this sense, settlement is also the colonization of time: it establishes a periodization scheme where Indigenous ways of being and knowing belong to a time before colonization (Rifkin 2017), a point of underdeveloped time, even as Indigenous ways of living are coterminous with settled ones.

The social life of land relations in the Ecuadorian Amazon can be told through such an ontology of settlement. As Wasserstrom and Bustamante (2015) indicate, "the push and pull of external forces" along Ecuador's Amazonian frontier over the past 150 years have shaped nation-state-Indigenous land relations. While, during the nineteenth century, Amazonian peoples thrived in relative isolation from the newly independent nation-states, throughout the twentieth century, the Ecuadorian government sponsored and endorsed land categorization and allocation schemes that redefined Indigenous activity and life-generating spaces in the Amazon as *tierras baldías* ("empty, unused lands") and welcomed non-Amazonian peoples to occupy and exploit these lands via productive and extractive activities. In the early twentieth century, for example, the expansion of the rubber extraction frontier forced Amazonian peoples out of their ancestral homelands to escape exploitation and genocide. Between the 1880s and 1930s, the rubber boom meant Indigenous death and capture into rubber gangs in some cases, or fragmentation and flight for survivors, the latter pushed into the areas occupied by others, where they assimilated or were eliminated (Cabodevilla 1994). Later, with juridical instruments, such as the Law of Agrarian Reform and Colonization of 1964, vast areas of the Amazon were allocated to agricultural settlers under the mandate of giving land to "those who work it." In the late 1960s, with the discovery of crude oil deposits, the Ecuadorian State allocated Amazonian lands as concession blocks to oil companies. Infrastructure such as fences and roads, bolstered by land titling policies, facilitated deforestation, settler encroachment, and Indigenous dispossession. Missionization played a role in these practices of occupation via Indigenous elimination too. Catholic and evangelical Protestant missions often reordered the presence of Amazonian peoples into protectorates that settled them as "civilized Indians." The concentration and sedentarization of formerly seminomadic, dispersed groups of Indigenous people facilitated the fragmentation and invasion of their lands, disrupting social and ecological connectivity and exacerbating overuse and degradation. In some instances, Native Amazonians consented to settlement, forced by the common sense of development and modernization of the new, dominant settler society. In other cases, they refused it and were forced to leave their ancestral lands and families and move deeper into the forest to protect themselves—what government officials and settlers often refer to as peoples who chose to live in "voluntary isolation" (Lu, Valdivia, and Silvia 2017).

Land is central to the encounter between the settled Waorani woman and the WVI, though not in the same way as a settler ontology maintains. As Burow et al. (2022) describe, settler colonialism works through ontological foreclosures, that is, ideologies, moral codes, and technologies of governance that negate Indigenous ontologies of land and, in doing so, bound land as an object that can be alienated and claimed, "always bound up in the historical discursive apparatuses of the State" (67).

North American Indigenous scholars seeking to decolonize land relations have pushed against the universality of this settler ontology as well and propose that Indigenous environmental governance is grounded in relational ontologies that exceed binary dualisms of subjects and objects. For example, in discussing relationships with the land, Opaskwayak Cree scholar Shawn Wilson (2008, 80) writes: "Rather than viewing ourselves as being *in* relationship with other people or things, we *are* the relationships that we hold and are part of." Anishnaabe scholar Leanne Betasamosake Simpson (2017) similarly argues that to re-create Indigenous ways of being, meaning, and knowing, we should be concerned not only with the content of practices but also with re-creating the conditions within which learning—as a verb—takes *place*. This is what Mohawk and Anishinaabe scholar Vanessa Watts (2013, 21) calls Place-Thought: "Where place and thought were never separated because they never could or can be separated," and where "land is alive and thinking and that humans and nonhumans derive agency through the extensions of these thoughts." Along similar lines, Cherokee scholar Brian Burkhart proposes an Indigenous philosophy of place where "nativeness," like all identities, is lived in *locality,* that is, as a voice rooted in "being-from-the-land and knowing-from-the-land" (2019, chap. 14). Nativeness, he argues, is not about belonging to something called a "nation"—an abstraction that characterizes settler location—but in being, meaning, and knowing *rooted* in the land. "Cultures and nations," he proposes, "do not speak, except as through the power of locality" (chap. 15); speaking with a Native voice is speaking from particular experiences of being human in the world, from a locality in its *present place.* For Wilson, Simpson, Watts, Burhkart, and other North American Indigenous scholars, land is an unbounded ground of kinship, and human beings are intertwined with this relational ground.

In this chapter, we showcase stories shared about charged encounters in Keweriono, one of the settled Waorani communities that are experiencing recurrent encounters with WVI, that not only resonate with this Indigenous ontology of land but also express Waorani ambivalences, fears, and consciousness at and of the boundaries of settler and Indigenous land ontologies. We start with the interview with the Waorani woman who saw and spoke with WVI.[2] Collaborative research and education partnerships with this community since 2011 afforded documentary filmmaker Keith Hayward, researcher Emilio Rojas, and one of the authors (Ciara Wirth) the privilege of listening to multiple accounts of encounters with the WVI since as early as 2014. On several occasions, these accounts were heard only days, and sometimes only hours, after the encounters. In the filmed interview featured in this chapter, this Waorani woman and her two older sisters living in the village rested in the outdoor kitchen. One sister listened while she worked on chambira palm handcrafts, while the other sister periodically helped interview and sometimes translated for her younger sister. On one occasion, she reminded her in *waoterero* of details of the story she had previously heard from her but that the woman had not yet recounted in the film footage.

"Being Waorani" in Settler Times

In *waoterero*, non-Waorani are called *cowore*, or "cannibal," and Keweriono (also spelled Quehueiri-Ono) means "the river of the cannibals," a name that might reference countless raids and counterraids, waged in areas north of the Keweriono River, between Waorani and Zaparoan groups (Rival 2002).[3] This community is in a narrow valley of the Shiripuno River (formerly known as the Keweriono River), dominated by a series of hills. Built up around an airstrip constructed by the Waorani in the early 1990s and resurfaced with river-rock by an ECORAE development project in 2011, the village was founded on land raised up a distance from the river. The waters of the Shiripuno River can rise and fall sharply. After only two days of steady rainfall, the river can rise four meters, transforming the lowlands into a vast marsh, felling riparian trees, and stealing Waorani canoes. Then, just as quickly, the river can recede, exposing newly configured beaches and clay cliffs, as well as treefall obstacles that complicate canoe transportation. Going with the current, high water levels, and an outboard motor, the river journey from Keweriono to the bridge at the Auca/Tiguino Road, an oil road that bisects Waorani territory, is at best about three hours but can easily take an entire day.

The forests traversed within Waorani territory along this journey remain populated with wildlife and bear the signature of Indigenous management—swiddens in various stages of succession and high concentrations of useful tree species emblematic of agroforestry. Waorani subsistence is still based on swidden agriculture, with manioc (*Manihot esculenta*), a starchy tuber, consumed many times a day as a fermented, often premasticated drink called *tepae*. Plantain, corn, peach palm (*Bactris gasipaes*), peanut, and sweet potato are also important cultigens. Protein is acquired through hunting (especially of peccaries, woolly

FIGURE 3.1. The elder who decorated this spear with his own feathers said he had recently found it in the forest after encountering a group of WVI while hunting to the south of his community. He admired the spear's beauty, especially the very long barbed tip.

Photographed in Keweriono on July 12, 2018, by Ciara Wirth.

monkeys, and toucans using blowguns for arboreal game, spears for terrestrial animals, or shotguns for both) and fishing (mostly with plant-derived poisons) (Yost 1991). Foraging for wild fruits, nuts, and tubers provides important nutrients. Yost (1981) described their "semipermanent sedentarism" as a cyclic movement between locations in which manioc gardens were at different stages of maturity. This form of dispersing their land use over a wide area was a reaction to high levels of intra- and intertribal warfare. Smaller gardens and lower intensity of trail use made it more difficult for raiding groups to locate housing sites, and if a raid did occur, the raided group could flee to a location where food was available.

The fundamental unit of Waorani society is the *nanicabo*, a residential unit of thirty to fifty related kin living in a long house. A *nanicabo* was economically self-sufficient and autonomous, characterized by ubiquitous sharing within the residential unit and minimal exchange with the outside (Rival 1992). Typically, a *nanicabo* was composed of an older man (after whom it was named), his wives, one or two married daughters and their children, his unmarried children, and one of his brothers and the latter's family. The preferred marriage pattern being uxorilocal, married sons rarely lived with their parents (Rival 1992, 109). Some older Waorani claim that at one time the various Waorani groups all lived peacefully together, but some incident caused them to split and disperse. Hostility created three groups: one going "downriver," one "upriver," and one "overland." Thus—according to this legend—the once unified group split into various *nanicaboiri*, which grew to have hostile internal relations as a result of killings and vendetta. The geographic terms "downriver," "upriver," and "overland" are used by the Waorani even today and have been adopted by outsiders to designate the particular dispersed or subgroup populations (Kelley 1988, 26). Most Waorani have been in sustained contact with the outside world beginning in 1958. They live in nucleated villages where distantly related and nonkin live in close proximity, taking advantage of infrastructure and services, such as education, transportation, and healthcare: a stark contrast to the mobile, extended

FIGURE 3.2. Warorani children playing in the Shiripuno River near the community of Keweriono.

Photo by Matt Goff.

family *nanicabo*. However, at least two *nanicaboiri*, the Tagaeri and Tarome-nane, remain in voluntary isolation. The cultural and physical survival of these WVI are the most threatened by resource extraction (e.g., oil, logging, agroindustry), deforestation, defaunation, and urbanization in Ecuador's northern Amazon.

"Are You Really Waorani?"

In the encounter opening this chapter, the settled Waorani woman, sensing her life in danger, insists on the power of her locality: "I am not an outsider, I am Waorani, I am from here." Throughout the interview, she thinks back to the encounter, explaining that while they asked her for food, pots, and the location of relatives, she thought they were going to kill her. She recounts:

> Another woman came to ask me, "You are really from here. You were born here?" I got scared. Many times, when they visited, I got scared. I thought I will live, or God will help, or I will die, I thought. And she said, "Now we are going to go. The next month when we come, have pots ready, and cups, and plantain. If you don't do this . . . we will take a kid, a small child with us."
>
> "We aren't civilized. We live in the forest," they told me. I just listened.
>
> Then another woman came to me. "Is it true that you are Waorani?" she asked. "I think you are lying to us. You are *cowori*," she told me. She pulled me like this [she gestured that the woman pulled on her hair when she asked].
>
> "I am not *cowori*," I said. "I am truly Wao," I said.

This insistence on being from this "place-thought" (Watts 2013) resonates with the relational ontologies described by North American Indigenous scholars. It signals a rootedness that verifies her identity as Waorani and, therefore, not an outsider. It also registers how WVI are forcing contact with settled Waorani in ways that unsettle their relationship with the state and as a survival strategy that depends on a common identification with place-thought. *Leave her, let her carry her daughter. She is like us. Let her speak.*

"We are the living forest," as the WVI man emphasized, is a phrase commonly used by settled Waorani leaders to describe the feel and recognition of ancestry as lived permanence through activities such as living together, moving freely, and sharing an abundance of forest resources with kin—like Waorani ancestors (*durani bai*) did. The moniker "forest people" is counterposed to "civilized"

Waorani, as Waorani negotiate their contemporary identities and the WVI represent living reminders of *durani bai*. However, for the WVI, distinctions between "civilized Waorani" and "civilized outsider" are quite different. In the communication recounted by the twenty-three-year-old woman in Keweriono, common ancestry and physical symbolism appear to be paramount for establishing the veracity of relatedness. Identity, for example, can be verified visually by examining the distendedness of earlobes, an indication that the "civilized Waorani" is, in fact, "Waorani" and not an "outsider." Requests for food and pots are more than an act of strong-arming to acquire desired goods, even though these demands, if unmet, might belie a threat of physical harm. Instead, acceptance of kinship encourages demand sharing, a practice common among Waorani kin. For the WVI, determining whom to trust, whom to avoid, and whom to neutralize are acts of discernment with much at stake. Ultimately, these concerns dictate how the WVI navigate space—both social and environmental. As the extended conversation between WVI and a resident of Keweriono indicated, the WVI recounted occasions where they considered attacking outsiders they saw traveling by canoe, as well as kidnapping the young granddaughter of the elder who took their spear but instead practiced restraint out of fear of retaliation.

Tellingly, while the settled Waorani of Keweriono share and debate these stories of encounter, the state authority charged with protecting the WVI and the Waorani federation, NAWE, appears to dismiss them, claiming there is insufficient evidence and suggesting these claims are made up by settled Waorani to back up their own solicitations for food and other goods from the state. The stakes are high, as state recognition of WVI presence in this region would strengthen ancestral claims to land, which could jeopardize exploratory and extractive petroleum activities, both underway and planned.

Settled Waorani often refer to WVI by the names of the individuals who lead them in the choice to isolation. While at least four groups of WVI are recognized—the Oñomenane, the Huiñetare, the Taromenane, and the Tagaeri—they are collectively referred to as the Tagaeri and/or Taromenane. Many Waorani are aware that some of these groups may have diminished or disappeared due to violent confrontations and disease, and some could have grown, split, and rearranged. Some Waorani believe they can trace their ancestry to some of these WVI families. The interview with the Waorani woman shows how tracing these common ancestries is one way in which settler ontologies are disrupted:

> They came down here [she indicates to the outdoor kitchen where she was sitting in a hammock] and one man said, "You aren't truly Waorani. You are an outsider. You are wearing clothes."

I said, "We are not from the city, I am Waorani."

And then he told me, "So if you are Waorani, why are you using clothes?" He had spears, around thirteen spears here [she indicates across her left shoulder] and in his other hand [she indicates to her right hand] he had another. He wanted to spear me.

Another man said, "Leave her alone. It turns out she is our family." He came down from my home and said how it was getting late, getting dark, we are going to leave, and go sleep over there [she gestures]. "It turns out she is my family. But others are not family. They are enemies. We are making you like a guide. Others will not kill you. Now we are going to take your pots." I was left with nothing, no pots, no cups. And they asked, "Do you know Nampa?" he asked me.

"I don't know Nampa," I said.

"I am Nampa," he said [she gestured, touching her chest and smiling]. "I am Tepa's brother, and another sister is Wanongi, and the last sister was Aboke." He said, "Look, look there she is." They tilted my head by the hair, and I looked. He said, "Other people we won't trust. We only will trust you. We have a lot of respect for you. If you tell other outsiders, or your other neighbors, they will destroy us. Other people are bad. Other people don't respect. We are going to tell people [from our group] that they shouldn't spear you."

"Don't Kill Her, She Is Family"

When the WVI ambushed the twenty-three-year-old woman in her home, she said they asked her to keep this encounter a secret from her neighbors and the outside world. They told her they were afraid others would seek them out and harm them. She eventually chose to tell other villagers in Keweriono about this encounter. While some residents expressed doubt about whether this encounter actually transpired, many parents asked their children to travel in groups and to remain close to the village center in their playful forays. Fear was highest immediately after encounters occurred, but village life broadly returned to normal weeks afterward, until the next reports of encounters were broadcast.

In the twenty-three-year-old woman's testimonial, the question of who are "true Waorani" is raised on multiple occasions. Today, the question of what it means to be Waorani, and who can call themselves "Wao" is a topic of heated dispute as it relates to positions of leadership, access to territory, and monetary claims on extractive industries and environmental NGOs. To some, fluency in their common language, *waoterero*, is insufficient to claim Waorani identity. During an electoral assembly that occurred in Keweriono in December 2016, for example, a healthy debate developed over who could be considered a candidate for president of the nationality. Some argued that only Waorani whose parents were both Waorani qualified, while others argued that at least one parent needed to be Waorani. Many settled Waorani identify themselves as fierce warriors; however, few individuals alive today have engaged in combat personally.

Related to these conversations about who is Waorani is the contentious issue of rights to land. Several residents are married to individuals from the Amazonian Kichwa nationality, and in at least two cases, the extended families of these non-Waorani individuals have relocated to live, cultivate, and hunt in Waorani forests (Lu and Silva 2015). Many of these new residents neither speak nor understand *waoterero*. And to the northeast of Keweriono, the Shuar father-in-law of one Waorani man was verbally gifted over forty hectares of land in Waorani territory where he says he plans to ranch livestock. This Shuar man, married to a Waorani woman, has reportedly invited some of his relatives to live with him, although it does not appear his plans to raise cattle have expanded beyond clearing a few hectares of forest and planting invasive grasses for cattle grazing. While none of the residents of Keweriono has acted to restrict this use of their territory, several are concerned and displeased about allowing non-Waorani access to Waorani lands. A few Waorani individuals have jokingly argued (often in the context of wanting to acquire a second spouse as was done *durani bai*) that Westerners would make ideal spouses because they rarely know how to hunt or garden, and it would be unlikely that they would bring their extended families to live in Waorani lands—not to mention the possible economic benefits. As the twenty-three-year-old woman recounts:

> One elder man was angry. He did not want to come close. He asked, "Are you really Waorani?" He came running toward me with heavy footfalls and he grabbed my shoulder.
>
> "Yes, I am Wao," I said. I was scared. He touched my clothes and said, "She is not Waorani. She is a *cowori*. Kill her, kill her. Did you come to kill or just be here?"
>
> The other man Nampa said, "No, no, no. She is our family, let her talk." He was blocking him like this [with his arm out]. I thought I was going to die. They were discussing among themselves. Their voice was thick, and one of them was very serious. Nampa crossed his arm out to block him, and another woman said, "We are going to go." Another woman said, "Leave her alone. If you spear her, others here will come after us, leave her alone." They were arguing among themselves. And another one came to see me. He grabbed the front right of my shirt and ripped it. "Leave it, don't pull, don't pull," shouted another. I was scared.

And just then my brother-in-law arrived [on the airstrip]. It was almost 4 p.m., and they were coming out to play soccer. He had his cellphone out with earbuds in his ears. He didn't hear. I shouted his name, "Come see, come see! People from the forest are coming. Come see quickly." I was shouting in Spanish.

But the other people said, "Don't shout. We aren't doing anything to you. We are just taking the pots and food. But don't tell others that we came." And then they said, "Ohh, there are the outsiders. Come on, come on; let's escape quickly into the forest."

And one man didn't want to return to the forest. "Is it really true that you are Wao?" he asked. "Yes," I said, "My grandmother is Tepa, and she lives downriver."

"Well then," he said, "I am going to stay here in this home [he indicated to her home]." But others did not want to. A young woman said, "Let's go and return another time." I think he wanted to stay and civilize like us.

I went running to my sister's home, west, along the airstrip. I told my sister, "People from the forest came, and they had no clothes." I went there afraid. I went to tell everyone in the village. They came to see, but there were only footprints left.

Reportedly, the WVI visited this same woman again sometime in the last two weeks of December. According to this woman's older sister's father-in-law, he had not believed her accounts of the WVI visits were true. But one day, he had rolled his wheelchair to the airstrip traveling west along the airstrip and stopped a short distance before arriving at her house when he saw one WVI man. As he told this account, he laughed heartily as he remembered seeing a WVI man hiding in the trees near the airstrip. Soon after spotting him, he saw the man trip and fall, his spears clattering to the ground. He got up quickly, gathered up his spears, and ran back into the forest.

Only Footprints and Spears

From the summer of 2018 through the summer of 2019, the woman's older sister (also the daughter-in-law of the elderly man who saw the man trip with his spears) reported seeing evidence of WVI activity in her garden. She knew WVI had taken plantains from her garden because of the way the banana plants were bent over. This technique for harvesting plantains was used when the Waorani did not have machetes. Aside from these signs, direct encounters in Keweriono were not reported again until February 17, 2019. As with other narrations of encounters, settled Waorani are precise. On this date, a twelve-year-old boy ran home, excited, drenched, scared, and out of breath, accompanied by his equally wet and shaken nine-year-old brother. They had been playing on a beach opposite the river to his home with their ten-year-old male cousin when a group of WVI emerged from the forest. One WVI woman came from the eastern side of the beach, while a large group of WVI approached from the western side of the beach. Upon seeing them, he and his younger brother jumped into the river, where they knew there was a particularly deep pool of water. The WVI managed to grab ahold of their cousin, but he squirmed out of their grasp and leaped into the river to join his cousins. All three boys swam quickly downriver to the nearest riverine trail leading to the village airstrip and paths to their homes. The twelve-year-old boy saw one WVI woman had followed them into the river but had only gone as deep as her knees, and then she returned to the beach.

The boys' father, who listened to this account intently, posited that the WVI probably did not venture deeper into the river because they do not know how to swim and that area is particularly deep. Upon hearing this story, he indulged his curiosity and headed out alone to check out the place where his sons had seen the WVI. He brought his cellphone just in case he might be able to catch an image of them. When he arrived, they were gone, but they had left many footprints. He took photographs of these footprints with his phone. This all occurred during a day when it was raining off and on. During this time, and in the months following this encounter, Waorani in this settled village expressed their belief that the WVI come close to the village when there is thunder and rain. It is interesting to note that the same is said of jaguars, who are believed to walk along Waorani trails and behave more brazenly, even violently, when it rains. When he returned home, he and his brother-in-law discussed the encounter and theorized that the WVI, who have, up until this point, always approached from the south, could be crossing the river in places where the river is low and they can wade across. They think that the WVI might be using a trail that they had recently constructed to the north of their territory.

In these accounts of WVI encounters with settled Waorani in Keweriono, specific families have been targeted. These encounters began with one matriarch and patriarch who lived on the outskirts of the village in 2014. All WVI encounters since then have involved the daughters of this couple and their extended family. The youngest of these daughters, who used to live for many years adjacent to her elder parents on the outskirts of the village, has been the primary focus of recent encounters, the only ones in Keweriono involving verbal exchange with WVI. The most recent WVI encounter that occurred on the beach on February 17, 2019, is the first to involve a more distant relative—the second cousin who was grabbed but managed to escape. The selectiveness of these encounters may play a role in the lack of widespread consensus among settled Waorani that the WVI were active in the area. First-hand testimonials appear to have aided in convincing other community residents to also share their stories.

Intentional withholding and secrecy contribute to the growing uncertainty and disbelief in the veracity of the encounters. In Keweriono, some residents tell some things to their neighbors (e.g., show the footprints) but keep other things secret. When a Keweriono elder took a WVI spear he found in the forest, he chose to keep it secret from other Keweriono residents and Waorani government officials. He said he feared it would be taken from him and sold by others. He also wanted to maintain it as proof to secure government aid for village medical emergencies, like that which befell his late wife, who died from snakebite.

Both the WVI and the Waorani residents of Keweriono demonstrate a mixture of fear, curiosity, and wonder in their interactions with each other.[4] While another Waorani community chose to relocate their homes out of fear of WVI violence, in Keweriono, the early accounts of WVI activity were all recounted with excitement. The twenty-three-year-old woman who was visited by the WVI on multiple occasions had, several years before, excitedly traveled to the site where her uncle had seen the WVI with the hope she might catch a glimpse. However, when the WVI ambushed her at her home and held her by the hair, she was very scared and thought she would be killed. Her fear, and that of her sister, was evident on their faces as they ventured with trepidation into the forest on the outskirts of her home to show traces of WVI presence.

Institutions of "Protection"

The Directorate of Protection (state authorities in charge of overseeing that precautionary measures are followed to protect WVI) and the Waorani Federation NAWE do not believe the settled Waorani's recounting of the exchanges detailed here, deeming their stories fabricated to secure food and other objects, such as pots, axes, and lanterns, for themselves. Monitors from the Directorate of Protection have made field visits to the sites of reported WVI encounters to search for "definitive proof" that the WVI were, in fact, involved. During these verification visits, these monitors have conducted in-depth interviews with the settled Waorani who have professed involvement in these encounters. However, it seems that in the absence of clear physical evidence, these accounts are not considered sufficient proof to warrant official state recognition that some WVI are, in fact, residing in or moving through the western part of Waorani territory. Meanwhile, the communities directly involved in these events (and their neighbors) openly disagree with the state office and NAWE through the media, social organizations, local governments, and the Ombudsman's Office.

Ecuadorian government officials visited Keweriono in July 2018, after three unknown and non-Waorani men descended on the village of Keweriono the night before, uninvited. The officials of the Directorate of Protection team recorded reports of this visit. Rumors swirled as to the intentions of these unexpected visitors, including drug traffickers, mercenaries paid to execute Waorani opposing oil extraction or who had financial debts, and FARC militants looking to uncover the drugs that had been buried to the south when a drug plane crashed in their territory decades before or seeking revenge against Waorani who had killed and buried some of their comrades. These unknown men arrived at approximately 10 p.m. on July 26, 2018. They walked around one residence, stole some food, and banged on the one closed bedroom door. A Waorani woman, alone in that room with her four youngest children, was terrified, and shouted for her dog to come and scare them away. Her father-in-law, a wheelchair-bound polio survivor, was in his home a few yards away but did not hear her call. Finally, the men left, and soon after, she and her children ran to her father-in-law's home to try and calm down and sleep. Later that night, this woman's younger sister and her husband and daughter, residing a five-minute walk away, heard the men outside their home. They said it sounded like the men were going to enter, but their dogs began to bark, and they left. The next morning, the men of Keweriono got together and tried to track the footprints. Everyone in the village was scared because these men appeared to be very good at hiding their tracks. They were able to trace them to the river's edge, but not any farther. One resident found a pair of their especially large rubber boots.

No one in the village slept well for the next three nights. Children were told to stay close to the village and always travel in groups. People slept with machetes at their side. A few men in the village said that another community had experienced these sorts of visitations recently, and a commission from the Ecuadorian police and the Ecuadorian Ministry of Interior went there to document reports of these visits. According to a Keweriono resident present at these meetings, the police were scared to go into the forest and look for these men, and one high-ranking official told them they should kill and bury these men if they encountered them. They said this official told them that they (settled Waorani) would be better at dealing with the problem and that any reports the officials would make of this activity could result in retaliation by the invaders. The Waorani who heard this information interpreted this as a capitulation and dereliction of duty on the part of the Ecuadorian government, and they complained that they should be given tools and ammunition to protect their villages if this was going to be the government's stance. However, when the precautionary measures team came to Keweriono, they said that their program had no funding of its own and they had to go through long bureaucratic processes to even acquire the funding to provision their office with toilet paper. They recognized that these uninvited visitors to Waorani territory were a possible threat to the WVI, if they were, in fact, in the area, but never indicated how to deal with this threat.

Waorani Land Ontologies

We make two interrelated observations about the social life of land based on the encounters between settled Waorani and WVI detailed here. First, the increasing number of encounters (violent and nonviolent) is a result of shrinking Waorani lifeworlds due to decreased access to land resources, which is associated with expanding frontiers of resource extraction. Through state practices of territorial reordering, settled Waorani are recognized as an "Indigenous nation" of the sort described by Burkhart. Under the ideology of *pluriculturalidad* and adherence to legal instruments such as the Ecuadorian Constitution (Art. 57) and the ILO Convention 169, Ecuadorian agencies demarcate protection territories and earmark funds to provide (limited) access to basic resources, such as housing, schools, and medical posts, to settled Waorani. Oil companies also provide such resources, often under the guise of corporate responsibility. In exchange, the Waorani who accept the terms of settlement consent to resource extraction and undertake concomitant changes in settlement patterns and mobility. This "bounding of space" in settler ecologies of petroleum extraction fractures not only landscapes and Indigenous territories but also social relations. The ancestral lands of the Waorani, fiercely defended for generations, now represent one of the remaining natural resource frontiers in Ecuador. Government schemes for restructuring space employ multiple, often contradictory, strategies for implementing and maintaining borders, which almost inevitably propagate colonial hierarchies (Lu and Silva 2015). The borders of oil concessions shift and expand, alongside changes in administration and policy, as corporate holders of concessions change hands and the price of oil fluctuates. The Waorani do not hold sovereign control over their legally titled and communally held territories; they cannot receive royalties from oil extraction, obstruct oil development on their land, or carry out extraction themselves. For the Waorani, oil exploitation catalyzed the devaluation and insecurity of endogenously managed resources—forests, game, rivers—replacing these with manufactured resources provided by oil companies and state entities. While communities themselves are more sedentary and fixed in space, socioeconomic mobility entails spending more time in periurban or urban areas. Sharing between households has declined as a result of increased dependence on the market and ecological degradation, and with it, a powerful mechanism to reaffirm cultural identity, food security, and social ties (Lu and Silva 2015).

WVI, however, refuse to participate in such settlement schemes. Under Ecuadorian law and through the lobbying efforts of Indigenous rights advocates, WVI are recognized as peoples with a protected status. In 1999, a reserve called the Tagaeri-Taromenane Intangible Zone (or ZITT in Spanish) was created to protect their right to land by forbidding the presence of extractive activities and settlement (fig. 3.2), though its establishment has been a long and controversial process due to oil concession areas (Pappalardo 2013). In 2007, following the massacres of WVI in 2003 and again in 2006, precautionary measures to reinforce the protection of WVI were sought, which resulted in the demarcation of a buffer zone of 10 km around the ZITT perimeter to mitigate the impact of activities by non-Waorani. In this additional protected area, timber and oil extraction are prohibited, while hunting, fishing, and traditional use of biodiversity are permitted as ancestral activities among Waorani.

The 2008 Constitution, a signature achievement of the Correa Administration, was the first in the world to recognize the rights of people in voluntary isolation, stipulating in Article LVII, Paragraph 21 that: "The territories of the peoples in voluntary isolation are of ancestral possession, irreducible, and intangible, and all extractive activity is prohibited therein. The state shall adopt measures to ensure their lives, see to it that their self-determination and decision to remain in isolation are respected, and see to the observance of their rights. The violation of these rights will constitute the crime of genocide, which will be defined by law" (Asamblea Constituyente 2008, 43).

In addition, the Inter-American Commission on Human Rights (IACHR) commissioned a monitoring team to report on outsider activities in the ZITT (IACHR 2014). Yet commercial enterprises are gaining access to more and larger tracts of tropical forests within the boundaries of the ZITT, bolstered by state policies aimed at stimulating economic development in the region. As a result, more and more rainforest is lost to oil extraction, colonization, cash cropping, cattle production, and urbanization (Lu and Bilsborrow 2011). The current moment of resource frontier expansion in Ecuador is forcing WVI to confront their Waorani kin who are settled, increasing the number of encounters between them (Lu, Valdivia, and Silvia 2017).

Second, encounters between Waorani and WVI point to the limits of an outsider/insider logic in structures of settlement. In the accounts related by Keweriono residents, encounters between settled Waorani and WVI, who are likely both kin and unfamiliar relatives, are expressions of incomplete settlement. The

Ecuadorian State, however, "sees" settled Waorani and WVI as different kinds of humans, requiring different responses when harmed (Vera 2012). Whites, *mestizo* Ecuadorians, and foreigners receive the highest protection from the state, and if members of these human groups were killed by settled Waorani, full prosecution would result. For Miguel Angel de Cabodevilla (2007), settled Waorani are part of the nation-state's time-space: they participate in and depend on the institutions of settlement (education, religion, and public works and services) that alienate them from the experiential learning of living in the forest (Rival 2000). Settled Waorani, by recognizing the authority of the state (Lu, Valdivia, and Silvia 2017), become disentangled from "forest living" and develop dependencies and responsibilities toward it—they become citizens with enforceable political claims and rights within the nation-state's legal and moral framework.

In contrast, WVI are not seen as being on the path to Ecuadorian citizenship. They are often described as anachronistic relics of ancestral lifeworlds that have not yet made the "leap" to modernity (see Deloria 1969). Their presence is ghostly; they can only be detected by remotely sensed imagery, noises, objects left behind, or footprints evaluated and validated by state-recognized experts (Ministerio de Justicia Derechos Humanos y Cultos [MJDHC] 2013). Among state institutions representing the rights of WVI, such as the Ministry for Justice, Human Rights, and Religious Affairs (and later on, the Secretariat of Human Rights), WVI land-life relations are narrated more like a temporal experience outside of "settler time" (Rifkin 2017)—normalized nonnative presence, influence, and occupation—which opens the possibility of WVI elimination (Álvarez 2017). Thus, in some cases, areas meant to protect WVI rights to land, such as the Yasuní National Park (YNP) and the ZITT, have been cartographically modified in state-created maps to erase WVI presence and facilitate resource extraction expansion in the name of national interest (MJDHC 2013). For Cabodevilla, this leads to a "misguided" state agenda towards WVI, exemplified in its decision to drill for oil in the YNP—lands occupied by the Taromenane—a decision that precipitated the March 2013 massacre. For Marchi, Aguirre, and Cabodevilla (2013), the only way that WVI will survive their relationship with settlers is if the state stops recognizing the WVI as peoples with a protected status and instead includes them as citizens. Doing so, they argue, would recognize their rights as Indigenous peoples. Implicit in this argument is that isolation and refusal of settlement no longer protect their right to land.

The encounters we examine in this paper go beyond this logic of Indigenous state recognition. Specifically, they illustrate settled Waorani consciousness. Settled Waorani often reminisce about *durani bai*: the ways they used to celebrate, the collaborations between husband and wife, the healthy foods they used to eat, the respect between relatives, the ways they kept intruders out of their territory, and the fortitude, skill, and both physical and mental strength of young women and men of times past. Now, they lament that their settled bodies have become soft; youth are fickle; girls have babies out of wedlock, abandoned by their male partners and not properly cared for; and many young people lack the autonomy and skill to maintain their own gardens and provide for themselves through hunting and gathering. The violence and fear of past times of warfare are also remembered and often romanticized.

For settled Waorani, WVI are living reminders of times past, physically and behaviorally different, even considered mythical beings possessing supernatural powers. The WVI are lighter skinned, settled Waorani say, because they live primarily under the cover of the forest canopy and their skin does not darken under the sun from time spent playing and traveling along the river. They are taller, some settled Waorani say, because they still exclusively eat the rich food of the forest. There are also rumors that the WVI have large feet and mask their footprints by taking large steps and wrapping their feet with leaves, like a sort of shoe.

Until recently, settled Waorani in the western reaches of Waorani ancestral territory admired the WVI from afar, in the abstract, comfortable in their belief that the WVI would not relocate to the forests that they themselves frequent. However, over the last seven years, fear and uncertainty have been added to this wonder and curiosity, as more and more individuals have had direct encounters with the WVI by their homes and involving their families. The unpredictable and uneven nature of these encounters and their secrecy, requested out of fear and/or political motives, has created an uneven, shifting milieu of belief and doubt.

When in-person testimonials such as the one analyzed in this chapter are given to state agencies and Indigenous organizations, they are often ignored. However, more and more stories are emerging about people coming out—or lured out—of isolation around the world (Kluger 2015). Such encounters are not limited to Ecuador but also occur in Brazil and Peru, where there is a surge in sightings and raids by people in voluntary isolation (Lawler 2015). As public and private enterprises seek economic growth through the construction of hydroelectric dams, mines, oil pipelines, transmission lines, and highways, "there is no part of the Amazon that is not under some kind of pressure" (Pringle 2015, 1081), pushing isolated peoples to "the last remnants of intact forest [. . .] in the most secluded areas" (Lawler 2015, 1076). Food shortages, conflicts with people working in extractive industries, such as loggers and oil/gas workers, illness, and intertribal violence may now be forcing isolated people from their hideouts, seeking contact out of desperation. The case study we present, one of the most detailed accounts of the Waorani of Ecuador, offers a way of seeing these encounters not just as acts of desperation but as efforts to adapt, to connect, and to understand.

Where the settled Waorani and the WVI *are* matters to how their lives are valued in the context of the Ecuadorian nation-state. WVI are selectively (not always mistakenly) erased from the land, rendered invisible or hypothetical when their existence unsettles the settlement of land ontologies. The presence of the WVI in the northwestern portion of Waorani territory, occupied by the greatest density of settled Waorani, has implications for petroleum extraction in the region.[5] WVI embody a blend of social, cultural, and environmental capital, making them powerful symbols of the need for forest conservation and the costs of continuing extractivism. The social and cultural viability of the Taromenane and other WVI is uncompromisingly tied to the lands where intact rainforest ecosystems remain. For the Ecuadorian State, the protection of WVI—unparalleled in their isolation, invisibility, and vulnerability—is important to the administration's identity as a guarantor of human rights and, more generally, a champion of social justice. Yet they are irrefutably known only through violence and body counts, and even then, the state decides not to recognize or acknowledge them.

While the case of the Waorani cannot (and should not) be generalized for all peoples in voluntary isolation, the tenuous and emotion-filled negotiations between separated kin offer insights into the political and affective terrain of land-life claims. In the case of the Waorani, settled communities recognize themselves through their encounters with WVI, a recognition that affirms their connections to place-thought and other forms of sociality that are being gradually lost. It is also important to note that the settled Waorani of Keweriono have not abandoned their village. They remain alert and attentive to WVI reaching out, not attacking them, but waiting. We can speculate about these decisions and how recognition and misrecognition play a role in the self-discipline of groups. Settled Waorani might fear the possibility of state action against them if they attack WVI; they fear state interventions that limit their autonomy. At the same time, WVI did not attack or kidnap settled Waorani, even though they wanted to, in fear of retaliation.

Stories of gruesome killings between settled Waorani and WVI are stories about the ending of WVI life and lifeworlds perpetuated by Ecuadorian settler society. In this chapter, we counter these narratives of endings by focusing on ongoing encounters rife with feelings of untrustworthiness, impending threat, and the dissuasive power of kin recognition, which carry with them the potential for transformation. These are stories of not-yet-deadly encounters, which point to a different register of land-life potentials. Through ethnographic approaches, we represented encounters rich with emotions (fear, curiosity, apprehension, excitement) that recognize settler Waorani time-space consciousness. For now, these encounters are moments of shifting place-thought relations, moments forced by the ongoing abstraction of land as an object of exploitation, and where the settled Waorani are unprepared but developing modes of communicating with WVI, no longer as an abstracted "other" but as distant families with kin obligations and responsibilities.

NOTES

1. Typical accounts of encounters with WVI center on incidents of bloodshed. For example, the *Newsweek* article titled "After All the People We Killed, We Felt Dizzy" (Horne 2014) centers on the attack in late March 2013 of members of a family group called the Taromenane, one of a handful of WVI in Ecuador's Amazon, by settled Waorani living along an oil road in Yasuní National Park (YNP). The massacre was an act of revenge by settled Waorani, precipitated by the death a few weeks earlier of two of their elderly relatives, who had been speared after the Taromenane confronted them about allowing oil activities in their territory. We describe elsewhere (Lu, Valdivia, and Silvia 2017) the details and context of both attacks, drawing on media reports and the first-hand accounts published by Marchi, Aguirre, and Cabodevilla (2013) in their book *Una Tragedia Ocultada (A Hidden Tragedy)*.

2. This Waorani woman allowed the documentary filmmaker Keith Hayward and the anthropologist Emilio Rojas to film her account of this experience. Hayward and Rojas were working with Wirth on a long-term educational project with Waorani youth.

3. The language of the Waorani, *waoterero*, is considered a linguistic isolate, without identifiable links with the recognized language families. Names of rivers are important social markers reflecting connections to place. The Waorani village of Toñampare means "Toñae's stream" and Quihuaro means "Quihua's river" (Lu 2001).

4. The mixture of curiosity and fear within individuals is not homogeneous among the WVI themselves, and whether to approach peacefully or defensively is a topic of disagreement according to the Waorani in Keweriono and Wentaro who have spoken directly with the WVI. According to the wife of a man who had direct encounters with the WVI in Wentaro, there are two separate WVI groups visiting Keweriono and Wentaro and there are tensions within and between the groups.

5. Narco-trafficking also impacts the safety of settled Waorani villages, a situation which has largely been ignored by the Ecuadorian government and one with significant implications for the mobility and autonomous living of WVI.

REFERENCES

Álvarez, K. 2017. "Presiones a los territorios de los Tageiri, Taromenane y otras familias no contactadas en la Amazonía Ecuatoriana." *Ciencia Política*, 12 (24): 97–114.

Asamblea Constituyente. 2008. *Constitución del Ecuador*. https://www .asambleanacional.gob.ec/documentos/Constitucion-2008.pdf

Burkhart, B. 2019. *Indigenizing Philosophy through the Land: A Trickster Methodology for Decolonizing Environmental Ethics and Indigenous Futures*. East Lansing: Michigan State University Press.

Burow, P. B., Brock, S., and Dove, M. R. 2022. "Unsettling the Land: Indigeneity, Ontology, and Hybridity in Settler Colonialism." In *Indigenous Resurgence:*

Decolonialization and Movements for Environmental Justice. Edited by J. Dhillon, 59–76. New York: Berghahn Books.

Cabodevilla, M. A. 1994. *Los Huaorani en la historia de los pueblos del oriente.* Coca, Ecuador: CICAME.

Cabodevilla, M. A. *El exterminio de los pueblos ocultos.* 2nd ed. Quito, Ecuador: CICAME, 2007.

Cabodevilla, M. A., R. Smith, and A. R. Toledo. 2004. *Tiempos de guerra: Waorani contra Taromenane.* Ecuador: Abya-Yala.

Coulthard, G. S. 2014. *Red Skin, White Masks: Rejecting the Colonial Politics of Recognition.* Minneapolis: University of Minnesota Press.

Deloria, V. 1969. *Custer Died for Your Sins: An Indian Manifesto.* Norman: University of Oklahoma Press.

Horne, B. 2014. "After All the People We Killed, We Felt Dizzy." *Newsweek*, January 6, 2014. https://www.newsweek.com/after-all-people-we-killed-we-felt-dizzy -225424.

IACHR (Inter-American Commission on Human Rights). 2014. *Tagaeri and Taromenane Indigenous Peoples in Isolation.* Ecuador: Inter-American Commission on Human Rights.

Kane, J. 2012. *Savages.* New York: Vintage.

Kelley, P. M. "Issues for Literacy Materials Development in a Monolingual Amazonian Culture: The Waodani of Ecuador." Master's Thesis, University of British Columbia, 1988.

Kluger, J. 2015. "Is It Ethical to Leave Uncontacted Tribes Alone?" *Time*, June 4, 2015. https://time.com/3909470/tribes-uncontacted-ethics/.

Lawler, A. 2015. "Making Contact." *Science* 348 (6239): 1072–1079.

Lu, F. E. 2001. "The Common Property Regime of the Huaorani Indians of Ecuador: Implications and Challenges to Conservation." *Human Ecology* 29 (4): 425–447.

Lu, F. E., and R. E. Bilsborrow. 2011. "A Cross-Cultural Analysis of Human Impacts on the Rainforest Environment in Ecuador." In *Human Population: Its Influences on Biological Diversity.* Edited by R. P. Cincotta and L. J. Gorenflo, 127–151. Berlin: Springer Verlag.

Lu, F. E., and N. L. Silva. 2015. "Imagined Borders: (Un)bounded Spaces of Oil Extraction and Indigenous Sociality in 'Post-Neoliberal' Ecuador." *Social Sciences* 4: 434–458.

Lu, F. E., G. Valdivia, and N. L. Silva. 2017. "Oil, Revolution, and Indigenous Citizenship in Ecuadorian Amazonia." In *Political Economy of Latin America Series.* New York: Palgrave Macmillan.

Manuel, A., and Grand Chief R. M. Derrickson. 2015. *Unsettling Canada: A National Wake-Up Call.* Toronto: Between the Lines.

Marchi, M. de, M. Aguirre, and M. A. Cabodevilla. 2013. *Una Tragedia Ocultada.* Coca, Ecuador: CICAME.

Melendez, A. 2013. *Isolated Amazon Indians Under Pressure in Ecuador.* Inter Press Service News Agency, June 5, 2013. http://www.ipsnews.net/2013/06/isolated -amazon-indians-under-pressure-in-ecuador/.

MJDHC (Ministerio de Justicia Derechos Humanos y Cultos). 2013. *Plan de medidas cautelares para la protección de los pueblos indígenas en aislamiento Tagaeri-Taromenani: Informe sobre posibles señales de presencia de pueblos indígenas aislados en los bloques 31 y 43 (ITT).* http://www.geoyasuni.org/wp-content /uploads/2013/09/All3MJDHC.pdf.

Moreton-Robinson, A. 2015. *The White Possessive: Property, Power, and Indigenous Sovereignty.* Minneapolis: University of Minnesota Press.

Pappalardo, S. E., M. de Marchi, and F. Ferrarese. 2013. "Uncontacted Waorani in the Yasuní Biosphere Reserve: Geographical Validation of the *Zona Intangible Tagaeri Taromenane (ZITT).*" *PLOS ONE* 8 (6). https://doi.org/10.1371/journal .pone.0066293.

Pringle, H. 2015. "In Peril." *Science* 348 (6239): 1080–1085.

Rifkin, M. 2017. *Beyond Settler Time: Temporal Sovereignty and Indigenous Self-determination.* Durham, NC: Duke University Press.

Rival, L. M. *Social Transformations and the Impact of Formal Schooling on the Huaorani of Amazonian Ecuador.* PhD diss., London School of Economics, University of London, 1992.

Rival, L. M. 2000. "La escolarización formal y la producción de ciudadanos modernos en la Amazonía Ecuatoriana." In *Etnicidades.* Edited by A. Guerrero, 315–366. Quito, Ecuador: FLACSO.

Rival, L. M. 2002. *Trekking through History: The Huaorani of Amazonian Ecuador.* New York: Columbia University Press.

Robarchek, C. J., and C. Robarchek. 1997. *Waorani: The Contexts of Violence and War.* Belmont, CA: Wadsworth Publishing.

Simpson, L. B. 2017. *As We Have Always Done: Indigenous Freedom through Radical Resistance.* Minneapolis: University of Minnesota Press.

Spivak, G. C. 1988. "Can the Subaltern Speak?" In *Marxism and the Interpretation of Culture.* Edited by C. Nelson and L. Grossberg, 66–111. Champaign: University of Illinois Press.

Tuck, E., and K.W. Yang. 2012. "Decolonization Is Not a Metaphor." *Decolonization: Indigeneity, Education, and Society* 1 (1): 1–40.

Valdivia, G. 2018. "Translations of Indigeneity: Knowledge, Intimacy, and Performing Difference in Ecuador." *Development and Change,* 49 (5): 1347–1358.

Vera, C. A. "Taromenani, el exterminio de los pueblos ocultos." Produced by Camara Oscura. January 26, 2012. Feature documentary, 59:51. https://vimeo.com /35717321.

Wasserstrom, R., and T. Bustamante. 2015. "Ethnicity, Labor, and Indigenous Populations in the Ecuadorian Amazon, 1822–2010." *Advances in Anthropology* 5: 1–18.

Watts, V. 2013. "Indigenous Place-Thought and Agency amongst Humans and Non Humans (First Woman and Sky Woman Go On a European World Tour!)" *Decolonization: Indigeneity, Education & Society* 2 (1): 20–34.

Wilson, S. 2008. *Research as Ceremony: Indigenous Research Methods.* Black Point, Nova Scotia, Canada: Fernwood.

Wolfe, P. 2006. "Settler Colonialism and the Elimination of the Native." *Journal of Genocide Research* 8 (4): 387–409.

Yost, J. A. 1981. "Twenty Years of Contact: The Mechanisms of Change in Wao ("Auca") Culture." In *Cultural Transformations and Ethnicity in Modern Ecuador.* Edited by Norman E. Whitten, 677–704. Urbana: University of Illinois Press.

Yost, J. A. 1991. "People of the Forest: The Waorani." In *Ecuador in the Shadow of Volcanoes.* Edited by M. Acosta-Solis, 96–115. Quito, Ecuador: Ediciones Libri Mundi.

4

WHAT IS LAND? ONTOLOGY, PRACTICE, AND INDETERMINACY

Paul Nadasdy

What is land? This deceptively simple question has no straightforward or easy answer. Anthropologists have long recognized that people conceive of and relate to land in myriad ways. One common way is to view it as "property," a kind of thing that can be subdivided, owned, and controlled by humans, either individually or collectively. Whether they work their land for generations or turn it over for a quick profit, so the story goes, individual property owners tend to view land as something external to themselves, an asset or commodity that they—as autonomous social agents—are free to use, rent, or sell as they see fit. But this is something of an illusion; as property theorists have long noted, property is not so much a relationship between people (owners) and things (owned) as it is a relationship among people mediated by things. Indeed, Tania Li (2014) points out just how much work—physical, legal, conceptual—must be done to strip land of its social entanglements and transform it into a stand-alone resource or commodity. Similar considerations apply to the other side of the ownership relation: social theorists have made it clear that far from being the "atom" of society, the autonomous property-owning "individual" is itself an effect of power and property relations under capitalism (Foucault 1980; see also Macpherson 1962; Marx 1972; Okin 1989). And the supposedly clear distinction between owner and owned becomes even harder to maintain if we shift our gaze to forms of collective ownership, even under capitalism. Whether we look at corporate lands, National Parks, or REIT funds, ownership relations become murky. In such cases, it is impossible to identify a single autonomous agent with full discretion over how to dispose of his or her property; rather, agency is distributed over a

range of actors, and the identities of these collective owners (whether corporations, nations, or groups of shareholders) are as much an effect of the property
relation as is the possessive individual. This suggests that the very notion of property is closely bound to a particular set of cultural understandings and practices. Indeed, Marilyn Strathern (1984, 1988) famously argued that because the
European notion of property is contingent on a distinction between subject
(the owner) and object (the owned), it is inappropriate to apply it in cultural
contexts where such a distinction does not apply. Instead, she argued, any attempt to understand property relations cross-culturally must take into account
the radically different ways that humans construct notions of personhood.

This comes as no surprise to anthropologists working with Indigenous
peoples, many of whom claim not to "own" the land on which they live, but to
be *of* it, to be inextricably bound up in relations of kinship and reciprocity that
mutually constitute not only lands and peoples but animals and plants as well.
It is not just that land is bound up in—and productive of—human social relations (although that is certainly the case, see e.g., Bastien 1978; Myers 1991; Basso
1996; Biersack 1999), but also that land itself, or at least certain landforms, along
with animals and plants, are often viewed as "other-than-human" persons—to
use Hallowell's felicitous phrase—imbued with agency, even sentience (Hallowell 1960; Povinelli 1995; Anderson 2000; Borrows 2010, 245–248; Watts 2013;
de la Cadena 2015; Di Giminiani 2018). In its capacity as a person, land can be
a powerful actor in its own right. It can enter into social relations with human
people, including relations of kinship. It can provide care, demand respect, mete
out punishment. From such a perspective, it is even possible to view land itself
as an owning subject, reversing the usual relations of ownership (de Coppet 1985)

Anthropologists have long remarked on the resilience of such beliefs in the
face of colonialism and commented on their ongoing social importance, noting
that people continue to act based on their strongly held beliefs in other-than-
human persons. For decades, however, anthropologists tended to view such beliefs as just that: beliefs. Secure in the supposition that, whatever Indigenous
people themselves may believe (and however socially useful those beliefs may
be), land, animals, and plants are not really persons who can react to—and interact with—humans as subjects themselves. The tendency was to view such understandings as particular cultural constructions of nature, not as accurate
descriptions of nature itself. Over the past couple of decades, though, this has
begun to change. The arrogant, if often implicit, presumption that anthropologists have knowledge of the world, while the people we study have only belief
(or worse, *superstition*) has come in for increasing criticism. In response, many
anthropologists have sought alternative ways to frame Indigenous people's understandings of—and engagements with—the land and animals that avoid

reducing them to a set of cultural "beliefs." Indeed, many evince a wariness of framing the issue in epistemological terms at all—precisely because of the way epistemology assumes the existence of a (single) objective world that can be known/represented differently (and sometimes wrongly) by different knowers. Instead, they have increasingly framed the issue in ontological terms.

Anthropologists grappling with questions of ontology now argue that we must "take seriously" what our interlocutors tell us about the nature of the world—and that to do so, we should accept their assertions about sentient landscapes and animal persons, for example, as literal statements of fact that tell us something not only about their society and belief systems but also about the nature of reality itself. Since such statements often contradict standard anthropological assumptions about the nature of the world, however, this necessarily raises a host of thorny theoretical and political questions. How are we to reconcile the fact that some people regard the landscape as sentient, for example, while others do not, without reducing this difference to a matter of knowledge or worldview (i.e., epistemology)? One way of answering this question, which has received a great deal of attention in recent years, is to assert that different peoples inhabit different incommensurable—and only partially connected—realities, or worlds. I refer to this as the "multiple worlds thesis."

I begin this chapter with a close critical examination of the multiple worlds thesis. Although its proponents claim to be decolonizing social theory, I show that it is, in fact, beset by significant political as well as theoretical problems. I illustrate these with reference to my own ethnographic research in the southwest Yukon. I then suggest that, by shifting the focus from multiplicity to indeterminacy, we can avoid the pitfalls associated with the multiple worlds thesis while leaving open the possibility that radically different understandings of the world might reveal something important about the nature of reality.

The Multiple Worlds Thesis

In her recent influential work with Indigenous people in the highlands of Peru, Marisol de la Cadena (2010, 2015), one of the foremost proponents of the multiple worlds thesis, introduces us to two ritual specialists, Mariano and Nazario Turpo, and their complex social and political relationship with *Ausangate*, a powerful sentient mountain, which plays an important role in local and even national politics.[1] Refusing to characterize the Turpos' understanding of *Ausangate* as a set of cultural "beliefs" (much less as "superstition"), de la Cadena insists that *Ausangate* and other *tirakuna* (or "earth beings") are real. Drawing on Eduardo Viveiros de Castro's (1998, 2004) notion of multinaturalism, she argues that the reason Mariano and Nazario see *tirakuna*, where government officials, for example, see only mountains, is that they inhabit different worlds. What is at stake, she says, "are views *from* different worlds, rather than [different] perspectives about the same world" (de la Cadena 2015, 110). The political stakes here are potentially high. If a mountain, say, is really a sentient other-than-human person, we are likely to think differently about the prospect of mining it than if it is just a mindless collection of rocks and minerals to be used as its owners see fit. Indeed, if the land is really sentient, then the very concept of landed property begins to look suspiciously like part of a larger colonial project of disenchantment, one that objectifies the land to justify its exploitation.

De la Cadena views standard academic and political discourses as deeply implicated in the colonial process. Ideas about what constitutes land, knowledge, and politics, for example, are suspect because they are specific to a particular world—the world of colonialism and state power. Such terms have altogether different meanings in the world of Mariano and Nazario, a world where mountains are powerful other-than-human actors who play an active role in the political struggles waged by the human members of their *allyu*. This world is completely alien to Mariano's leftist urban allies, for example, who dismissed as mere superstition his efforts to enlist the help of *Ausangate* in their joint struggle for land reform. By arguing that Mariano and Nazario live and function in a completely different world, de la Cadena seeks to deprivilege the concepts held by Mariano's leftist allies, politicians in Lima, and many academics. In this way, she draws attention to their colonial nature. This is necessary, she suggests, because these different worlds are not equal. What Mariano and Nazario call "knowledge" (about *Ausangate*, for example) is reduced by scientists, politicians, and other relatively more powerful actors to mere "belief." By contrast, de la Cadena argues that Mariano and Nazario, too, possess "knowledge," but it is knowledge "of" and "in" a completely different world. This strategy has the benefit of decentering or relativizing standard ways of conceptualizing land, knowledge, and politics; our conceptualizations of these may be valid, she suggests, but only in the world where they were generated. There are other worlds out there—like the one inhabited by Mariano and Nazario—where different rules and concepts apply.

But if different peoples inhabit different realities, how is communication—to say nothing of politics—across worlds even possible? If we want to understand what happens in a cross-world encounter, say between Mariano and his leftist allies, says de la Cadena—again drawing on Viveiros de Castro, we need to focus on the process of "equivocation," that is, (mis)communication across worlds. Equivocation emerges, she says, when "different perspectival positions—views *from* different worlds, rather than perspectives about the same world—use the same word to refer to things that are not the same [e.g., *Ausangate*/mountain]" (de la Cadena 2015, 110).

De la Cadena goes on to argue that equivocation—and cross-world communication more generally—is only possible because these different worlds are not completely separate from one another. Taking inspiration from Marilyn Strathern's (1991) notion of "partial connections"—and Annmarie Mol's (2002) elaboration on the idea—de la Cadena argues that the different worlds inhabited by Mariano on one hand and his leftist allies on the other are "more than one, less than many." That is, the world of *Ausangate*—the earth being—and *Ausangate*—the mountain—are not *completely* distinct from one another. In Mol's terms, they "hang together."

In his analysis of caribou management efforts in Labrador, Mario Blaser (2016), too, draws on the notion of partially connected multiplicity to argue that despite appearances, Euro-Canadian wildlife managers and Innu hunters are not actually trying to manage the same thing. Wildlife managers, for their part, seek to manage caribou (dumb animals), while Innu hunters focus instead on managing their relations with *atîku* (caribou-persons). Here, Blaser explicitly adopts Annmarie Mol's "praxiographic" approach to the constitution of "objects." In her influential 2002 ethnography, Mol notes that the disease atherosclerosis is not quite the same thing for vascular surgeons as it is for pathologists or hematologists. What is more, the different atheroscleroses are not completely compatible with one another. It is not simply that different kinds of doctors have different "perspectives" on the same thing (atherosclerosis), she argues, because that would imply that atherosclerosis exists "out there" as an independent stand-alone entity. Nothing, she maintains, exists in and of itself. Rather, every object is related to others through the practices that enact it (Mol 2002, 53–54). In the clinic, for example, surgeons and patients enact atherosclerosis by reporting complaints, experiencing pain while walking, and feeling a weak leg pulse; in the pathology lab, by contrast, pathologists enact it by manipulating amputated legs, dies, slides, and microscopes.

In an analogous move, Blaser (2016, 558) argues that *atîku* and caribou emerge from different "material-semiotic assemblages": "*Atîku* emerges from an assemblage that involves *atanukan* [stories], hunters, the sharing of meat, generosity, a spirit master, and so on; caribou emerges from an assemblage that involves the discipline of biology, wildlife managers, predictive modeling, calculations to balance environmental and economic concerns, and so on." Caribou/*atîku*, he claims, are an equivocation. Like different versions of atherosclerosis and *Ausangate*/mountain, they are different things, yet they hang together as "more than one, less than many." From there, it seems but a small step to argue, as Blaser does, that wildlife biologists and government officials inhabit a different reality from Innu hunters: one of which is inhabited by caribou, the other by *atîku*.[2]

According to proponents of the multiple worlds thesis, it is precisely the partial connectedness of worlds that enables cross-world communication via equivocation (e.g., de la Cadena 2015, 110). But, as de la Cadena herself suggests, such acts are fraught with danger. If translators do not realize they are translating across worlds, and if their translation work takes place in the context of unequal power relations (that legitimate only one of those worlds as "real"), then translation of this sort becomes a colonial act. Cross-world translation can never be perfect; it always leaves an untranslatable excess, and in the world inhabited by state actors, scientists, and academics and backed up by state power, that remainder gets cast as "belief" or "superstition" and so falls out of the realm of the political (de la Cadena 2015, 205, 249). The antidote, scholars like de la Cadena and Blaser suggest, is the development of a "cosmopolitics" (a term they adapt from Isabelle Stengers) that explicitly acknowledges the existence of multiple worlds and recognizes political conflict as "emerging among partially connected worlds" (de la Cadena 2010, 362).

Although I am sympathetic to the decolonial politics motivating the use of the multiple worlds thesis, I am uncomfortable with this approach on both theoretical and political grounds. To see why, I turn now to my research in the southwest Yukon. At first glance, this is an ethnographic setting that would seem ripe for the discovery of multiple worlds and cross-world encounters like those described by de la Cadena and Blaser.

Multiple Worlds in the Yukon

Like other parts of the North American Subarctic, the Yukon is full of other-than-human persons. I have written extensively about how Indigenous hunting there involves a set of understandings and practices that many Indigenous people view as central to maintaining an ongoing social relationship among human and animal people (e.g., Nadasdy 2003, 2007). In their broad outline, these beliefs and practices are very similar to those Blaser describes for Innu caribou hunters, so it would be very easy for me to construct an account analogous to his, in which biologists live in a world inhabited by moose, while Indigenous Southern Tutchone hunters inhabit one peopled by *kanday* (with the moose/*kanday* equivocation essential to communication across these two worlds). There are also "earth beings" in the Yukon, although they are somewhat less prominent in Yukon politics than they appear to be in Peru. Anthropologist Catharine McClellan, who conducted research in the southern Yukon in the 1940s and 1950s, noted that Yukon Indian people conceived of the land as animate and even sentient: "[. . .] the landscape is not simply the inert product of physical forces, dotted with the animate species familiar to us. Rather, many parts of it are highly sensate and full of indwelling power. Various sections of it are under the special control of powerful beings or *yek* who are easily angered. Human beings must do their best to use the resources of their country without bringing upon themselves the major or minor disasters which can so easily follow inattention to the required observances of the 'beings' who make up or control the landscape" (McClellan 1975, 88).

More recently, Julie Cruikshank (2005) has written eloquently about glaciers, one especially animate group of earth beings that inhabit the region. Although she does not invoke the multiple worlds thesis (nor use the term "earth being"), Cruikshank juxtaposes different understandings of glaciers: they are at once the physical entities studied by glaciologists, the forbidding symbols of sublime nature celebrated by Romantic poets, and the powerful sentient beings encountered by Tlingit and Athapaskan travelers. In the process, she refuses to privilege—or dismiss—any particular view, arguing that the erasure entailed in such a dismissal is the essence of colonialism. Instead, she treats the glaciers evoked by Tlingit storytellers as having the same ontological status as those brought into being by the narratives of climate scientists.

Catharine McClellan's interlocutors told her that other landscape features, too, such as mountains and rivers, could sense and interact with people. According to McClellan, moieties "owned" particular lands—including certain fishing sites, landforms, and important hunting areas—and had the obligation to "care" for them. As I discuss elsewhere (Nadasdy 2017, 99–104), McClellan's (tentative and qualified) use of the term "ownership" in this context (which seems to have been following local usage) connotes neither relations of property nor jurisdiction; rather, it is a way of acknowledging that moieties had a responsibility to manage social relations among humans and the powerful other-than-human beings in those areas. This not only meant ensuring that human people in the region interacted in appropriate ways with animal-people, but it also involved communicating with, honoring, and sometimes placating rivers, mountains, and other powerful and sentient landforms by holding potlatches in their honor or performing other ritual practices (McClellan 1975, 483–485). Yukon Indian people saw themselves as intimately bound up through relations of kinship and reciprocity with all of these other-than-human people. Far from being "resources" to be "managed" by those humans exercising jurisdiction/ ownership over them, the land and animals were—and in some contexts still are—regarded as important political actors in their own right.[3]

Today, while many Yukon Indian people continue actively to maintain proper social relations with animal people (Nadasdy 2007), this is less the case for what de la Cadena calls earth beings. It is true that people do still sometimes tell stories that feature sentient landforms, and at times, they orient their activities accordingly. I was warned more than once, for example, never to cook with grease in the vicinity of a glacier, which is widely thought to anger them (Cruikshank 2005). People also pointed out different mountains to me, each with a different "personality." Some are benevolent, some are evil and should be avoided, and some can control the weather and, thus, are dangerous when angered. Talk of sentient landforms, however, is relatively rare, and it has been many decades since a potlatch was held to placate a river or mountain. I never heard anyone invoke sentient mountains or glaciers in a political context, such as land claim negotiations (in contrast to animal-persons, whom they do sometimes invoke). Indeed, some, though certainly not all, Yukon Indian people dismiss talk of sentient mountains as the superstition of their ancestors. Yet, I suspect few Yukon Indian people would agree with the assertion that land is "just" dirt and rocks.

Indeed, Yukon Indian people have repeatedly emphasized the fundamental and constitutive role of land in their way of life. In 1973, for example, the Yukon Native Brotherhood (later renamed the Council for Yukon Indians) presented the Canadian government with *Together Today for Our Children Tomorrow* (1973), the document that initiated Indigenous land claim negotiations in the Yukon. In it, they emphasized the central importance of land to their way of life: "Without land, Indian People have no Soul—no Life—no Identity—no Purpose. Control of our own Land is necessary for our Cultural and Economic Survival." Yet, they did not frame their interests as a matter of ownership but, rather, as a need to protect it for "our children and for our children's children in perpetuity" (31), and I have provided accounts elsewhere of Indigenous elders who objected with anger to the suggestion that people can "own" land (Nadasdy 2002, 247) or that different groups of Indigenous people historically had exercised exclusive jurisdiction over bounded territories (Nadasdy 2017, 210–211). Many Yukon Indian people continue to regard both ways of relating to the land—property and jurisdiction—as morally suspect (at least in some social contexts) precisely because they contradict the values of sharing and reciprocity that, to some extent, still structure social relations among human and other-than-human persons. While most still maintain that they have a special relationship to the land, that they are still, in the words of one Inland Tlingit woman, "part of the land, part of the water" (McClellan et al. 1987, 1), Yukon Indian peoples' way of life has changed dramatically over the past eighty years, and the nature of their relationship to the land and animals has changed correspondingly.

Yukon Indian people do not all share a unitary vision of proper human-land-animal relations and likely never did. For starters, notions of property and jurisdiction are now commonplace in the Yukon. Many Yukon Indian people are now private landowners (and those who do not own land themselves certainly understand and generally respect the property rights of others), and the recent negotiation of land claim and self-government agreements (modern treaties) has led to the rise of self-governing First Nations, Indigenous polities that themselves exercise jurisdiction over bounded territories. Whether they like it or not, all Yukon Indian people regularly enact relations of property and jurisdiction in their everyday practices (Nadasdy 2017). What is more, Yukon Indian people sometimes (e.g., in their capacities as Yukon politicians, mining company employees, or wildlife technicians) *act* as if mountains are just rocks and moose are just moose—at least at certain times, in certain social contexts—even if at other times and in other contexts they act differently. Any blanket assertions to the effect that Yukon Indian people and Euro-Canadians inhabit different worlds—one that contains sentient mountains, glaciers, and *kanday* and another that contains only rocks, ice, and moose—necessarily ignores history and steamrolls ethnographic complexity. The situation, it would seem, is far more dynamic, complex, and heterogeneous than can be captured by the multiple worlds thesis.

A Proliferation of Worlds

Michael Cepek (2016) has argued convincingly that anthropologists concerned with questions of ontology tend to flatten ethnographic complexity in their quest to produce the clean examples of "radical alterity" they require for ontological theory building (see also Bessire and Bond 2014; Hunt 2014; Graeber 2015). To this, I would add that the tendency toward ethnographic simplification is not simply instrumental; it is essential if the multiple worlds thesis is to remain at all coherent. If we are supposed to accept our interlocutors' particular understandings and practices as diagnostic of the existence of alternate worlds, then ethnographic heterogeneity presents a serious challenge because it leads—almost inevitably—to an uncontrolled proliferation of worlds. If two ritual practitioners, for example, have slightly different ways of relating to— and so enacting—*Ausangate* (so that *Ausangate* is slightly different for each of them), or two hunters have different ways of enacting *atîku*, then worlds proliferate. Just how many worlds are there? Does everyone live in their own private, though partially connected, world? Barring that extreme, how are we supposed to distinguish variation among worlds from variation within a single world? How much variation in understanding and practice is required to produce separate worlds? It is hard for me to view the uncontrolled proliferation of ever smaller but still homogeneous worlds as a viable solution to the problem of ethnographic simplification identified by Cepek and others.

Problems with the multiple worlds thesis run even deeper, though, because heterogeneity exists not only at the level of society. What of the Yukon Indian hunter who cultivates social relations with *kanday* and also works for her First Nation's wildlife management office managing moose populations? Or the hunter who will not fry fat near a glacier, who also owns his own plot of land and helps survey First Nation settlement lands? In which world do they live? Do they live in hybrid worlds populated by both *kanday* and moose, earth beings and property? Or do they somehow regularly switch from one world to another depending on whether they are enacting *kanday*/earth beings or moose/property at any given moment? If the latter, how are we supposed to understand world-switching of this sort?

Finally, the problem of ethnographic heterogeneity plagues all the worlds variously conjured by proponents of the multiple worlds thesis, not just the Indigenous ones. It is all well and good to claim that "Euro-Americans," for example, live in a world in which land is an inert entity that is amenable to human ownership and control; but then how do we account for so "western" a phenomenon as the national homeland? For Euro-American nationalists (including those who own their own land), land is neither inert nor separable from humans. Rather, it is the "geo-body" of the nation, to use Thongchai's (1994) evocative phrase, redolent with memories, histories, and stories that together constitute the lifeblood of the nation. Those histories animate the landscape, endowing it with "mythical content and hallowed sentiments" (Williams and Smith 1983, 509). The soil itself, infused with the bodies and blood of the nation's ancestors, is sacred, part of the very being of those who make up the national collective (Verdery 1999). Just as Mariano and Nazario Turpo, through their relational practices, continually enact *Ausangate* as a sentient earth being, so, too, nationalists, through their everyday and ritual practices, enact the homeland as an entity that inspires love, patriotism, and even a willingness to sacrifice one's life in its defense. National homelands, it seems, are earth beings too. They can even "own" people: "[. . .] the concept of a homeland implies a nationalist vision of the globe and of interstate relations, in which specific communities 'belong' to particular territories and states by a sort of natural right" (Williams and Smith 1983, 509; see also de Coppet 1985).

So, do nationalists inhabit a world peopled by earth beings? The only way proponents of the multiple worlds thesis can deny such a claim, it seems to me, is to assert that nationalism—unlike, say, Indigenous practices associated with earth beings—is "just" a matter of culture/ideology. But on what basis would we relegate one set of beliefs and practices to the realm of culture while elevating another to the status of ontology? To complicate things even further, it seems that nationalist and Indigenous ways of relating to the land are not even necessarily incompatible with one another. Elsewhere (Nadasdy 2017, 195–197, 234–247), I have argued that the rise of Yukon First Nation nationalism (which has accompanied the formation of First Nation states) is not so much *creating* the sacred links between Yukon Indian people and their homeland as it is reframing them in national—rather than (just) kinship—terms. Indeed, sentient landforms—with all their complicated ties of kinship to other beings who reside in the homeland—can prove welcome additions to the nation. But which world(s) do land-owning Yukon Indian nationalists inhabit? And what if they are wildlife management bureaucrats and hunters to boot?

Indeterminacy and Complementarity

How, then, can we rescue the laudable political project of decolonizing knowledge from the morass of multiple worlds? Fortunately, there is another approach that has been largely (though not completely) overlooked in the rush to multiply worlds. As it turns out, one need not stray far from the literature on multiple worlds to find an approach that avoids many of the pitfalls just discussed. In fact, although proponents of the multiple worlds thesis draw heavily on Annemarie Mol's influential work on the ontology of atherosclerosis, Mol herself never invokes the notion of multiple worlds. Although vascular surgeons, pathologists, and hematologists all enact atherosclerosis in slightly different—and sometimes incompatible—ways, she never suggests, as a result, that they inhabit different worlds. In keeping with her focus on practice, Mol conceives of atherosclerosis as more of a process than a thing; it never just exists "out there," independent of the practices through which it is enacted; instead, it is something that happens (in the clinic, for example, or the pathology lab). So, for Mol, the fact that each version of atherosclerosis is slightly incompatible with the others is not a case of different "things" being slightly incompatible with one another; rather, it is a matter of incompatible practices. To enact atherosclerosis in the pathology lab, for example, the pathologist requires an amputated leg he or she can use to prepare slides, which, under the microscope, show evidence of blocked leg arteries. Such practices are utterly incompatible with the clinic, where surgeons would never amputate a leg just to determine whether a patient suffers from atherosclerosis. The surgeon must enact the disease in a different way, a way that does not always correspond perfectly with the atherosclerosis of the pathology lab.[4] The apparent "multiplicity" of atherosclerosis, then, is an artifact of our insistence on seeing the world as composed of "things," rather than relations and processes. It is only if we insist on conceiving of atherosclerosis as a stand-alone object—which, Mol asserts, it is not—that "it" appears multiple; it becomes fuzzy, hard to pin down because it looks and acts a little bit differently depending on the particular set of practices (and associated assemblage of other objects, e.g., knives, slides, dies, and microscopes) used to enact it.

As it happens, Mol's praxiographic approach resonates powerfully with early twentieth-century debates among physicists over the nature of reality. One such debate concerned the nature of light, which by the early twentieth century had become the subject of intense controversy. Physicists had carried out well-designed and convincing experiments that conclusively and reliably showed light to be composed of particles. Yet other equally well designed and convincing experiments showed light to be a wave. The problem is that waves and particles are very different kinds of phenomena; it is impossible for something to be both a wave and a particle at the same time. As it turns out, while experiments can be designed to demonstrate either the wave or the particle character of light, no experiment can demonstrate *both at the same time*. So, the nature and properties of light (particle or wave) depend entirely on the experimental apparatus. Viewing this state of affairs through the multiple worlds thesis, we might be inclined to claim that some physicists live in a world where light is a particle, while others live in a world where it is a wave. In such an account, light would be an equivocation that facilitates but also troubles cross-world communication. This is not, however, the solution favored by physicists and philosophers of science.[5]

Karen Barad (2007, chaps. 3 and 7) credits Niels Bohr with the solution to the problem just described, a solution that was experimentally confirmed in the 1990s. Discarding one of the basic ontological assumptions of classical physics, Bohr argued that light is not a stand-alone entity with a set of given properties "out there" in the world waiting to be observed and measured by independent subjects. Rather, it is fundamentally bound up with what Barad calls the "agencies of observation," the specific material practices used to observe/measure it. "As a matter of principle," she notes, "there is no unambiguous way to distinguish between the 'object' and the 'agencies of observation.' No inherent/Cartesian subject-object distinction exists" (114). The ontological implication of this is that the world is not composed of independent objects with inherent properties but rather of what Bohr referred to as "phenomena." He used this term to signify the essential wholeness of the interaction between the "objects" under investigation and the "agencies of observation" (427, n. 47). As such, they are "the basic units of existence [. . .] ontologically primitive relations—relations without preexisting relata" (333). Any attempt to isolate the "thing-in-itself"—by asking, for example, "What is light?"—without specifying the material practices used to observe it, is to break apart the phenomenon, the basic unit of existence. The object-in-itself is, according to Bohr, "indeterminate." That is, if one does not specify the experimental apparatus one is using to observe light, then the nature of light is indeterminate; it can be either particle or wave. Given a particular experimental apparatus, however, the properties of light become determinate; it becomes a wave, or it becomes a particle . . . in a particular experimental context. "Indeterminacy," as Bohr uses it, implies incompleteness rather than uncertainty.

Central to Bohr's notion of indeterminacy is the incompatibility of experimental apparatuses. Recall that it is impossible to design an experiment that demonstrates both light's wave-like and particle-like properties *at the same time*. One must choose, and until one does so, the nature of light remains indeterminate. Once the choice is made, however, the nature of light becomes determinate. It is a wave. Or it is a particle. But only in that particular experimental context. In Bohr's terms, the wave and particle behaviors of light are "complementary" (or mutually exclusive). This implies that the nature of the observed phenomenon changes with corresponding changes in the apparatus of observation (Barad 2007, 106). This is a fundamental challenge to the ontology of classical physics and to many people's everyday view of the world (since it upends many of our most basic assumptions about the nature of causality, for instance, and the distinction between subject and object), but it does not require the invocation of multiple worlds.

In this same vein, the principles of complementarity and indeterminacy can be used as the basis for constructing a viable alternative to the multiple worlds thesis.[6] It is fairly straightforward, for example, to translate Mol's argument into the language of indeterminacy. We have already seen that the material practices by which atherosclerosis is enacted in the clinic are incompatible with those used in the pathology lab. So, is atherosclerosis pain when walking? Or is it evidence of blocked blood vessels under a microscope? As in the wave/particle debate, it cannot be both at the same time; in the absence of specific material practices, atherosclerosis remains indeterminate. It could be either pain when walking or blocked blood vessels. Only once a particular set of material practices has been chosen can atherosclerosis be enacted either as pain when walking or as blocked vessels under the microscope. In Bohr's terms, these mutually exclusive versions of atherosclerosis-in-practice are complementary phenomena. Each is real yet incomplete; one learns nothing about the pain of atherosclerosis in a pathology lab.

One can treat the ethnographic examples used to provide evidence of multiple worlds in much the same way. Recall Mario Blaser's (2016, 558) assertion that *atîku* and caribou emerge from different "material-semiotic assemblages." These sound suspiciously like Barad's "agencies of observation" or Mol's material and discursive practices for enacting the "reality" of atherosclerosis. In the absence of specific material-semiotic assemblages, *atîku*/caribou (the object-in-itself)—like light and atherosclerosis—is indeterminate. Only once those practices are specified does the phenomenon become determinate. It is caribou. Or it is *atîku*. Caribou and *atîku* are complementary phenomena. As such, each is a "basic unit of existence" rather than a different cultural "take" on some invariant external object. One cannot enact both at the same time, because the material and discursive practices needed to enact them are incompatible. *Ausangate*/mountain is indeterminate in this same way. Any effort to distill out the "agencies of observation" (be they Nazario Turpo's offerings or geological surveys) renders the object-in-itself indeterminate. There is no need to invoke multiple worlds to take Indigenous peoples' understandings of the land and animals "seriously." As complementary phenomena, neither earth being nor mountain is more "real" than the other, but both are incomplete. One can learn nothing about *Ausangate*'s politics from a geological survey.

The indeterminacy framework has several advantages over the multiple worlds thesis. Because it does not force us, despite ourselves, to focus on objects-in-themselves, it avoids many of the theoretical problems associated with the multiple worlds thesis. For one thing, there is no proliferation of worlds because indeterminacy does not require multiple worlds, only incompatible material and semiotic practices. And without the need for multiple worlds, there is no pressure to flatten the ethnographic record so as to produce distinct, homogenous, and radically other worlds. Indeed, Henry Sharp (2001, 47, 65–73) has shown, in his analysis of human-animal relations among the Denésuliné (Chipewyan), that indeterminacy does not require radical alterity at all. Animals, it turns out, are indeterminate even *within* Denésuliné ontology. That is, it is not only caribou/*atîku* (or, in Denésuliné, caribou/*etθhen*) that are indeterminate, but plain *etθhen* are too. The multiple worlds thesis can only accommodate the heterogeneity of practices that give rise to apparently multiple versions of *etθhen* by generating a world for each and leaving Denésuliné people to straddle those worlds. Indeterminacy helps us understand everyday heterogeneous practices in Euro-American society too. Land is indeterminate. Depending on the set of material and semiotic practices through which it is enacted, a piece of land can either be property or part of the national homeland, though never quite both at the same time. The practices that enact property as a phenomenon and those that enact the national homeland are complementary. There is no need for landowners to inhabit a different world than nationalists, only for them to engage in different practices.

Indeterminacy and Colonialism

At this point, one might reasonably ask how appropriate it is to use an approach that emerged from turn-of-the-twentieth-century debates in quantum physics as the basis for trying to understand—and hopefully combat—ongoing forms of colonial violence, which, after all, is the laudable goal pursued by proponents of the multiple worlds thesis. On the face of it, there seems to be a vast gulf between rarefied academic debates among theoretical physicists nearly a century ago and the ongoing and systematic erasure by settler colonial governments of Indigenous ways of knowing and being in the world. For one thing, the quantum mechanical debate over the nature of light—for all its ontological significance—was a narrow one among an elite group of highly educated physicists who shared a broadly similar way of being in and understanding the world. Is Bohr's solution still useful when the debate is thrown open to encompass different kinds of people who may subscribe to very different understandings and objectives? And what about power? Bohr's notion of indeterminacy does not take power relations into account at all. There is no real reason why it should have; after all, wave physicists were not bent on dominating particle physicists and destroying their way of life. Yet that is precisely the situation we confront in trying to transport his solution into a colonial context.

In the southwest Yukon, for example, the creation of the Kluane Game Sanctuary (parts of which later became Kluane National Park) physically separated people—for more than a generation—from a large swath of their traditional lands. During that time, their mere presence in the sanctuary was punishable by fines and imprisonment. This caused grave hardship; the Canadian government had to truck beef to the village of Burwash Landing to prevent starvation. In addition to depriving local Indian people of access to food, the sanctuary also undermined relations between humans and other-than-human persons in the region. Because hunting is a social relationship between human and animal people, the ban on hunting necessarily disrupted those relationships. Fortunately, all the animals present in the sanctuary can also be found outside of it, so those relationships survived, if in attenuated form. Many of the sentient landforms I mentioned, however, including all of the glaciers, are located within the bounds of the sanctuary/Park, so those relationships were even more severely diminished. It is hard to maintain a social relationship with other-than-human persons when you are prohibited from going anywhere near them. And while the Canadian government was physically separating Kluane people from other-than-human persons in the sanctuary, it was also forcibly removing their children and shipping them off to mission schools, where they were explicitly taught to reject the "superstitious" beliefs and practices of their elders. In these Christian schools, beliefs involving other-than-human persons were regarded as demonic and specially marked for eradication.

At first glance, there does not seem to be much of a parallel between this co-lonial history and the wave-particle debate. But some of the differences fall away if we take a somewhat longer historical view of light. As it turns out, the wave and particle theories of light are hardly the only ways Western scholars have understood and enacted light over the centuries. Though of relatively recent vin-tage, both theories have their roots in ancient Greek texts (Lindberg 1978), and the nature of light and vision was long the subject of intense scholarly debate. Medieval Christian theologians, for example, puzzled over how God could have created light on the first day—but then waited until the fourth to create the sun and stars. This apparent contradiction, combined with passages in the Book of John (1:6–9) that equated Christ with light, led some to conclude that light has a spiritual as well as physical aspect (McCarthy 1976, 65–67). In his doctrine of Divine Illumination, for example, Augustine viewed light as the cognitive princi-ple, a notion still with us today in the powerful metaphorical connection linking light, sight, and knowledge (Salmond 1982). Later Christian theologians adopted Islamic scholar Ibn Sina's distinction between *lux* and *lumen* to differentiate be-tween the physical and spiritual aspects of light, a distinction sometimes still in-voked to mark the difference between light's physicality and its sociocultural meanings (Ingold 2005). With the emergence of modern optical science in the seventeenth century, light was gradually stripped of its spiritual, social, and psy-chological aspects, henceforth to be analyzed purely in terms of its physical prop-erties (Smith 2015). The process of "disenchanting" light, like the disenchantment of other forms of matter around this time (Merchant 1980), had an important political dimension. Gradually, various "experts" whose views on the nature of light had had to be considered were marginalized, their views dismissed as "un-scientific." Light became a *mere* metaphor for knowledge, which it certainly had not been for Augustine, and only certain kinds of practices (e.g., those involving lenses, prisms, and diffraction gratings) were deemed appropriate for getting at the true nature of light. Other practices (those involving the Bible and Augus-tine's *Confessions*, for instance) were prohibited from the study of light-in-itself because they were viewed as productive only of human belief or understanding (whether metaphorical or mistaken).

A Bohr-inspired approach to this history would suggest that there is more to the indeterminacy of light than the complementarity of its wave and particle forms. There are other complementary phenomena as well. With a material-semiotic assemblage that includes the Bible and Augustine's *Confessions*, for example, it is possible to enact the phenomenon of light as an emanation of the divine. By Bohr's time, however, such phenomena had long since been banished from scientific thought and practice, which concerned itself only with physical waves and particles. Those older ways of enacting light are not merely incompatible in a *logical* sense with the waves and particles (as, one might argue, the latter two are with each other). Rather, they were actively undermined and rendered "unscientific" and so banished from the realm of debate. This, historians of science tell us, was a political process as much as an intellectual one. Similarly, the material and discursive practices through which Indigenous people enact sentient earth beings and *kanday*, for example, are not just *logically* incompatible with those that enact mountains and moose. Rather, settler colonial governments have carried out a sustained assault on the material and semiotic practices of Indigenous people that rendered them irrational, illegal, or both. Indeed, settler colonialism is itself a set of material and semiotic practices geared to the material domination of lands and peoples. The "disenchantment" of the land and animals (like the disenchantment of light) was part of a larger effort to dominate and control the natural world, in this case by transforming them into resources for exploitation and exchange (Merchant 1980; Watts 2013). This enabled the accumulation of capital, which augmented settler state power vis-à-vis Indigenous people and, thus, reinforced the supposed superiority of their view of the land and animals. Euro-American understandings of mountains and moose seem "truer" to many of us precisely because they are linked to the material and semiotic practices of colonial domination.

I began this paper with the question, "What is land?" It should be apparent by now that I regard this question as a deeply problematic one, because it takes for granted the idea that the object-in-itself (land) exists independently of the material and semiotic practices through which it is enacted. Like the question "What is light?" it breaks apart the phenomenon, the smallest unit of existence. As we saw, it makes no sense to ask what light *is* without specifying the apparatus used to observe/enact it. This renders suspect any ontological claims to the effect that light is "really" one thing (e.g., a wave) and that those who view it instead as something else (a particle) are succumbing to superstitious beliefs, or that particle-beliefs—as opposed to wave-beliefs—are part of a culturally constructed nature, socially useful perhaps but not reflective of "reality." Instead, as complementary phenomena, light waves and particles are equally "real"; both can tell us something important about the world, though neither is a perfect reflection of the world-in-itself. Both are also necessarily partial; we can learn nothing about light's wave-like properties if we enact it, in practice, as a particle. To learn about those properties, we need a different set of material and semiotic practices. And this argument is valid for other enactments of light as well. From the vantage of indeterminacy theory, any assertion to the effect that Augustine's divine light, for example, was "really" just photons seems almost willfully obtuse. The phenomenon Augustine was describing arose out of yet another set of material and semiotic practices; it was not the sort of thing that could have been either verified or disproven by experimentation with a diffraction grating.

The same can be said of land. It makes little sense to ask what land *is* unless one specifies the material and semiotic practices through which it is enacted. Indigenous people's enactments of sentient landscapes are no less "real" than are the other kinds of land enacted by geological surveyors, real estate agents, and nationalist politicians. None of these can be chalked off as "just" cultural constructions. Rather, they are all complementary phenomena; each is "real" to those who enact them, and each provides important—if always only partial—insights into the nature of the world. We can no more learn about land as a sentient actor by surveying it than we can discover its elevation above sea level by holding a potlatch in its honor. Because they are complementary phenomena, each of these different ways of enacting land offers us a way of knowing the world that is necessarily inaccessible to us when we enact the others instead. Those who consign sentient landscapes to the realm of superstition condemn a whole range of material and semiotic practices (along with the constellation of knowledge, values, and ways of being in the world that authorize and give them meaning) as ignorant and primitive while implicitly valorizing other such practices as somehow enacting "truer" versions of reality. Indeterminacy provides a way to avoid this colonial perspective and suggests, instead, that Indigenous ways of being in and enacting the world are worthy of study not because they are interesting cultural constructions or because they are diagnostic of alternate worlds but because they can help us understand important aspects of the (one) world in which we all live.

NOTES

I am grateful to participants at the "Social Lives of Land" workshop at Cornell for their questions and comments on the earliest version of this chapter. Special thanks are due to Robert Nichols, the paper's official discussant at that workshop, for his extremely insightful comments. Thanks, too, to the volume editors for all their hard work and to Norman Easton, Marina Welker, and the anonymous reviewers for their careful readings and useful suggestions. Finally, I would like to thank the people of Burwash Landing, Yukon, for their friendship, guidance, and patience over the years. This chapter is based on research funded by the Wenner-Gren and National Science Foundations.

1. For a few other influential—though all slightly different—statements of the multiple worlds thesis, see Blaser (2013, 2016), Henare et. al. (2007), and Viveiros de Castro (1998, 2004).

2. In fact, this move is often undertheorized in the literature. This is a problem, for as we will see when we examine Mol's (2002) work in more detail below, it is quite possible to write about the multiplicity of an object without invoking multiple worlds. For one (in my view quite problematic) attempt to theorize how "the things-in-themselves may dictate a *plurality* of ontologies," see Henare, Holbraad, and Wastell (2007, 2–7).

3. For an extended discussion of animals as political actors, see Nadasdy (2016).

4. Most of the time, there is no way to know whether or not the two versions of atherosclerosis correspond, since very few patients who visit the clinic have their legs amputated and sent to the pathology lab; most doctors just assume that if an atherosclerotic leg diagnosed in the clinic were to be sent to the pathology lab, it would show evidence of atherosclerosis there too. Usually, when pathologists do get to examine an amputated leg, Mol notes, the two versions of atherosclerosis do coincide, but this is not *always* the case (Mol 2002, 44–46).

5. One apparent exception is Thomas Kuhn, who famously argued that "though the world does not change with a change of paradigm, the scientist afterward works in a different world" (Kuhn 1970, 121). Since he uses successive transitions from particle to wave and from wave to quantum mechanical theories of light as examples of paradigm shifts, it is possible to read him as claiming that scientists who subscribed to the wave theory of light and those who saw light as a particle inhabited different worlds. In fact, however, his claim is more complex and ambiguous, as suggested by the fact that he uses "world view" and "world" interchangeably (e.g., the chapter in which he makes the above claim is titled, "Revolutions as Changes of World View," and it is peppered with statements such as: "Whatever he may then see, the scientist after a revolution is still looking at the same world" [129]). Kuhn's point is that the choice between paradigms is not merely a matter of competing interpretations of some "fixed" nature, because interpretation is an activity that can only take place within—and based upon—the ontological assumptions of a paradigm. After a paradigm shift, scientists not only see the world differently but ask different kinds of questions, perform different kinds of experiments, and produce different kinds of data (which they then interpret). As a result, the "objects" of scientific inquiry do not stand alone, independent of the paradigm's ontological assumptions or the experimental practices and apparatuses to which they give rise. Rather, "objects" (whether pendulums, oxygen, or light waves) themselves emerge—and are inseparable—from the material-semiotic practices through which they are enacted.

6. To the objection that a principle governing subatomic particles is irrelevant to the world of human interactions, Barad, herself a theoretical physicist, notes that "there is no theoretical basis or empirical evidence for the belief held by some that the laws of quantum mechanics apply only to the restricted domain of microscopic objects and that the laws of classical mechanics apply to the macroscopic domain. On the contrary, the overwhelming empirical success of quantum mechanics suggests that it is a theory that *supersedes* Newtonian physics" (Barad 2007, 324; see also 110). She herself then goes on to import Bohr's insights to the realm of social theory through an explication of what she calls "agential realism" (see especially chap. 4). It is also worth pointing out that Bohr himself was of the opinion that the principle of complementarity was applicable in the sociocultural realm (see Bohr 1939).

REFERENCES

Anderson, D. 2000. *Identity and Ecology in Arctic Siberia: The Number One Reindeer Brigade*. Oxford: Oxford University Press.

Barad, K. 2007. *Meeting the Universe Halfway: Quantum Physics and the Entanglement of Matter and Meaning*. Durham, NC: Duke University Press.

Basso, K. 1996. *Wisdom Sits in Places: Landscape and Language Among the Western Apache*. Albuquerque: University of New Mexico Press.

Bastien, J. 1978. *Mountain of the Condor: Metaphor and Ritual in an Andean Ayllu*. Eagan, MN: West Publishing Co.

Bessire, L., and D. Bond. 2014. "Ontological Anthropology and the Deferral of Critique." *American Ethnologist* 41 (3): 440–456.

Biersack, A. 1999. "The Mount Kare Python and His Gold: Totemism and Ecology in the Papua New Guinea Highlands." *American Anthropologist* 101 (1): 68–87.

Blaser, M. 2013. "Ontological Conflicts and the Stories of Peoples in Spite of Europe: Toward a Conversation on Political Ontology." *Current Anthropology* 54 (5): 547–568.

Blaser, M. 2016. "Is Another Cosmopolitics Possible?" *Cultural Anthropology* 31 (4): 545–570.

Bohr, N. 1939. "Natural Philosophy and Human Cultures." *Nature* 143: 268–272.

Borrows, J. 2010. *Canada's Indigenous Constitution*. Toronto: University of Toronto Press.

Cepek, M. 2016. "There Might Be Blood: Oil, Humility, and the Cosmopolitics of a Cofán Petro-Being." *American Ethnologist* 43 (4): 623–635.

Cruikshank, J. 2005. *Do Glaciers Listen? Local Knowledge, Colonial Encounters, and Social Imagination*. Vancouver: UBC Press.

De la Cadena, M. 2010. "Indigenous Cosmopolitics in the Andes: Conceptual Reflections beyond 'Politics.'" *Cultural Anthropology* 25 (2): 334–370.

De la Cadena, M. 2015. *Earth Beings: Ecologies of Practice across Andean Worlds*. Durham, NC: Duke University Press.

De Coppet, D. 1985. "Land Owns People." In *Contexts and Levels: Anthropological Essays on Hierarchy*. Edited by R. H. Barnes, D. de Coppet, and R. J. Parkin, 78–90. Oxford: JASO.

Di Giminiani, P. 2018. *Sentient Lands: Indigeneity, Property, and Political Imagination in Neoliberal Chile*. Tucson: University of Arizona Press.

Foucault, M. 1980. *Power/Knowledge: Selected Interviews and Other Writings, 1972–1977*. New York: Pantheon Books.

Graeber, D. 2015. "Radical Alterity Is Just Another Way of Saying 'Reality': A Reply to Eduardo Viveiros de Castro." *HAU: Journal of Ethnographic Theory* 5 (2): 1–41.

Hallowell, I. 1960. "Ojibwa Ontology, Behavior, and Worldview." In *Culture in History: Essays in Honor of Paul Radin*. Edited by S. Diamond, 19–52. New York: Columbia University Press.

Henare, A., M. Holbraad, and S. Wastell. 2007. "Introduction: Thinking through Things." In *Thinking Through Things: Theorising Artefacts Ethnographically*. Edited by A. Henare, M. Holbraad, and S. Wastell, 1–31. Routledge.

Hunt, S. 2014. "Ontologies of Indigeneity: The Politics of Embodying a Concept." *Cultural Geographies* 21 (1): 27–32.

Ingold, T. 2005. "The Eye of the Storm: Visual Perception and the Weather." *Visual Studies* 20 (2): 97–104.

Kuhn, T. *The Structure of Scientific Revolutions*. 2nd ed. Chicago: University of Chicago Press, 1970.

Li, T. M. 2014. "What is Land? Assembling a Resource for Global Investment." *Transactions of the Institute of British Geographers* 39 (4): 589–602. https://doi.org/10.1111/tran.12065.

Lindberg, D. 1978. "The Science of Optics." In *Science in the Middle Ages*. Edited by D. Lindberg, 338–368. Chicago: University of Chicago Press.

Macpherson, C. B. 1962. *The Political Theory of Possessive Individualism: Hobbes to Locke*. Oxford: Clarendon Press.

Marx, K. 1972. "On the Jewish Question." In *The Marx-Engels Reader*. Edited by Robert C. Tucker. New York: W. W. Norton.

McCarthy, E. *Medieval Light Theory and Optics and Duns Scotus' Treatment of Light in D. 13 of Book II of His Commentary on the Sentences*. PhD diss., University of New York, 1976.

McClellan, C. 1975. *My Old People Say: An Ethnographic Survey of Southern Yukon Territory*. Vol. 1–2. Canada: National Museum of Man.

McClellan, C., L. Birckel, R. Bringhurst, J. Fall, C. McCarthy, and J. Sheppard. 1987. *Part of the Land, Part of the Water: A History of the Yukon Indians*. Vancouver: Douglas and McIntyre.

Merchant, C. 1980. *The Death of Nature: Women, Ecology, and the Scientific Revolution: A Feminist Reappraisal of the Scientific Revolution*. New York: Harper and Row.

Mol, A. 2002. *The Body Multiple: Ontology in Medical Practice*. Durham, NC: Duke University Press.

Myers, F. 1991. *Pintupi Country, Pintupi Self: Sentiment, Place, and Politics Among Western Desert Aborigines*. Berkeley: University of California Press.

Nadasdy, P. 2002. "'Property' and Aboriginal Land Claims in the Canadian Subarctic: Some Theoretical Considerations." *American Anthropologist* 104 (1): 247–261.

Nadasdy, P. 2003. *Hunters and Bureaucrats: Power, Knowledge, and Aboriginal-State Relations in the Southwest Yukon*. Vancouver: UBC Press.

Nadasdy, P. 2007. "The Gift in the Animal: The Ontology of Hunting and Human-Animal Sociality." *American Ethnologist* 34 (1): 25–43.

Nadasdy, P. 2016. "First Nations, Citizenship and Animals, or Why Northern Indigenous People Might Not Want to Live in Zoopolis." *Canadian Journal of Political Science* 49 (1): 1–20.

Nadasdy, P. 2017. *Sovereignty's Entailments: First Nation State Formation in the Yukon*. Toronto: University of Toronto Press.

Okin, S. M. 1989. *Justice, Gender, and the Family*. New York: Basic Books.

Povinelli, E. 1995. "Do Rocks Listen? The Cultural Politics of Apprehending Australian Aboriginal Labor." *American Anthropologist* 97 (3): 505–518.

Salmond, A. 1982. "Theoretical Landscapes: On Cross-Cultural Conceptions of Knowledge." In *Semantic Anthropology*. Edited by D. Parkin, 65–87. Cambridge, MA: Academic Press.

Sharp, H. 2001. *Loon: Memory, Meaning, and Reality in a Northern Dene Community*. Lincoln: University of Nebraska Press.

Smith, A. M. 2015. *From Sight to Light: The Passage from Ancient to Modern Optics*. Chicago: University of Chicago Press.

Strathern, M. 1984. "Subject or Object? Women and the Circulation of Valuables in Highlands New Guinea." In *Women and Property, Women as Property*. Edited by R. Hirschon, 158–175. New York: St. Martin's Press.

Strathern, M. 1988. *The Gender of the Gift: Problems with Women and Problems with Society in Melanesia*. Berkeley: University of California Press.

Strathern, M. 1991. *Partial Connections*. Lanham, MD: Rowman & Littlefield Publishers.

Verdery, K. 1999. *The Political Lives of Dead Bodies: Reburial and Postsocialist Change*. New York: Columbia University Press.

Viveiros de Castro, E. 1998. "Cosmological Deixis and Amerindian Perspectivism." *The Journal of the Royal Anthropological Institute* 4 (3): 469–488.

Viveiros de Castro, E. 2004. "Perspectival Anthropology and the Method of Controlled Equivocation." *Tipití: Journal of the Society for the Anthropology of Lowland South America* 2 (1): 3–22.

Watts, V. 2013. "Indigenous Place-Thought and Agency amongst Humans and Non Humans (First Woman and Sky Woman Go On a European World Tour!)." *Decolonization: Indigeneity, Education & Society* 2 (1): 20–34.

Williams, C., and A. Smith. 1983. "The National Construction of Social Space." *Progress in Human Geography* 7 (4): 502–518.

Winichakul, T. 1994. *Siam Mapped: A History of the Geo-Body of a Nation.* Honolulu: University of Hawai'i Press.

Yukon Native Brotherhood. 1973. *Together Today for Our Children Tomorrow.* Yukon Native Brotherhood.

5

THE AUTOBIOGRAPHY OF A TRANSYLVANIAN LAND PARCEL

From Late Feudalism to Postsocialism

Katherine Verdery

The beneficiary of the entail, the eldest son, belongs to the land. The land inherits him.

—Karl Marx

'Are'are people do not own the land. The land owns 'Are'are people. The land owns men and women; they are there to take care of the land.

—'Are'are Paramount Chief Eerehau

In the turbulent period following the breakup of socialist regimes in Eastern Europe and the Soviet Union during the 1990s, special effort went into rectifying the property order of socialism: disposing of the collective property forms that had been scraped together from citizens' prior possessions and labor. The chief problem of doing so was how to restore the ownership of houses—nationalized from before or constructed later with collective resources—the values of state-owned enterprises, similarly derived, and land that had been confiscated, expropriated, or "donated" to state and collective farms. As the process was envisioned, these were all objects or values to which people held rights of certain kinds, now to be replaced with other rights.

Property rectification envisioned people as having biographies in which restitution aimed to repair prior injustices. For example, people who had owned land and been forced to donate it to collective farms without compensation might now, later in their lives, receive it back. These biographies included stories of the movement of the objects and values in question from one group of people (households) to another (the party-state and its collective farmers) and then another (individual owners). In the commonsense way of conceptualizing these processes, human beings stand at the center and are defined by the things they have, had, or lost. The things move from one person to another; people stay put. Hidden in this commonsense conception is the fact that nothing actually "moves" except control of the rights being exercised. But might there be some benefit to turning the commonsense view upside down—using property restitution to think differently about property in land? That is, although we may think of things moving and people staying put, in our experience, it is rather that people move, and land, factories, and houses stay put. Not that these objects are completely unchanging: land, for instance, absorbs and is transformed by the labor of the people who work on it. To think of it as something that is transacted, however, is to fall into the illusion of commodity fetishism that focuses attention on objects rather than on the relationships that intersect in them.

It is appropriate, then, to examine not just the people whose biography we should write but the land. What people passed across its surface? How did they belong to it and it to them? How did it serve as the embodiment or palpable manifestation of those relations? Even this phrasing is problematic, however, for it assumes that land and persons are separate, whereas, in fact, they may form a single comprehensive whole. Indeed, the hope of communist parties was to _create_ such comprehensive wholes, in which people would collectively become embodied in the total fund of socialist property, rather like the kin groups on clan land.

To see this requires questioning the customary definition of property as relations among persons by means of things. First, to speak of "person," "thing," and "relations," presupposes an object-relations view of the world, which assumes that to separate persons from things is unproblematic. But is it? We can go further, questioning the very notions of "person," "thing," and "relation." Standard property theory assumes that persons are bounded units consistent through time, but what if they are not?[1] If we call into question the unity of "persons," then we must reassess the entire nexus of "persons-things-relations" central to the property concept. What is a "thing"? Do "things" have agency?

Even the idea of "relations" can be problematized: What kinds of relations does a property analysis include? Overwhelmingly, because the tendency has been to presume that persons and things are recognizable and separate, establishing a property relation has meant overcoming while affirming that separateness: the thing is united with some persons as against other persons who are excluded from it. But how about relations of _consubstantiality_, in which persons and things are not seen as clearly bounded and separate but as participating in one another? Consubstantial relations merge the substance of "person" and "object." One's land parcel contains the sweat, blood, and intentionality of one's ancestors, which in turn nourish one's substance.[2] A consubstantial relation of persons to land would, therefore, be one of _coconstitution_, as in the three parts of the Holy Trinity. This is very different from the object-relations view of, say, land in a commodity economy.[3]

This chapter is a very preliminary effort to explore these questions from the point of view of the "object" land. It rests on a remarkable document discovered during research into property restitution in "Transylvania: The Autobiography of a Parcel of Land." This autobiography was reconstructed from fragments found in the land register for the Transylvanian village Aurel Vlaicu.[4] Reading it provides an angle of vision on property issues that is refreshingly different from the standard story of land "privatization," in which people who had lost their land later recuperate it. Perhaps a word about the land register will clarify the situation.

Transylvania, a hilly region that in 1918 became the northwestern third of present-day Romania, had previously formed part of the Habsburg Empire and the Kingdom of Hungary. This history frames the autobiography of our land parcel, for beginning in 1794, Habsburg officials initiated cadastral surveys and land registers throughout the empire. The system was completed in Transylvania in 1870. In Romanian, the register is known as *Cartea Funciară* (the Land Registry Book) or, for short, CF—the form used in the present account. In the other parts of Romania that Transylvania joined after World War I, this sort of land registry did not exist; within present-day Romania, therefore, only in Transylvania could an autobiography like the present one exist.

The CF serves as a system not only of evidence about landholdings but of publicity concerning real estate transactions.[5] Organized around the cadastral system of numbered plots corresponding to a map, it treats the topographic identity of a parcel of land as a fixed element independent of the persons who own it or hold use rights to it.[6] It is this quality of the CF—its emphasis on land rather than (or alongside) persons—that makes it the biographer of parcels (or parcels-plus-persons) rather than of the people who relate to them. This will be clearer from a description of the actual files.

The CF for a given community consists of numbered dossiers, each referring to a holding; each change in the status of that holding brings a corresponding change in the relevant dossier. With each transaction in the CF, the transactor receives an "extract" noting the parcel's topographic number and the number of the dossier, but this paper is not a title; it is merely the placeholder of one, title being lodged in the CF notation itself. If an owner loses the piece of paper, the CF dossier entry serves as adequate verification of title; nowhere is the registration organized by people's names. Unlike the registry system employed in the other parts of Romania, in which what unifies entries on a page is the date when people formally recorded land transactions, a page in Transylvania's CF is unified by the landholding unit to which it refers.[7] The page contains only those persons who have enjoyed a certain relation to that holding and only the dates on which that relation changed.

The specificities of the Transylvanian system derive from its Habsburg origins. Motivated by imperial revenue hunger, these land records strengthened the empire in its competition with colonial states. Thus, the system emphasizes the revenue-generating resource, locates it in a grid of such resources, and identifies on a map those who are responsible for turning over the revenue. This reading forces us to modify somewhat the claim above that the CF privileges the parcel. Because the feudal system (still partly in force when the CF was first set up) made land subject to entail, it was the property not of individuals but of kin groups, members of which had prior claim to any holding that was leaving the hands of the noble immediately responsible for it.[8] In a sense, land and its persons were one being, and this was the unit privileged in the CF.

We can see this from the first page made for each dossier when the CF was set up. On it are the names of the household head and his wife, usually listed as "equal coproprietors," and all the members of their household; any other people exercising an ownership claim (such as the noble co-owner); the topographical number and size of their house-plot in the residential part of the village; and the topographical numbers and sizes of every plot of land they worked at that time, with an indication of its use (arable, meadow, hayfield, or vineyard). This document, then, creates a social being we might refer to as the "family holding," an entity in which persons and land parcels form a complex whole authorized by the state that is recording it.[9] Starting from this whole, the CF narrates the fate of its constituent pieces of land. Each transaction involving one of those pieces (sale, dowry, inheritance) opens a new dossier, the entries of which are in chronological order by the operations performed on that parcel. Family members disappear from this narration, but pieces of land never do. As the stable element from the original dossier, land "moves" into a new dossier only if a piece of the original holding is split off for some new owner, with whom it forms a new organic unity in the registration system. If we take the point of view of land, then, rather than of owners, we see succession and sale not as a process in which land passes among people but as one in which land is fixed and people move across it.

The manner of CF registration means that, in the CF for any given settlement, there will be some files linking the original family holding of the 1870s to a person now alive. Thus, the CF dossier is a biography whose subject is the relationship between a subset of persons (many of them kin and affines) and a set of parcels. It lends itself easily to being read as a narrative, chronologically organized, that records the changing relations of parcels to persons.[10] The condition for entry into that narrative is that something happens to a parcel. The CF, as the prime operator of property relations, creates social subjects (parcels and their persons), authorizes their relation, and organizes the relation as a history. While the individual dossier does this for a family holding, the entire CF of a settlement does it for that settlement, which constitutes a unity defined by the total set of dossiers that give the biographies of a specific set of adjacent parcels.

State power, in the form of the registration (the CF), mediates and guarantees these relations of family holdings and village community. Conversely, what unifies the CF itself is its story of parcels as connected with both persons and the state. It is important to remember that using the CF foregrounds the view of the state in constituting the parcel's character. The CF is not just a scribe but is empowered by states of different kinds as a mediator and biographer in the history of changing agrarian economies. As state forms succeed each other, the meaning and character of "a parcel" change (something the CF entries do not make explicit).

If a "parcel" is seen as a changing concatenation of land and people, then a complete account of our parcel—let's call it 572/2—should include explaining the historical events that surround it. The CF has operated in an Eastern Europe whose land-person relations have often changed through multiple wars, border modifications, land reforms, and emancipations. In the 1850s and 1860s, serfdom was abolished; after World War I, country borders were redrawn, with land reforms and exchanges of population; the same things occurred after World War II, with the arrival of communists; and the collapse of socialism in 1989–1991 changed land relations once again. Our parcel does not "understand" what drove these changes (a land reform, for instance) and does not attempt to explain them; it can only reflect on their consequences.

This, then, is the basis for the following recollections, which emanate from changes in the land regime of Transylvania. The editor takes the viewpoint of the parcel and its associated persons, understood as an actor with a certain consciousness, and explores the changing nature of that consciousness as the socioeconomic environment changes. To what extent does this parcel have agency, and how does that manifest itself and change over time? How do its relations with humans change as well? What does it mean to think of land as a "property object," and how does that relation evolve? These matters are our implicit concern here.

The Autobiography

I dwell in the space known as Transylvania, in a village called Vlaicu. This village, known in documents since the thirteenth century, has been part of the Habsburg Empire, the Hungarian Kingdom, and now Romania. Lest I be thought a rural hick with no claim to anyone's attention, let me say that I have a very cosmopolitan past, and it has taught me much about the world. I have had deep connections not just with serfs and peasants but with great nobles, who spent much of their time at the court in Vienna or Budapest and were active in the politics of the Transylvanian Principality as well.

Autobiographies have been written since Antiquity in various forms. Because much of my story precedes this, I must adopt an anachronistic persona in writing about my early life. This begins with my name: since I know that an autobiography must have a subject, I will call myself "Moshia" [moh SHEE a], although for the past 150 years, I have been known as "572/2." From the moment I acquired clearly fixed edges, I have occupied a surface of 15 yokes, 416 fathoms, (or 8.5 hectares) in subsequent reckoning.

Conventionally, an autobiography has a beginning. My case accommodates that standard with difficulty. As physical stuff in a specific location, I have been around for thousands, perhaps millions, of years—even though my humous parts (like the cells of human bodies) have washed away and been renewed so often that the "I" who address you now is scarcely the same as that first piece of what would, eons later, become a Transylvanian landscape. Most of those erosions and reshapings occurred long before I was part of a village with a name, Binținți (or Benczencz), for the nobleman then residing there.[11] The name stuck until the 1920s when they changed it after the local son, Aurel Vlaicu.

The main question of my beginning is, "When did I become a parcel of land?" Or, before that, "When did I become recognizable?" I could mark that beginning with the start of settled agriculture, when I entered into permanent relations with the human beings who have ever since worked me with their tools while renewing my vitality with their root crops and manure. In this particular neighborhood, for many centuries humans came and went, driven off into the hills by now one, now another invader. My parcelness began to stabilize only with the onset of what humans call feudalism, which developed in these parts after about 1100 CE. Before then, I was not a well-defined entity but formed great, unbroken expanses with others like myself, our contours bleeding over into one another. I am not saying this was bad, merely that it was not parcelness, which requires relations with humans. Collectively, we maintained an inchoate sense of landness without edges. These gradually emerged as feudal nobles became landlords and acquired people to work their land. In other words, my parcelness does not precede assemblages of social relations but is a function of them.

Things become sharper only when I gain a biographer to jog my memory, but that came late in 1865 or 1870. This biographer (I refer to him as CF) is fully authorized for such work: employed by the state, he is very careful about dates and people and about how they increase on my surface. Since CF began writing about me, he has had three makeovers, giving him a total of four different personalities, of which the first was by far the most serious. That one was employed by the Austro-Hungarian Empire and lasted fifty years. The next one appeared after 1918, an agent now of the Romanian Kingdom that had taken Transylvania from that empire. Following this, around 1948, came another makeover whose agent called himself a "communist," and he basically quit writing at all. Worse, he tried to get rid of me altogether as a separate being with contours. The final makeover after the 1989 "Revolution" that got rid of the communists has brought only confusion, but at least people are paying attention to me again, and they are consulting those earlier versions to be sure they get me right.

Because of the differences among these several makeovers, which gave CF different styles of writing and thinking about me, I will divide my story into four periods corresponding to each one. I will call them "late feudalism" (ca. 1820–1918; ed. n.), "interwar capitalism" (1918–1948), "socialism" (1948–1989), and "postsocialism" (1989 on).

There is one other thing you should know about me before I continue: I like to mix myself with human beings. Together with them, I have felt that we have a purpose in life, a potential that must be fulfilled. I am happiest when I feel myself to be one with them and always strive to accumulate them. Sometimes I do this by force of attraction, sometimes I am helped by laws and states. People feed, care for, and groom me so that together, we can bring forth crops in abundance. In appreciation for their help, I let them take some crops for themselves and their animals to eat. I think of these people as mine, for once a man mixes his labor with my substance, as I understand it, this makes him my property.[12]

Late Feudalism

I said earlier that, before about 1100 CE, there was not much distinguishing among parcels of land but only great expanses of fields cultivated episodically. Yet around this time, these expanses seemed somehow to grow more powerful and attractive, drawing onto ourselves noble warriors with whom we forged special connections. Being warriors, they themselves could not care for us as we wished, and so we made a compact: as long as they made sure we always had people, we would make sure they had enough to eat. To keep the bargain, they gave us serfs, who would work us with plows and teams of oxen, then feed us seeds and manure. All these were my people—warrior-lord and serfs—though in different ways. But the lord also considered the serfs _his_ people, even though it was my relation with them that produced food; thus, our claims overlapped.

Over time, we parcels gradually took on special roles and, in the process, began to become more particularized, more clearly defined as entities. Some of us ("allodial" lands) reserved ourselves strictly for our lord's use, while others ("urbarial" lands) worked out an exchange with specific serfs. Urbarial parcels felt very attached to their serf families; I, for my part, felt as one with them, our boundaries murky. Our relationship was not one of "land over there" and "people over here," "owning" or working on the land; it was rather a relation of shared substance, my people feeling their labor and that of their ancestors as part of both them and myself.

Following an epidemic in 1815–1817, I needed some new people and attracted the interest of one Pavel Vlaicu. I know his name because an 1820 census lists him as a serf; at that time, he was taking care of some 5.6 of my hectares.[13] My remaining 2.9 hectares stayed as allod, part of the lord's immediate estate, until, over time the lord released to me some serfs (*inquilini*), named Romcea, Grozav, and Rusu, with their families.[14] Romcea united with 1.5 of my hectares, and the remainder went to the other two. As with the Vlaicus (and unlike the master), they mixed themselves with me in a labor process. The job of the three *inquilini* was to provide manual labor on the allod at least three days a week. Pavel used the word *moshia* for me, a collection of land plus people, indicating a relation of kinship: he fed me lots of corn, much more nourishing than the wheat the lord preferred, which always leached me dry after a few seasons.[15]

In speaking of the different kinds of people with whom I had different relations, I have left out the most important: the "lord," with his immediate family and lots of interested kin. Who was this lord? In general terms, he thought of himself as my master, having rights over me granted by the king. His serfs called him *stăpân* (master) and my relationship with him *stăpânire*, "mastery" or "rule." But from my point of view, the master is mine, someone to whom I have special rights: he dies, and I inherit his sons and daughters.[16] It is *I* who have the rights, not *he*. My own particular lord for a time was Count Lajos Teleky, from one of Transylvania's greatest noble families. The ones in Binținți for the following two generations were also called Lajos Teleky; I inherited each of them from his father.

This is how things were in the middle of the nineteenth century: I had a noble family—the Telekys—and four serf families, the Vlaicus and the three *inquilini*, with several children each and many grandchildren. I had rights of different kinds to each of them; Count Lajos also had rights to the serfs. His rights sometimes overpowered even mine: he could move the serfs elsewhere or refuse to let me inherit their heirs. That was one kind of change. The other important one came when each count died, with the ensuing "transmission of the estate." I would inherit more masters—theoretically, often quite a large number—some of whom might renounce our relationship in favor of siblings, while others would insist on staying with me at all costs, precipitating great quarrels. Something like that could occur with the death of a serf, too.

Then, something astounding happened. In retrospect, it was the beginning of a long process in which we parcels were losing our force of attraction upon our lords. It began with the urbarial parcels. In 1848, I was stunned to learn that the nobles in the Hungarian parliament had decreed an "emancipation," freeing Count Lajos and his family from all land but their allods (2.9 of my hectares). The nobles had promised themselves some "compensation," money to be paid by the government; the compensation would enable them to start new forms of lucrative enterprise that were then emerging. It seemed the noble families wanted to be emancipated from their ties to serfs on urbarial land and would henceforth feed themselves only with the *inquilini* or by paying people to work for them. Another way to put it is that the social connectedness of the allods had proven stronger than those of the urbarial parcels among us, for the allods held onto both their lords and the *inquilini*, who had to continue working for the lord's family as before.

In a way, losing the count simplified my life. Our relationship always tended to be abstract; he was not around much, and he did not take a lot of interest in me. Pavel and his heirs were different. Over time, I had grown very attached to them; in some sense, they and I were not fully separate beings but somehow conjoined, part of each other, sharing substance and labor. This made for a very special relationship that gave both of us agency, including the ability to bring forth crops. They groomed and fed me, encouraged me to produce, and then lifted the crops off my surface. They left corn stalks for me to eat and brought out their animals to nourish me with manure. I had come to feel of one substance with these people more than with the Lajoses, and I think that feeling was reciprocated. Let me explain.

Consider how the Vlaicu family and I first appear in CF's biography. When it began, around 1870, there was only one male Vlaicu, Luca, who headed a household. He appears on the cover sheets of dossier no. 74 as follows:

Coproprietors in equal parts:
>   1876 1. Vlaic Luca and his wife
>   2. Vlaic Ioana, b. Carașca
>
>   . . .
>
>   14. n.t. 202 house
>   n.t. 203 garden
>   n.t. 204 hayfield
>   15. [various topographical numbers (n.t.) for parcels out in the fields]

This makes a unity of their household and myself plus other parcels. This unity appears best in the variations wrought upon my name, Moshia, which show that my people's ideas about their relations to each other and to me were tightly fused.

A series of Romanian words share the root *moş-*, from which my name comes. They include *moş*, grandfather or elder; *moaşa*, midwife; *strămoşi*, ancestors; *moşteni*, to inherit; and *moşia*, landed family estate. This means that people work from a single root to talk about ancestors, land, inheritances, and birth. A scholar who lately visited these parts was heard to say that such connections are not rare in the world, to wit (this from a place called Melanesia): "[P]eople are strongly subordinated to the land, that is, to their ancestors who are buried there. Land is part of the genealogical origin of each living person and is not simply soil but rather an entity always fused with the ancestors, under whose joint authority the living are placed."[17]

I think this idea fits both the relation of the peasants to us parcels and also that of the feudal lords: the second was the model for the first. It appears in that 1820 census, in which serfs speak of their relation to the parcels they care for as "*noi ţinem moşia*" ("we hold an estate") using the same word they used for what the lords took care of. (They seem to forget, though, that it is *we* who hold them— after all, what else does "tied to the soil" mean?) We and they formed an indissoluble link that was eroded only after the emancipation of the serfs and then only with time.

So where do I find myself around 1870, the time CF starts his job? First, my edges have been sharpened, giving me a much clearer sense of where and what I am. Surveyors had been around before now, but never like this: the state sent whole teams of them, along with soldiers, to make sure no one could bribe the topographers to move the boundary a bit this way or that. They used very fancy instruments, gave each of us parcels our own number (572 for me), made an amazingly detailed picture of the edges they had measured, and handed all that over to CF. There, they gave me my very own folder: no. 102. From now on, when my Vlaicus multiplied and "subdivided" me, I would get little extra numbers and letters: 572 would become 572/1, 572/2, 572/3, etc., then 572/2/a, 572/2/b, and so on, for all of Luca's children and grandchildren whom I managed to hang onto. The extra numbers and letters were a source of pride for me; they showed I was good at holding onto people. They also showed that my relations with people were partible.

Alongside this, by about 1870, one layer of relatedness (to the Telekys) has thinned, meaning Count Lajos cannot interfere in the life of the Vlaicus or in my tie with them, which has thickened. Because they no longer have to feed the Telekys, they decide to take even better care of me, so I reward them with more food that they either eat or take to the market. With my *inquilini*, nothing much is new: the family of the Count can still demand work out of them in exchange for their house plot or even remove them from it altogether. Or even, as they say, "sell" it—that is, take money from someone in order to get me another person and then be free. This shows that I am still powerful and they do not dare to emancipate themselves from me without getting in their place someone who will pay them money to be in bondage to a parcel.

In fact, testimony to the thinning of our connection, Count Lajos now does just that: "sells" me. Like so many other nobles, ever since the emancipation he has been unable to make ends meet and has been getting further into debt. He decides that he hates the land and wants to dissolve our relationship altogether. In 1888, the count takes a huge amount of money—well over 10,000 forints—from a Lajos Kovacs, who moves in. Thus, Count Lajos has been emancipated and is gone.

These developments have serious consequences for my *inquilini*, whom I have been carrying ever since the emancipation as they pay their yearly labor dues to the count. With the Romceas, I have been slowly able to strengthen my connection, helping them make enough money so they can give some to the count and be rid of those obligations for good. Now, they devote all their attention to me instead. (The other two *inquilini* have disappeared.)

Meanwhile, things are not going well with the new Lajos. He turns out to be fairly uninterested in me, and now he is in debt too. A bank comes in and tells him they are taking money from a group of new people and emancipating him from me entirely. Scarcely eight years after he moved in, he is moving on. But the new people—I will call them Germans—what an amazing lot! They arrive in carts, just like gypsies.[18] A lot of other parcels are gaining them too (about a hundred hectares' worth), not just me. From what we gather, they had been living in Hungary, but they had had too many kids and wanted more space. My impractical Lajoses and that bank had given them their chance.

These Germans and I got along famously. They knew how to cultivate better than anyone I ever had. They gave me a lot of manure, and they made careful rows with holes, putting one seed in each instead of just scattering the seeds around the surface as the Vlaicus and the Romceas did. They plowed more deeply, bringing fresh air and water to clods of earth stagnant and caked from neglect. They planted not just the usual corn and wheat but tasty clover and fodder beets and other food that invigorated me and made the animals grow faster. In a word, my interactions with these people improved us both.

With all these emancipations and sales, though, we parcels were becoming like objects; people thought they could do whatever they liked with us, as if we had no common history, no personness. Some say it was the "money economy," but I say it is people's increasing arrogance: they have come to see me as "nature," and as having nothing to do with their superior selves, our "masters." Little do they realize that if I do not feel respected and properly tended, I give back less. Herein lies our agency: an unhappy parcel grieves the loss of that oneness of being and withholds its fruits. The problem was worse with the remnants of the old aristocracy, who took money from new entrepreneurial types, hoping to make a profit from sugar beets or rapeseed; when this failed, they would take money to bring in new people and then leave, just as if we had never had a relationship. The only ones who seemed to feel something of that old consubstantiality were the peasants. Most retained a touching sentimentality, seeing in us the repository of their ancestors' blood and sweat.

We could tell, though, that even they were beginning to think of us as objects to be transacted. At first, this mainly took the form of trying to get more of them on us ("making families"). This could be good, but it could also become very heavy, and they might stop feeding us well or not be able to afford animals to give us manure. Our relationships with them were the simplest we had had: no labor obligations, no complex tiers of people expecting different kinds of loyalty, just us and these ever-proliferating families. When they got too numerous or had saved enough, they could usually find someone of the old or new elite to take their money and persuade us parcels to take them on. But soon, that would change: what they would call "land hunger" was just around the corner. We parcels warned them to stop multiplying, but to no avail.

Then, once again, the state stepped in to confuse things utterly as it had before. There had been a war, at the end of which we got the news that our Transylvania was becoming Romanian. All those agents of the Habsburg and Hungarian states were technically out of work, so CF began to change as they brought in the new Romanian agents.

Interwar Capitalism

The new Romanian state had decreed a "land reform," aiming to get rid of all those unproductive Hungarian and Romanian peasants and bring in for us a bunch of new people: land-poor villagers who had fought in the war and "owned" no parcels but were now able to feed themselves, which they had had trouble doing. With the land reform, the remaining Hungarian aristocrats, along with newly wealthy Romanians, were to be "expropriated." By this, they meant that some people—people are always at the center of things, in their telling—were to lose rights over land so others could get them instead.

I was lucky: the whole reform pretty much passed me by, given my Germans (*they* were *my* reform). Nonetheless, I too felt the reform's effects. What were they? First, a lot more surveying, those pointed tripods sticking into our sides like tiny swords. Second, the parcels that had had less peasant weight and better caretaking suddenly acquired numerous new families, a lot of whom did not really know much about what a parcel needed. Moreover, these folks were too poor to bring with them the plows and animals any self-respecting peasant owns, so the care of parcels deteriorated further. Third, and in consequence, there followed even more taking of money and exchanges of people, as some of the new ones just could not make it. We had scarcely any time at all to get attached to these new ones; they might leave at any moment. Their inexperience and lack of funds led to further erosion of the already-weakened idea of shared substance and more treating of parcels as objects; losing these people hardly hurt at all. But we parcels missed those feelings of connectedness that used to make it a pleasure to bring forth food for our people.

It seemed to take forever for things to settle down from the reform, for CF to get the papers in order, and for people to get what they needed to work us with and start winning our goodwill. Meanwhile, peasants were finding it hard to sell crops for their debts, taken on to acquire parcels, which everyone was now seeing as "objects." Thus, yet more money was exchanged, and new people arrived. One advantage of the situation was that people began raising more animals, which kept their value better than grain did. It was good news for us parcels: now we could gorge ourselves on manure and give really great harvests.

Socialism

Some years later, we parcels once again found ourselves wounded by the boots of armies—German, Romanian, and Soviet. The government declared "requisitions" to feed all those boot-wearers; this made our families anxious, and they tried to persuade us to give up more food so there would be enough for them as well. It was a pretty exhausting time for everyone, parcels and people alike. There was yet another "land reform," in which lots of new people were brought onto parcels "expropriated" from other people. Supposedly, the other people thrown out were the richest, the ones whom many parcels loved but who were now called "exploiters." We were very upset indeed, for these were the only people left who sometimes showed a trace of the old feelings of connection with us. I had been conjoined for almost 150 years with the Vlaicu family; their sweat and tears had soaked into me for centuries. Now, they were "expropriated" from me.

The people we got now were—as before—war veterans and people who felt no connection with us. But now we had to take them or risk not being cared for at all. With each land reform, our agency was diminished, as the government imposed people on us at will rather than allowing us to attract new ones through social relationships. It took a while for me to realize that more was going on than just the replacement of my favorite humans: we began to hear that a new government had come in, run by people called communists. They had been behind the reform, and now they continued it, taking more rich peasants away from us and giving us new ones, most of them in impecunious circumstances, who, as it turned out, would not be good caretakers.

What happened next was the low point in my existence as a parcel—in fact, nearly the *end* of that existence: the communists declared "collectivization." They began by saying that anyone who wanted to be rid of their parcels should just come over and say so; then, when few people went, they started moving people from the parcels they loved and giving them to other, worse parcels, farther away. Eventually, they took away all the people I owned, even the new ones I had scarcely gotten to know. Worse, the disruption of my social relationships with people diminished my power to attract and, for the first time, I could not get any new people to come. It seemed that my agency was draining away. At the same time, so was my consubstantial relation with people, for all along, that relation had flourished through their recognition of me, and that was lost.

You might have thought that I would like collectivization with its creation of a new whole, consisting of people and parcels, but no: collectivization was the most catastrophic event of my existence. It altogether severed me from my human beings. Henceforth, no more "tied to the soil" in any form whatsoever. Humans had finally emancipated themselves from us in full. From now on, no parcel would have its own people to take care of it, but everyone would supposedly do that together for all the parcels combined. Moreover, the idea was that somehow all these people should feel conjoined not to specific parcels but to *all* of us parcels as a group. So they got rid of every sign of our individuality—tore out hedges, cut down trees, pulled up boundary stones, plowed up streams and ditches, and removed almost everything that would allow our people to recognize us. In a word, our very parcelness was destroyed. Then they plowed us in huge, multi-parcel fields, often changing our very configuration in the process.

I got the feeling that many peasants did not like this new arrangement, but I most certainly did not. You might think that surprising, given my expressed nostalgia for consubstantiality: here we were being invited to a more transcendent form of "person-object relations" that were not commodified. I did not like it, first, because I had always resisted being made an object and had found my agency increasingly diminished as that process advanced. Second, I did not like it because the newly proposed consubstantiality was fake: despite the reforms, there were still many parcels that felt quite attached to their earlier peasants (who loved them in return), and there was a lot of mutual pining. Third, unlike other times when people left us because they wanted to be free of parcels, a lot of these people did not want their freedom from us at all.

Finally, fourth, with all the pining and our residual shock at having no people of our own, we had lost our raison d'être—bringing forth fruits to exchange with our special people—and the crop situation was consequently bad. Lacking their exclusive tie with us, people did not feel like feeding and grooming us properly anymore: we no longer had what it took to bring forth our fruits. We had gotten used to having some individuality, too, and found it both painful and disturbing to have our people taken away and our edges erased, plowed over. No longer sure who and where we were, our sense of consubstantial relations began to wither.

With the 1945 land reform that had freed the Germans of their ties to land, the communists had been careful to tell CF all about it and to write the new people into the register. By the time collectivization got going, though, this was too time consuming. Moreover, they said, now that people would be completely free of the tyranny of parcels, there was no need to tell anyone about changes in person-parcel relations. No one wrote anything down anymore. CF was deeply dismayed by all this and lost his ability to tell stories about parcels and their people. I, too, entered into some kind of stupor and can barely remember anything that happened during that time. It is as if losing my special people killed off my ability to reflect on myself or to remember them and their ancestors. I cannot tell you how many grandchildren my former "owners" had. For the first time, I am utterly adrift. Socialism has brought about my complete commodification.[19]

Things proceed like this for years. The caretaking continues to be bad—no, it gets worse for a time, and instead of delicious manure, they start feeding us with bags of some powdery chemical that burns as it goes down. Sometimes, one of my old people will walk on me, and I feel a faint stirring of recognition. But I get the sense that they, too, have adopted the communists' disdainful attitude to me and are now interested only in factory work. Why, some of my people even told a visiting anthropologist that "if someone tried to give us back our land" (*sic*), they would not even want it anymore, much though they had hated to lose it to the collective. They have gotten used to being free of land, and now some of them like it that way.

Meditating upon what sort of future there can be in this regime, I feel my parcelness, my very will to live, quietly ebbing away. It occurs to me that I had a similarly inchoate feeling eons ago, before the coming of the feudal lords with their various serfs. Is it possible, I wonder, that a "parcel" like me does not exist outside the assemblages of social relationships in which we are embedded? Perhaps I do not *antedate* those relations—that is, "I" was not sitting around waiting for people—but came into being *as a function* of them. It was their recognition that made me a parcel when groups of people joined me in social relationships based on joint activity. Now, the relationships are completely different and not very sustaining. No wonder I feel groggy and disoriented.

Postsocialism

Fortunately, it did not last. To everyone's astonishment, suddenly the communists are gone, at least in name. The new leaders are looking for ways to make people see them as different from their predecessors, and they settle on—what else?—another "land reform." They want to give back to us parcels our parcelness and re-create our connections to specific families instead of this collectivist stew of the past forty years. I am very excited, but I have one big question: How will our people or their children possibly return to us parcels, given that we have lost our edges? Our identities have grown so weak with all the confusions of these years that we no longer exert any power of attraction: too many emancipations. Worst of all, we have no guides, for after the 1945 reform, CF became afflicted with terminal amnesia.

My doubts are soon confirmed. First, the law, known as Law 18/1991: in that typical human-centric way, it "gave" everyone whose families had "owned" parcels the right to claim them back. The name for this was "property restitution," but to me, it was *people* restitution: the re-creation of some kind of bond—howsoever loose—between me and specific persons from before. And what with the kinship stuff in the law, it was not just about re-creating a bond with individuals: in some cases, I was repossessing whole lines of ancestors too.

Given that many had been saying they liked their freedom and would not want ties to parcels, I had feared they would not even try to recreate their bond with us. But I believe that we parcels gradually regained some of the initiative that had been stripped away. As our borders were restored, we began to recover agency, calling to our people to awaken our connection. Interestingly, the first people to restore their familial parcels were those who had had more of us. It was as if reexperiencing the pull of landownership from multiple parcels, these wealthier peasants had suddenly been reconstituted as owners by reliving their previous bonds to us. And once they got started, everyone else piled in. I felt rejuvenated.

Sadly, the feeling was not to last. Most peasants no longer had the tools they needed to work on parcels, and troubles establishing their claims led to their turning their new parcels over to the "association" (a postcollective form of cultivating collectively) to resolve quarrels. Here I was: supposedly reconnected to these people, but not actually involved with them in a daily way. I began to realize that the years of the collective farm had deepened the "object" attitude of these villagers: many had lost all memory of how to be one with a parcel and saw it as merely a source of sustenance. For me, this was a bitter realization. I had always loved my people and enjoyed thinking of the chain of ancestors and descendants that connected me with them over the decades; it was this connection that made me a parcel, and its prevalence in the interwar years made that my favorite period.

Now, though, it seems that my love is not requited. Sure, my people liked knowing I was there, but when they argued about where my edges were and who should "have" me because of their ancestral ties, I do not think they were manifesting a deep attachment: they were using the language most suited to getting access to some crops, an important source of security in those uncertain times. In a word, it was just talk. Suddenly, I felt lonelier than I could have imagined possible in the era of "property restitution."

How about CF? Has he regained his capacity to tell stories, to ground people in parcels? Yes and no. At first, CF was happy to see people writing things down again and making new maps despite the countless quarrels and the millions of court cases. But he has begun to see problems, too: the biography of this region, with its special biographer and its villages divided into parcels, has been disrupted. It is not just that, once again, writing down one's parcels has become very costly, and people do not always do it. Worse, the new maps being made with their new numbers bear no relation at all to the numbers in the old records! Therefore, it will be impossible to connect the two sets of biographies across that ocean of communist-induced amnesia. CF and I agree that this has potentially serious consequences for people. If, as some say, humans' sense of self comes from telling their biography and connecting it to other such tellings around them—the biography of their nation, say, or their ancestral clans—then would not a ruptured biography make for a ruptured sense of self?

It is depressing to think that after hundreds of years of intimate symbiosis with humans, I am left longing for their affection, while they see me as just a thing. The communists, despite their fall, have truly completed the emancipation of parcels from their people; there is no going back. Parcels have lost their centrality to agrarian life and livelihood seeking. Most people see value elsewhere now: they invest themselves not in their relations with the earth but in trinkets, clothing, cellular phones, or shares of some factory. They will eat wheat from Hungary or America and chickens raised on drugs and hormones; they will say they have "joined Europe" and are too modern to think about parcels. More than that, if they work land at all, they will use chemicals and powders instead of tasty manure, and rather than improving the land, they will end up killing it. But worst of all, they will not notice that one cost of forgetting the deep value of parcels is that people's connections with one another diminish. Parcels contained human relationships: many people tied to ancestral parcels means many people tied to each other. No more.

Maybe they see this as part of their emancipation—and maybe I should take this to heart, rejoicing in my liberation from the weight of all those people, the sting of all their sweat, the burden of bearing crops. A life without them would be a life without effort. I could become not a parcel but a nameless element of a tranquil landscape.[20]

NOTES

1. Especially influential in raising this question has been the work of Marilyn Strathern, who posits the notion of "dividuals"—not bounded units but partible assemblages of the multiple social relations in which they participate. See, e.g., Strathern (1988).

2. For an example of this kind of relation, see Vitebsky (2005).

3. I am speaking of conceptions of land that do not objectify it, as a commodity economy would. Absence of a commodity economy may be a precondition of consubstantiality.

4. Historically known as Binţinţi (pronounced "beenTSEENTS," later "owREL VLYku"). See Verdery (1983, 1994).

5. Comparable systems can be found elsewhere, such as in Java, for instance.

6. Burghelea n.d. [1994], vol. 1, 145.

7. This system keeps records under the names of the persons who hold the rights. Each entry gives the date, the name of the transactor, a reference to the piece of land in question, and the operation performed (sale/purchase, inheritance, dowry). The land to which those rights obtained is described in terms of its neighbors or natural and man-made features of the landscape; the description is written on a deed, which is held by the owner. There is no master map.

8. If the land was collectively held by the kin-group, entail meant that separating some part of the land from the whole was almost impossible. The Austrian registration system gained comprehensiveness following the emancipation of the serfs in 1848–1854, which created several different categories of peasant relations to land based in the feudal division between *urbarial* and allodial land. *Urbaria* were the lord's lands that had been given in usufruct to categories of serfs, who paid him for its use. Allodia, by contrast, were lands the lord worked directly with the labor of serfs and various kinds of cottars and day labor. To hold this labor he might grant them use-rights to a patch of the allod.

The emancipation of the serfs gave those on urbarial land proprietary rights to the holding they had worked. Cottars and laborers working on the allodia, however, received no proprietary rights. On the CF dossiers created after impropriation, the former allodial lands were listed under the joint names of the lord and the peasant by whom the land had been used; the title page of the dossier often listed, as well, *the feudal obligations still owed by these dependents*. Emancipated urbarial serfs, by contrast, were listed as full owners. The obligations of allodialists to their former masters were finally revoked in 1896.

9. "Family" refers here to the coresident kin-based group (usually husband, wife, children, and sometimes a senior parent).

10. Thus, if my grandfather inherited from his parents' five-hectare holding a one-hectare piece (with a single topographic number, say, 10), the dossier in which that hectare was listed in his grandparents' name—say, dossier no. 27—would gain an entry referring the reader to a new dossier number, say, no. 532; at my grandfather's death, if the property was divided equally between my father and his brother, my father's portion (10/a) would be recorded in dossier no. 532, and an entry would send the reader to a new dossier, no. 824, for his brother's share (10/b).

11. The first known reference to Benczencz comes from 1291. See Zimmermann and Werner (1892, 185–186).

12. Cf. Locke (1960, bk. 2, chap. V, 27:4–7).

13. In 1820, Habsburg authorities undertook an inquiry into the labor conditions of serfs throughout the empire. Known as the "Cziráky Conscription," it provided the names of all heads of *urbarial* serf households, the extent of their house plots and arable lands, and declarations concerning the labor dues each serf-owning noble demanded of their serfs.

14. Unlike an *urbarial* serf, who received both a house plot and plots of land to work, an *inquilinus* received only a cottage in exchange for his labor; he might eventually acquire some land.

15. This word incorporates both land and people (e.g., *mos* means ancestor, *mosia* a landed estate, and *mosteni* to inherit).

16. One cause of the excessive fragmentation of Transylvania's noble estates was that, according to ideas of entail, which governed the inheritance of land, inheritance was partible, and daughters appear to have inherited alongside sons at least some of the time. See Verdery (1983, 164).

17. See Coppet (1985, 81).

18. This is how local lore (including that of the Germans themselves) remembers the arrival of the Swabians colonized by the bank that took over the Kun and Kovacs/Teleky estates.

19. See Martha Lampland (1995) for a similar argument about the commodification of labor under socialism.

20. I owe a major debt to the late Mr. Iván Christ of the Hunedoara County state notary's office in Deva, Romania, for his generous help in teaching me about the Cartea Funciara. Many thanks also to Elizabeth Dunn and Nancy Peluso, as well as participants in the conference, for numerous helpful comments.

REFERENCES

Bourdieu, P. 1990. *The Logic of Practice*. Stanford, CA: Stanford University Press.

Burghelea, D. 1994. *Drept funciar și cadastru român*. Vol. 1. Iași: Ed. Moldova.

Coppet, D. de. 1985. "Land Owns People." In *Contexts and Levels: Anthropological Essays on Hierarchy*. Edited by R. H. Barnes, D. de Coppet, and R. J. Parkin, 78–90. Oxford: JASO.

Grimm, J. A. R. von. 1863. *Das Urbarialwesen in Siebenbürgen*. Vienna: Friedr. & Moritz Förster.

Lampland, M. 1995. *The Object of Labor: Commodification in Socialist Hungary*. Chicago: University of Chicago Press.

Locke, J. 1960. *Two Treatises of Government*. Cambridge: Cambridge University Press.

Mitrany, D. 1930. *The Land and the Peasant in Rumania: The War and the Agrarian Reform, 1917–1921*. NY: Greenwood.

Strathern, M. 1988. *The Gender of the Gift: Problems with Women and Problems with Society in Melanesia*. Berkeley: University of California Press.

Verdery, K. 1983. *Transylvanian Villagers: Three Centuries of Political, Economic, and Ethnic Change*. Berkeley: University of California Press.

Verdery, K. 1994. "The Elasticity of Land: Problems of Property Restitution in Transylvania." *Slavic Review* 53 (4): 1071–1109.

Vitebsky, P. 2005. *Reindeer People: Living with Animals and Spirits in Siberia*. Boston: Houghton Mifflin.

Zimmermann, F., and C. Werner. 1892. *Urkundenbuch zur Geschichte der Deutschen in Siebenbürgen, Vol. 1: 1191–1342*. Hermannstadt: Franz Michaelis.

Part II
MATERIALITIES AND MOBILITIES

6

FROM SAND TO LAND

Laura Schoenberger

This chapter is about sand and land as both form and process. Land has long been argued to be unique from all other resources because it does not move: "Land is not like a mat. You cannot roll it up and take it away. It has a presence and location" (Li 2014, 584). However, new processes of "making land" through large-scale land reclamation projects have made sand into that mat. "Constructed land" describes a class of phenomena involving extensive morphological alterations of the earth's surface by displacing large quantities of material, like sand, gravel, rock, and soil, to create buildable or inhabitable land where there was no land before. Terms such as "man-made land" and "artificial land" are used alongside expressions such as "earthworks" and "terraforming" that encompass technologies of land construction, such as cutting and filling, leveling, dredging sand, and stabilizing and compressing soil. All of these terms relate to the many typologies of modified landscapes, of which land reclamation, the practice of pouring material into the sea to create land, is one (Topalović 2014, 52). Land creation, the earthworks deployed to create new buildable land, and the technology of altering the morphology of the landscape are all territorializing processes that manipulate the material bases of territory to create both terra and extend land control. Mining the sand needed to create land is its own form of geoengineering: 50 billion metric tons of sand is extracted from quarries, pits, rivers, coastline, and the marine environment each year, making it the largest volume of solid material extracted globally (United Nations Environment Program [UNEP] 2019).

Singapore is known as the largest land reclamation project in the world, and it is the world's biggest importer of sand for construction (Topalović 2014, 51). Because Singapore has focused its land reclamation efforts on expanding its coastline and creating new territory, borders—both territorial and maritime—shift and expand outward along with the newly constructed land. Much attention has been given to the ways that Singapore has increased its landmass by importing enormous quantities of sand for land reclamation, but less has been done to explore the implications of what it means to lose the material substance of territory to processes that displace it elsewhere. Scholars have examined the remaking of the landscape in border regions through earthworks (see, e.g., Nyers 2012) but have tended to focus on manipulating the borderlands of adjacent states. Less explored are questions about the movement of material that chips away at territory in one location and gets shipped off to make territory in other countries. Even the language of the dredging industry obscures this relationship by labeling the places where extraction occurs as "sand borrow areas" (see Schaart 2008). In these "sand borrow areas," the extraction of sand is not necessarily identified as a loss of land or loss of the material basis of territory. This may be because sand is mobile and oftentimes submerged under water at the moment of extraction, and, thus, the material is not sufficiently "land-like" before it is manipulated by geoengineering practices.

Cambodia became a major supplier of sand to Singapore, accounting for nearly one-third of its imports after neighboring Malaysia and Indonesia instituted bans on export due to overexploitation (DESA/UNSD 2018). Over a ten-year period, Cambodia went from exporting almost no sand to being one of the top ten global exporters of sand, with 97 percent going to Singapore (RFA 2017). Dredging operations consisted of rampant, uncoordinated work to strip one province of coastal sand, along with sand taken from estuaries and rivers, which, taken cumulatively, erodes the material basis of the overall landmass in an uncertain and unpredictable fashion. To understand how sand extraction is articulated with ongoing resource struggles, I explore the processes to assemble and "make up" sand as a resource and deploy it into making land (Bridge 2009; Li 2014). Attending to the different ways sand is known and how the practices and technologies assembled to extract and transport it developed helps to make sense of how the rush on sand was not enrolled into land-based grievances and territorial concerns during the heyday of its extraction in Cambodia. I draw upon insights from the resource materialities framework (Richardson and Weszkalnys 2014) to put the processes of sand dredging for land reclamation into a relational perspective by examining the multiple ontologies of sand. This entails a shift away from a tendency to focus on the commodity status of resources toward considering what else they might be at any point in time (and place). Such an approach facilitates an examination of processes at the Cambodian node of the assemblage that transform sand into a resource through its extraction and sale so that it can be further worked upon by the land reclamation assemblage at the Singaporean end to be made into land. It also helps to explore questions of how sand can be land at one point of the assemblage and "not land" at another point. In particular, what might be standing in the way of seeing the material in land-based and territorial terms in extraction sites?

To answer these questions and to understand how the sand mining sector took shape and articulated with the rush on other resources in Cambodia, I draw from primary and secondary data. Interviews were conducted with twenty-five residents of areas with intensive sand mining in March 2018 (fourteen months after bans on dredging for export came into effect) to gather people's reflections on dredging in the coastal region of Southwest Cambodia. All interviews were conducted in confidentiality, and the names of interviewees are withheld by mutual agreement. Secondary sources, including the campaigning work by international and national NGOs, policy changes at regional and domestic levels, political disputes documented by the Cambodian press, and reported international trade data, were analyzed. I also draw from my past research with rural people living in land-conflict areas (2010–2015) and how these local struggles articulated with national campaigns to reveal the scale of land dispossession (Schoenberger 2015, 2017; Lamb et al. 2017; Schoenberger and Beban 2021).

This chapter proceeds as follows. The first section reviews new developments in the literature on territory, which advocate for increased attention to its dynamism and materiality and how thinking volumetrically can expand the analysis. I then consider sand's unique materiality in the second section and how this contributes to its ontological multiplicity. The third section outlines how land reclamation megaprojects take shape and the technological developments that extract huge volumes of sand so that land reclamation can reach greater scales. The fourth section gives an overview of land reclamation's role in Singaporean state building and the volumes of material imported from across the region to create Singaporean land. The chapter then turns to the Cambodian side of the assemblage for its remainder. How sand extraction took shape, the practices that characterized the sand rush, and how it was informed by past resource enclosures are detailed in the fifth section. The sixth section scales down to the local level to examine how the sand mining assemblage took shape in coastal Cambodia and explore what it is about sand that meant it was not enrolled into ongoing land and territory movements. I detail different attempts to draw attention to the negative impacts of sand mining and the unique characteristics of a winning strategy that exposed the discrepancies in recorded trade between Cambodia and

Singapore that revealed widespread underreporting of the volume of sand extracted and shipped off. This campaign, which emphasized volumetric calculations and the shadowy economy of the trade, led to intense scrutiny of the sector and an eventual ban on sand exports.

Material and Volumetric Territory

Questions and arguments raised in the recent volumetric and material turn in the literature on territory suggest that exploring the ways in which coasts, seabeds, swamps, and islands—spaces notable for their indeterminacy, dynamism, and fluidity—might expand thinking about territory, power, and nature. This body of work emphasizes the materiality of territory and its dynamism, turning toward analyzing terrain and giving greater attention to "rivers, oceans, polar regions, glaciers, airspace, and the subsurface—both the subsoil and submarine" (Elden 2017a, 10). Drawing from work in physical geography, advocates of the material turn have argued for more attention to the distinction between form and process in order to understand the ways in which terrain is dynamic (Elden 2017a). This also facilitates the examination of work done by the state to transform territory by draining swamps, damming rivers, extracting resources, and reclaiming land—work that physical geographers term "anthropogeomorphology," or the study of the human impact on geomorphology. The material turn is thus argued to better take into account the power of natural processes and resources, the dynamics of humans and environment, and the interrelations that "produce, continually transform and rework the question of territory and state spatial strategies" (Elden 2017b). Indeed, projects to reshape terrain require logistics: the political and legal require the scientific and the technical (Elden 2017a).

In thinking through territory in terms of its physical and political material, Elden argues that terrain—like *terra* and conventional understandings of territory—"might be seen as too tied to dry land, to the form rather than the process, the static rather than the indeterminate or the dynamic" (Elden 2018, 15). To get at the land-sea interface, it is helpful to keep this emphasis on dynamic processes and to go beyond two-dimensional cartographic imaginations to stress the vertical or volumetric as part of thinking productively about "height and depth, space not just area" (Elden 2018, 15; Peters, Steinberg, and Stratford. 2018). This shift away from flat, surface, areal senses of political-legal geography toward three-dimensional spaces also facilitates more attention to temporality (Elden 2013a, 2013b). Similarly, incorporating the vertical element of volume into territorial thinking requires an emphasis on materiality that does not reinforce a sense of matter as fixed and grounded (Steinberg and Peters 2015).

These arguments for volumetric thinking and considering how territory works "at depth" are also directly relevant to the vertical and volumetric nature of mining, in this case for sand, and working to build up sand deposits to create land (Bridge 2013). Land reclamation projects are inherently vertical: they begin by pouring layers upon layers of sand on shallow parts of the seabed until enough volume is amassed that the sand rises above the surface of the water to produce areal space. Here, the "volumetric," a term used in cartography and physics, is helpful as it indicates "the mechanisms of calculating, measuring, surveying, managing, controlling, and ordering (the metric) that constitute the political technology of territory, understood as volume" (Elden 2017a, 21).

This volumetric turn also reflects the roles that mining and extraction play by mixing the different planes of surface and netherworld into forms of vertical rupture and displacement—a dynamic that can be harnessed to manipulate territory by moving vast quantities of material (Bridge 2013). This manipulation is an exercise of power-exercising-power through technologies of calculation, visualization, and manipulation deployed around volume (Bridge 2013). Gavin Bridge (2013) argues that volume may be even more useful as an organizational problematic when it is considered as a spatial form of property that is in contrast to two-dimensional areal expressions in which resources tend to be imagined as fixed territory. Instead, a spatial form that is "quanta-based" (typically volume, sometimes weight) and refers to ownership rights asserted over commodities in motion or in storage can better capture rights given to material in "flux" that have a weaker link to place (Bridge 2013, 57). Such quanta-based rights are developed by the processes created by the state to grant licenses for sand extraction. Companies acquire ownership rights to the sand itself in the moment of extraction since property rights are exerted on the volumes that can be moved and displaced. In the case examined in this chapter, the calculations surrounding recorded measures of weight and volume in international trade logs became key to sand struggles, as I examine in later sections.

Sand As a Material and a Resource

Sand is the earth in a loose, light, shifting, mobile, and fragile form, determined not by its origins but by its size (Beiser 2018; Nieuwenhuis 2018). Sand is a loose grain of any hard material with a diameter between 2 and 0.0625 millimeters, as defined by the most commonly used geologic standard, the Udden-Wentworth scale (Beiser 2018, 6). The grains can be made from ground stones, degraded sea-shells and corals, or volcanic lava, but the vast majority of all sand grains on Earth, 70 percent, are quartz and formed by the erosion of geologic features. Quartz is a form of silicon dioxide (SiO_2, also known as silica).

Sand has a number of particular qualities. First, it is a transient component of the ever-changing earth that is part of how landmass and territory are formed and consolidated. Second, it is both buried and suspended, equally at home in water, land, and air, and able to move in between. Third, it can move freely and without territorial interference and constraint, but it can also come to rest, ac-cumulating as riverbeds, seabeds, or islands, or compacted to form sandstone. Loose silt and dust can seep through cracks and crevices, the swirling body of *terra* falling outside of state control and able to traverse national borders (Nieu-wenhuis 2018). Fourth, sand has a temporality—sometimes slowly shifting, marking the passing of time, and at others whirling as powerful and devastating storms (Nieuwenhuis 2018; Kothari and Arnall 2019). Human and nonhuman agents are entangled in shaping the pace, form, extent, and direction of flows in sand—determining where sand accumulates and where it flows out to sea (see Kothari and Arnall 2019 for an examination of these processes in the Maldives). In marine environments, waves, currents, and tides—ongoing or cyclical changes and rhythms that might be hourly, tidal, daily, and seasonal—continually wash sand onto and offshore, while exceptional events, like tsuna-mis and storm surges, can shift tons of sand in a moment, sometimes removing a whole beach (Puotinen et al. 2016; Kothari and Arnall 2019). Sand can also be worked upon to be forced into a configuration that expresses fixed and grounded qualities through processes like beach replenishment or land recla-mation. Such processes to reconfigure sand are part of turning sand from a natu-ral material, or "thing that is already," into a resource that takes shape according to the knowledge and infrastructure needed to extract, refine, transform, and transport it (Richardson and Weszkalnys 2014).

The marketization of sand at increasing scales is perhaps the most significant human influence on coastal spaces in recent years (Kothari and Arnall 2019). In 2016, the sand industry was valued at US$1.71 billion globally (DESA/UNSD 2018). Extraction is often uncontrolled. Sand is being bought, sold, and trans-ported on an unprecedented scale and speed, building new assemblages of people, materials, and environments along the way (Kothari and Arnall 2019). The priva-tization and enclosure of sand are also complicated by its tendency to be hid-den, either under water or comprising the "underground."

In the case study examined in this chapter, sand is ontologically different at each end of the assemblage and at different points in time; sand is a material part of the natural world, then a resource for extraction, before it becomes the material basis for new constructed land. To analyze these shifts, it is helpful to draw from the resource materialities framework developed by Richardson and Weszkalnys (2014, 16), which encompasses consideration of four key points: "First, resource ontologies, that is, assumptions about the nature and affordances of the 'things that are already' and their participation in making local, regional, national and global scales; second, the different ways in which specific resources are known; third, the infrastructures designed to extract resources and those needed to refine, transform and transport them; and fourth, how resources are experienced by people who work with, transform, or . . . ingest them."

Later sections of this chapter detail the unfolding of this resource history to show an interplay and contest between different ontologies, sand as "out there" and sand as constituted—through arrangements of substances, technologies, discourses, and practices deployed by different kinds of actors—as a resource and then as land (Richardson and Weszkalnys 2014, 16).

Constructing the Assemblages to Mine Sand to Create Land

Mining and extraction are not just about moving quantities of earth but are an exercise of power that involves technologies of calculation, visualization, and manipulation deployed around volume (Bridge 2013); this is particularly pronounced in land reclamation megaprojects. The process and technology of reclaiming land from the sea is well established: the Dutch have built artificial land since the eleventh century; expansion of the island of Manhattan began in 1646; shallow areas of the San Francisco Bay were filled in the 1850s; and land reclamation has been used to build large portions of Marseilles, Hong Kong, and Mumbai (Hassler 2014; Beiser 2018). Coastlines across East Asia, the Persian Gulf, Western Europe, and North America have all been altered by land reclamation, and although concern for the environmental consequences has increased, developing countries and rapidly growing economies are aggressively pursuing land reclamation projects that dwarf historical examples (Wang et al. 2014; Beiser 2018; Chen, Wei, and Peng 2018). Researchers using satellite data to analyze where water has been converted to land, and vice versa, found that 33,700 km^2 of coastal land has been created since 1985 (Donchyts et al. 2016)—a size roughly equivalent to Jamaica or the US state of Connecticut (Doyle 2016).

Acquiring the sand for reclamation requires dredging, an excavation activity that is carried out underwater in shallow seas, estuaries, rivers, and lakes to remove sediment from the waterbed. Although most dredging occurs to supply the construction and land reclamation markets, dredging can also be conducted under the justification of widening or deepening waterways for better passage of ships or to reduce flooding. Sand dredgers use either mechanical scoops or hydraulic suction pumps to lift sand to the surface and onto barges for transport. Technology advances since the 1970s—in the form of bigger dredging ships equipped with extremely powerful pumps that can dredge deeper, as well as more precise technology to deposit sand onto predetermined places—have made it easier and cheaper to pursue land reclamation (Beiser 2018). In a thirty-year period from 1965 to 1994, the amount of material that the largest dredgers could hold more than tripled, and by the late 2010s, the amount has grown nearly ten times (Beiser 2018). Shipping technology and trade networks allow sand to be transported over short and long distances such that "new land can be constructed at will" (Hassler 2014). Meanwhile, developments in sand-blowing technology have made land reclamation faster: it is now possible to reclaim 1 km^2 of land from the sea in about twenty days (Ge 2009, cited in Wang et al. 2014). Taken together, the costs of building new land have dropped significantly, and, according to the International Association of Dredging Companies, new seafront land can be built for less than $536 per square meter, which is significantly cheaper than the market price for existing land, provided "good quality sand is available within a reasonable distance" (Beiser 2018, 175). In addition to being a tool of state-led modernization drives, coastal land reclamation projects can be pursued by webs of substate and supranational actors consisting of dredgers, contractors, developers, overseas investors, and property speculators and politicians at every scale (Comaroff 2014).

The pursuit of land reclamation is putting enormous pressure on the natural environment. At sites of land reclamation, the scale of such projects far outpaces the speed and exceeds the scales at which the coastal and marine ecosystems can readjust and restore, resulting in loss of coastal wetland areas, significant coastal landscape fragmentation, loss of biodiversity, reduced water purification ability, and increased water pollution and harmful algal blooms (Wang et al. 2014). Meanwhile, the scale of the demand for sand has led the UNEP (2019, 15) to label it "one of the major sustainability challenges of the twenty-first century" because it is "one of the least regulated activities in many regions."

Coastal earthworks are underway throughout Asia, some of which are so large they encroach on and have the potential to remake sovereign borders (Comaroff 2014). In many instances, state projects to create "new land" through megascale land reclamation have been central to twentieth-century modernization, development, and state-building goals (Choi 2014; Topalović 2014). The next section of this chapter details the central role of land reclamation in Singaporean state building.

Land Reclamation in Singapore

Reshaping the natural shoreline is an enormous undertaking in Singapore, and land reclamation projects have been a tool to create landmass, assert state power, and enact modernity. Land reclamation has a long history in Singapore and can be traced back to colonial projects undertaken in the nineteenth century (Hassler 2014), but the role of such projects and their scale really took off in the post-Independence era. Singapore's first leader after independence held up land reclamation as a signifier of the successful transition "from third world to first" (quoted in Hassler 2014, 15), and the country aggressively pursued land reclamation such that its territory has increased by one-fifth since 1965 (Koninck 2017). To date, the scale of Singapore's sand works has exceeded the figural archipelagos of Dubai, with much of the city's Central Business District occupying what were once the straits separating Singapore and Indonesia (Comaroff 2014). Land reclamation is an ongoing pursuit with goals of reaching a 30 percent increase (compared to pre-Independence landmass) or an additional seventy square kilometers in the country's original land area by 2030 (Milton 2010; Koninck 2017). Scaling down to examine each constructed square kilometer is helpful in trying to picture the volumes of material involved: estimates suggest that it takes 37.5 million cubic meters of fill, or the loads of approximately 1.4 million dump trucks, to create this areal landmass (Milton 2010; Comaroff 2014).

Despite efforts to ascertain the volume of sand dredged domestically and internationally for land reclamation in Singapore using geoengineering reports and trade statistics, there is no certainty about the exact volume dredged from different seabeds and coastlines, just like there is no certainty about the precise depths of offshore land reclamation (see Hassler 2014, 18). Scholars estimate that since 1925, between 1,940 million and 2,825 million cubic meters of volume were moved to construct the land that comprises Singapore's 2012 boundaries. Most of this material, in the range of 1,270–2,157 million cubic meters, was used to add 138 km^2 of offshore land reclamation (Hassler 2014). And of this, it is estimated that at least three-quarters of the created land is comprised of imported sand and materials or "built on foreign soil" (Topalović 2014, 52).

Initially, projects to reshape Singapore's topography sourced the material locally from inland terrain, but as resources and opportunities became scarce in the 1980s, the sand hinterland spread to its regional neighbors (Hassler and Topalović 2014). Since the 1990s, the sand poured into reclamation projects tends to be sourced from course sea sand extracted from coastlines in the region, particularly Malaysia (until a ban on exports in 1997), Indonesia (until 2007), Cambodia (until 2017), as well as Vietnam, the Philippines and Myanmar. At the peak of extraction in the seas between Indonesia and Singapore, 77 percent of the world's sand dredgers were on site, and mining was so intense that at least twenty-one Indonesian islands were wiped off the map (Milton 2010). As a result, an emerging geopolitical narrative is that Singapore has begun to absorb surrounding territory (Comaroff 2014).

Making Sand into a Resource for Extraction in Cambodia

Shortly after Indonesia banned exports of sand, Cambodia became a hotspot of sand extraction and trade, a process that rapidly transformed sand from a material into a resource to be captured by the well-connected. The assemblage formed to exploit sand as a resource was informed by the historical and material environment and followed processes of "becoming" that "happens when the constituents of the resource assemblage shift and change, when elements are drawn into the assemblage and others expelled" (Richardson and Weszkalnys 2014, 15). The assemblages formed to capture natural resources to accumulate capital and amass power through patronage-based distributive practices have reconfigured several times in the postconflict period around trees, fish, and land (Le Billon 2000, 2002; Sneddon 2007; Un and So 2009, 2011; Milne 2015; Diepart and Schoenberger 2017). Resource extraction in Cambodia is organized by state-granted concessions and licenses; the first state-issued license to dredge sand was granted in 2006, and so began the rush on sand (CCHR 2016).

The Cambodian sand rush took off in late 2007, shortly after Indonesia banned the export of coastal sand (Global Witness 2009; CCHR 2016), and the trade in sand skyrocketed. The technology and infrastructure quickly relocated to Cambodia, with nearly all dredgers imported into the country over a three-year period from 2007 to 2009 (DESA/UNSD 2018). Licenses to dredge specified the depth of activity and allocated companies the rights to dredge particular rivers and coastal areas. Geographically, dredging for export was concentrated in borderland areas that were also resource frontiers with relatively small populations and often was confined to areas only accessible by boat. The empirical material that informs this chapter focuses on dredging in the hotspot of Koh Kong province in Southwest Cambodia, which was the center of the trade and national debates around sand. There, mined sand would not necessarily be brought to shore; instead, it was often directly transferred onto larger offshore barges for export. Once the assemblage took shape, Cambodia went from exporting almost no sand to shipping 80.2 million metric tons between 2007 and 2016 (DESA/UNSD 2018).

Although the assemblage to extract sand quickly took shape, the industry was characterized by secrecy and allegations of improper activity. This murkiness was written into the legal framework guiding sand mining: the 2001 Law on the Management and Exploitation of Mineral Resources specifically states that all applications, reports, and plans concerning exploration and exploitation are confidential (Global Witness 2009, 2010). This makes it challenging to identify the actors involved and the volumes and locations specified in extraction licenses that underpin the trade in sand. Research suggests that a mix of companies are involved in the trade, with backing from a range of actors, inclusive of local entrepreneurs, firms connected to politicians, and various regional companies (Global Witness 2009, 2010; CCHR 2016; Lamb et al. 2019). Key players in Cambodian politics shaped the trade in sand, with one local senator described as a "referee" for all sand contracts a role that placed him at the center of payments from offshore buyers to onshore dredgers (Global Witness 2009, 31–33, 2010). The boundaries between legal and illegal dredging were also regularly blurred: licensed dredgers commonly operated outside of their licensed parameters; companies often turned to mining under the cover of night during license suspensions; and unlicensed dredgers proliferated (Taing and Mom 2015; CCHR 2016). Since granting the first dredging license, the policies surrounding sand have also been in a state of constant change, with even the governance and oversight of the industry shifting from one ministry, the Ministry of Water Resources, to another, the Ministry of Mines and Energy (MME) (Hul 2015a; CCHR 2016). The Prime Minister stepped in to make this rearrangement in the midst of uproar around several controversial riverbank collapses blamed on sand dredging (Hul 2015b). Shortly after this appointment, the MME revealed that only thirty-seven of the 142 active sand dredging companies held licenses (RFA 2015).

Taken together—frequent policy changes, lack of public records, the secrecy of dredging activities undertaken by both licensed and unlicensed operators—it is difficult to accurately ascertain the state of sand dredging, including its shifting locations, the companies involved, and the networks established between dredgers and government officials (CCHR 2016). A 2016 report on sand dredging by the Cambodia Center for Human Rights found that the practice was widespread and uncontrolled throughout Cambodia's rivers, estuaries, and coastal regions and that the scale and intensity of dredging were facilitated by weak governance and rampant corruption. One campaigner described arrangements formed around dredging for export as: "The companies, which in reality are no more than criminal syndicates working hand in hand with powerful government officials, declare a tiny portion of the actual sand exports. This allows them to make vast amounts of profits, which of course must be shared with those in government who provide 'protection services to them'" (quoted in Paviour and Aun 2016).

Efforts to raise awareness at the start of the sand trade garnered media attention (see, e.g., Global Witness 2009, 2010) but did not result in sustained local
or international efforts to document sand extraction, and the issue was dwarfed
by the land grabbing debates, which Cambodia was an epicenter of in this period
(Schoenberger, Hall, and Vandergeest 2017). During the decade that dredging
for export was the most active, it was largely omitted from efforts to map, count,
and document how resources were captured, which is noteworthy because this
time period overlaps with the sustained work by nongovernment actors to cata-
log and map the concessions granted for land, forests, and fisheries and the licenses for mining and oil and gas exploitation.[1] The remainder of this chapter
examines tensions around how the sand mining assemblage took shape to explore what it is about sand that meant it was not enrolled into ongoing land and
territory movements.

Struggles around Sand Extraction

It took nearly one decade for the struggles around sand mining to hit a winning
strategy and get sustained attention. At the outset, sand extraction was framed
as an environmental problem with impacts on fisheries and livelihoods (Global
Witness 2009, 2010; Marschke 2012), and within two years of dredging taking
off, villagers started to complain that dredging was to blame for riverbank collapses leading to loss of houses and farmland (Sam 2009). Affected communities raised their grievances and protested using established tactics employed by
environmental and land-based social movements, namely signing petitions to
multiple levels of government, requesting governmental investigations, and
working their networks to raise awareness of what was happening (Marschke
2012). These small-scale protests were considered to be effective and responsible for the 2009 Sand Trafficking Decision that banned dredging rivers for export but allowed for sand dredging to continue to supply local demand and
contained an exception for where "sand gathered and replenished itself naturally" (quoted in Sam 2009). In the months that followed, the Prime Minister
repeated his ban with warnings about dredging's destructive impact on nearby
areas and raising concerns: "I am afraid that history will put the blame on me
for the sales that will have a destructive impact on our islands" (quoted in Vong
2009). However, the following year, Global Witness (2010) exposed that the ban
had been completely flouted and sand exports from Cambodia's coastline had
actually increased.

This increase continued until coastal sand mining peaked in 2013 and 2014,
after which UN data illustrates a drop in sand exports that aligns with local

accounts of dredging activity. Interviewees characterized the peak by emphasizing the near-constant activity conducted by a large number of dredgers
that would clog up waterways to such an extent that the operations sometimes
blocked access to the sea for local fishing boats (interviewees nos. 3, 1, 17). During the peak of sand dredging, there were a number of flashpoints, including
accidents where dredgers and fishing boats collided, and smaller targeted protests (detailed later). Protests were fuelled by concerns about dredging's potential to seriously impact the stability of people's homes in instances where the
dredging operations came close to shore and caused riverbanks and riverside
farming to sometimes collapse into the water (interviewees nos. 2, 6, 13, and
21). Collapses were understood to be caused by dredging deepening waterways
and, thereby, allowing water to flow much faster than before (interviewees nos.
15, 17, and 20), and because mangroves were destroyed by dredging operations
(interviewee no. 15). Interviews with people working in the tourism industry in
the provincial capital also revealed worries that dredging would eventually cause
the beach and shoreline to collapse, leading to a potential downturn in tourism.
Overall, as sand mining operations continued and the sand was stripped, people
feared that dredging operations would only be possible if they moved closer and
closer to shore and to people's homes (interviewee no. 19) and that it would create
large-scale and inevitable destruction of bays and beaches (interviewees nos. 22
and 23).

Dredging also negatively impacted nonhuman territories, particularly the
habitats of fish, shrimp, and crab, as nearly all twenty-five interviewees emphasized. Dredging disturbs the seabed, increases turbidity, kills seagrasses (interviewees nos. 4 and 20), and was understood to make it impossible for crabs to
live in the area. Degradation of the natural environment was given further credence when the fish disappeared. Intensive dredging took place near, and at times
inside, a Cambodian Protected Area (Pream Krasoap Wildlife Sanctuary) and
an International Ramsar Site (Koh Kapic and Associated Islets) and also expanded into community-managed fishing areas. When dredging operations
expanded into areas used by fisherfolk, the practice caused widespread damage
to private property in the form of destroyed traps and gear.

In the mid-2010s, fishing families escalated their protest, going as far as creating obstructions and attempting to drag dredging operations out of estuaries.
In one instance, fishing families tied their boats to twelve barges and eight
transport boats to obstruct operations and organized to chase dredgers away
(Hul 2015c). They targeted dredgers known to be operating in spite of an ex-
pired license that was not valid for the area and were accused of "pump[ing] out
the sand and caus[ing] the mangrove trees to fall down," according to a fisherman active in the protest and quoted in the press (Hul 2015c). These efforts

were followed by attempts to work through formal channels to reach the Prime Minister, but when this proved a dead end, locals returned to direct action due to heightened concerns that dredging operations had gone too deep and were causing riverbank collapses as well as drops in crab and fish stocks (Aun 2015). Locals attempted to tow away barges transporting excavators and to chase dredgers out of the estuary, eventually seizing one barge and ordering the driver to tow away other barges that claimed to be "broken" (Aun 2015). These efforts drew national attention to the plight of coastal communities. Activists in the land, housing, and eviction movements started to lend their support to the anti-dredging effort, most notably the Boeung Kak activists, themselves the targets of urban lakeside evictions due to inland fills. A veteran activist emphasized that the antidredging movement was "to protect the national interests of the country," noting that "we saw that their situation was unfair and similar to our case" (quoted in Pech 2015). This is one of the rare instances where the link between sand dredging, the nation, and ongoing processes of land creation is articulated.

Around the same time that local protests escalated, a turning point in the domestic debates surrounding sand extraction came as a result of a campaign launched by the local activist network Mother Nature. The launch began with a Facebook post to announce that they "would like to create a new culture within Cambodia's civil society: having young activists ask Prime Minister Hun Sen questions related to the environment." To start, they proposed two questions:

1. How many millions of tons of sand has Cambodia exported in the last five years out of Koh Kong [Province], and at what price has this sand been sold?
2. How much revenue has the state received from the sale, and how are the funds being dispersed by the government? (Facebook, December 24, 2015).

The two core themes of these questions, namely the volume of sand removed and state management of extraction revenues (i.e., corruption), became the focal points for questions of how state governance of territory and resources applies to sand and its extraction. This initial post was followed shortly thereafter by Mother Nature's first of a series of "viral" sand videos featuring young activists speaking Khmer with English subtitles and posted to Facebook and YouTube.[2] As an activist, buried up to his neck in sand, explained in the video:

> You are likely wondering what I am doing buried in sand. The reason is to express my pain at seeing how many millions of tons of Cambodian sand continue being exported to Singapore every year, which is causing

severe environmental damage to our country's ecosystems, is a threat to Koh Kong's mangrove forests, and above all, has been destroying the livelihoods of the local communities for the past eight years.

Recently, many people have asked the Ministry of Mines and Energy for transparency and accountability regarding the total amount of sand exported from Cambodia to Singapore and the total amount of taxes the state has obtained (through this export of sand). Because the Ministry of Mines and Energy has ignored these calls for transparency, Mother Nature has conducted its own research.

According to official data from a United Nations website, we have obtained the following shocking results: The Cambodian government is reporting that it has exported a total of 2.6 million tons to Singapore in the last eight years, worth US$5.5 million. During that same period, Singapore's government reports that it has imported from Cambodia a total of 73 million tons, worth around US$700 million.

For this reason, Mother Nature would like to ask HE Suy Sem, Minister of Mines and Energy, as follows: Where has all this sand, worth several hundred million US dollars, gone? Mother Nature hopes that HE will give a public explanation regarding this issue to all Cambodians. Thank you and goodbye. (Facebook, October 8, 2016)

This video got 300,000 views and was followed by a series of videos using the same visual language of activists buried up to their necks in sand while detailing the discrepancies in UN trade data logs to reveal the systematic underreporting of Cambodian exports of sand to a series of importing countries. The videos introduced new variables, measures, and efforts to monitor something that was taken for granted and extracted without any oversight. The videos got significant attention, with some reaching up to 2.5 million views in a country of 16 million people. The campaign sparked online debates, and the issues raised were covered by national and international media outlets. Working through reported trade statistics was the "eureka!" in how to campaign for sand because the mismatch in the import and export data were "killer facts" (Oya 2013; Scoones et al. 2013) that could be harnessed to illustrate the volumes of sand exported and the scale of the trade as well as the shadow economy surrounding it.[3] As the NGO explains on its website: "Mother Nature pulled an ace from under our sleeve that played a vital role in killing off for once and for all the fraudulent and destructive extraction of marine sand. The method was simple and yet tremendously effective: we highlighted the massive discrepancies in recorded trade between Cambodia (as the exporting country) and other nations which had been buying the sand as importers."

These revelations sparked investigations by civil society groups (CSOs) and calls for action—including an immediate moratorium on issuing new licenses to dredge sand until research on long-term impacts could be conducted—and a review of all existing sand dredging licenses with revocation of companies that did not comply with environmental impact assessments (EIAs) or did not conduct EIAs in the first place (CCHR 2016). The need for increased transparency was also highlighted, and requests were made to the MME to make the license issuances and conditions publicly available and accessible online, along with the EIAs and hydrological reports related to dredging (CSOs 2016). Although the government agreed to a closed-door meeting with civil society organizations where they pushed for a suspension of coastal and estuary sand dredging and for a better system to manage the trade, the government did not budge (Hang and Paviour 2016). In particular, they refused to publish documents pertaining to sand licenses, including the names of the companies licensed to dredge. Emphasizing the frustration with the lack of transparency around the sand sector, one of the Mother Nature founders explained: "Where are the reports? We've been asking for months. If they really wanted to do things according to the book, they would release everything: EIA reports, hydrological reports, company names and numbers" (quoted in Runcie 2016). Frustration over the secrecy of the sector was also shared by competing ministries, and the mismatch in sand trade data and state revenues was a hot topic of debate in the National Assembly.

Intense scrutiny of the sector led to a temporary ban on exports in January 2017, followed by a signed formal decree in July, in which MME issued a set of guidelines detailing the permanent ban of sand exports from Koh Kong and invalidated all current licenses. MME officials explained that reassessments of environment and social impacts "indicate significant impact on the ecology and local communities if large scale dredging continues operating. That's why we decided to issue this" (quoted in Amaro and Phak 2017). And yet one of Mother Nature's posts just before the ban was issued might better get at the heart of the matter. The post showed satellite images of the numerous barges and dredgers mining and moving sand in Koh Kong province. The post tagged the MME and the Prime Minister and asked in the caption: "Who loses? Cambodia as a whole, which keeps getting smaller and smaller as millions of tons of sand are stolen from her every year. Who wins? Singapore, which keeps getting bigger thanks to our sand" (Facebook, December 7, 2016).

This chapter has responded to invitations in the territory literature to better account for the materiality of territory and to "think volumetrically" by exploring where this might lead through an examination of sand's role in land reclamation in Southeast Asia. Some of the new territory literature has pushed back at the easy connections between volume and earthy, grounded territory and the ways in which the *geo* in geology is used to characterize a material world of stable ontologies that persist in spite of transformations within the geophysical or social domain (Steinberg and Peters 2015). Sand does not have a stable ontology. When manipulated and reconfigured by geoengineering projects, sand is transformed from a material in flux into a volumetric arrangement that is worked upon in order to stabilize it and create a type of material strata and areal space that can be neatly bordered and contained in the form of "new land." As such, this case is useful in exploring the interplay between mobility and fixes, volume and area, land and sea.

This case has demonstrated the usefulness of thinking through sand's "distributedness" in terms of its material dispersal in time and place and how this informs its ontological multiplicity (Richardson and Weszkalnys 2014, 21). To become "land-like," sand had to be reassembled in massive quantities and arranged with substances (like aggregate) and worked upon through technologies, discourses, and practices to create new coastal land and, thereby, expand territory. Although sand is eventually constituted as land, its transformation into a resource for extraction was not connected to ongoing and intense debates around land grabbing and territory loss in Cambodia. When we look at the unfolding of the resource assemblage at the point of extraction, the removal of sand was not treated as a land problem but as a type of resource problem that was bound up in a wider view of watery ecologies before being transformed into a corruption problem based on secretive trade practices and the mishandling of revenues owed to the state. Sand was ontologically different from land before processes to enclose it were enacted. It was conceived of as one piece of the puzzle of coastal, estuary, and riverine ecosystems and landscapes in Cambodia but not their material basis. Extraction of sand did not threaten land's existence at the outset; instead, the effects of sand mining were first felt as disruptions to fisheries and nonhuman territories. This may also be an effect of the assemblage formed to extract sand and transform it into a resource, namely the barges dredging waterways and coastlines and the ferrying of boatloads of sand out to sea to be shipped by private actors to faraway and unseen places, which is an assemblage very different from the network of actors that shape land grabbing through large concessions granted for agribusiness (see Schoenberger and Beban 2018, 1346). Once the activity intensified, it threatened livelihoods based on fisheries such that sand became entangled and then pronounced in coastal livelihood concerns. As the impacts from dredging and its knock-on effects accumulated, erosion accelerated, riverbanks collapsed, and sand's role as a territorial substance took on new attention. Incidents of land collapse have been flashpoints in domestic debates over dredging and tied to renewed calls for oversight, rear-rangements of jurisdictional responsibilities, and renewed protesting efforts; but the geographically fragmented and unpredictable nature of collapse may have also contributed to sand extraction not attracting the sustained attention that land grabbing received.

Turning sand into land also required a specific set of techno-scientific schemes and Singapore's own assemblage of practices, expertise, and infrastructure. Ul-timately, it was practices of knowledge production, namely logs of import and export figures of weight, volume, and payments, that activists drew upon to sit-uate Cambodian sand into struggles over governance and exploitation of natu-ral resources. Here, this case makes clear how the calculations of territory (and volume)—the work to map, measure, weigh, control, and order—are not exclu-sively the domain of the state and shows parallels to activist work in the land sector to map and document concessions and existing smallholder land rights in Cambodia. Such calculations of territory can be harnessed to compel the state to govern its resources according to a logic more grounded in Foucauldian gov-ernmentality than the fire sale and elite-based looting of natural resources.

The particularities of coastal sand extraction in Cambodia also raise impor-tant questions for environmental politics. The case demonstrates the ways in which "registers of flow, volume, and containment" are increasingly used to se-cure and negotiate environmental futures by focusing on calculative and technical-legal practices (Bridge 2013, 57). Yet there are still important questions about how a decade of intensive and free-wheeling sand mining might affect the country's territorial integrity in the long term, especially as climate change is likely to accelerate the erosion of coastlines and beaches as sand is washed away with ever-increasing speed. How these manipulated spaces go on to withstand the mounting pressures of climate change, as well as future geomorphological processes, reinforce the usefulness of focusing on the stakes of earth processes to speak to larger questions of *geo*power, *geo*politics, and *geo*metrics (Elden 2013a).

NOTES

1. Examples of the multisector mapping and documentation efforts can be found on-line at http://archive.opendevelopmentcambodia.net/maps/ and https://www.licadho-cambodia.org/land_concessions/.

2. These videos can be viewed on Mother Nature Cambodia's website, https://mothernaturecambodia.org/our-videos-2016-2017.

3. The pattern of mismatched export figures from Cambodia and import figures from elsewhere was found to also characterize the data on Cambodia's wood exports which had a reporting gap of nearly $1 billion (Hang and Paviour 2016).

REFERENCES

Amaro, Y., and S. Phak. 2017. "Koh Kong Sand Exports Permanently Banned After Volume Discrepancies." *Phnom Penh Post*, July 12, 2017.

Aun, P. 2015. "Koh Kong Fishermen Resume Anti-Sand-Dredging Campaign." *Cambodia Daily*, August 13, 2015.

Beiser, V. 2018. *The World in a Grain: The Story of Sand and How it Transformed Civilization*. New York: Riverhead Books.

Bridge, G. 2009. "Material Worlds: Natural Resources, Resource Geography, and the Material Economy." *Geography Compass* 3 (3): 1217–1244.

Bridge, G. 2013. "Territory, Now in 3D!" *Political Geography* 34: 55–57.

CCHR (Cambodian Center for Human Rights). 2016. "The Human Rights Impacts of Sand Dredging in Cambodia." Briefing Note, September 2016.

Chen, Y., Y. Wei, and L. Peng. 2018. "Ecological Technology Model and Path of Seaport Reclamation Construction." *Ocean & Coastal Management* 165: 244–257.

Choi, Y. R. 2014. "Modernization, Development and Underdevelopment: Reclamation of Korean tidal flats, 1950s–2000s." *Ocean & Coastal Management* 102: 426–436.

Comaroff, J. 2014. "Built on Sand: Singapore and the New State of Risk." *Harvard Design Magazine* 39: 138–147.

CSOs (Civil Society Organizations). 2016. "Civil Society Open Letter Seeks Clarification Regarding Sand Exports." Letter to the Minister of Mines and Energy, October 31, 2016. https://cchrcambodia.org/media/files/press_release/641 _210otme_en.pdf.

DESA/UNSD (Department of Economic and Social Affairs/United Nations Statistics Division). 2018. UN Comtrade/International Trade Statistics Database. https://comtrade-un-org.proxy.bib.uottawa.ca/

Diepart, J.-C., and L. Schoenberger. 2017. "Concessions in Cambodia: Governing Profits, Extending State Power and Enclosing Resources from the Colonial Era to the Present." In *The Handbook of Contemporary Cambodia*. Edited by K. Brickell and S. Springer, 157–168. New York: Routledge.

Donchyts, G., F. Baart, H. Winsemius, N. Gorelick, J. Kwadijk, and N. van de Giesen. 2016. "Earth's Surface Water Change Over the Past 30 Years." *Nature Climate Change* 6 (9): 810–813.

Doyle, A. 2016. "Coastal Land Expands as Construction Outpaces Sea Level Rise." *Reuters*, August 26, 2016.

Elden, S. 2013a. "Secure the Volume: Vertical Geopolitics and the Depth of Power." *Political Geography* 34: 35–51.

Elden, S. 2013b. "How Should We Do the History of Territory?" *Territory, Politics, Governance* 1 (1): 5–20.

Elden, S. 2017a. "Legal Terrain—the Political Materiality of Territory." *London Review of International Law* 5 (2): 199–224.

Elden, S. 2017b. "Foucault and Geometrics." In *Foucault and the Modern International: Silences and Legacies for the Study of World Politics*. Edited by P. Bonditti, D. Bigo, and F. Gros, 295–311. London: Palgrave Macmillan.

Elden, S. 2018. "Foreword." In *Territory Beyond Terra*. Edited by K. Peters, P. Steinberg, and E. Stratford, 11–15. London and New York: Rowman & Littlefield.

Global Witness. 2009. *Country for Sale: How Cambodia's Elites Have Captured the Country's Extractive Industries*. London: Global Witness.

Global Witness. 2010. "Shifting Sand: How Singapore's Demand for Cambodian Sand Threatens Ecosystems and Undermines Good Governance." *Global Witness*.

https://www.globalwitness.org/en/archive/shifting-sand-how-singapores
-demand-cambodian-sand-threatens-ecosystems-and-undermines-good/

Hang, S., and B. Paviour. 2016. "NGOs Ask Government to Suspend Sand Dredging." *Cambodia Daily*, November 12, 2016.

Hassler, U. 2014. "Development Dynamics and Constructed Land: Singapore As a Model for a Purposeful Declaration." In *Constructed Land: Singapore 1924–2012*. Edited by U. Hassler and M. Topalović, 14–22. Singapore: ETH Zürich DArch and Future Cities Laboratory.

Hassler, U., and M. Topalović. 2014. *Constructed Land: Singapore 1924–2012*. Singapore: ETH Zürich DArch and Future Cities Laboratory.

Hul, R. 2015a. "Hun Sen Puts Mines Ministry in Control of Sand Dredging." *Cambodia Daily*, March 23, 2015.

Hul, R. 2015b. "Hun Sen Steps In to End Dredging Row." *Cambodia Daily*, March 24, 2015.

Hul, R. 2015c. "Fishermen Claim Victory against Sand Dredgers." *Cambodia Daily*, April 13, 2015.

Koninck, R. de. 2017. *Singapore's Permanent Territorial Revolution*. Singapore: NUS Press.

Kothari, U., and A. Arnall. 2019. "Shifting Sands: The Rhythms and Temporalities of Island Sandscapes." *Geoforum* 108: 305–314.

Lamb, V., M. Marschke, and J. Rigg. 2019. "Trading Sand, Undermining Lives: Omitted Livelihoods in the Global Trade in Sand." *Annals of the American Association of Geographers* 109 (5): 1511–1528.

Lamb, V., L. Schoenberger, C. Middleton, and B. Un. 2017. "Gendered Eviction, Protest and Recovery: A Feminist Political Ecology Engagement with Land Grabbing in Rural Cambodia." *Journal of Peasant Studies* 44 (6): 1215–1234.

Le Billon, P. 2000. "The Political Ecology of Transition in Cambodia 1989–1999: War, Peace, and Forest Exploitation." *Development and Change* 31 (4): 785–805.

Le Billon, P. 2002. "Logging in Muddy Waters: The Politics of Forest Exploitation in Cambodia." *Critical Asian Studies* 34 (4): 563–586.

Li, T. M. 2014. "What is Land? Assembling a Resource for Global Investment." *Transactions of the Institute of British Geographers* 39 (4): 589–602.

Marschke, M. 2012. *Life, Fish and Mangroves: Resource Governance in Coastal Cambodia*. Ottawa: University of Ottawa Press.

Milne, S. 2015. "Cambodia's Unofficial Regime of Extraction: Illicit Logging in the Shadow of Transnational Governance and Investment." *Critical Asian Studies* 47 (2): 200–228.

Milton, C. 2010. "The Sand Smugglers." *Foreign Policy*, August 4, 2010.

Nieuwenhuis, M. 2018. "Earth: A Grain of Sand against a World of Territory: Experiences of Sand and Sandscapes in China." In *Territory Beyond Terra*. Edited by K. Peters, P. Steinberg, and E. Stratford, 19–33. London and New York: Rowman & Littlefield.

Oya, C. 2013. "Methodological Reflections on 'Land Grab' Databases and the 'Land Grab' Literature 'Rush.'" *Journal of Peasant Studies* 40 (3): 503–520.

Paviour, B., and P. Aun. 2016. "Ministry Blames 'Ineffective Practices' for Over $400M in Missing Sand." *Cambodia Daily*, November 2, 2016.

Pech, S. 2015. "Boeung Kak Activists Join Koh Kong Protest." *Phnom Penh Post*, September 1, 2015.

Peters, K., P. Steinberg, and E. Stratford, eds. 2018. *Territory Beyond Terra*. London and New York: Rowman & Littlefield.

Puotinen, M., J. A. Maynard, R. Beeden, B. Radford, and G. J. Williams. 2016. "A Robust Operational Model for Predicting Where Tropical Cyclone Waves Damage Coral Reefs." *Scientific Reports* 6: 26009 (2016).

RFA (Radio Free Asia). 2015. "Cambodia Orders Temporary Halt to New Licenses For Sand Dredging." *Radio Free Asia*, March 25, 2015.

RFA (Radio Free Asia). 2017. "Cambodian Sand Could Build a Foundation for Legal Action in Singapore." *Radio Free Asia*, January 5, 2017.

Richardson, T., and G. Weszkalnys. 2014. "Introduction: Resource Materialities." *Anthropological Quarterly* 87 (1): 5–30.

Runcie, A. 2016. "Sand Dredging Licenses Secretly Soaring." *Phnom Penh Post*, May 25, 2016.

Sam, R. 2009. "Hun Sen Announces Ban on Sand Exports." *Phnom Penh Post*, May 11, 2009.

Schaart, J. "Mega Reclamations: Opportunities and Challenges." Presented at the CEDA Conference on Dredging and Reclamation, Doha, Qatar, May 2008.

Schoenberger, L. "Winning Back Land in Cambodia: Community Work to Navigate State Land Titling Campaigns and Large Land Deals." Presented at the conference on Land grabbing, Conflict and Agrarian-Environmental Transformations: Perspectives from East and Southeast Asia, Chiang Mai, Thailand, June 2015.

Schoenberger, L. 2017. "Struggling against Excuses: Winning Back Land in Cambodia." *The Journal of Peasant Studies* 44 (4): 870–890.

Schoenberger, L., and A. Beban. 2018. "'They Turn Us into Criminals': Embodiments of Fear in Cambodian Land Grabbing." *Annals of the American Association of Geographers* 108 (5): 1338–1353.

Schoenberger, L., and A. Beban. 2021. "Rupturing Violent Land Imaginaries: Finding Hope through a Land Titling Campaign in Cambodia." *Agriculture and Human Values* 38 (1): 301–312.

Schoenberger, L., D. Hall, and P. Vandergeest. 2017. "What Happened When the Land Grab Came to Southeast Asia?" *The Journal of Peasant Studies* 44 (4): 697–725.

Scoones, I., R. Hall, S. M. Borras, B. White, and W. Wolford. 2013. "The Politics of Evidence: A Response to Rulli and D'Odorico." *Journal of Peasant Studies* 40 (5): 911–912.

Sneddon, C. 2007. "Nature's Materiality and the Circuitous Paths of Accumulation: Dispossession of Freshwater Fisheries in Cambodia." *Antipode* 39 (1): 167–193.

Steinberg, P., and K. Peters. 2015. "Wet Ontologies, Fluid Spaces: Giving Depth to Volume through Oceanic Thinking." *Environment and Planning D: Society and Space* 33 (2): 247–264.

Taing, V., and K. Mom. 2015. "Gov't Clarifies Dredging Scope." *Phnom Penh Post*, January 29, 2015.

Topalović, M. 2014. "Constructed Land: Singapore in the Century of Flattening." In *Constructed land: Singapore 1924–2012*. Edited by U. Hassler and M. Topalović, 51–63. Singapore: ETH Zürich DArch and Future Cities Laboratory.

Un, K., and S. So. 2009. "Politics of Natural Resources Use in Cambodia." *Asian Affairs* 36 (3): 123–138.

Un, K., and S. So. 2011. "Land Rights in Cambodia: How Neopatrimonial Politics Restricts Land Policy Reform." *Pacific Affairs* 84 (2): 289–308.

UNEP (United Nations Environment Program). 2019. *Sand and Sustainability: Finding New Solutions for Environmental Governance of Global Sand Resources*. Geneva, Switzerland: GRID-Geneva, United Nations Environment Programme.

Vong, S. 2009. "Hun Sen Again Calls On Sand Export Ban, Study of Impacts." *Phnom Penh Post*, July 2, 2009.

Wang, W., H. Liu, Y. Li, and J. Su. 2014. "Development and Management of Land Reclamation in China." *Ocean & Coastal Management* 102: 415–425.

7

WASTELAND AND PARADISE GARDEN
Building Soil in the Brazilian Cerrado

Andrew Ofstehage

Ethnographic research with large-scale farmers and ranchers in Brazil entails a lot of riding around in pickups, traveling from field to field.[1] In my research with transnational soybean farmers in the Brazilian Cerrado, long rides in pickups from Luis Eduardo Magalhães to far-afield soybean fields near the escarpment that separates Bahia and Tocantins states afforded generous time to talk about business practices, farming techniques, and challenges of managing massive farms. It also provided space for patient, slow ethnographic conversation that encouraged learning about the everyday ethics of transnational farming that farmers expressed through offhand remarks and casual statements that spoke to their daily framing and interpretation of what was good and bad, valued and worthless, or progress and backwardness.

Early in my research, I accompanied David Hanson on his two-hour drive out to his isolated, 30,000-hectare farm. David migrated to Brazil to start his own soy farm after finding that starting a farm in Illinois was prohibitively expensive and working on the family-owned farm did not satisfy him. After preliminary introductions, explanations of my research, and biographical questions, our conversation moved quickly to focus on David's primary concern: government regulations on land and workers. He complained about the strict protections for worker living conditions on the plantation-like farm and the forest law, which required farmers to set aside 20 percent of their land as native, uncultivated Cerrado forest. Throughout the day, I returned to the topic of his forest reserve. Where is it? What does it look like? Do you and are you allowed to use this land for hunting and fishing? He dismissed these questions until he explained to me that he had never been to his reserve, did not know where it was, and gave it little thought. David's forest reserve, to him, was neither working land nor recreation nor worthy of conservation. David's lack of interest in the vegetation of the Cerrado follows through to his disregard for the soils of the Cerrado, which call for more intensive management than Illinois soils to become productive for industrial agriculture. The soils of the Cerrado require higher rates and more types of fertilizer, need soil amendments to decrease soil acidity, and benefit from the use of no-tillage. While farmers like David rarely think about their tracts of set-aside Cerrado savannah, they put a great deal of thought and work into making Cerrado soils productive for industrial crops.

Soil, the biophysical foundation of agricultural land, is often made invisible in land grab and foreignization processes. Borras Jr. et al. (2012) recognize the difficulty of defining land grabbing and global land grabs due to historical, political-economic, and cultural differences but outline three connected characteristics of current land grabbing. First, following Peluso and Lund (2011), it is essentially "control grabbing," or "grabbing the power to control land and other associated resources such as water in order to derive benefit from such control of resources" (Borras Jr. et al. 2012, 850). This entails a redefinition of land as a productive asset used for profit accumulation, not as a socially, ecologically, or culturally meaningful thing. Following Wolford (2010), they recognize that land is extracted and alienated from local markets and directed to global market production. Thus, the "land grab does not always require expulsion of peasants from their lands; it does not always result in dispossession" (Borras Jr. et al. 2012, 850). It does entail a taking of control over land. Second, land grabs may relate to large-scale land acquisition but also to large-scale capital investment. Third, the current land grab is a capital accumulation, which responds to interconnected food, energy, climate, and financial crises and the rise of middle-income countries in search of reliable or controllable sources of fuel and food. The focus of land grab scholars and activists centers on control, territory, and land but rarely speaks to what happens to the land after it is sold, appropriated, or stolen. Attention to the effect of land grabs on peasant and Indigenous communities, farm workers, and territorial sovereignty is well placed and necessary to understand and confront the consequences of land deals. However, understanding foreign farmers' engagement with soil furthers this engagement by doing two things. First, engaging with soil encounters recognizes land grabs for what they usually are: both a speculative investment (or grab) *and* a productive endeavor (Fairbairn 2020). As an investment property, it may be enough to gain control of land, but to make an investment property into a farm, the land must be made productive for agriculture. Second, by asking how foreign farmers engage with soil through farming practices and narrative discourse, we can better understand the mechanisms by which foreign landowners learn to manage new soils and give meaning to that work. This intervention reminds us that the social lives of land are also the social lives of soil.

David is one of thirty to forty US farmers who have migrated to the Brazilian Cerrado to produce soy, cotton, and corn. They are mostly young, white, unmarried men who had a connection to farming in the US Midwest but did not have land of their own nor enough capital to buy expensive farmland. In search of farming livelihoods, profit, and a little adventure, they toured land in Western Bahia, Brazil. There, they found expanses of flat, productive farmland that cost a fraction of Midwest farmland. They encountered the city of Luis Eduardo Magalhães—once little more than a rest stop and now the Brazilian capital of agribusiness. Luis Eduardo is an island of red, dust-covered concrete and half-finished roads in the center of the Brazilian Cerrado and at the frontier of soy production. US farmers courted investment, mostly from rural neighbors in the United States, and purchased massive tracts of Brazilian farmland. They reside in Luis Eduardo Magalhães, but their community extends to US-owned farms two to three hours away and to their home farming communities in the United States. The farms span from 3,000 to 30,000 hectares and are corporatized in their business structure but often family-owned and managed. The farmers themselves move easily across borders between family and investors in the US and workers and the farm in Brazil, sometimes splitting time between the management of US-based farms and Brazil-based farms. Local farmworkers maintain fields and farms, while farm owners occupy themselves with farm management decisions, paperwork, and management of investors and investments. Their flexible farming communities are transient, adding new hopeful members as others sell their land and return to the US. Landowners trade land as an asset with speculative and productive potential and treat it as a flexible commodity; yet the social and ecological life of the land materializes in surprising ways.

US soybean farmers frame the Cerrado as a wasteland to be redeemed in everyday remarks, investment pitches, and conversation. David's ignorance of his own Cerrado land is instructive of the ethical statements that lie just under the surface of social interaction. Statements made in casual conversation say a great deal about the speaker's worldview and ethical opinions. Yet how do these statements fit within a structure of systematic labeling of land as wasteland fit for development? What is the basis for making claims of value and waste? What is it being made productive for? Who is it being made productive for?

The social lives of land speak to themes of property, territory, and landscape narratives. Yet it cannot escape the material side of land. The biological life of land, including nematodes, rhizomes, and earthworms, sometimes enables plants to access water and nutrients and, at other times, parasitize crops. The physical aspects of land, including soil texture, chemistry, and depth, limit or enable crop production. A socioecological approach to land asks how land, landscapes, and soil are generated out of and in relation to social and material life. In this chapter, I use a socioecological analysis to ask how the "difference as deficit" model marks land with low soil fertility as wasteland. Transnational farmers compare the physical and biological properties of Cerrado soil to those of the US Midwest and find it lacking: soil acidity calls for "correction," low organic matter and soil moisture constrict farmers' use of tillage, and low levels of soil nutrients require additional fertilization. They mobilize this translation of differences into deficit to frame their work as skilled farm work and the land as wasteland in need of improvement and unfit for conservation. Transnational farming in Brazil is a relational process in which farmers do work on soil and soils do work on farmers, but it is also generative. Out of this experience, farmers develop fertilization and tillage practices to address soil differences in Brazil, models of industrial farming, and narratives of progress and waste, scaling up the socioecological life of Cerrado soils to global levels.

Wasteland(scapes)

The construction of land as waste, valued wilderness, or valued farmland shapes land use and guides public policy. Labeling land as neither productive nor worth conserving has significant consequences for land use, waste disposal, extractive industries, and infrastructure development. Mostly, white farmers and settlers have transformed both the Prairie of North America and the grasslands of South America into swaths of soy fields because of perceived suitability for industrial agriculture and unsuitability for anything else. And the farmers have not acted alone but in response to favorable public policies in the US and Brazil that encourage both migration to and cultivation of these grasslands. Labels of waste and value lend authenticity to development and conservation projects and delegitimize resistance. For example, agricultural development and a land rush in the Nacala Corridor of Mozambique are predicated partially on imagined wasteful land use by peasants and the potential of turning wasteland into productive territory (Wolford and Nehring 2015), despite counternarratives by Mozambican farmer organizations that industrial agriculture of the Brazilian Cerrado was the real wasteland. In fact, a member of the Mozambican Rural Association of Mutual Aid commented on his tour of the Brazilian Cerrado: "All we saw, for hundreds of kilometers, was huge soya fields. No farmers, no villages. There are no trees, and there is no animal life because heavy use of pesticides and fertilizers has turned the area into a desert. We were horrified to think that our home could become an empty wasteland like that" (Liberti and Parenti 2018). Landscapes of waste are defined by what they lack. The Cerrado before soy was home to Indigenous communities, highly endemic nonhuman plants and animals, and productive livelihoods suited to the environment; but it lacked a highly capitalized economy, built infrastructure, dense human populations, and high-growth forests like Amazonia. This lack became defined as waste and legitimized broad land use change. The bewildered Mozambican farmer in the Cerrado similarly saw a lack—"no farmers, no villages . . . no trees . . . no animal life"—and defined the soy fields of the Cerrado as wasteland.

Land dispossession often gains authority and legitimacy by delegitimizing current land use. Recently, former President Bolsonaro commented, "Onde tem uma terra indígena, tem uma riqueza embaixo dela. Temos que mudar isso daí" ("Where there is Indigenous land, there is wealth underneath it. We need to change this situation.") (Dolzan 2017). Similarly, as a student of agronomy at a Midwestern land grant college, I read assigned textbooks that told students that American Indians lost their land because they did not use it productively. I heard a strikingly similar comment from a USDA employee at the US Embassy in Brasilia. The financialization of agriculture is not just the abstraction of value and commodification of land but also the valuation of capitalist farm activities and the devaluation of noncapitalistic activities (Ofstehage 2018b).

Land is redefined in relation to new property regimes, erosion, financial investments, crop rotation, and labor regimes. Categories of underutilized, marginal, and "wasteland" enable land investment and development but require a forgetting of labor and life that dwelled there (Li 2014b, 592). Land is a sociomaterial thing that emerges out of human and nonhuman activity and meaning-making; those who control the land often have power over not only land use and access but also narratives of land (Peluso and Lund 2011).

Wasteland is a normative classification given to a defined area, which identifies it as neither productive, nor valuable, nor worthy of conservation. It is defined by landscape appearance, current land use, alleged infertility of soils, or, in some cases, arbitrarily (often as a colonial claim on land). The classification of wasteland discredits current occupants of the land from claims to the land, authorizes land use change, and disregards conservation. As part of the Netherlands East Indies, Sumatra defined a large portion of the region as "wasteland" (woeste land), as it was either jungle or in swidden agriculture and not permanent fields. This classification allowed land distribution and alienation (Stoler 1995, 23). Narratives of the Everglades portray it as "an unpopulated landscape that humans act upon" (Ogden 2011, 2). The Chinese government labels Tibet as a wasteland in reference to labor practices and landscape features. Land without agriculture was regarded by state bureaucrats as empty, and the state policy was to "attack the grasslands" and wage war against the earth (Yeh 2013, 64). Waste in India is "a long-standing, colonial-era label used to mark certain lands as vacant, idle, devalued, or unused and has historically erased the multiple-subsistence land uses of more marginalized, nonpropertied constituents" and is now mobilized by real estate developers to authorize land transfers (Balakrishnan 2021). Grasslands and low-growth forests, like much of the Cerrado, are particularly susceptible to narratives of waste and development (Oliveira and Hecht 2016). The Cerrado, as a wasteland, can be plowed, deforested, and denuded with minimal complaint because, as farmers often reminded me, the Cerrado is not the Amazon. Likewise, the people of the land do not merit protection because their culture, work, and economy have not fostered the kind of economic and agronomic production that is valued and respected. They are either paternalistically taught the agricultural ways of the settlers, removed from the land (forcibly or not), or otherwise marginalized on the landscape.

Narratives of waste and value can be connected to landscape, land use, and soils, yet it can also be a materially arbitrary and racially constructed thing (Voyles 2015). Diné people creatively resist and deconstruct prevailing narratives of Navajo land as toxic sites of waste (Powell 2017). White settler colonialists not only socially constructed the arid landscape of the Southwest as worthless, fit only for savage, violent, backward people, but also restricted shepherding, destroyed peach orchards in a blatant attempt to make it into a wasteland, and discredited and disallowed environmentally appropriate livelihoods. Environmental changes and colonial processes layer on top of each other in what Kyle Powys Whyte calls "vicious sedimentation and insidious loops" (2018). Environmental changes compound over time to impose settler land use, subject Indigenous populations to environmental degradation and risk, and erase, delegitimize, and ignore alternative relationships and uses with the land.

The American Prairie and Brazilian Cerrado share a narrative of conquest, development, and progress. Colonists in each place identified the respective frontier regions with "wilderness, emptiness, the savage, the Indian, the slave, the colonized, the atheist, the heretic, the weak, the backward," while "settled places" were identified as spaces of "civilization, the civilized, the crowded, the urban, the white man, the colonizer, the Christian, the strong, the advanced" (Amado 1990, 53). Yet what survives of the Prairie and the Cerrado is their potential to transform ordinary people into champions of enlightenment, democracy, the nation, and progress (Cronon 1992). This transposition of geography and temporality, connecting the nineteenth-century American Prairie to twenty-first-century

Brazilian Cerrado, allows farmers to embody practices and ideas of development and progress—neither place nor time is essentialized but rather generalized as a process of becoming.

Agricultural development and modernization in the Brazilian Cerrado is a long-held dream of the right-wing *ruralista* (rural caucus) political faction. In his proposed "March to the West," Brazilian president Getulio Vargas hoped to populate and modernize the Cerrado by funding agricultural research, incentivizing agricultural production, and building the marvel of Brasilia in 1937. Later, in 1955, Brazilian President Juscelino Kubitschek Oliveira built upon this, determined to "rationalize agriculture" and to extend the presence and visibility of the Brazilian state into the interior of Brazil, including the Cerrado and Amazonia (which the Brazilian military called "A land without men for men without land") (Oliveira 1955). In the late 1960s, the military government enacted an agrarian development project, POLOCENTRO (*Programa de Desenvolvimento dos Cerrados*), to incorporate the Cerrado into the national economy and to support rural producers through funding for infrastructure development and agricultural research. Concurrently, the government provided loans for land purchases on generous terms through the PROTERRA (*Programa de Redistribuição da Terra*) program (Jepson, Brannstrom, and Filippi 2010). In the 1970s, the Japan International Cooperative Agency (JICA) cooperated with the newly formed Brazilian Agricultural Research Corporation (Embrapa) to implement PRODECER (*Programa de Cooperação Nipo—Brasileiro para o Desenvolvimento dos Cerrado*) to provide financing and technical agronomy research and training to induce Southern Brazilian farmers to migrate to and settle in the Cerrado. Embrapa brought together scientists, technocrats, and investors to adapt Green Revolution practices for Brazil and make the "Miracle of the Cerrado" real (Nehring 2016). Both financial and research inducements drew farmers to "barren land where nothing can grow without neutralizing the soil with a large amount of lime and fertilizer" (Rodrigues 2016, 221). PRODECER had the goal of settling the Cerrado with farmers from the South and making the Cerrado a sacrifice zone to buffer deforestation in the Amazon. In 2015, the Federal Government passed the Agricultural Development Plan for "Matopiba" (the Brazilian States of Maranhão, Tocantins, Piauí, and Bahia) to support the expansion of soybean production in the Cerrado. The plan (decree no. 8447) committed the government to developing infrastructure, supporting agricultural research, and strengthening the rural middle class in the region.

These governmental and intergovernmental programs cannot be understood outside of the context of waste. In an edited volume on the Cerrado and sustainable agriculture (Hosono, Rocha, and Hongo 2016), the President of JICA reminds the reader of the growing global population before writing that "Brazil achieved an epoch-making breakthrough to become a net exporter of grain by converting barren land into one of the most productive agricultural areas in the world" (Tanaka 2016). The volume goes on to argue that this "epoch-making breakthrough" converted the "barren land" (Hosono, Rocha, and Hongo 2016, 6) of the Cerrado into not only a source of local employment and impetus to regional development but even a major factor in national poverty reduction and reduction of global hunger. All this with little environmental destruction and apparently little social displacement. The authors argue that the development of the Cerrado can be "regarded as a sustainable development model" (Hosono, Rocha, and Hongo 2016, 2).

Wasteland Soils

Waste is often ascribed to lands with certain land-use or landscape characteristics, as discussed below. I propose a third determinant of waste: soil quality. Biophysical soil processes (erosion, degradation, salinification, desertification) and properties (organic matter content, pH, clay-silt-sand texture) often escape observation and critique by social scientists, just as soil scientists often disregard political economy, social values, and capital (Engel-Di Mauro 2014). In this chapter, I center on two questions. First, how is soil quality mobilized in narratives of waste, value, and development? And second, how is "good" soil built, both socially and materially? Altogether, I will address how improving and building soils support claims of improvement, waste, and value and redefine both farmer and land.

A socioecological approach to soil asks how capital operates alongside social and ecological processes, sometimes in opposition, other times in conjunction, and often in ambivalent relationships. The mechanisms of capital combine with the character of crops, habits and desires, local and global prices, and droughts, diseases, soil, and other elements (Li 2014a). "*Terra preta do indio*" (black earth of the Indian) in Amazonia, for example, is an assemblage of soil chemistry, the fallout from the US Civil War, pre-Colombian Indigenous populations, and Caboclo communities today (Kawa 2016). Terra preta has a higher pH, more stable organic matter, and a higher concentration of plant-available phosphorous and other nutrients than the predominant soils of the region. This fertile soil is what soil scientists call anthropogenic soil; it was created by human hands. Indigenous communities added biochar to the soil, and this transformed it slowly from red soils with few plant-available nutrients to black soil high in organic matter and plant-available nutrients. Until a *confederado* sugar plantation owner (a US southerner who fled the United States for Brazil after the Civil War) alerted geologists about dark, rich soils peppered with artifacts in the1860s and Canadian geologist Charles Frederick Hartt connected rich soils and pottery to pre-Columbian settlements, Western scientists thought that communities were drawn to the soil, but later found the communities made it. Today, local farmers call farming in the black Amazonia earth *uma batalha* (a battle) in comparison with less fertile red Amazonian soils. Terra preta soils are more fertile, but they also demand greater labor because of increased weed and pest pressure. The common distinction of fertile/infertile or productive/unproductive soil assumes capitalist, productivist farming, and we do not see the same distinction here. Rather, soil becomes burdensome when it is overly fertile and thus attracts unwanted insects and plants and calls for greater labor.

Soil has its own history marked by human interaction, nonhuman species interaction, and millennia of weathering, erosion, and soil creation. Soils, then, do not exist as static, meaningless material but as living, remembering things with histories and memories of destruction, growth, and encounters. Soil has a life beyond taxonomic classification and management prescriptions. Colombian soil scientists commonly refer to Amazonian soils (besides terra preta) as poor and unproductive due to their high acidity, defining them according to their potential for agricultural production. Indigenous communities, however, perceive the same soils as neither static, nor powerless, nor even poor (Lyons 2014). Each collective—soil scientists and Indigenous farming communities—engages with soil. For soil scientists, it is classified as poor soil and considered a deficient means of production in need of improvement. Indigenous farming communities consider an ongoing entanglement of human and nonhuman actors as something to be engaged with but not necessarily improved. Progressive, productivist, and linear perspectives of soils fail to understand the roles of rest, relations with human and nonhuman actors, and the vitality of soil (Bellacasa 2015).

Soil surveys impose an abstract epistemology on land to remove people and practices and reinscribe it as land to be quantified and improved (Van Sant 2018). Claims of generic soil quality refer to the ability of the soil to grow predominant regional cash crops in monoculture and ignore societal and ecological difference factors, such as soil's role in supporting ecological life (noncash crop life). A diversity of soil classification systems coexist, most created by the state, but local, Indigenous-designed classification systems also exist. For example, a Purhépecha community in Central Mexico has developed a hierarchal soil schema based on soil as a living body composed of earth material, organic matter, and living organisms. While their soil maps mirrored USDA soil taxonomy maps, they differed in flexibility to allow for changing social and environmental contexts (Barrera-Bassols, Zinck, and Van Ranst 2006). In many cases, differences in soil are read as deficit or deficiency. State classification schemes are a kind of state discourse on value, which prioritizes fertility that supports certain cash crop production. Soil, its generation, and its generativity play an active role in the material and social life of wastelands.

Those who label the Cerrado as a wasteland do so because of its aboveground attributes—aesthetics, land use, biological life—but also of its toxic, infertile soils below the ground. Improving the soil and making it productive for industrial agriculture transforms the land into productive land, gives value to farm work, and marks farmers as skilled. Aesthetic, aboveground attributes are easily debunked as subjective—no inherent value of landscape, land use, biological life—and soil is less easily dismissed. Certain attributes make row crop agriculture difficult or impossible; land value (in terms of exchange value and use value) is more or less an expression of this fertility, as are soil surveys, but we can question if this is the only measure of soil health or soil quality. Improving soil requires hard, patient work and allows farmers to claim material improvement, expertise, and legitimacy. Material qualities of soil and physical work make row-crop production possible and give meaning to claims of improvement and value (of land and farmer). Soils are made by chains dragging through trees and adding minerals and nutrients from

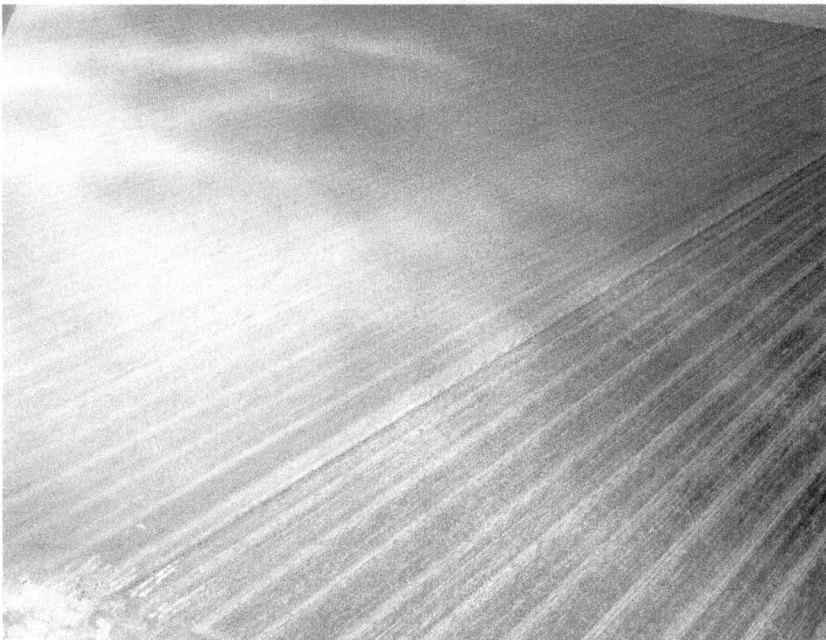

FIGURE 7.1.   A Cerrado field with its straight rows of plantation.

Photo by Andrew Ofstehage.

FIGURE 7.2. A Cerrado field.

Photo by Andrew Ofstehage.

near and far, but also through discursive moves that describe the transformation of toxic, infertile land into soil "apt for agribusiness."

Concerns with degradation are well supported in political ecology literature and foundational Marxist texts, but the theme of improvement of soils is often overlooked. Marx noted in *Capital* that "all progress in capitalistic agriculture is a progress in the art, not only of robbing the labourer, but of robbing the soil; all progress in increasing the fertility of the soil for a given time, is a progress towards ruining the lasting sources of that fertility" (Marx and Engels 1978, 416–417). Blaikie built on this tradition by connecting relations of power to relations between soil and ecosystems (Blaikie 1985). Yet Engel-Di Mauro argues that limiting analysis to human-induced degradation loses sight of both natural causes of degradation and of social and ecological processes of making soil. One community's degradation is another's improvement. In this chapter, I show how making "good soil" is an essential part of the process of development storytelling.

Making, Building, and Improving the Cerrado Soil

The "Miracle of the Cerrado" is a tried and true model of "making deserts bloom" to reduce world hunger (*Economist* 2016) by using intensive farming techniques without government subsidy or deforesting (not counting, of course, the Cerrado itself) for, "the great expansion of farmland [in the Cerrado] has taken place 1,000 km from the jungle [The Amazon]" (*Economist* 2010). Improving Cerrado soils was driven in part by the "March to the West" and in part by the need to find (or create) productive agricultural land in the wake of land inaccessibility and land degradation in the south of Brazil where farmers had denuded the land with minimal fertilization and care (Haesbaert 1998; Silva 2018, 426). But how were Cerrado soils, in fact, made productive for industrial agriculture? Soil constitutes a rich medium for sociomaterial cocreation of land. Soil is made up of minerals, water, air, living biota, and organic matter; it is also produced through human activity, given meaning by farmers, soil scientists, and extension agents, and deeply affects the ways farmers do agriculture. It is cocreative both physically and socially. It is produced by and produces tillers of the soil; it gives meaning to and is given meaning by farming; and it is creative of new techniques, skills, and models of farming.

A North American farm tour operator describes the Cerrado as a "vast wasteland" and "literally an inaccessible, useless wasteland [. . .] isolated from the rest of Brazil by lack of roads or other modern transport access." But the Cerrado is defined by more than its accessibility for outsiders and industrial agriculture. Cerrado landscape and soil are both diverse and dynamic; it includes dense stands of small trees (campo Cerrado), shorter, less dense stands of trees (campo sujo), and low bunch grass with widely spaced, dwarfed trees (campo limpo). In his 1956 dissertation, Reeshon Feuer identified 40 percent of soil in the federal district of Brasilia (in the center of the Cerrado) to be latasols of "excellent physical properties for agricultural crops, but reaction and nutrient status is often unfavorable." Cropping, he argued, was "not possible on the scrub-savanna uplands under a continuous cropping type of soil management, involving existing technique and management." Yet moderate yields would be possible with "use of rotations, mulches, cover crops, animal manures, and small amounts of industrial materials," while excellent yields would be possible on all latasols with "full use of scientific soil and crop management principles, machinery, and industrial materials" (Feuer 1956, 349). While outlining the same issues with Cerrado soils as other soil scientists, Feuer is unique in outlining them in relation to various types of land use.

Archeological evidence reveals a long history of thriving Xavante and Xevente communities in the region (Klink and Moreira 2002), and contemporary Indigenous communities celebrate the beauty of the Cerrado and identify a plenitude of nonindustrial, agricultural uses of the land (Miller 2019). But the vision of the Cerrado as a wasteland is not unique to foreign farmers, scientific experts, and short-sighted politicians in Brasilia. Schoolchildren in Brasilia espoused low identification with the region and little appreciation for the region's natural landscape. Though children with greater exposure to the Cerrado showed greater affinity, many echoed farmers and soil scientists in calling it ugly and empty (Bizerril 2004). Students in Barreiras, Brazil, represented the Cerrado in drawings as nonhuman spaces (with some exceptions in the past), stereotyped occupation (conflict, confrontation, degradation, people versus land), and futures of urbanization and desertification (Rigonato 2013).

Midwestern farmers have easily inserted themselves into the Cerrado. Agricultural practices have been easy to manage. One farmer recounted thinking the biggest challenge of farming would be learning plant names, insect names, and best practices, "but that's easy. You have crop scouts, agronomists, managers, and farmworkers that know everything here and tell you all you need to know, know how to operate machinery. The most important thing is city work—paperwork, legalese, culture. You need a good scout, a couple tractors, a couple good tractor drivers, and everything else is easy." Farmers hire out farm labor, live in towns far from their farms, and know little of their reserve Cerrado land, but they have strong opinions of it nonetheless.

The clearing of land and soil "development" (preparing land for soy cultivation) was not as easy. A father of an Iowa farmer in Western Bahia (also CEO of the farm company) said his first impression of the Cerrado was that it was "not much besides ten-foot trees and grassland," yet nearby limestone quarry for pH amendments, a necessary addition because "there was no fertility . . . soil profile goes down 100 feet deep." While he found the scope and scale of agriculture there impressive, he found the Cerrado itself worthless without amendments and "improvement." Farmers, investors, and farm tourists alike describe clearing ten-foot-tall trees in romantic terms. A tour guide for US agronomy students, prospective farmers, and investors in Brazil explained to me that one of the favorites for US farmers is the cutting of trees and watching them fall. Sitting in on this process was quite a difficult task for the tour guide because farmers are resistant to letting in others and are secretive, but most agricultural tourists consider it a mandatory tour stop.

Despite distinguishing themselves as serious, business-centered farmers, they still romanticized land clearing. A farmer described his clearing process and excitedly explained, "I don't know, where do I start!? When you're opening Cerrado, anytime you're opening new ground, it's like a hundred years ago in the Midwest, United States, or several hundreds of years ago in Europe or now in Brazil; you're gonna find different things. Number one, when you're opening land and it's full of trees, I don't know what's going on, on a 10,000-hectare farm, before you open it up you can't, sometimes there's pieces of ground you don't expect, root structures are something that you come across, that was a big problem for us." In his excitement, he told a clear story of the Cerrado soil, of transformation from rooty wilderness to developed land that resembles Midwestern and European farmland.

When this farmer arrived in Brazil, "there was no infrastructure," and it was "very primitive." It was an adventure, and land clearing represented a chance to transform the primitive. There are always surprises when you clear land—you never know what the topography or texture of the land is like until you remove the trees. Once the trees were removed, farmers were left with an unfamiliar and infamously poor soil to improve.

The dominant soils of the Cerrado are latosols (oxisols in USDA soil taxonomy and Ferralsols in the World Reference Base for Soil Resources). Latosols are defined by Embrapa as soils in an advanced stage of weathering and "*virtualmente destituidos*" ("virtually destitute") of primary and secondary minerals (Embrapa 2013, 93). Latosols are suited for mechanization due to the physical characteristics of the soil, have high water permeability, poor chemical characteristics, and are "apt for agribusiness" (Sano et al. 2007). They are generally well-drained soils and extremely deep; the topsoil rarely measures less than a meter, and there is little distinction between soil layers. They are strongly acidic (Embrapa 2013). Latosols are formed by the removal of silica and bases by weathering. Generally, they are soils with "*grandes problemas de fertilidade*" ("major fertility problems") (Sousa and Lobato 2004, 43). Limiting factors of latosols are low fertility, susceptibility to erosion, and low soil organic matter. Embrapa advises farmers to "correct" the soil with respect to acidity, aluminum saturation, and low fertility, to keep the soil covered (especially at the beginning of the rainy season), and to use conservation practices, such as *plantio direto* (direct planting, zero tillage, or no-tillage) whenever possible (Sousa and Lobato 2004). Measures to conserve land, such as no-tillage, and forest reserves were, much like American farmers' common perceptions of conservation on the Great Plains (VanWinkle and Friedman 2017), motivated by lower production costs and soil quality (Kawa 2021) more than stewardship in its own right.

Cerrado soils have very low levels of phosphorus and a low pH associated with high levels of aluminum toxicity (Kiihl and Calvo 2008). Embrapa found that fertilizing with high levels of lime ($CaCO3$) could "correct" the pH of the soils, and high levels of phosphorous fertilizers drastically increase soil productivity. Inoculation of Cerrado soils with *Bradyrhizobium* allowed biological nitrogen fixation by soybean plants to eliminate necessary nitrogen fertilization (Alves, Boddey, and Urquiaga 2003). Further, no-tillage soy production (production without the use of field cultivation) became widely adopted by farmers to maintain soil moisture, reduce soil erosion, and reduce production costs (Kiihl and Calvo 2008). No-tillage farming in the Cerrado has resulted in both increasing carbon stocks in the soil (increased organic matter that aids in increasing water-carrying capacity, among other things) and increasing soil microbial life (Green et al. 2007) compared to conventional tillage. While fertilization and tillage practices increased soil productivity, Brazilian soybean yields increased by 54kg/ha per year from 1984 to 2005, due primarily to improvements in hybrid seeds developed for the low latitudes and high acidity of the Cerrado and resistant to plant diseases and pests (Almeida et al. 1999). More recently, Brazil has allowed the planting of GMO seeds and Monsanto's RoundUp Ready soybean seeds, and Bt Cotton seeds have become commonplace (Motta 2016). This, along with no-tillage practices, has further encouraged the use of pesticides as the primary form of pest management.

Sanchez places the improvement of Cerrado soils as part of the first major improvement of tropical soils. He writes that "the area was thinly populated with extensive cattle growing and was supposed to be useless but became highly productive and, in thirty years, increased the area of production by 58 million hectares, doubled average crop yields, and quadrupled total grain production" (Sanchez 2019). What makes the first major improvements in tropical soils unique is that they overcome soil constraints through the application of fertilizers, soil amendments, and irrigation to meet crop requirements. Temperate region-educated agronomists modified western farming practices for the tropics and considered only the production function of soils while paying less attention to other ecosystem functions. Fertilizer research concentrated on nutrient uptake by crops, and little attention was paid to the fate of nutrients in soil and their loss to groundwater or the atmosphere (Sanchez 2019). This model is what I call the "difference as deficit" model, in which the difference between soils of North America and Europe and soils of the Global South are described not in terms of difference but in terms of lack or deficit. The solution, once soil is analyzed, is to build, develop, and improve the soil to bring it in line with the physical properties of temperate soils. The goal is to make these soils productive for industrially produced cash crops.

Farming is easy for transnational farmers in Brazil. They hire agronomists and managers to advise and direct the work and farmworkers to do the work, but they recognize that developing the land is hard work (Ofstehage 2016, 2019). Jacob Miller explained:

> We didn't realize at the time how much it took to really develop the properties and it, it takes years, it's not even a matter of just adding fertilizer, it takes years to build up the fertility and soils and, and build'em up to the point where you produce optimal yields so we kinda learned about that the hard way. But, you know there's a benefit to that though, 'cause if it's newer ground or raw land it sells, the value of it is a lot less, so it sells at a lot lower price so a lot of the value of the land could be dictated by how old it is or what it could produce so that's a . . . I guess you have to weigh those.

After clearing the land, farmers add large amounts of lime and gypsum the first year and then supplement with phosphate, potash, magnesium, nitrogen, and lime thereafter. They also integrate no-tillage cultivation, which minimizes or eliminates tillage in fields to conserve soil moisture and increase organic matter in Cerrado soils (Ofstehage and Nehring 2021). This means more attention to soil testing, an understanding of controlling fungal plant diseases, and an agronomically and economically informed approach to insect pest management. One US farmer similarly described a process of learning, not imposition:

> A lot of guys who come here, I've seen them come and go. They think they're going to bring the United States to Brazil. That doesn't work. What you've got to do is do a little bit of both. You've got to get a guy who knows what he doesn't know and nothing else. You bring your know-how because you can't get too far on the other side. You can't be too much saying, "Well, I know more than the other guy," and just farm the way you want to because there are things here that are different that you need to learn. On the other hand, you can't get too far on the other side saying, "I need to learn from the Brazilians," because a lot of the Brazilians that are doing this are learning, too. Agriculture in this place is different than Paraná. It's different than Rio Grande do Sul, and it's even different than Mato Grosso. Bahia has its own little characteristics you need to learn just like I'm sure Iowa does or Nebraska does or South Dakota does.

This farmer and his father, as well as many American farmers, had arrived in Brazil with agronomic, business, and life plans, but they found that they had to adapt to the realities of farming in Brazil, or return to the US unsuccessfully. When they arrived, they "realized pretty quick there is no way that's going to happen." "We completely changed what we were thinking. And I have no regrets, but you've got to learn."

Another farmer in nearby Tocantins recognized the need to adapt to the way Brazilians farm and to adapt to the Cerrado. He listed micronutrient fertilization, pH management, and fungicide application as practices he had adopted in order to adjust to the complications of farming in Brazil and to the "weakness" of the soils:

> It's a lot more difficult to farm there. The level of technology that is applied at the agronomic level is much higher in terms of just balancing the soil [pH], micronutrients, and then we're doing multiple applications of chemical, of fungicide. We're doing foliar fertilization. We're doing stuff that here the top-end guys are experimenting with, and it's a fact of business in Brazil that you have to do it . . . Here, the soils are so weak that you have to spoon-feed the soil. You can't afford to just throw fertilizer on it. And then you're dealing with issues of fungicide, so it's a lot more complicated to farm there . . . In terms of agronomics, honestly I don't really think that I bring much to the table there. I rely on our agronomist to tell me what he thinks we should do and my overall knowledge of agriculture just to say, "yeah, that makes sense."

Comparatively, Midwestern row-crop farms often only fertilize with nitrogen, phosphate, and potassium and are just now transitioning towards minimal tillage.

> [In Illinois] you can almost skip applying fertilizer for a year, whereas down there you literally can't. There are severe limitations: the areas with new soil. There's an area where we took out a new pasture, and the fertilizer bander got clogged up, and so fertilizer wasn't applied in spots. Where the fertilizer skipped, the plants were four to five feet off the ground, and the other plants were one to two feet tall. The newer the soil, the more you have to add fertilizer. You're talking about 440 kilos per hectare, moving a lot of products and tendering a lot of products.

Soil quality is recognized as good when it supports organisms above- and belowground, processes exchanges of matter, and provides habitat; yet the exact balance between above- and belowground processes leads to different concepts of soil quality. Engel-De Mauro defines soil quality as "the extent to which a soil, with given intrinsic properties, nonhuman organisms, and relative degree of human alterations, enables the fulfillment of survival needs of every human being, understood both biophysically and socially (Engel-Di Mauro 2014, 57). Yet a productivist might define soil quality in relation to how well it supports specific cash crops in conjunction with industrial inputs. An ecological definition might focus on how well soil supports endemic and indigenous species of plants, animals, fungi, and insects. The distinction between fertile and infertile is based on the production of certain cash crops, not a reference to the overall health or quality of the soil. Regardless of whether the soil supports certain ecologies or livelihoods, it is called infertile if it does not support industrial agriculture. Even if it is made to be productive, it is still viewed as inferior and in need of redemption. This distinction allows farmers to claim that their practices are again improving the land and gives them firmer ground from which to claim so. It even allows them to claim they are caring for it, that the land is "in need of care."

This skill gained in learning to develop, build, and construct soil changes the soil; it also changes the farmer. Many spoke of their eventual return to the United States after they could afford to purchase land or take over their family's farm. I would ask about what practices they would bring back, and many focused on business practices of hiring for work, focusing on the managerial aspect of farming, and keeping tidy records of accounting and business transactions. Others also brought up soil management techniques they gained in Brazil. The fickle and needy soils of the Cerrado had taught them the need for consistent soil testing, extensive fertilizer applications, minimizing tillage, and keeping track of pH levels of the soil. This reminds us that the soil is also doing work on farmers.

Waste is built on social and material life and has social and material consequences, and soil is also social and material, not to be lost sight of in discussions of land (Kawa 2016). Industrial agriculture in the Cerrado is not just erasure but generative of new meanings and relationships (Ofstehage 2018a). The soil takes on different characteristics and meanings, and the farmer becomes a new subject (pioneer, business farmer, transnational farmer, and expert soil manager) with new skills, identity, expertise, and relationships (Cordeiro 2018).

Farmers frame the Cerrado as wasteland to minimize destruction (for *this* is not the Amazon, and *this* does not count as deforestation), legitimize their authority (they are there to build the soils, create jobs, and improve the region), and impress potential investors, the Brazilian public, and the American public. Wastelanding is purposeful, not disinterested. It is based strategically on material reality (landscape, economy, and soil), but this is best described as an identification of difference. That difference then needs to be mobilized by discourse and/or violent action.

The Cerrado is named wasteland based on the appearance of the land and vegetation but also its lack of infrastructure and farm fields. The landscape, according to transnational farmers, is not beautiful or worthy of protection like the Amazon. This allows them to claim improvement (Li 2007) without destruction.

In reminding me that it is not the Amazon, they declare two positions. First, that they recognize the value of conserving the Amazon, and second, that the Cerrado is not similarly valued. Because, as they say, there was nothing here before (in terms of recognizably valuable natural space, built environment, or recognizably valuable livelihoods), they provide space to complain about the forest law because it is only protecting ugly, twisted, stunted trees.

Soil difference is normal in all agroecologies. No fields are homogeneous, and no soil is the same, but these differences can be masked in many cases. Soy production in Argentina, for example, can be done "by email" using agrochemicals, genetically modified crops, and hierarchically structured workforces (Lapegna 2016). But when these differences cannot be ignored, as in the case of the Cerrado soils managed by young farmers raised on dark soils of Illinois, Iowa, and Indiana, farmers are tasked with making sense of the difference and making do with the difference. Farmers, in this case, respond by adopting new soil management techniques but also by building narratives involving infertile wasteland and pioneering farmers. These wasteland "stories" (Morris 2021) mobilize the material realities of soil as matters of progress and development.

NOTES

1. This research would not have been possible without generous funding from the Wenner-Gren Foundation, Fulbright IIE, and the UNC-CH Graduate School. I thank the participants of the Social Life of Land Workshop, the members of the Wendy Wolford writing lab, and Wendy Wolford herself for comments and critique of earlier versions of this paper, and the coeditors of the Cornell Series on Land that organized this volume.

REFERENCES

Almeida, L. de, R. Kiihl, M. Miranda, and G. Campelo. 1999. "Melhoramento da soja para regiões de baixas latitudes." In *Recursos Genéticos e Melhoramento de Plantas para o Nordeste Brasileiro*. Edited by M. A. de Queiroz, C. O. Goedert, and S. R. R. Ramos. Mimeo, Brazil: Embrapa

Alves, B. J. R., R. M. Boddey, and S. Urquiaga. 2003. "The Success of BNF in Soybean in Brazil." *Plant and Soil* 252 (1): 1–9.

Amado, Janaina, Walter Nugent and Warren Dean. 1990. "The Frontier in Comparative Perspective: The United States and Brazil." Working Paper No. 188 of the Latin American Program of the Woodrow Wilson International Center for Scholars. Washington, DC: Latin American Program of the Woodrow Wilson International Center for Scholars.

Balakrishnan, S. 2021. "Narratives of Waste: The Fictions and Frictions of Land Commodification in Liberalizing India." In *Land Fictions*, 104–123. Ithaca: Cornell University Press.

Barrera-Bassols, N., J. A. Zinck, and E. Van Ranst. 2006. "Local Soil Classification and Comparison of Indigenous and Technical Soil Maps in a Mesoamerican

Community Using Spatial Analysis." *Geoderma* 135 (November): 140–162. https://doi.org/10.1016/j.geoderma.2005.11.010.

Bellacasa, M. P. de la. 2015. "Making Time for Soil: Technoscientific Futurity and the Pace of Care." *Social Studies of Science* 45 (5): 691–716.

Bizerril, M. X. A. 2004. "Children's Perceptions of Brazilian Cerrado Landscapes and Biodiversity." *The Journal of Environmental Education* 35 (4): 47–58.

Blaikie, P. M. 1985. *The Political Economy of Soil Erosion in Developing Countries.* London, UK: Longman.

Borras Jr., S. M., J. C. Franco, S. Gómez, C. Kay, and M. Spoor. 2012. "Land Grabbing in Latin America and the Caribbean." *Journal of Peasant Studies* 39 (3–4): 845–872.

Cordeiro, M. S. S. 2018. "Pioneiros, Fundadores e Aventureiros—a Ocupação de Terras em Rondônia." *Revista de Antropologia* 61 (1): 125–146. https://doi.org/10.11606/2179-0892.ra.2018.145519.

Cronon, B. 1992. "A Place for Stories: Nature, History, and Narrative." *The Journal of American History* 78 (4): 1347–1376.

Dolzan, M. 2017. "'Não podemos abrir as portas para todo mundo', diz Bolsonaro em palestra na Hebraica." *Estadão*, April 3, 2017. https://politica.estadao.com.br/noticias/geral,nao-podemos-abrir-as-portas-para-todo-mundo-diz-bolsonaro-em-palestra-na-hebraica,70001725522.

Economist. 2010. "The Miracle of the Cerrado." August 26, 2010. http://www.economist.com/node/16886442.

Economist. 2016. "Feeding the Ten Billion; Agricultural Technology." June 9, 2016. https://www.economist.com/leaders/2016/06/09/feeding-the-ten-billion.

Engel-Di Mauro, S. 2014. *Ecology, Soils, and the Left: An Ecosocial Approach.* New York: Palgrave Macmillan.

Fairbairn, M. 2020. *Fields of Gold: Financing the Global Land Rush.* Ithaca: Cornell University Press.

Feuer, R. 1956. *An Exploratory Investigation of the Soils and Agricultural Potential of the Soils of the Future Federal District in the Central Plateau of Brazil.* Ithaca: Cornell University.

Green, V. S., D. E. Stott, J. C. Cruz, and N. Curi. 2007. "Tillage Impacts on Soil Biological Activity and Aggregation in a Brazilian Cerrado Oxisol." *Soil and Tillage Research* 92 (1–2): 114–121.

Haesbaert, R. 1998. "A noção de rede regional: Reflexões a partir da migração 'gaúcha' no Brasil." *Revista Território* 3 (4): 55–71.

Hosono, A., C. M. C. da Rocha, and Y. Hongo. 2016. *Development for Sustainable Agriculture: The Brazilian Cerrado.* New York: Springer.

Jepson, W., C. Brannstrom, and A. Filippi. 2010. "Access Regimes and Regional Land Change in the Brazilian Cerrado, 1972–2002." *Annals of the Association of American Geographers* 100 (1): 87–111.

Kawa, N. C. 2016. *Amazonia in the Anthropocene: People, Soils, Plants, Forests.* Austin: University of Texas Press.

Kawa, N. C. 2021. "A 'Win-Win' for Soil Conservation? How Indiana Row-Crop Farmers Perceive the Benefits (and Trade-Offs) of No-Till Agriculture." *Culture, Agriculture, Food and Environment* 43 (1): 25–35. https://doi.org/10.1111/cuag.12264.

Kiihl, R., and E. Calvo. 2008. "A soja no Brasil: Mais de 100 anos de história, quatro décadas de sucesso." In *Agricultura Tropical: Quatro Décadas de Inovações Tecnológicas, Institucionais e Políticas, Ed. by A. Albuquerque and A. Silva, Embrapa Tecnologia Da Informação.* Edited by A. C. S. Albuquerque and A. G. da Silva. Brasilia, DF: Embrapa.

Klink, C. A., and A. G. Moreira. 2002. "Past and Current Human Occupation, and Land Use." In *The Cerrados of Brazil: Ecology and Natural History of a Neotropical Savanna*. Edited by P. S. Oliveira and R. J. Marquis, 69–88. New York: Columbia University Press.

Lapegna, P. 2016. *Soybeans and Power: Genetically Modified Crops, Environmental Politics, and Social Movements in Argentina*. Oxford: Oxford University Press.

Li, T. M. 2007. *The Will to Improve: Governmentality, Development, and the Practice of Politics*. Durham, NC: Duke University Press Books.

Li, T. M. 2014a. *Land's End: Capitalist Relations on an Indigenous Frontier*. Durham, NC: Duke University Press.

Li, T. M. 2014b. "What Is Land? Assembling a Resource for Global Investment." *Transactions of the Institute of British Geographers* 39 (4): 589–602.

Liberti, S., and E. Parenti. 2018. "Mozambique Won't Be Mato Grosso." *Le Monde Diplomatique*, June 7, 2018. https://mondediplo.com/2018/06/14mozambique.

Lyons, K. M. 2014. "Soil Science, Development, and the 'Elusive Nature' of Colombia's Amazonian Plains." *The Journal of Latin American and Caribbean Anthropology* 19 (2): 212–236.

Marx, K., and F. Engels. 1978. *The Marx-Engels Reader*. Edited by R. C. Tucker. New York: W. W. Norton & Company.

Miller, T. L. 2019. *Plant Kin: A Multispecies Ethnography in Indigenous Brazil*. Austin: University of Texas Press.

Morris, M. L. 2021. "Ground Fictions: Soil, Property, and Markets in the Colombian Conflict." In *Land Fictions*, 86–103. Ithaca: Cornell University Press.

Motta, R. 2016. "Global Capitalism and the Nation State in the Struggles over GM Crops in Brazil." *Journal of Agrarian Change* 16 (4): 720–727.

Nehring, R. 2016. "Yield of Dreams: Marching West and the Politics of Scientific Knowledge in the Brazilian Agricultural Research Corporation (Embrapa)." *Geoforum* 77 (December): 206–217.

Ofstehage, A. 2016. "Farming Is Easy, Becoming Brazilian Is Hard: North American Soy Farmers' Social Values of Production, Work and Land in Soylandia." *The Journal of Peasant Studies* 43 (2): 442–460.

Ofstehage, A. 2018a. "Farming out of Place: Transnational Family Farmers, Flexible Farming, and the Rupture of Rural Life in Bahia, Brazil." *American Ethnologist* 45 (3): 317–329.

Ofstehage, A. 2018b. "Financialization of Work, Value, and Social Organization among Transnational Soy Farmers in the Brazilian Cerrado." *Economic Anthropology* 5 (2): 274–285.

Ofstehage, A. 2019. "Transmission of the Brazil Model of Industrial Soybean Production: A Comparative Study of Two Migrant Farming Communities in the Brazilian Cerrado." In *In Defense of Farmers: The Future of Agriculture in the Shadow of Corporate Power*. Edited by J. W. Gibson and S. Alexander, 289–324. Lincoln: University of Nebraska Press.

Ofstehage, A., and R. Nehring. 2021. "No-till Agriculture and the Deception of Sustainability in Brazil." *International Journal of Agricultural Sustainability* 19 (3–4): 335–348.

Ogden, L. A. 2011. *Swamplife: People, Gators, and Mangroves Entangled in the Everglades*. Minneapolis: University of Minnesota Press.

Oliveira, G., and S. Hecht. 2016. "Sacred Groves, Sacrifice Zones and Soy Production: Globalization, Intensification and Neo-Nature in South America." *The Journal of Peasant Studies* 43 (2): 251–285.

Oliveira, J. K. 1955. *Diretrizes gerais do plano nacional de desenvolvimento.* Belo Horizonte: Livraria Oscar Nicolai.

Peluso, N. L., and C. Lund. 2011. "New Frontiers of Land Control: Introduction." *Journal of Peasant Studies* 38 (4): 667–681.

Powell, D. E. 2017. *Landscapes of Power: Politics of Energy in the Navajo Nation.* Durham, NC: Duke University Press.

Rigonato, V. D. 2013. "As representações sociais dos cerrados: Um estudo de caso no colégio Alexandre Leal Costa, no oeste da Bahia." *Boletim Goiano de Geografia* 33 (2): 239–258.

Rodrigues, R. 2016. "PRODECER: An Innovative International Cooperation Program." In *Development for Sustainable Agriculture*, 220–234. New York: Springer.

Sanchez, P. A. 2019. *Properties and Management of Soils in the Tropics.* Cambridge, UK: Cambridge University Press.

Sano, E. E., L. A. Dambrós, G. C. Oliveira, and R. S. Brites. 2007. "Padrões de Cobertura de Solos Do Estado de Goiás." In *A Encruzilhada Socioambiental–Biodiversidade, Economia e Sustentabilidade No Cerrado.* Edited by L. G. Ferreira Jr., 85–100. Goiânia: Editora UFG.

Santos, H. G. dos, et al. Embrapa. *Sistema Brasileiro de Classificação de Solos, 3a Edição.* 3rd ed. Brasilia, DF: Embrapa, 2013

Silva, C. M. da. 2018. "Entre Fênix e Ceres: A Grande Aceleração e a Fronteira Agrícola No Cerrado." *Varia Historia* 34 (65): 409–444.

Sousa, D. M. G. de, and E. Lobato, eds. 2004. *Cerrado: Correção Do Solo e Adubação.* Planaltina: Embrapa.

Stoler, A. L. 1995. *Capitalism and Confrontation in Sumatra's Plantation Belt, 1870–1979.* Ann Arbor: University of Michigan Press.

Tanaka, A. 2016. "Foreword." In *Development for Sustainable Agriculture: The Brazilian Cerrado*, 10–11. New York: Palgrave Macmillan.

Van Sant, L. 2018. "'The Long-Time Requirements of the Nation': The US Cooperative Soil Survey and the Political Ecologies of Improvement." *Antipode* 53 (3): 686–704. https://doi.org/10.1111/anti.12460.

VanWinkle, T. N., and J. R. Friedman. 2017. "What's Good for the Soil Is Good for the Soul: Scientific Farming, Environmental Subjectivities, and the Ethics of Stewardship in Southwestern Oklahoma." *Agriculture and Human Values* 34 (3): 607–618. https://doi.org/10.1007/s10460-016-9750-z.

Voyles, T. 2015. *Wastelanding: Legacies of Uranium Mining in Navajo Country.* Minneapolis: University of Minnesota Press.

Whyte, K. 2018. *Settler Colonialism, Ecology, and Environmental Injustice.* Oxford, NY: Berghahn Journals.

Wolford, W. 2010. *This Land Is Ours Now: Social Mobilization and the Meanings of Land in Brazil.* Durham, NC: Duke University Press.

Wolford, W., and R. Nehring. 2015. "Constructing Parallels: Brazilian Expertise and the Commodification of Land, Labour and Money in Mozambique." *Canadian Journal of Development Studies/Revue Canadienne d'études Du Développement* 36 (2): 208–223.

Yeh, E. T. 2013. *Taming Tibet: Landscape Transformation and the Gift of Chinese Development.* Ithaca: Cornell University Press.

8

MOBILE LABOR, SHIFTING LAND REGIMES, AND SOCIAL REPRODUCTION IN EAST JAVA, INDONESIA

Nancy Lee Peluso

Migrations from villages were not a very rare thing in Java. Even the *sikep* [land-holding villagers] had trouble retaining a large number of *numpang* [dependent workers], since they could easily apply for opening land. There was under Mataram [Kingdom], after all, a relative shortage of labor.

—Ong Hok Ham, 1975, emphasis added

This has always been a place of people coming and going.

—Paing, small farmer, founder's grandchild, interview in Jambuok, 2019

Cece secured a job as a domestic worker in Hong Kong in 2000 and left behind her natal and extended families on a montane tea plantation in East Java, Indonesia. Like other worker families in rural Java, hers was still feeling the effects of the 1997 Asian Economic Crisis: economic slowdowns, violence in cities and the forests, and the postponing of urban construction projects (Breman and Wiradi 2002; White and Boomgaard 2016). Starting her first two-year contract, Cece had no idea that she would be in Hong Kong for another eighteen years, returning only five times, a few weeks at a time between contracts. Her work as a babysitter and housekeeper enabled her husband Wijoyo to buy a small plot of village land, construct a house, and move their little family off the plantation. Remittances she sent also helped pay their considerable debts, put their two children through high school and college, acquire and maintain forest land for growing fodder, and subsidize daily household expenses while Wiyono grew a stable of dairy cows. Cece's wages helped her two siblings and her parents to move off Java and resettle in Sulawesi and Kalimantan, where they acquired plots of land that would eventually be titled. When Cece's parents returned to the tea plantation to care for her ailing maternal grandmother, Cece paid their way. Though all these family members worked where they lived, mobilities and the income from these had shaped their everyday lives, work, and livelihoods: their means of social reproduction.

Born into a long line of landless plantation workers dependent on the tea plantation for basic shelter and work, Cece's work in Hong Kong for eighteen years enabled her entire natal family to move off the plantation. Her nuclear family could buy a small plot of village land on which Wiyono built a house. Cece's friend, Tini, had worked for twelve of the previous eighteen years in Hong Kong before returning home for good in 2018. Like Cece, Tini was born on a tea plantation, descended from several generations of mobile laborers without formal rights to land, and married a man born in the forest plantation to which her parents had moved when she was a child. The two women's older daughters worked transnationally or in Tulung Agung city; both women's incomes helped buy small plots of urban or rural land to build homes. Their mobilities as laborers have further enabled the social reproduction of their families.

Land-labor relations, as well as the three land regimes discussed here—agricultural plantations, forest plantations, and private or village land—have long been central to studies of agrarian change in Java, Indonesia, and the nation's colonial predecessor, the Netherlands East Indies.[1] Although numerous available studies and reports attest to the mobility of Java's rural populations, past and present, the implications of such mobility, particularly among landless laborers of late, have less often been explored. In a recent paper, Gidwani and Ramamurthy (2018) examined the mobilities of women of two different castes in India, demonstrating how labor migration from rural to urban worksites has generated new means of social reproduction for what they call semiproletarian families. Cece and Tini's stories demonstrate how the transnational migration of plantation workers and their family members has contributed to economic changes, agrarian practices, and their families' social reproduction and well-being. This chapter thus takes on the challenge of thinking about what Bernstein has dubbed "the agrarian question of labor" (2004) by looking historically at how mobile laborers and other mobile rural actors have influenced the social lives of land (see also Sunam 2020). These are complex relationships that differ across the three land regimes treated here and from one part of Java to another.

The remittances earned by Cece, Tini, and Tini's daughter Farah are contributing to new patterns of land access, use, and control due to new forms of mobility by members of plantation worker families and by new investments of labor and capital in land-based resource productions on and off the forest and tea plantation lands. At different historical moments and conjunctures, I explore some of these shifting connections on the three land regimes in these uplands, including "privately" held

FIGURE 8.1. Sumber Pandan Plantation headquarters, now Sumber Alam, 2019.

Photo by Nancy Peluso.

village land, privately managed tea plantation land, and the mahogany and pine plantations that have constituted production forest land. Buying village land for housing or agriculture was beyond the reach of landless plantation workers before transnational and other forms of long-distance labor migration became part of their lives and landscape histories. Labor mobilities have also made new forms of agrarian production possible for the poor and the proletarian, specifically the purchase of dairy cows. Cows, in turn, have transformed the uses and users of forests, agricultural plantations, and private lands (Peluso and Purwanto 2018).

Of course, mobility does not always render or represent a positive change, nor does transnational migration always end well! Women, in particular, sacrifice long years they could have spent together with their families. Laborers' agency has interacted not only with (structural) conditions of possibility but also with the different conditions and pathways of labor mobility, contractual work conditions, and regional political economies.

I tell this story of labor's mobility and landlords' attempts to fix or tie mobile laborers to themselves as employers and to the land on which laborers work through the figure of the *numpang*. Numpang are landless, dependent laborers whose existence and presumed mobilities are always produced in relation to a landowner or institutional landlord; each is a different class position. Numpang is a positionality in class relations based on control or lack of access to land (Ong Hok Ham 1975). It has been conceived as a patron-client relationship (Scott 1976;

Blusse 1984). Numpang and their "peasant" landlords, known in the nineteenth century as *gogol*[2] in lowland villages of Tulung Agung, are mentioned in the fourteenth-century chronicle about kingship and rural life in Java translated by Pigeaud (1960) as well as in early studies of changing rural lives under precolonial and colonial rule by Moertono (1981) and Ong Hok Ham (1975). It is an ancient concept and relationship, transcending periods of labor abundance as well as labor scarcity.

Numpang, like Cece, Wiyono, Tini, and their forebears, and *tuan tanah* (or landlords) like those we will meet below, have populated the three upland land regimes constituting the montane district where we conducted fieldwork. Often running from oppression themselves, private landholders became landlords by arriving first in the early to mid-nineteenth century to clear forests and stake claims (Pigeaud 1960; Moertono 1981; Elson 1994). They were followed by mostly private coffee plantations along Java's East-West volcanic spine, whose managers took on roles as institutional landlords to resident plantation workers (Breman 2013; White and Boomgaard 2016). The last institutional landlords were foresters who oversaw the enclosure of montane land in the 1930s for the enclosure of the last forests on Java, establishing state-run forestry plantations in the 1950s (Nyoman 2004; Peluso and Purwanto 2018). Numpang is always a relational category connected to a landlord, whether a private individual, a household, or an institution. These relations were also related to land—or lack of certain kinds of it.[3] The landholders called *petani* (today translated as both "peasant" or "farmer") were differentiated during the colonial and postcolonial eras by terms describing their house and yard landholdings as well as their agricultural landholdings. Those with agricultural land were called *kuli kenceng* or *kuli gogol* (the local terms); those with only house and yard land were known as *kuli setengah kenceng* or *kuli mburi*.[4] Numpang were also differentiated: those living in houses they built on a landholder's land were referred to as *numpang*, while those without any access to land and living in the house of the landholder were called *numpang dalem*, *numpang rumah*, or *nggenger* (the latter being a derogatory term in one of our research villages and not in the other one).[5]

Numpang have always been expected to provide some kind of labor in exchange for their temporary access to land, even if just to build a small house on someone else's land. Across the centuries and these three contemporary land regimes, the nature of these obligations has changed. Yet what is striking across time is that numpang have been consistently regarded as temporary settlers *because of* their presumed mobilities: "always coming and going," as Paing states in the epigraph above. Since the 1930s, the term has been used to indicate a sharecropper (one who numpang to farm on someone's land without ownership rights in the land) (White 2018). Today, the word numpang is most commonly used to refer to workers living in settlements on state or private forest or agricultural plantations (Nyoman 2004; see also Besky 2017). Further complicating matters, adult children working on their parents' land that they had not yet inherited also called themselves or were called numpang.

The puzzle invoked here has to do with why the category of numpang has had such a long and robust life, traveling through space and time and withstanding multiple changes in political economies and ecologies. How does such a precolonial institution, developed to enable elites to extract surplus from scarce labor by fixing them in place to work, persist under today's conditions of labor surpluses and land scarcities? How does it travel into the territorialized property regimes of contemporary capitalism? How does such a word remain a part of late(r) capitalist land regimes, in which free labor presumably relegates tied labor to the dustbin of history? The answers to all these questions have to do with the ways that the social and economic relations between mobile laborers and landholders are reproduced and repurposed.

I have selected four "mobility moments" to discuss related transformations of Mt. Wilis's uplands as private, forest, and plantation regimes, and I show how numpang fit into each of these. I begin where the oral histories we collected on Mt. Wilis brought us: with labor mobilities that began just after the Java War (1825–1830) that strengthened Dutch territorial control in Java's "outer provinces" of Madiun and Kediri in East Java. In Moment One, peasants, numpang, and coffee planters traveled to the upland forests of Mt. Wilis and converted forest cover to dry field crops and, eventually, coffee. Peasants with land rights in the irrigated lowlands paid land taxes with their labor. During the period called the Cultivation System, they or their numpang labored on commodity crops, including coffee, monopolized by the Dutch colonial state but often grown by entrepreneurs who rented customary or state land (Fasseur 1992; Elson 1994). Coffee attracted pioneers, small and large entrepreneurs, and laborers into these volcanic uplands.

In Moment Two, beginning in approximately 1890 and running through 1940, land boundaries between and within forest lands, private/customary lands, and plantation lands (leases from state lands) were formalized. The 1930s land registration and legislation of forests were key to this period. Coffee rust led many plantations, including those discussed here, to change their primary commodity crops to tea, rubber, and kina (quinine). The idea of resident workers as numpang traveled from customary/private lands to the agricultural plantations.

Moment Three saw a great increase in the number of numpang and their radical reduction, all between the 1940s and the mid-1980s. During the Japanese Occupation, workers were ordered to cut tea bushes to their stumps and plant corn and castor oil, while some plantation workers were told to clear parts of the forest that the colonial state had recently reserved and occupy it. After the wars, both the Forest Service and the tea plantation owners reappropriated the land and places to build houses for anyone willing to work. By the 1970s, the worker settlements had grown well beyond the plantations' capacities to provide work. Beginning in the mid-1970s, the state-sponsored resettlement program, Transmigration, significantly reduced the numbers of numpang living on all three land regimes.

In Moment Four, from the late 1980s through 2020, nearly all households in all three land regimes were raising dairy cows, while one or more members have worked transnationally or on other Indonesian islands. These mobile workers, most numpang, have changed the land in all three regimes, shifting their relationships with private and institutional landlords. Migrant laborers, particularly those working transnationally, numpang while they work elsewhere. They have invested their savings in housing and education for their children, helped family members migrate, and invested in dairy cows and other livestock.

History's lessons about class relations and social mobility suggest this may be a fleeting moment. Nonetheless, a generation of mobile landless and land-poor laborers has achieved what their mobile ancestors never could. Some, like Cece's extended family, are no longer numpang.

Some Notes on Mobilities, Land Taxes, and Laboring Subjects in Nineteenth-Century Java

> [E]vidence places question marks against the commonly held notion that Javanese peasants were firmly and immutably rooted in the village of their birth and the graves of their ancestors [. . .]. Many peasants, even those who held land, did not feel themselves only bound to a particular place; given the generally threatening and unsettled nature of peasant life [and] . . . in the knowledge that there were plentiful opportunities for livelihood elsewhere in labor-deficient and land-rich Java, they probably considered migration, whether temporary or permanent, as an option which did not necessarily mean a serious disruption in their lives (Elson 1994,10–13).

This passage from Robert Elson's brilliant book (1994) shows that, despite the relative land abundance of nineteenth-century Java, many laborers, traders, artisans, and small landholders were mobile in Java's nineteenth century and before. At the century's start, Java's population was approximately three million people; it grew to an estimated 30 million by the turn of the twentieth century. These numbers are paltry compared to the island's population of 150 million in the first quarter of the twenty-first century (Hirschman and Bonaparte 2012). Many parts of eastern Java, especially the volcanic mountains stretching across the island's center and the southern coastal mountains, were relatively unsettled forest frontiers in the mid-nineteenth century, as most of the island's population was concentrated in its western half (Breman 2013; Bosma, pers. comm. 2018). Nevertheless, class relations built around land control, or lack thereof, already defined social relationships (Ong Hok Ham 1975; White 1978). The people called numpang, as mentioned in the introduction to this paper, were the ones without long-term control of land (Pigeaud 1960; Moertono 1981).

Numpang were landless, dependent, mobile, and assumed-to-be-temporary laborers who constituted "the lowest level of rural society" (Ong Hok Ham 1975, 169). Elson (1994, 166) defined them by drawing on Veth (1875, vol. 1, 658), who described Java's eighteenth- and nineteenth-century numpang as "a very numerous class of people who have next to nothing of their own, have no right to a share in the communal land, and are dependent for their livelihood(s) on the labour [sic] of their hands." Individuals or couples in search of work were most likely to numpang by building a house in a landholder's yard, or even *numpang rumah*, living inside a welcoming landowner's dwelling. Being dependent on the land of another thus represented a settled moment in the trajectory of a mobile laborer's life in or through the uplands. Numpang were not the only mobile rural people. As Elson (1994) explains: "In some cases, people used a settled community as a base from which they periodically ranged in search of a better livelihood. [In other cases] an altogether different style of mobility from that of usually settled people was provided by the substantial numbers of unattached Javanese who lived transient and rootless lives, wandering from place to place in search of employment or fulfillment" (11,13).

Land controllers were those Elson called "usually settled people," for whom mobility was often temporary and circular. His "unattached Javanese" meant those not bound by the labor taxes that lowland agricultural landholders had to pay. Both scholars nuanced these categories, of course, yet both suggested that mobility was shaped as much by class as it was reproductive of it, even before the nineteenth century; mobility was not limited to the underserved. Unlike corvee and forced laborers coming to the uplands from lowland areas, many of these unattached Javanese traversing the upper slopes of Mt. Wilis were coming from and going to other montane areas along a network of footpaths, which were the highways for horses during colonial-era management.

The tropical forest habitats of tigers, deer, pumas, wild boar, and monkeys that challenged Javanese farmer pioneers, settlers, and early coffee planters in the eastern part of the island's montane forests had largely disappeared from these Tulung Agung mountains by the end of the nineteenth century (Ong Hok Ham 1975; Boomgaard 2001). These wilder habitats were replaced by small clearings for houses and eventual family compounds with yards, followed by clears for unirrigated fields, planted in cassava, corn, and upland rice, and, where suitable, the construction of terraced and irrigated fields (Ong Hok Ham 1975). Subsequently and concurrently with pioneer settlement, coffee gardens (*koffietuinen*) were planted on rented peasant or "waste" land during what I call the Cultivation System for simplicity's sake.

The Cultivation System was not a singular policy or governmental practice; it was constituted by multiple "systems" of commodity production that varied by region and crop but was meant to valorize Java's land (Fasseur 1992). Still remembered today as "the forced planting era" (*jaman tanam paksa*) or "forced labor era" (*jaman kerja paksa*), historians usually date "the System" as extending from 1830 to 1860, which was true for indigo, sugar, and cotton, all produced in the lowlands. Due to its profitability, the "Coffee System," or *Koffiestelsel*, was formally extended until 1890 (Elson 1994). Under this same system, forced teakwood deliveries were extended to 1865 or 1870 (Peluso 1992). Some sources claim that forced labor in the coffee plantations of Tulung Agung continued through 1915 (*Dinas Pariwisata dan Kebudayaan Kabupaten Tulungagung* 2007).

After 1832, "non-Native" entrepreneurs (Europeans, Eurasians, and Chinese) could plant coffee "gardens" on state-claimed "waste" or on rented peasant land.[6] They were not formally allowed to buy or own "native" customary land but were permitted to rent land from landholders.

In addition, some lowland village and district heads cleared upland forests to plant coffee gardens in the uplands, worked by corvee laborers from lowland villages (Elson 1994).

The Cultivation System's institutions of forced cultivation of monopolized commodity crops and forced coffee delivery increased the demand for laborers—at a time when labor was scarce in an absolute sense. Hence, it was handy, to say the least, to have lowland landholders pay taxes *in the form of such corvee labor* in exchange for their access to the irrigated land on which they grew paddy rice. Labor taxes could be "paid" in the upland coffee gardens. Further, upland landholders were required to plant coffee on one-fifth of their land—this was also seen as a tax. And here is the connection to numpang: allowing mobile laborers to numpang facilitate the "payment" of land taxes by engaging them in the labor of coffee cultivation.

Throughout much of the Cultivation System, unclaimed and uncultivated montane land, most under forest cover, remained abundant, while labor remained scarce (Blusse 1984). While some people we will meet in the next sections were fine with being numpang, the numpang unhappy with their circumstances could run away into the upland forest and clear it for their own shifting or permanent cultivation—or attach themselves to a more tolerable settler landlord (Ong Hok Ham 1975). Decades later, when plantations allowed workers to construct small shelters (*pondok*) for themselves or their families on the plantation lands, the plantation became an institutional landlord.

Until the Agrarian Act was passed in 1870, such mobility was supported by policies that allowed newly cleared and cultivated forest land to remain tax-free for three years as an incentive to bring "waste" land into production. This benefitted many of the "unattached"; not everyone wanted to deal with the in-kind taxation obligations that went with access to fields in the lowlands (Ong Hok Ham 1975; Elson 1994). As a result, numpang in this eastern frontier region occasionally enjoyed some leverage with their landlords (Van Schaik 1986; Hefner 1990).[7] Swidden cultivators who preferred the mobile life could clear forests, work the land for three years, and then sell it, moving off to another section of the forest to clear (Elson 1994). We heard of some pioneers making extensive land claims, then working with others to clear portions of their claim, and later "selling" those plots to those who helped clear them for a goat or two (Pak Juno July 2018, and Mbah Amita 2019, interviews with the author).

The cold uplands of Mt. Wilis remained settlement frontiers until the end of the nineteenth century, in the sense that new settlers and mobile laborers continued clearing forests even after the Agrarian Act in 1870 technically forbade such clearing. The Agrarian Act and subsequent policies created a formal-legal category of "State Lands"—which included all uncultivated and unoccupied land (also known as "*woeste*" or waste). That was the *Domeinverklaring* part of the Act (Peluso 1992) that claimed colonial land sovereignty. The other part of the Agrarian Act was the establishment of a legal mechanism through which agricultural enterprises—a.k.a. plantations—held by Europeans and Chinese could formally lease state land for seventy-five years to grow specific commodities (Boomgaard 1989; Breman 2013). The terminology of waste that referred to all unleased and unsettled state land in the uplands was replaced with "Bosch," and the Forest Service or Boschwezen became another kind of state landholder. One after the other, the three montane land regimes—private/customary farming and settlement lands (*tanah yasan*), agricultural plantations, and another half-century later, plantation forests—came to benefit from the same sort of tied labor known as numpang.

In the first mobile moment to which we now turn, mobile laborers establish these foundational patterns.

Mobile Moment 1, 1830 to 1889. Peasants, Numpang, and Coffee Planters

> As long as land was abundant, the cost of devising exclusive rights for the farmer to its use remained too high [. . .]. As such, the thirty-year period of the Cultivation System represents a more or less controlled transitional stage in which the personal type of authority was replaced by the territorial one.
>
> —Leonard Blusse, *Itinerario*

Both labor relations and means of access to land were different between Java's uplands and lowlands, in part because the uplands were settled much later. As in other parts of Kediri, Mt. Wilis's uplands may have been settled, vacated (due to political violence), and resettled many times, as suggested in Bergsma's *Eindresume* (1883), as well as in Pigeaud (1960), and in Carey (1976).

That said, it seems that only a smattering of settlers, rice farmers, and Dutch officials were living in settlements around the small upland village called Sendang in the early to middle nineteenth century when Mat Ngali, his sturdy wife, and his baby son in tow, arrived on Pandan Ridge. They had walked from a district west of Yogyakarta known as Bagelen, more than 300 kilometers away, a Qur'an in one hand, a bush knife (*parang*) in the other. His great-granddaughter, Mbah Amita, asserted to my assistant and me in 2018 that Mat Ngali's arrival was the settlement's origin moment. She said that when her intrepid ancestor arrived, the land was "all forest," and other long-term residents confirmed that no other settlers had yet opened land on that ridge. Ngali's family had walked forty days and nights, stopping along the way to borrow space to sleep in the corner of a stranger's house, against a wall inside a mosque, or to roll out a mat on a porch or in someone's yard—all ways they could temporarily numpang or occupy someone else's space (Mbah Amita, interview with the author, July 2018).

Pandan, the site where Mat Ngali settled, was named after the fragrant leaf or grass that grew abundantly in the section of the woods he cleared to farm (Pak Sumaji, interview with the author, 2019). He cleared trees and other plants to make a shelter, building a simple house of bamboo and wood with a grass roof. Within a week of the family's arrival, two couples showed up from a lower elevation settlement in Sendang (about a six-kilometer walk) and, in Bu Amita's words, "asked if they could numpang" on Mat Ngali's land (interview with the author, July 2018). They were not looking for land, Bu Amita insisted; they were looking for work and a place to shelter from the rain and miasmic vapors that rose up from the lowland swamps that had given the district its name—*Ngrowo*.

Over time, Mat Ngali and his numpang constructed rain-fed fields, terracing the slopes below Pandan Ridge, after, of course, the numpang had built themselves small huts (*pondok*) to live in with their wives.

The Java War had led to several "Outer Districts" (*Mancanegara*), such as Kediri and Madiun, coming under Dutch colonial authority, triggering both the establishment of direct (territorial) rule and migrations from other areas by different classes of people (Bosma 2019). Land in Java was governed on the Dutch colonials' assumption that it belonged first to the Javanese kings and later to the "successor sovereign," the Dutch monarch. With the almost immediate establishment of the Cultivation System, private entrepreneurs, potential settlers, and temporary farmers and workers were attracted to the forested frontier lands of East Java, including the various flanks of Mt. Wilis (Bergsma 1876, vol. 2, 218). Before that, a few mobile cultivators had been drawn to the uplands despite the high-elevation cold and foggy forest conditions caused by the lowland swamps. Dating back roughly through the family genealogy provided by Bu Amita, we estimated that her ancestor arrived in Pandan within a decade or so of the Java War. Unlike Mat Ngali, not all visitors came to stay; thus, the names and traces of mobile folks without local descendants or stories have been lost.

Javanese rulers had long imposed labor taxes on lowlanders to whom they had granted access (use rights) to paddy rice land. When the Dutch took control of Madiun and Kediri, they added onerous new labor obligations. Ong Hok Ham (1975, 179) calculated that these new obligations in Madiun increased land taxes from sixty-six to ninety person-days per year after the imposition of direct rule. When corvee laborers began performing corvee labor at higher and colder elevations than where coffee was planted, lowland numpang repurposed to fulfill these obligations would have been exposed to new opportunities for acquiring land and work (Hefner 1990; von Schaik 1994; Breman 2013). Some likely ran away from oppressive landlords.

Mobilities ramped up, and access to land changed. In some places, the onerous land taxes paid in labor led to the consolidation of individually held paddy lands into communal holdings to which access was rotated. Lowland numpang, who became such communal land shareholders, thus took on more of the labor obligations attached to paddy rice land. In upland Pandan, where there was no irrigated paddy land at the time and no communal production, the requirement to plant coffee may have led some landholders, like Mat Ngali, to give land to the numpang that had cleared it (Bu Amita, interview with the author, July 2018; Bergsma 1876, vol. 2).

As early as 1831, the Chinese Captain of Kediri Residency and a Dutch partner rented some 360 *bahu* (meaning, literally, 360 "shoulders" of land, each bahu being about seven-tenths of a hectare) of state land on the Mt. Wilis volcanic outcrop known locally as *Sapu Angin* (West Wind). The coffee garden and subsequent plantation established by the Chinese captain adopted that name for much of the next eighty years.[8] Dutch, Scottish-Javanese, and Chinese entrepreneurs rented peasants and wasteland in the vicinity as well. These companies benefited from forced labor to clear forests, plant, tend, and harvest the coffee trees on monocropped plantations; smallholder forest clearers planted coffee in "hedgerows" or in partially cleared forests (Van Schaik 1986). The annual number of coffee trees to be planted in a year was determined by the Dutch Resident of Kediri, while his Javanese underlings—the Regents (*Bupatis*) and village heads (*Lurah*)—determined landholders' planting obligations, which varied according to the amount of land they controlled (Elson 1994). An 1879 map of Kediri, for which data were collected in 1866 (before the Agrarian Law), shows fairly detailed land uses, including *koffietuinen* (coffee gardens) planted on rented peasant lands and in the understories of forested areas closest to the small settlements in the mountain's higher reaches. In addition, sometime before 1890, planters began to intercrop cinchona trees with coffee on Sapu Angin and the other adjacent coffee gardens and plantations, often to provide shade for coffee while producing quinine bark (Bussy 1892).

Between 1830 and 1870, even as planters were clearing forests and growing coffee, Javanese pioneers into the uplands cleared patches of forests to build houses, construct home gardens, make swidden fields, and plant or work the coffee gardens (Elson 1994). Some of our interlocutors talked about their ancestors being hired to clear horse and carriage paths or to carry coffee from the higher elevations to the government storehouse in Sendang. Reciting another familiar story, a current resident of Pandan Ridge told us his grandfather migrated up the mountain from a drought-plagued area on the south coast, stopping in Sendang to numpang in a *sawah*-rich settlement. He married one of the landowner's daughters. Two decades later, one of his sons sought his fortunes at a higher elevation (in Pandan), and another became village head in Sendang (Pak Juno, interview with the author, June 2019).

In sum, through the first half of the nineteenth century, hamlets or settlements on Mt. Wilis were founded by settlers seeking new land or escaping epidemics, war, or repressive labor arrangements. Not all who cleared forests to cultivate wanted to settle for the long term—many came for a few seasons or years and moved on (Elson 1994; Pak Juno, interview with the author, 2019). Dozens of people we interviewed said that their predecessors walked in seeking work, not land. Tied to labor obligations or not, mobile Javanese workers, as well as short- and long-term settlers, changed the mountain landscape. They transformed tropical montane forests into settlement compounds, private fields, agroforestry plots, and plantations until the Cultivation System finally came off its coffee high to compost on the slopes of Mt. Wilis.

Mobile Moment 2, 1890 to the 1930s. Planters, Peasants, and Labor Brokers to Land Managers

> In general, the population in Kediri [Residency], especially in the Regencies of Ngrowo and Trenggalek, was in favor of individual ownership. Not only did people want to retain that type of possession where it existed, but in most villages where communal property was found, they wanted to see it converted into individual property (*tanah yasan*).
> —Willem Bergsma, *Eindresume*

According to her eighty-year-old granddaughter, Bu Manis lived in the high-elevation settlement (900 meters above sea level) of Pakem from the early 1890s until she died in 1955 (Mbah Sutinah, interview with the author, 2019). Manis left her first husband behind in Pulung, Ponorogo, after a violent argument. Separated, barefoot, and pregnant, she walked across the ridges from the west and up into their higher elevations into Pakem with her three young children in tow. Pakem was the last high-elevation area to be carved out of "wasteland" for settlement and cultivation that would be incorporated with the rest of the Jambuok hamlet into the village of Nglurup in approximately 1917 or 1918.[9] What the space occupied by Pakem looked like before 1893 remains unclear. It may have been planted in coffee or corn by mobile cultivators with no intention of staying. It may have housed mobile workers or low-level managers of the Cultivation System "plantation" as forced laborers made montane pathways and planted coffee at Sapu Angin. The land may have been part of the original forested parcel rented to the Chinese Captain and a Dutch partner for coffee production. Clearly, however, in 1893, Pakem was under construction just outside the formal bounds of the relatively new *erfpacht*, or plantation lease. It was designed to be a settlement area for plantation managers, technicians, and foremen to live with their families (Soeter 1893).

Manis married the man in charge of forest clearance and construction known as Surontani, an aristocrat and contractor from Sragen, Central Java, according to his granddaughter. Eventually, the couple controlled most of the settlement and agricultural land created from the forest. The land was inherited by the five children the couple had together and the four that Manis had borne with her first husband. As the plantation grew and changed from coffee to tea production,

Bu Manis packed up ample baskets filled with leaf-wrapped packets of rice and savory side dishes she cooked every day, selling them to workers and foremen in the plantation's upper reaches. Allegedly the only woman to own a horse in the area, she rode with her wares into the steeper elevations to some 1,200 meters above sea level. She traversed the network of forced-labor-built horse and foot paths connecting Sapu Angin, Penampean, and Mringin plantations, through clustered worker houses. She connected plantations through her own mobile labor, mobile in a different way than her grandchildren would ever be (fig. 8.2). Some plantation workers were numpang on her land or in her house. Even as a major landholder and landlord, Manis depended for income and part of her own family's reproduction on the mobile workers that the plantations attracted and on the mobility she enjoyed to live well in this montane settlement.

Sapu Angin was not the first plantation for which Manis' husband, Pak Surontani, cleared forest for settlements and cultivation; he specialized in such work (Mbah Sutinah, interview with the author, June 2019). Surontani generated ongoing demands for laborers to clear, burn, plant, make terraces for fields, and construct buildings inside and outside the leased coffee lands. In earlier years, and well past the 1890s, men like Surontani would have had access to forced laborers, including convict labor, to help construct the upland plantations and the new settlements of workers and managerial staff (Elson 1994; Shipman 2006).

Surontani knew Manis's two brothers, who worked as labor brokers/foremen (*mandor*) (Mbah Sutinah, interview with the author, 2019). They had moved to this part of Mt. Wilis from Pulung, Ponorogo, like Manis. The labor foremen shuttled encumbered workers on foot or on horseback up the mountain from gathering places in the low and middle slopes to various coffee plantations to perform the labor taxes they owed (Pak Slamet, interview with the author, 2015). The brothers supervised laborers on multiple coffee plantations[10] before settling down in Pakem, Jambuok, Pandan, or other *kampong* adjacent to plantations (Mbah Paing, interview with the author, January 2019).[11] Such labor brokers were well positioned to acquire land in the uplands as a result of their work. Their shuffling of laborers between plantations during the forced labor period foreshadowed the subsequent free laborers' movements between plantations in search of the "best" terms of work (Pak Sulim 2015 and Pak Bando 2018, interview with the author).

The extension of the Cultivation System for coffee until 1890 had other implications for the implementation of certain tenets of the Agrarian Act of 1870. Powerful men like Tan Kok Tong, the Chinese captain of Kediri, put off formally leasing the plantation's coffee land until 1889, postponing the transition to free laborers longer than any other coffee plantation on the southeastern slopes of Mt. Wilis (Bussy 1892). That may be why the wages on the plantation were surprisingly low, as Soeter wrote in his 1893 report to the Semarang inspection service on the sale of Sapu Angin. Unpaid forced laborers were still part of the labor force (Shipman 2006).

After Sapu Angin shifted to tea from coffee in 1915 and a small tract of land was added to the plantation's area, its name was changed to "Sumber Pandan" (Bussy 1915). The labor force shifted as well. More single women—the daughters of smallholders from other hamlets—sought work picking tea. These more privileged women, even daughters of smallholders having more status than landless working-class daughters, lived as *numpang dalem*, inside the homes of the households of the landholding class—often occupying the homes of Manis or her nine adult children. These women, in particular, were not derided for their numpang status; it was known that their families had some land. They performed some household labor, likely without being "ordered" to do so. Moreover, the work would not be called "work" or "labor." They helped cook on occasion, served visitors, or swept their host's yard before or after they picked or sorted plantation tea each day from 6 a.m. to 2 p.m. (Mbah Bhakti, interview with the author, June 2019). Many found spouses in the households they occupied; indeed, I often wondered if a prearranged marriage was the intent of the arrangement.

Meanwhile, poorer mobile women and men, those who were landless and without local connections, sought to live on the plantation—the other numpang arrangement of the times.

The coffee-turned-tea plantation subsequently weathered economic fluctuations before and after the 1918 flu pandemic—another period of labor shortage and loss. That same year, the upland settlements of Pakem, Pandan, Jambuok and their agricultural lands were consolidated with three lower-elevation hamlets (Nglurup, Sumberejo, and Babat) into Nglurup village (*desa*). That same year, the *lurah*, or village head, married Canthur, the beautiful daughter of Manis and Surontani (Mbah Sutinah and Mbah Yando, interview with the author, 2018, 2019). The marriage both symbolized and cemented the territorial union of Nglurup as an administrative village and of Lurah Sademo, the first village head.

In the 1930s, peasant landholdings/claims were subjected to a new logic of land ownership as well as new forms of state territorialization (Vandergeest and Peluso 1995). Plantations that were already leased remained intact, while the forest was formally bounded, mapped, and legislated. Just as territorial village consolidation came late to these upland districts, the land registration process came relatively late to Nglurup. Colonial officials had begun Java's land registration process in 1911 (Breman 1980). This was when *tanah yasan* (individual or family customary holdings) became *tanah pemajekan* (taxed land). Yet formal measurement and registration began in 1931. The property map that accompanied the land register of Nglurup was produced in 1933. Peasant land was now burdened with taxes in cash; gone were the formal labor obligations attached to lowland irrigated rice fields and the percentages of coffee, rice, and other harvests delivered to Javanese officials or Dutch authorities as rents on the land. New ways of seeing this land valorized it: the types, sizes, borders, improvements (e.g., terracing or irrigation), and relative quality of agricultural fields and settlement land (yards and houses) were all formally recorded in the colonial land register, along with each plot's assessed values. Failure or refusal to pay taxes on a land parcel meant the state would confiscate it and the plot would change status, becoming a part of the state forest lands.

Agrarian scholars of Indonesia found that the 1930s were remembered by residents as a time when plantation workers were more prosperous than peasants despite the global recession (Wertheim 1969; White 1983, 2018). Workers' cash wages could buy twice as much as before, as prices of peasant crops/staple foods crashed. However, this was only true if they kept their jobs—huge numbers were laid off (White 2018). Experience in our research sites verified this impression, but the number of people who were laid off has not been possible to trace. Yet although full-time, resident plantation workers had no land of their own and had been numpang by definition for several generations, elderly landholders descended from Manis and Surontani often described mobile workers living on the plantations as "lazy" and "spoiled," complaining that workers "worked shorter hours than cultivators and had only to wait for their salaries."

During the 1930s, formal, state-authorized boundaries demarcated all three land regimes, with lines drawn between the village territory and the state forest and, on state land, between the state forest and the tea plantation. The formal boundaries demarcating the state forest created management districts designated for protection and production (Peluso and Vandergeest 2001). This difference would affect where people could live in the future, but only as numpang and only with the permission of their forester landlords. Forest boundaries in this part of Mt. Wilis were among the last the Colonial Forest Service formalized in all their Java holdings, the final boundaries approved in 1938–1940 (Seksi Perencanaan Hutan Wilayah Kediri 2013).[12]

As early as 1931, the Colonial Forest Service made plans to clear the land designated as production forest, intending to create forest plantations (Goor and Kartasubrata 1960). Forest species were those that produced hardwood logs, pulp, or resins. The creation of permanent forests was meant to forever alter the practice of peasants claiming land by clearing forest cover. On the lands acquired from land claimants who could not afford taxes, the foresters prioritized planting fast-growing seedlings. In addition, they established a living nursery for mahogany, a valuable hardwood forest species that could claim the land as forest

FIGURE 8.2.   Painting of two land regimes: Forest Plantation and Private Village Land.

Painting by Darji (used with permission).

over the long term once it was outplanted. However, World War II's Pacific war and the Japanese Occupation encroached on the foresters' plans for rapid planting of mahogany plantations.

The movements of workers to the forest plantation from nearby tea and rubber plantations and from afar, as well as the formalization of the forest and private land regimes, set up the forest as a third formalized land regime, housing numpang in a new form (see fig. 8.3). World War II was already casting its shadow across the Pacific Ocean and over the South China Sea.

Mobile Moment 3, Japanese Occupation to 1980. Forest and Plantation Interruptus

During the Pacific war, the Japanese invaded Indonesia in 1942 and occupied Java. For three and a half years, they transformed Javanese labor and land relations, pushing back against the proprietary systems recently established on the three upland land regimes. The Japanese occupied the Sumber Pandan tea plantation's buildings and mobilized workers and other village residents—numpang as well as landholders—to cut back the tea trees on Sumber Pandan's concession. They changed the arable and plantations' primary crops to corn, castor oil, and cassava. They commandeered private and forest land for the same crops. They took

50 percent of the harvests from private lands and forest lands and 100 percent of the harvest on plantation lands (local interviews; Sato 1994). Told by the Japanese to occupy or reoccupy forest and some plantation lands, landless and land-poor villagers once again began to use the land taken away from them the decade before, grazing small animals, farming, building shelters, and taking refuge in forest areas and upper reaches of the plantation.

The Japanese also invoked a new species of forced labor: sending Javanese to the Tulung Agung coasts to build a giant culvert, diverting the waters of Ngrowo Regency's notorious swamps[13] and ending the flooding of agricultural land in the lowlands once and for all (local interviews with the author; Sato 1994). Like labor brokers of an earlier era who had marched lowlanders up the mountain to work in coffee, upland village and hamlet officials were responsible for organizing laborers forced to walk to the steamy, hot, mosquito-infested coast. Laborers toiled in extreme heat and humidity, were poorly fed, and died by the thousands in the malarial, cholera-ridden coastal swamps. Few who made this journey returned to their upland homes; many who made it back died within a week or so of their return (local interviews with the author, 2018).

Shortly after the end of the war, the Dutch returned to reclaim Java. President Sukarno had declared Indonesian independence in 1945 within days of the Japanese surrender. However, the Dutch attacked, and an anticolonial revolution began. Among other aggressive acts, the Dutch bombed many plantations, including the tea plantation and the adjacent hamlets of Pakem and Jambuok. The revolutionary forces prevailed with the assistance of the UN and the US, the Dutch conceded, and Sukarno oversaw the formation of the Republic of Indonesia in 1950.

After the wars, foresters also returned. The new Forest Service tried to pick up where its predecessors left off: turning production forest land into plantations and finishing planting out forest species seedlings on the lands they acquired during the 1930s. The *magersari*, or workers' settlement area, was cleared. Like numpang, the term *magersari* originated under precolonial Javanese rule and implied a class relation around access to land. Magersari referred originally to the concept of land "borrowed" from the Javanese king by his subjects (Moertono 1981). Like the Javanese kings who ruled before the colonial state, and like plantation managers and peasant proprietors before them, the local foresters assumed the role of land controllers and patrons, who granted the workers access to forest work and to land on which they could live. The numpang class was now a fixture of all three land regimes under the modern political organization of the nation-state.

When designing the magersari in the 1950s, the returning Indonesian foresters did not want the forest land they had acquired before the Japanese Occupation to be "mistaken" for a "hamlet" on village land. Workers' access was not free: "rent" was paid in labor. Forestry work here was men's work, so it was men who were tied to the forest to labor (Peluso and Purwanto 2018). With some 560 hectares of extant forest to convert into a mahogany plantation, work was guaranteed for a long time to these laborers and others in other parts of the adjacent forest village. In the production forest/plantation, workers in the 1960s were still clearing and reforesting tracts, logging and replanting whole sections of the forest at a time, year after year. They were paid low cash wages, but workers won priority access to logging and reforestation work and had places to live, albeit as numpang, in the magersari.

The magersari-dwelling forest workers had to pay for their access to space for housing with their labor, while the access to the space for housing was part of their pay as forest workers. Each household in the magersari had to provide a forest plantation worker to do forest work—logging, thinning, seedling carrying, reforestation, and, later, collecting resin—or risk eviction from the magersari. The women did the bulk of the social reproduction work: cooking, raising the family, and finding some local work as market traders or agricultural laborers. Yet they also engaged in reforestation, both in planting the forest species and some dry food crops between the primary forest plantation species.

Mobile laborers, war widows, and other uprooted Javanese sought work at the tea plantation just after the Japanese Occupation (1942–1945) and during the Indonesian Revolution (1945–1949). Many were attracted by the opportunity to numpang/live on the plantation during those times of crisis. Some walked up the steep mountain road from Tulung Agung and Sendang; others traversed the mountains. These mobile laborers needed work; at the same time, Pak Hong, the struggling owner-manager of the Sumber Pandan tea plantation, needed workers.

Pak Hong had resumed control of the 250-hectare tea plantation in need of rehabilitation, yet faced a labor shortage caused by the 1940s events and the ongoing war. While tea trees had been cut back as the Japanese repurposed the plantation, buildings, including his family's houses, were destroyed during the Dutch bombing. Pak Hong, and later his son Pak Tik, became regionally renowned for providing jobs and housing to anyone willing to work. They also allowed workers to grow food along the riverbanks where the plantation was not permitted to cultivate tea. In the 1950s and 1960s, a worker's access to a small plot of land within the plantation's land to grow corn reduced the effects of low wages; it made Sumber Pandan seem "a good place to work" (local interviews with the author, 2019). Landless laborers working and living on the plantation became all the more beholden to the plantation manager.

During the wars, Pak Hong's wife and children fled to Bandung, West Java, to take refuge. In 1958, Hong's oldest son, Pak Tik, boarded a train to Tulung Agung and headed to Sumber Pandan with five technicians from Bandung's plantation district who knew how to grow cabbage, carrots, potatoes, patchouli, and other essential oils. A few years later, nearly thirty contract laborers from the West Java city followed, planting vegetables on Sumber Pandan's plantation grounds between tea trees. They taught local workers and farmers to plant vegetables and improve their care of the tea. Most returned to Bandung when their two-year contracts were up.

One technician, Cece's father, married a local tea sorter and numpang on the plantation (Pak Tik, Pak Sulin, and Cece, interview with the author, 2015–2018). Cece's father helped Pak Tik consolidate worker houses in a single settlement on the plantation side of the border, moving resident workers who had originally lived in smaller clusters in the higher elevation parts of the plantation. Allowing access to housing made the tea plantation managers seem more worker friendly and conveniently reproduced the labor force. It also allowed them to consolidate the tea growing spaces in a single large block.

Pak Tik also provided work that appealed to the "elites" of the hamlets nearest the plantation (Pakem, Pandan, and Jambuok); they came to work for the plantation as contract foremen. Each one was allocated spaces to clear and refurbish the tea plants. They had their own work crews on the plantation's land, creating work for local women and men. The temporary foremen paid the workers for the hours they worked and sold the tea and firewood to the plantation. When the plants were revitalized, local women picked and sorted the tea and sold it back to the plantation. As in earlier times, women in the settlement and in the other hamlets surrounding the forest did mostly household reproductive work—unpaid—collecting firewood and forest foods, such as bamboo shoots, ferns, and leaves, and fodder for their cows and goats; some did agricultural labor for their neighbors with land.

Further complicating matters of life and livelihood in the early 1960s, all of Java suffered extended droughts, rats overrunning fields, and extensive malnutrition. While many adults and children in neighboring areas were afflicted with beriberi, the workers of Sumber Pandan and the surrounding hamlets proudly claimed they had none or very little. The 1960s rural labor demonstrations, unilateral actions in Java and Sumatra, and violent movements against forests and plantations gained little traction in Pak Tik's tea plantation. In turn, the protections, work, living spaces, and political support that Pak Tik offered to all workers at the tea plantation helped, some suggest, to keep the plantation from being targeted for political violence (neither the attacks by the peasant organizations and the Indonesian Communist Party nor the army-led rural genocide). The violence and genocide that wracked the Regency of Tulung Agung and all of East Java in late 1965 and 1966, including the plantations to the east and west of Sumber Pandan, did not land here (e.g., Sulistyo 2000).

Both the tea plantation and the magersari experienced exponential growth in the aftermath of the 1960s violence; hundreds of people migrated looking for work and safety. The number of worker houses on the tea plantation grew to some 200 households, and the magersari expanded far beyond its intended borders and houses to 109 or so households. Pak Tik and the forest liaison in the magersari found work and new land uses for all of them. The expansions could not, however, continue on, as we see in the next section.

In this third mobile moment, many men and women circulated for work between the tea and forest plantations to sufficiently socially reproduce their families and themselves as plantation labor. They transformed Mt. Wilis's slopes into monocultural plantations of agricultural or forest species. They built and occupied settlements on borrowed land—the magersari and the tea workers' settlements—but remained landless and numpang by definition. Except in the loftiest protected forest areas, all that remained of the tropical montane forest were the names of vegetative giants and fragrant grasses, attached now not to flora but to the monikers of the surrounding high-elevation hamlets.

Mobile Moment 4, 1978 to 2020. Agrarian Transformations and Transnational Labor Formations

The late 1970s began a turning point for the workers and farmers of these montane hamlets, the tea plantation, and the magersari. Until recently, the upland area had been a destination for mobile laborers to work and/or live, building and rebuilding the tea and forest plantations. This abundance of work promised good prospects for socially reproducing their families by numpang on private plantations or forest land. In the late 1970s, however, the mahogany plantation was mature and establishment labor nil. Illegal logging in the plantation and above in the protection forest wase rampant. The tea plantation could no longer support all willing laborers with a living wage. The mountain became a "migrant-sending area"—a source of mobile, circular laborers and permanent migrants from government-sponsored and spontaneous migration. By the end of this mobile moment, money earned in far-flung work destinations financed the social reproduction of household and family economies in their places of origin.

Increased timber extraction and conversion of many of Indonesia's extensive tropical rainforests to industrial agriculture on other islands created opportunities for work and settlement, mechanisms for mobility, and narrative justifications for the government's giving Indonesian land outside Java to Javanese, Sundanese, and others living in "more crowded" regions, like Java and Bali. The promise of work and land, narratives about shortages of "skilled" labor outside Java, and the labor surpluses on Mt. Wilis drove landless workers and the underemployed to go. Transmigration areas in Sumatra and Kalimantan expanded from their early allocations of land for smallholder agriculture to state-led, then public-private, and finally corporate industrial agriculture to these sites (Robison 1989; Robison and Hadiz 2004). Decades later, successful transmigrants offered work to family members back in Java; many signed up to labor on plantations and helped relatives rebuild their houses.

Over two decades, Pak Gending, a Sendang subdistrict official, personally recruited and accompanied hundreds of transmigrant families to project areas outside Java. Upon arrival, the sponsored migrant-settlers received 1.5 or 2 hectares of land, some cleared of forest, some not. By 1985, twenty-some resident families left the Sumber Pandan (tea plantation) settlement; another thirty abandoned their numpang status on private lands in Nglurup Village, and about seventy or more left the magersari. Local plantation managers, landholding villagers, and foresters faced major changes in the labor pool. As Pak Gending saw it, for the first time, "numpang no longer had to numpang" (local interview, 2019). He described transmigration as a "leveling mechanism," allowing previously landless and dependent laborers "a decent life."[14] With glee, he said, "big farmers, tea plantation managers, and the foresters hated me because I drained their labor pool" (Bapak and Ibu Gending, interview with the author, June 24, 2019).[15] Pak Gending was only partially right: a long-term effect of transmigration was to end numpang on private land, except among children waiting to inherit their parents' land. Numpang as pay for work, however, remained a fact of life for people living on the tea and forest plantations.

Pak Gending went so far as to state that the subdistrict office expected that private landowners would be assuaged by government projects enabling elite villagers to buy dairy cows on credit. Elites were targeted because cow recipients had to provide written proof of land ownership. The first hundred New Zealand Holsteins were allocated in 1982. "We couldn't keep people working here," the plantation's financial manager said. "I lost [labor] to the cows" (Bu Mita, interview with the author, August 2019). The story of the cows and their ubiquitous importance across these montane hamlets is not straightforward (see Peluso and Purwanto 2018).

Cece and Tini's families were still numpang on plantation land when the dairy cow project began. Yet both their fathers and Cece's husband, Wiyono, were among the first plantation residents to raise dairy cows. Most elites who received allocations of dairy cows were unwilling to invest in the labor to take care of them; they sought "share-ranchers." In exchange for collecting fodder, milking the cows, and delivering raw milk to the refrigerated collection station (on foot or by bicycle), share-ranchers received half the income from the milk produced and took possession of the first calves; the second calf was for the cow owner. Thus, when Tini's father moved his family to the magersari, it was partly to have more space and time for the cows he was taking care of. Wiyono and his father-in-law continued working at Sumber Pandan, making cow pens on their plantation housing plots. As the tea plantation's fortunes declined, Wiyono and other workers sought ways to move off the plantation.

By the time I began research here in 2015, every household in the magersari had at least one dairy cow, and government and private industry had put in place complex infrastructures in the region to collect and sell milk, provide supplements, and feed, buy, and sell the livestock. Moreover, the forest's understory—the space between the pines replanted in the early 1980s (that began resin production in the early to mid-1990s)—was almost entirely planted in elephant grass for fodder. An informal property system had arisen in the forest understory (Peluso and Purwanto 2018). Some magersari residents sold grass to cow owners to people from outside the magersari (see fig. 8.3 for a map of current households in the magersari).

Three years after Cece began working in Hong Kong in 2000, Wiyono purchased a small plot of private/taxable land, an acquisition made possible by Cece's second two-year contract as a Hong Kong housekeeper. Wiyono hired a contractor and built a solid house, the first on private land in either of their natal families for at least four generations. In a corner of their small yard, Wiyono built a stall and milking station to house his cows. He paid magersari residents for access to three large plots of elephant grass in the understory.

The broad expansion of dairy production to the landless, dependent laborers (numpang) of the magersari and the tea plantation was made possible by the wages of the many women who went to work in Hong Kong, Singapore, and Taiwan as part of the transnational domestic labor force. Men's mobile labor was more constrained: many were tied to the locality for work. As mentioned above, living in the magersari entailed at least one household member working for the State Forestry Corporation (*Perhutani*). Their daughters and wives often became labor migrants. Placement agencies provided loans and infrastructure for migration overseas; domestic workers repaid these over the first six months of their two-year work contracts (Silvey 2006; Elmhirst 2011).

Tini and her husband, Sukanto, lived in the magersari with the latter's parents for some years until she left for Hong Kong in 2000. Her remittances enabled her husband to "buy" a house site in the magersari from a family that had transmigrated.[16] In 2004, Tini's wages as an elder caregiver in Hong Kong enabled Sukanto to buy a small plot of private residential land adjacent to Cece and Wiyono's in Jambuok. Tini also financed the construction of a beautiful house of

PEMUKIMAN WILAYAH MAGERSAREN
Proyeksi: Geografi, Datum: WGS 1984

FIGURE 8.3.   Aerial view of Magersari and house sites, 2016.

Map by Anita.

permanent materials in the magersari, bought a motorbike to carry grass from the forest for the cows and take her daughter to school, helped support her adult siblings and parents, and bought several dairy cows that her husband raised and then sold to finance the initial house construction. When she returned in 2017, she bought five more pregnant dairy cows.[17] She also used savings to complete the house construction in the magersari and sponsored a three-day wedding feast for her son.

For now, Tini and Sukanto have chosen to continue living as numpang in the magersari, in their house built from her remittances. Forest policy has also changed regarding the work requirements for living in the magersari: as long as the forester's pine resin quota is met each month, the foresters will allow the current families to stay. Sukanto prefers not to do the heavy work of tapping and hauling pine resin; husband and wife collect grass grown between the main species on the forest land for their cows and sell milk. They have built stalls and a milking station that holds five adult cows next to their refurbished house. They pay a "sharing" fee to the foresters for the forest plots where they planted grass. The elephant grass now extends throughout the forest plantation's understory and has been written into the local forest management plan (Peluso and Purwanto 2018; Lukas and Peluso 2020). New, informal work institutions are developing, allowing some men to "specialize" in resin collection while others tend their cows, goats, and fodder production on the forest lands. Almost every household with women under forty has made do with their absence to earn wages in Hong Kong, Taiwan, or Singapore.

Tini's eldest daughter chose to skip high school and seek work as a live-in babysitter in Hong Kong.[18] Like the older women who inspired her, Farah lives in the home of her Hong Kong bosses. Part of her salary is room and board. In this way, she is also a numpang, a live-in housekeeper. After four years, she returned to Jambuok briefly between contracts in 2017 to buy a residential property in a coveted roadside location within a mid-elevation village, an investment for a future house site. She returned to Hong Kong on another contract and came back in 2019 when a plot adjacent to hers became available.

Circular labor migration has become embedded as a cultural practice, as a means of saving money or acquiring small amounts of productive capital that change lives. Land and cows require far more capital than forest or tea plantation workers could ever accumulate in the past. For young people, for women and men like Marko, who said to me, "I have the soul of a wanderer," labor migration is what they do: to live, to build families, and to improve their living conditions as they socially reproduce their migration-plantation worker families in new ways that fit the times. With her savings from Hong Kong, Marko's wife also bought the tiny plot of village land that her mother had previously sold to pay for her cancer treatments years ago. It is still in fallow, sporting just a few cassava plants and some chilis grown by nearby relatives, but it is theirs for the future, secured by a title.

While there were many problems with the implementation of the transmigration program (not discussed in detail here), it provided land and work to many of those who moved—helping truly landless and land-poor workers get land, places to live, and opportunities for work. But it was the ability to own dairy cows—milk-producing proxies for savings accounts—together with further remittances from transnational migration to Hong Kong, Singapore, and Taiwan that accelerated the rising standards of living for the proletarian poor who remained in these upland environments. Mobility powered these improvements, however incremental. Elephant grass fills the understory on forest land and has replaced rice in fields; there is at least one dairy cow and a cow pen doubling as a milking station in every yard. Bamboo shacks and wooden dwellings have been replaced by more permanent housing on plantations as well as on private lands. The land has been reshaped by labor's mobilities and remittances in ways that make many different varieties of household social reproduction viable.

In this chapter, I have shown how three regimes of land-based production in Java, Indonesia—forests, agricultural plantations, and private land—have been made and remade by mobile laborers under different historical political and economic conditions. Mobile laborers in this story did not just "come and go"; they transformed the mountainside and moved away from old-fashioned relations of dependence. The chapter begins and ends with the stories of two women whose relatively long-term transnational mobile labor enabled both their natal families and their nuclear families to move off the local tea and pine plantations for the first time in at least three generations, buying land and investing in other agrarian resources with both use and exchange value. The paper thus addresses in part the challenge set forth by Henry Bernstein (2004), calling for more scholarly attention to the agrarian question of labor. Cece and Tini were not the only ones to benefit from new migrations; mobility became empowering for many of the landless women laborers and families.

In telling this story through life histories, I have made a case for the importance of place-based history to understanding a persistent form of land-labor relations, called numpang, a positionality closely associated with (assumed) mobilities. Through the centuries, landless Javanese numpang have been tied to various "kinds" of land (upland, lowland, private, family, and institutional land) and landholders, including smallholders, private plantation owners/managers, and state forest plantation managers. Manifest initially in lowland Java and in virtually all regions of precolonial *and* colonial Java, the obligations of numpang changed in uplands cleared of forest by peasant cultivators and agricultural plantations. After colonial authority gave way to both the Japanese Occupation and the anticolonial revolution, leading to the formation of the Republic of Indonesia, numpang-landholder relations took a new form in dramatically changed land uses and within structurally reconfigured power relations on the land, particularly in upland forest plantations. As political economies and the materialities of resource productions changed, so did the class-like nature of numpang-landholder relations and the ways in which mobile labor moved into, out of, and across this and other montane landscapes.

Territorialization of state and private land control did not eliminate the practice of securing and controlling mobile laborers through the precolonial relationship of numpang (see Blusse 1984). Rather, numpang-landholder relationships continued to characterize the land-labor relationships in all three regimes. Moreover, as the experiences of hundreds of other interviewees on Mt. Wilis have shown, the conditions of plantation work and where workers live as numpang have much to do with the possibilities of transcending their initial, and often ongoing, dependent numpang status. Long-distance mobile work has made new conditions of possibility for laborers in numpang families on forest and agricultural plantation land without formal land rights. Many are using their earnings from transnational and transinsular mobile labor to buy land for housing and livestock, some leaving behind their numpang status. These are not privileged migrants—most, like Cece and Tini, started as proletarians descended from proletarians.

Mobilities have shaped and reshaped work and land in myriad ways, as they have remade the southeastern slopes of this mystical mountain in East Java. From Mat Ngali to Manis and Surontani, from Cece and Wijoyo to Tini and Sukanto, from land and labor contractors to foresters and plantation managers, what all these workers and small landholders had in common was their mobility. Each "moment" depicted here focused on people who were able to maneuver within the structural constraints of landlessness and dependence on private and institutional landlords. I do not deny that the risks and dangers of mobile work and of transnational and transinsular migration are formidable; they cause many to fail. Yet it was not until very recently that numpang and mobile labor could enable more than simple reproduction of families and a work force. Transnational migration has largely changed that in this locale, enabling the poorest domestic workers to save enough money to buy dairy cows, fix their houses, and support their families.

NOTES

1. Some examples include Geertz (1963), Ong Hok Ham (1975), White (1983, 2018), Hart (1986), White and Wiradi (1989); Hart, White, and Turton (1989), Peluso (1992), Elson (1994), Rachman (1999); and Breman (1980, 2013).

2. The term was *Sikep* elsewhere in Java, as in Ong Hok Ham (1975).

3. *Numpang* is the root of an Indonesian (and Javanese) word that can be a verb or a noun. *Menumpang* is the formal Indonesian verb, *penumpang* the formal noun; both usages are usually spoken as *numpang*. The word has other common uses referring to

being a passenger on any kind of vehicle, or living in the home of one's employers, for example, as with maids in Hong Kong or Jakarta.

4. Interviews with a former forest settlement head, a former Islamic official, and other local elders (2015, 2018).

5. See Moertono (1981) and Ong Hok Ham (1975) for more on this; also Elson (1994) and Blusse (1984). Bergsma (1876) also discusses these relations.

6. The Dutch considered the sultans sovereign rulers and owners of the land. The sultans granted land to *Bupatis* (called Regents by the Dutch). In turn, the Bupatis allocated use rights in the land to the "peasants" known as *sikep* (in Madiun Residency) or *gogol* (in Kediri Residency), and by other regionally varied names. Some writers question whether "peasant" is the best way to describe the positions of these gogols, as they were actually small-scale labor managers (e.g., Ong Hok Ham 1975). In Ngrowo/Tulung Agung Regency, gogols were allocated use rights to cultivate lowland rice paddies based on their claims to control a number of numpang and their labor. Rural class differentiation was thus centrally related to both land control (or lack thereof) *and* labor control from well before the fourteenth century (Pigeaud 1960).

7. But see Breman (2013) that Li (2017) draws on to discuss the horrific conditions faced by coffee workers in western Java's Priangan Residency.

8. Besluit (Government Decision) Bt July 18, 1890–1914 for rental of Sapoe Angin. From ANRI.

9. Stories from several of Manis' grandchildren indicate that the clearing and construction of Pakem were still in progress when she arrived. Several said there was still "much forest" around. I estimate that Manis arrived between 1890–1894. This guess comes from combining the estimated date of birth of Manis's fourth child—the first one born in Pakem—by his daughter (she said 1894 or 1895) with the statement of an inspector for NHM (Nederlandsche Handel-Maatschappij) who submitted a letter/report in 1893, stating that the Sapoe Angin plantation manager's house was under construction that year (Soeter 1893).

10. Specific stories we heard from their grandchildren invoked plantations, such as Sumber Petung, Penampihan, and Mringin.

11. Though we do not yet have written evidence, it is likely that lowland *sawah* holders or their numpang from Karangrejo, Dono, Tugu, Picisan, and Sendang villages worked at the various coffee plantations on the southern facing upper slopes of Mt. Wilis: Besowo, Penampihan, Sapu Angin, Mringin, and Djaejan.

12. The forest had been claimed by state decree in 1866 (Statsblad voor Houtbossen) but not immediately reserved or exploited because of the forest wood's low commodity value (Soepardi 1959).

13. Rowo means "swamp" in Javanese.

14. "*Dulu ada cemburuan social lalu para kuli belajar mereka bisa hidup layak kalau pergi.*" ("In the past there was social jealousy; the workers learned they could live a better life if they left.")

15. "*Sampai-sampai saya dibenci sama petani-petani besar dan Pak Tik karena tenaga kerjanya dipindah keluar.*" ("I was even hated by the large farmers and Pak Tik because their workers were moved away.")

16. Such compensation is still commonly paid when places or sites for residence change hands in the magersari: the land cannot be sold because it is classified as forest land.

17. For six years in the middle of these eighteen, Tini lived in the magersari.

18. Her older brother migrated to work some five hours away at a bread and cake maker's shop in Surabaya where he met his future wife, another migrant worker from Gendingan, down the mountain and near the city of Tulung Agung.

REFERENCES

Bergsma, W. B. 1876. *Eindresume van het bij Gouvernements besluit dd. 10 Juni 1867 no. 2 Bevolen Onderzoek naar de Rechten van den Inlander op den Grond op Java en Madoera*. Batavia Centrum: Verslag Ernst Wasmuth, A.-G.

Bernstein, H. 2004. "'Changing Before Our Very Eyes': Agrarian Questions and the Politics of Land in Capitalism Today." *Journal of Agrarian Change* 4 (1–2): 190–225.

Besky, S. 2017. "Fixity: On the Inheritance and Maintenance of Tea Plantation Houses in Darjeeling, India." *American Ethnologist* 44 (4): 617–631.

Blusse, L. 1984. "Labour Takes Root. Mobilization and Immobilization of Javanese Rural Society Under the Cultivation System." *Itinerario* 8 (1): 77–117.

Boomgaard P. 1989. *Children of the Colonial State: Population Growth and Economic Development in Java 1795–1880*. Amsterdam: Free University Press.

Boomgaard P. 2001. *Frontiers of Fear: Tigers and People in the Malay World, 1600–1950*. New Haven: Yale University Press.

Bosma, U. 2019. *The Making of a Periphery*. New York: Columbia University Press.

Breman J. 1980. "The Village on Java and the Colonial State." *Journal of Peasant Studies* 9 (4): 189–240.

Breman, J. 2013. *Mobilizing Labour for the Global Coffee Market: Profits from an Unfree Work Regime in Colonial Java*. Amsterdam: Amsterdam University Press.

Breman J., and G. Wiradi. 2002. *Good Times and Bad Times in Rural Java*. Leiden: KITLV Press.

Bussy, J. H. de. 1890–1940. *Handboek voor Cultuur-en Handels-Ondernemingen in Nederlandsch-Indië*. Amsterdam: J. H. de Bussy.

Carey, P. 1976. "The Origins of the Java War (1825–30)." *The English Historical Review* 91 (358): 52–78.

Dinas Pariwisata dan Kebudayaan Kabupaten Tulungagung. 2007. *Tulung Agung dalam Rangkaian Sejarah dan Babad*. Tulung Agung: Pemerintah Daerah.

Elmhirst, R. 2011. "Migrant Pathways to Resource Access in Lampung's Political Forest: Gender, Citizenship and Creative Conjugality." *Geoforum* 42 (2): 173–183.

Elson, R. E. 1994. *Village Java under the Cultivation System, 1830–1870*. Southeast Asia Publication Series, no. 25. Sydney: Australian Association of Asian Studies Series in association with Allen and Unwin.

Fasseur, C. 1992. *The Politics of Colonial Exploitation: Java, the Dutch, and the Cultivation System*. Translated by R. E. Elson and A. Kraal. Edited by R. E. Elson. Ithaca: Cornell University Press.

Geertz, C. 1963. *Agricultural Involution*. Berkeley: University of California Press.

Gidwani, V., and P. Ramamurthy. 2018. "Agrarian Questions of Labor in Urban India: Middle Migrants, Translocal Householding and the Intersectional Politics of Social Reproduction." *The Journal of Peasant Studies* 45 (5–6): 994–1017. https://doi.org/10.1080/03066150.2018.1503172.

Goor, C. P. van, and J. Kartasubrata. 1982. *Indonesian Forestry Abstracts: Dutch Literature until about 1960*. Wageningen, NL: Centre for Agricultural Publishing and Documentation.

Hart, G. 1986. *Power, Labor, and Livelihood*. Berkeley: University of California Press.

Hart, G., B. White, and A. Turton. 1989. *Agrarian Transformations*. Berkeley: University of California Press.

Hefner, R. 1990. *The Political Economy of Mountain Java*. Berkeley: University of California Press.

Hirschman, C., and S. Bonaparte. 2012. "Population and Society in Southeast Asia." In *Demography of Southeast Asia*. Edited by L. Williams and P. Guest. Ithaca: Cornell University Press.

Kelly, P. F. 2011. "Migration, Agrarian Transition and Rural Change in Southeast Asia." *Critical Asian Studies* 43 (4): 479–506.

Lukas, M., and N. L. Peluso. 2020. "Transforming the Classic Political Forest: Contentious Territories in Java." *Antipode* 52: (4): 971–995.

Middleton, T. 2019. "The Recursive Lives and Death of Cinchona in Darjeeling." In *Frontier Assemblages*. Edited by J. Cons and M. Eilenberg. Hoboken, NJ, and West Sussex, UK: Wiley.

Moertono, S. 1981. *States and Statecraft in Old Java: A Study of the Later Mataram Period, 16th to 19th Century*. Modern Indonesia Project Monograph Series Publication No. 43 (rev. ed.). Ithaca, NY: Cornell Southeast Asia Program.

Nyoman, N. 2004. *Magersari: Dinamika Komunitas Petani-Pekerja Hutan dalam Perspektif Antropologi Hukum*. Malang: Universitas Brawijaya dengan Universitas Negeri Malang Press.

Ong Hok Ham. 1975. "The Residency of Madiun: Priyayi and Peasant in the Nineteenth Century." PhD diss., Yale University.

Peluso, N. L. 1992. *Rich Forests, Poor People: Resource Control and Resistance in Java*. Berkeley: University of California Press.

Peluso, N.L., and P. Vandergeest. 2001. "Genealogies of the Political Forest and Customary Rights in Indonesia, Malaysia, and Thailand." *Journal of Asian Studies* 60 (2): 761–812.

Peluso, N. L., and A. B. Purwanto. 2018. "The Remittance Forest: Turning Mobile Labor into Agrarian Capital." *Singapore Journal of Tropical Geography* 39 (1): 6–36. https://doi.org/10.1111/sjtg.12225.

Pigeaud, T. G. T. 1960. *Java in the 14th Century: A Study in Cultural History*. Vol. 4. The Hague: Martinus Nijhoff.

Rachman, N. F. 1999. *Petani dan Penguasa: Dinamika Perjalanan Politik Agraria Indonesia*. Yogyakarta: Insist Press.

Robison, R. 1989. *Indonesia: The Rise of Capital*. Australia: Asian Studies Association of Australia.

Robison, R., and V. Hadiz. 2004. *The Politics of Oligarchy in an Age of Markets*. University of Hong Kong Southeast Asia Series. London: Routledge.

Rush, J. 1990. *Opium to Java: Revenue Farming and Chinese Enterprise in Colonial Indonesia 1860–1910*. Ithaca: Cornell University Press.

Sato, S. 1994. *War, Nationalism, and Peasants: Java under the Japanese Occupation, 1942–1945*. London: Routledge.

Scott, J. 1976. *The Moral Economy of the Peasant*. Berkeley: University of California Press.

Scott, J. 2013. *The Art of Not Being Governed*. New Haven: Yale University Press.

Seksi Perencanaan Hutan Wilayah. 2013. *Rencana Pengaturan Kelestarian Hutan*. Kesatuan Pemangkuan Hutan KPH Kediri. Buku A. Jombang: Perum Perhutani.

Shipman, P. 2006. *The Man Who Found the Missing Link: Eugene DuBois and His Lifelong Quest to Prove Darwin Right*. New York: Simon and Schuster.

Silvey, R. 2006. "Geographies of Gender and Migration: Spatializing Social Difference." *International Migration Review* 40 (1): 64–81.

Soepardi R. 1959. *Hutan dan Kehutanan dalam Tiga Jaman*. Jakarta: Departemen Kehutanan.

Soeter. 1893. "Letter to the Semarang Inspection Service." Nationaal Archief, Den Haag, Nederlandsche Handel-Maatschappij (NHM). Access no. 2.20.01, Inventory no. 7951.

Sulistyo, H. 2000. *The Forgotten Years: The Missing History of Indonesia's Mass Slaughter. Jombang-Kediri 1965–66.* N.p.

Sunam, R. 2020. *Transnational Labour Migration, Livelihoods and Agrarian Change in Nepal: The Remittance Village.* New York: Routledge.

Van Schaik, A. 1986. *Colonial Control and Peasant Resources in Java.* Den Haag: CIP-Gegevens Koninklijke Bibliotheek.

Vandergeest, P., and N. L. Peluso. 1995. "Territorialization and State Power in Thailand." *Theory and Society* 24 (3): 385–426.

Vandergeest, P., and N.L.Peluso. 2006a. "Empires of Forestry: Professional Forestry and State Power in Southeast Asia, Part 1." *Environment and History* 12 (1): 31–64.

Vandergeest, P., and N.L. Peluso. 2006b. "Empires of Forestry: Professional Forestry and State Power in Southeast Asia, Part 2." *Environment and History* 12 (4): 359–393.

Veth, P. J. 1875–1882. *Java, Geographisch, Ethnologisch, Historisch.* Haarlem: Erven F. Bohn.

Wertheim, W. F. 1969. "From Aliran towards Class Struggle in the Countryside of Java." *Pacific Viewpoint* 10 (2): 1–17.

White, B. 1983. "Agricultural Involution and Its Critics: 20 Years Later." *Bulletin of Concerned Asian Scholars* 15 (2): 18–36.

White, B. 2018. "Marx and Chayanov at the Margins: Understanding Agrarian Change in Java." *The Journal of Peasant Studies* 45 (5–6): 1108–1126.

White, B., and P. Boomgard. 2016. *Dari Krisis ke Krisis: Masyarakat Indonesia Menghadapi Resesi Ekonomi Selama Abad 20.* Yogyakarta: Gadjah Mada University Press.

White. B., and G. Wiradi. 1989. "Agrarian and Nonagrarian Bases of Inequality in Nine Javanese Villages." In *Ranah Studi Agraria: Penguasaan Tanah dan Hubungan Agraris* (Agrarian studies: land tenure and agrarian relations). Edited by G. Wiradi, B. White, W. L. Collier, M. Soentoro, C. Manning, & M. Shohibuddin, 296–344. Yogyakarta: Sekolah Tinggi Pertanahan Nasional (National Academy of Agrarian Affairs), University of California Press.

9

"INCOMPATIBLE WITH A PROGRESSIVE AGRICULTURE"

The Role of Manioc in Colonial and Postcolonial Visions for Land and Labor in Mozambique

Wendy Wolford

At 7:00 a.m. on Friday, December 2, 2016, Jaime picked me up outside my hotel in Nampula, the dusty capital of the province of the same name in northern Mozambique.[1] The road from Nampula to the much smaller town of Ribaue is one of the few paved roads in good condition in the province. We drove fast and made it to the Dutch Agricultural Development & Trading Company (DADTCO) collection site early.

DADTCO is a Dutch company that is moderately famous in Mozambique for having developed a mobile manioc-processing unit (MPU). The unit consists of a conveyor belt that loads freshly dug and cleaned manioc roots into a machine that pulps, mills, and cleans the manioc and then expresses the water to create small blocks of pure starch. These blocks have multiple uses but are primarily destined for distillation into a beer called Impala. DADTCO partners with the International Fertilizer Development Center (IFDC), a somewhat poorly named research NGO allied with the Ministry of Agriculture's research agency, the Agricultural Research Institute of Mozambique (IIAM), to assist farmers in two different regions of Mozambique.[2] Given that farmers here have been planting manioc for centuries, the researchers and DADTCO were not really teaching them how to grow the root crop from scratch. Rather, they were teaching them how to plant manioc in ways that matched the rhythm and needs of a newly developing market (Gengenbach 2019).

The DADTCO collection site in Ribaue sits right off of the main road, surrounded by fields of manioc, the head-high, tell-tale knobby stalks standing silently at attention, their sparse green leaves providing little shade for the soil.

The day was already hot—full sun and no wind. It would rain later that afternoon, but unless someone told you it was raining, you would not know because the drops were as hot as the air. When we pulled in, several men in a pickup truck were loading manioc roots onto the conveyor belt. A small covered area with two tables and plastic chairs sat off to the side; two young women waited with a small cash box, a ledger, and a laptop to make note of any manioc deliveries. No one paid much attention to me as I wandered around the MPU and eventually plopped down into an empty chair under the tent. As I sat there, writing field notes and taking pictures, activity began to pick up. Jaime brought news that a government minister would be visiting shortly (people thought it was the Minister of Agriculture, but it turned out to be the Minister of Transportation and Commerce). All of the workers at the DADTCO mobile processing unit were quickly given blue hair nets, and a few were given brand new red gloves still clipped in the middle with plastic ties. People looked at the equipment oddly, as if at a loss, but upon Jaime's urging, gamely put the nets on their heads and the gloves on their hands.

At 9:30 a.m., the Minister pulled up in an SUV along with a convoy of trucks. Surrounded by a group of bodyguards, reporters, and others, he looked the machine over, asked Jaime if any Mozambicans had a share in the company (the answer was no), and then went over to the tented area. A farmer who had brought in a load of manioc roots that morning sat in front of one of the tables and looked startled when the Minister clapped him on the shoulder with a hearty greeting. The Minister asked him how much land he had planted in manioc this season. The farmer blinked but eventually answered, and the Minister said, still heartily, "Well, you're going to plant more next time, right? You have to expand!" The farmer responded that he would plant more "if he had the *força* [strength]." At that moment, as he sat somewhat limply on his chair, it seemed very unlikely that he would indeed have the strength, but the Minister said, "Of course you have the *força!*" Facing the audience, the Minister said that what the farmer had planted this season, he had done with one arm—and he held up one of the farmer's arms in demonstration—but now the farmer would have to plant with the other arm too! Everyone, including the farmer, nodded in agreement at this nonsensical statement, and the Minister and his incredible retinue marched off, getting back into their cars and driving away in less time than it had taken for the men working the machines to get their new gloves on.

Manioc is the most widespread food crop planted in Mozambique today. A study of the way in which colonial and postcolonial government officials, scientists, and aid workers have treated the tuber sheds light on colonial and postcolonial aspirations for the land and people of the region.

When the Portuguese tightened their rule over the territory in the early twentieth century, natural scientists, government administrators, and self-styled businessmen toured the region, evaluating the land for its agricultural potential. Reports submitted to the newly formed (1908) Department of Agriculture praised the beauty and certain fertility of the land in Mozambique but warned that it would only bear fruit if the local residents could be made to work.[3] The Portuguese—the poorest of the European colonizers—anxiously discussed the commodity crops that could successfully launch the territory into the global market. They imagined well-organized landscapes with row crops managed by European estate owners and tended to by local residents. They dismissed the ability of locals to farm independently, arguing that indigenous groups favored "uncivilized" crops like manioc because they were easy to grow, requiring little technique and providing easy calories months after planting.[4] The history of manioc in the country is thus a history of empire itself; a story, I argue, of naturalizing and neglecting local crops and people in an attempt to bend both to the service of tropical commodities for the global market. This history of neglect explains how manioc could be so widespread and yet receive so little attention from those tasked with improving colonial and postcolonial agricultural production.

In the chapter that follows, I describe the story that the Portuguese told about manioc in the early days of the colony: that manioc production was a natural extension of local peoples' incapacity to farm and their propensity for an easy life. I then offer a counterstory, arguing that dependence on manioc was not "natural" but increased in direct relation to the increase in plantation crops and colonial rule, serving as food for laborers, prisoners, and refugees. This is a study of absences, prompted by my sifting through the archives of the main agricultural research agency in the country, trying to understand why manioc—the most important food crop in the colony—was only rarely and partially counted in official surveys and why systematic research on varieties, diseases, and production techniques was never undertaken until it was almost too late. Only in the 1990s, when drought and disease reduced manioc supplies, causing mass famine and illness as people ate toxic tubers in desperation, was a multicountry research effort marshaled in defense of the plant. These efforts continued the colonial tendency of downplaying local farmers' abilities to manage their land, focusing on breeding rather than on in situ farm practices that might have mitigated the spread of disease. With the release of new varieties and international attention, manioc became interesting as a market commodity, and new projects sprang up to commodify and process manioc at scale. Local farmers gravitated toward these market projects in part because they offered the best access to new varieties. The projects, however, have had difficulty succeeding, and I argue that this is because they are predicated on farmers producing manioc on the land in a way they never had before, in efficiently ordered rows with preset harvest times and an emphasis on production quantity over other characteristics of the tuber, such as quality of the foliage (which people boil and eat), hardiness, and flavor (Gengenbach et al. 2018; Gengenbach 2019). In essence, plans for expanding this market required local farmers to trade one externally imposed naturalization for another: *the native* for *homo economicus*. Both naturalizations positioned local farmers as laborers on someone else's land in a commodity regime to which they otherwise did not belong (Wolford 2019).

I tell the story of manioc in part as an intervention against a masculinist tradition of writing world histories through the lens of single commodities purported to have shaped the international system. From Sidney Mintz's (1986) powerful epic on sugar (see also Moore 2000) to studies of cotton (Beckert 2015), silver (Moore 2010), and corn (Warman 2003), commodity histories are almost always plantation crops or resources produced in large-scale, usually extractive sites intended for export. These triumphant histories define the world system by the crops or resources that dominated the market, influenced labor relations, and defined imperial ambitions. They have contributed much to our understanding of agricultural production, national development, and the world system, but the fixation on dominant crops leads to a fetish of both scale and market and obscures the importance of "support crops" that make dominance (both agronomic and political) possible. A study of manioc illustrates the ways in which an otherwise unremarkable plant knits together a vast array of production strategies and aspirations on the land. Manioc is not itself a plantation crop; it is a "hidden crop" (O'Connor 2013), an escape crop (Scott 2009), a "life-sustaining crop" (Gengenbach 2019), one that has supported both plantation production and itinerant subsistence production among poor households.

The research for this chapter comes from the archives and the field. I originally went to Mozambique in 2013, following the Brazilians who traveled to the country to aid in what they saw as the agricultural transformation of the next frontier: Africa (Wolford and Nehring 2015; Wolford 2015, 2019). Over the next four years, I returned repeatedly to Mozambique, spending six months in Maputo in 2016 on a Fulbright research grant and six months in Lisbon, Portugal, working in the archives.[5] While in Mozambique, I conducted over sixty interviews with research scientists, aid workers, and government employees. I also spent time in several different rural communities and, alone and with research associates, conducted over one hundred interviews. Upon returning from Mozambique and Portugal, I have transcribed, translated, and coded these interviews; the arguments I make in this chapter result from both my qualitative observations and conversations and patterns in the data.

It's Only Natural: Of Course the Natives Love It

Manioc (also known as cassava, yuca, or arrowroot, as well as the plant that gives us tapioca) is a perennial woody shrub that grows anywhere from five to twelve feet tall. The many (thousands of) varieties are classified as sweet or bitter, depending not on the taste of the tuber (which can be misleading) but on the level of hydrocyanic acid (HCN). Bitter varieties contain cyanogenic glycosides that are toxic if not cooked or dried correctly. Although the sweet varieties have the advantage of a slightly shorter growing season, in addition to not being poisonous, the bitter varieties tend to yield larger roots and can be left in the ground longer (Karasch 2008). The manioc plant yields well in soils that are low in fertility, particularly in the acidic soils of northeastern Mozambique. Manioc propagates vegetatively and grows well in wet or dry conditions. It requires relatively little work, grows belowground—so has natural protection from pests (including locusts, monkeys, and the state)—and can be left in the soil for up to three months after reaching maturity. The peel is the richest in proteins and fats, but most people peel away the tuber because it is quite tough, difficult to clean, and, as if that were not enough, tastes like bark.

As numerous as the advantages of manioc are, the crop does not appear to have dominated local diets in Mozambique until well into the twentieth century. The exact date and route by which manioc was introduced into East Africa is not well known.[6] When introduced into East Africa, manioc was originally incorporated into a local diet rich in diversified grains, legumes, and meat. Early accounts of the region from European travelers describe the bountiful gardens, filled with sorghum, millet, groundnuts, and squashes (Jones 1959). As British Consul for Portuguese East Africa and author R. C. F. Maugham wrote in the early 1900s: "In the neighbourhood of the older established villages one finds planted, in addition to the food-producing cereals, ground nuts (*Arachis hypogeia*), the castor-oil plant (*Ricinus comunis*), melons, pumpkins, cucumbers, gourds, of which serviceable household and other utensils are fashioned, sweet potatoes, manioc (cassava), tobacco, tomatoes, red pepper, and kidney beans. In addition to the foregoing, pineapples, pawpaws, bananas of various kinds, and, more rarely, lemons, limes, and sugar-cane. Numerous other wild fruits are gathered and eaten in their season, but their native names would convey but little to the reader at home" (Maugham 1906, 288–289).

In 1913, Robert Nunez Lyne, a British agronomist who served briefly as Director of the Department of Agriculture (1910–1912), described the plants cultivated by "Indigenous" (his term) farmers in his guide for "the intending settler and investor," (28) as including "manioc, pigeon peas, groundnuts, sweet potato, yams of enormous size, citrus, cashew, bananas, tobacco, turmeric, tonniers, castor oil, and sesame" (36).

Increasingly, however, manioc production came to overshadow these varied gardens. The full extent of manioc production historically is difficult to estimate definitely, given that little official investigation was ever done of indigenous farm production, but by 1970, "manioc, cultivated throughout the province, can be considered the food crop that occupies the greatest area" (Mota 1970, 23).[7] Despite the earlier evidence of diversified farm production, European observers argued that reliance on manioc was "natural" because of the plant's agronomic characteristics and the local resident's purported laziness and disorganization in farming methods.

As the agronomist Teresa P. Mota wrote, echoing the general sentiment in the archives: "[manioc's] expansion is primarily due to the easy method of production (à fácil cultura) and good productivity in varied climatic conditions and in almost all soils [. . .]" (Mota 1970, 23). A widely distributed compendium of best agricultural practices argued that "the popularity of this plant, among the Indigenous in all of Africa, is due to its vigorous growth, to its certain and good yield, to its resistance to drought or dryness, to the limited and easy work that it requires as well as the ease with which it can be kept in the soil which, together with its long harvest season, allowed the roots to be collected according to necessity" (Costa and Ferrinho 1964, 88). In general, the Portuguese thought it was natural for local inhabitants to gravitate to manioc because the plant's agronomic characteristics lent it to habits they saw as foreign and primitive. They disparaged what they saw as the lack of private property and the regular migrations from one plot to another where people harvested manioc "opportunistically" when it was time to move on.[8]

This manner of working the land—with the long fallow periods of shifting cultivation often referred to as primitive or rustic—struck the Europeans as extraordinarily wasteful and appeared to legitimate European colonization. As Robert Nunez Lyne (1913) said, "Generally, the African method of cultivating is to till the ground in patches so that while a lot of land is occupied, a little of it is used. This wasteful system, or want of system, is, at bottom, the reason why Europe has appropriated Africa in accordance with the maxim, 'The tools to him that can use them'" (48). Even as attitudes began to change somewhat in the 1950s and 1960s, and more researchers argued in support of local agriculture, shifting cultivation was still officially seen as highly primitive and an obstacle to "progress." An official survey of agricultural practices in 1964 argued that fallows needed to be "eliminated because they are not economical and they are incompatible with a progressive agriculture and they will not aid us in our goal" (Barradas 1962, 30).

Forced Labor: The Marriage of Manioc and Cotton

Manioc may be the ultimate "famine reserve" crop (Jones 1959; Scott 2009), but it has serious deficiencies. It is low in necessary nutrients, and the bitter varieties contain sufficiently high levels of cyanide that they are toxic if not processed correctly after harvesting. Manioc is best if it is one of many elements of a diet, providing starch, while other goods like peanuts, squash, and horticultures provide the balance. In the early 1960s, Salvador Nunes conducted one of the first studies of the nutritional contents of different varieties of manioc in order to assess the potential for expansion. He found corn and sorghum to be significantly better for calories, protein, and iron, as well as considerably less toxic (see Table 1 below). Nunes assumed that local inhabitants chose to plant and eat manioc because they appreciated the ease of its cultivation despite the nutritional deficits: "Effectively, the low or trace percentages of protein and fat put manioc in the category of "unhealthy food" (*alimentos desequilibrados*), but the Native (autochthone) is interested in manioc for its carbohydrates, easy cultivation, and low cost of production, and this brings him to consider manioc a basic subsistence good" (Nunes 1964, 137).

Disparaging manioc served the dual purpose of dismissing local farmers (who could be dismissed as not farming at all because planting manioc required no effort) and dismissing indigenous rights to land. The irony is that manioc production grew not because its agronomic characteristics mirrored the natural desires of the local population; rather, manioc production grew because it was the subsistence food that colonial rulers used to prop up the labor force. Manioc was

TABLE 9.1. Nutritional content per 100 grams

	MANIOC (FRESH)	MANIOC (DRY)	CORN	SORGHUM
Water g	62	12	11.5	12
Protein raw g	.70	2.00	10.00	10.00
Fat raw g	trace	trace	4.50	3.00
Calcium g	25	55	20	25
Phosphorous mg	50	110	200	280
Iron mg	.50	1	4	5
Thiamin mmg	20	50	450	500
Riboflavin mmg	70	70	140	120
Niacin g	.6	1.2	1.5	3.5
Calories	144	328	360	347

Source: Salvador Nunes (1964, 138)

the crop chosen by government officials, plantation owners, police officers, and military commanders to feed those under their control. From African slaves in the sugar mills of Brazil to plantation laborers across Africa to prisoners captured by opposition forces in Mozambique, manioc was the food of choice (Geffray 1991, 66; Karasch 2008, 183).

Providing cheap food was an important part of securing the cheap labor upon which colonial Mozambique's ambitions depended. This quote from Governor General Mousinho de Albuquerque (written in 1899 and published in 1913) summarizes a common sentiment of early Portuguese rulers in Mozambique:

> One of the most difficult problems and, at the same time, the one whose resolution is most insistently imposed on Africa is, without doubt, that which results from the necessity of using Indigenous labor and the difficulties that their habits of indolence common to all wild things (*selvagens*) present. The climatic conditions of the province of Mozambique [. . .] make it impossible to use the European immigrant not just as an agricultural worker but in many violent jobs, because they will not last in that climate. For these jobs, therefore, the Native is indispensable, leaving the European just with the role of leading them" (99).

In this context, manioc was the key to unlocking the potential of local labor, particularly in relation to the most significant commodity crop in the territory: cotton. Cotton was planted in Mozambique from the 1700s on, and historical records document the twinning of cotton and manioc. As R. C. F. Maugham wrote, "From 1765 to 1799, the destinies of the country were in the hands of one Balthazar Manuel Pereira do Lago, who caused the erection of buildings answering to our town halls and established, in the more important centres, assemblies similar to our municipal councils. The cultivation of cotton and manioc became obligatory, and many *feiras* (places of exchange and barter) were founded throughout the colony" (Maugham 1913, 24).[9]

Cotton production increased in the 1900s as the Portuguese tightened control of their overseas territories and looked to cotton production in Mozambique to ameliorate the country's dependence on imports (Newitt 1995). Conditions on the cotton plantations were harsh for the workers—Allen Isaacman (1996) calls the plantations the "Mother of Poverty," and manioc became necessary for both subsistence and survival. As Isaacman (1996) writes, "many peasants supplemented their meagre diets by eating roots and tubers and planting manioc which, though of lower nutritional value than other food crops, required only a minimal amount of labor" (594). The historian Merle Bowen emphasizes this: "In most parts of the country, forced crop production led peasants to change from the cultivation of grains such as sorghum, a labor-intensive subsistence crop, to cassava, a less labor-absorbing and less nutritious crop. Cassava also interfered less than sorghum or millet with the agricultural calendar of commodity crops like cotton or rice" (Bowen 2000, 36). Manioc was usually planted by Indigenous farmers themselves, although the records in the monthly magazine, the *Gazeta do Agricultor* (Gazeta), maintained by the national agriculture and veterinary services, suggested that manioc was also planted by colonists who wanted to employ local residents and needed to plant manioc "to sustain the staff" (*Gazeta do Agricultor* March 1951, 191). Bridget O'Laughlin (2002) argues that, in Mozambique, "the development of plantations created a demand for cheap staple foods—principally maize and dried cassava—which was not satisfied by [European] settler farms" (518).

Manioc production increased further when government control over cotton production intensified with the abolition of the privately owned "royal companies" in the mid-1940s (Saraiva 2009). "Soon, the diet basis of the local population was based on manioc, a less demanding crop but also a less nutritive one. Famines started to show up in the cotton regions, and in 1951, in the Mogovolas, some two to three thousand people died from starvation" (54).

By the 1960s, planting manioc and cotton together was the official recommendation. In a government-produced "Introductory Manual for Agricultural Knowledge in Mozambique" that outlined which crops would do well in different regions, the author suggested that "if one is going to set up locally an industry of cotton textiles, it will be necessary to increase concomitantly the industry of manioc, to make use of the subproducts" (*Manual de iniciação* 1962, 108). Land area planted in manioc on non-Native farms (what were referred to as "civilized" or European agriculture) tripled between 1941–1942 and 1951–1952 (from 1,178 hectares to 3,614 hectares) (Esteves 1957, 11). On the eve of Independence, manioc production was estimated at 2,400,000 tons per year in fresh roots, whereas corn (the preferred food crop of the Europeans and also coveted by local residents) was registered at 450,000 tons per year, principally produced in the higher regions and Sul do Save (Martins Santareno 1973, 16).

For the colonial administration, manioc consumption represented the laziness and improvidence of local residents as well as the ideal crop to keep them alive and working. It was suited to local agronomic conditions, complemented cotton production, and required little aid or research. It made a certain form of colonization possible, one suited to the particularities of the Portuguese empire, a relatively impoverished empire (compared to other Europeans in Africa) with scarce resources for settlement or development and a great desire to wring surplus from the territory for investment back in the center (Newitt 1995). Manioc allowed forced labor to sustain itself, if just barely, justified by a racialized naturalization of so-called Native habits and crop characteristics.

It's Native and Natural, So No Research Needed

In spite of the fact that manioc is the number one crop produced in Mozambique by quantity, there has been relatively little agronomic or socioeconomic research into the plant or market. In 1960, the official handbook on farming in Mozambique reported: "The study of varieties existing in Mozambique has still not been done even though we are already working on introducing varieties from other countries" (*Manual de iniciação* 1962, 182). Scientists and others employed by the National Agricultural Services did not seem aware of the basic uses of manioc by local people.[10] Technical recommendations for production were desultory; in 1961, the Gazeta (vol. 13, no. 144) provided this advice for how to plant in sandy soil: dig a hole. And "the harvest is very easy, especially in sandy soil. Just pull the stem up and to the sides, shaking it each time until all of the roots are pulled out. If, by chance, some roots are left in the ground, use a hoe to take them out" (138). In his dissertation investigating Indigenous agriculture in 1960, Armando Lourenço Rodrigues wrote: "Even in poor land, it's enough to stick the stalks in the ground at convenient intervals, to get a reasonable harvest" (Rodrigues 1960).

In 1953, a farmer wrote to the Gazeta to ask about the possibility of processing manioc on his farm. His question and the answer were published in the "Consultations" section of the Gazeta, illustrating the general lack of infrastructure or capacity for manioc: "A complete and precise answer to that question would be so much work and vast that it's outside of the scope of the Gazeta" (vol. 5, no. 9, 179–180). The author of the "Consultations" section could think of no better advice than to provide the name of an extension agent who worked with a local banana cooperative and who might be of help.

In 1970, however, the Technical Planning and Economic Integration Commission of the Province of Mozambique recommended that manioc yields needed to be improved through improved varieties and planting techniques, so IIAM made a "first pass" (*um primeiro passo*) at coordinating research efforts (Mota 1970, 23). IIAM selected the best varieties from a collection of eighty stored in the Agronomic Station of Nhacoongo (in the southern province of Inhambane), selecting for resistance to the mosaic virus, productivity, and attractiveness to consumers. They sent these to the Namapa Agronomic Station in northern Mozambique to see how well they would do in that environment. "With a little interest," the head of the commission wrote, "and some effort to improve the manioc crop in Mozambique, one could entertain the hypothesis of reaching international markets" (28).

That same year, however, J. A. L. Martins Santareno (then Provincial Secretary of Lands and Settlement) asked for information about work done on manioc in the territory and a year later received a twenty-three-page report that highlighted the weakness of agronomic research in Mozambique that "doesn't have logical planning or the confidence that [experiments undertaken] will be continued" (Leitão 1971, 1). The report outlined manioc studies that had been undertaken as early as 1943 and repeated in 1957, but the results of these were unreliable because of "the lack of continuity and of method" (3). Many of the experiments were wasted or useless without additional work. Overall, the author of the study concluded that more work needed to be done and that it was important to outline from the beginning whether the study was geared towards traditional agriculture or business-oriented agriculture (*agricultura patronal*), as these would likely require different methods and approaches.

After Independence in 1975, the primary program for funding research and extension in agriculture was the Mozambique-Nordic Agricultural Program (called MONAP for short). MONAP was coordinated by the Swedish International Development Cooperation Agency, SIDA, and funded by a consortium of foreign donors. MONAP was a ten-year, multi-million-dollar program focused on comprehensively improving the infrastructure for agriculture, silviculture, and veterinary services around the country. The program did not, however, include research on or assistance for manioc, with the exception of limited assistance for marketing manioc (Adam et al. 1991, 101). The crops included were instead ones that favored an urban and even export market, such as corn, peanuts, soy, beans, wheat, rice, sunflower, *Crotolaria* (rattleweed, grown as a cover crop), and cotton.

Mozambique has occasionally pushed for research on manioc, but this has generally not been considered feasible for cross-regional projects. For example, in the Agricultural Productivity Program for Southern Africa, the multicountry (Zambia, Malawi, and Mozambique) program funded by the World Bank, researchers in Mozambique initially suggested that the country focus its contribution on manioc, but the other countries were not interested in the tuber, which was considered of interest primarily for former Portuguese colonies (IIAM, interview with the author, 2016). As a result, Mozambique became a Center of Excellence for rice.

Research scientists I interviewed in Mozambique explained that the lack of research into manioc was due to the continued division of projects into ones focusing on market crops or ones focusing on subsistence crops. Another way of putting this was that most projects focused on "emerging" farmers while others targeted poor farmers (mirroring the division between "civilized" and Native farmers under the Portuguese). Manioc research falls into the latter category and, therefore, warrants very little research despite being the largest single source of calories in the country.[11] Researchers at the lead agencies and organizations, such as IIAM, the International Institute for Tropical Agriculture (IITA), and others, tend to develop technologies for wealthier farmers—such as plantations, mechanization schemes, and extension advice delivered through smartphones—while nongovernmental organizations such as the Cooperative League of the USA and the Cooperative for Assistance and Relief Everywhere in Mozambique work on programs for the poor—*coisa dos pobres*, as the lead for FAO Mozambique called them—such as farmer field schools, conservation agriculture, and savings associations.

Researchers, policy makers, and farmers alike were sold on the "green revolution" coming to Mozambique, with its promise of high-yielding plant varieties, mechanized agriculture, and access to modern markets. The independent Mozambican government has seen this intensification as the solution to this very serious problem of smallholder poverty. Such imaginaries have been fundamental to colonial and postcolonial aspirations for Mozambique for over a hundred years now (Shankland and Gonçalves 2016). Rhetorically, the government is focused on reducing hunger and improving nutrition, but most people agree that it is still following strategies that focus on production and productivity (USAID, interview with the author, 2016; Wolford 2019).

In the 1990s, manioc began to get more attention across Africa because an outbreak of Cassava Brown Stripe Disease (CBSD) badly affected manioc production, and people across southern Africa were greatly endangered. International organizations like IITA began the research effort to tackle CBSD, starting in Nigeria and expanding outward. There were two options for treating CBSD, according to the IIAM/Save the Children/USAID document outlining the success of the manioc breeding program begun in the mid-2000s. One option was to work with clean material (in situ selection by farmers, getting rid of the infected material, and replanting clean stalks), and the other was breeding. There was good evidence of the former succeeding in other countries, such as Tanzania (Hillocks 2003), and the official handbook (*Manual de iniciação* 1962) of the 1960s reported that "taking stalks from healthy plants is the best means of preventing disease that we have available now, given that we do not have resistant varieties" (183). But the scientists involved in the initial program decided that a program focusing on land management would not work in Mozambique because, according to the IIAM/Save the Children/USAID document, such farmer-centered approaches do not "typically succeed in developing countries, especially in ones as poor as Mozambique. Success normally depends on having a well-defined commercial sector that can provide seeds and operate in an economic environment that is well institutionalized. Outside of this, the pressure of root rot in the districts severely affected is so high that it is unlikely that a program of clean seed by itself will be successful" (9).

The Director of IITA, however, suggested that the focus on breeding was a result of the international network in which manioc research got started. In an interview conducted in IITA's Nampula compound, I asked the Director whether there was a conversation about better management as opposed to better varieties, and he responded: "No, basically, they identified the problems in the different countries—and most projects are like that. We identify where the problems are, and the country offices write the proposal, and then we look for funding. The network on cassava was a regional approach, where Malawi—it was seven African countries, Nigeria, Mozambique, and others—but basically the problems are mostly the same [in all of the countries], so they came in here, and the breeders did the breeding and got new materials—and the new varieties [come] with management [guidelines] and then also capacity building of the research system" (IITA, interview with the author, December 8, 2016).

From interviews across IIAM, it was clear that international emphases on breeding dominated the agenda. Breeding might have been the best option in the case of CBSD, but it was often done without attention to the demands of the farmers themselves, instead focusing on the genetics and pathology of the plant. One of the scientific leads of the manioc program in the early 2000s said they lost time because they tested varieties that were not what the producers said they wanted and ignored local varieties that had some clear advantages.

"An example I give is one I saw with the producers in Mongicoal [a small town in the province of Nampula]. We were working with cassava and, at the end of the season, at the end of the study, you know, as researchers, we said 'that,' 'that,' 'that,' [points as if indicating stalks of manioc] okay, that was okay for us . . . But the producers didn't always choose what we recommended! [. . .] He already had his focus. He said, 'I want this variety, that, that, and that' [points in the other direction]. They did their thing, but when we looked at the varieties [they wanted], they were not always the resistant ones, and we said, 'but there's disease, there's this, there's that.' And as time went on, we released new varieties, more of the researchers' but some of the producers'. Over time, we have seen that the producer's variety had a very desirable architecture for production, although every now and then they discover the disease on the root or some such . . . That is, the new variety is not fully resistant, but it tolerates the disease [well]. Maybe we would have saved a lot of time . . . if we had given the producer directly what he wanted. And on the other hand, the researcher's variety has been developing as a very woody plant, and it has . . . certain architectural problems, while the producer's does not. Today, I give my hand [to the producer]" (IIIAM, interview with the author, September 23, 2016).

As this long quote suggests, while research on manioc was finally set into motion by the Brown Stripe disease across southeastern Africa, the focus was on the science rather than on the farmers themselves or on land management techniques that might have enabled the farmers to plant more fields with a healthier distribution of crops.

Making Money? Manioc and the New Supply Chain

As new manioc varieties were researched and developed, initiatives for marketing the most productive varieties emerged. The most well-known initiative is the one that I describe in the introduction to this chapter: the initiative to create a mass-marketed beer from manioc roots. The beer, called Impala after the small African antelope, is distilled by Cerveja de Moçambique, SA (CdM), a subsidiary of the largest beer conglomerate in the world, Anheuser-Busch InBev. The initiative involves two other organizations: the IFDC, which provides training to the farmers so that they can plant most effectively according to the needs of the buyers, and DADTCO, the Dutch company that operates the MPU and works directly with farmers to purchase manioc in two regions of Mozambique, including Nampula where this chapter begins.

IFDC and DADTCO began working together in 2004 in Nigeria. DADTCO came to Nampula in 2011. The biggest problem the three organizations have run into with the project in Mozambique is not the market for the beer, which is very popular; rather, it is the supply of manioc. That supply would be the problem is surprising in a country where manioc still occupies the largest number of hectares of any single crop, but IFDC, DADTCO, and CdM require the supply to conform to certain characteristics; namely, the manioc must be delivered in specified quantities (not too much or too little) at specified times. This requires a different approach to production from what the farmers are familiar with, as manioc has always served as the reserve crop, valued for its capacity to sit in the ground until needed.

IFDC and DADTCO, therefore, select farmers carefully. They promote the project over the radio, through Field Days at the local agricultural experiment station, and through "awareness-building sessions" (*sensibilizações*) or quick informational meetings. Farmers are required to sign statements that they will plant as they are told to, using new varieties and methods provided by IFDC.

They are given orientations around creating a nursery, selecting good stalks, planting, timing, spacing, and harvesting. IFDC works with a small set of particularly active community members they call mobilizers (also commonly called facilitators or animators in aid circles, although each of these has a slightly different meaning). These community members have a little more land than the others and are selected for their higher capacity for both production and leadership. These mobilizers encourage the rest of the community to use proper methods and provide their harvest on the right day and in the right manner. The emphasis on timing is critical, as manioc begins to ferment roughly twenty-four hours after the roots are pulled from the ground. If fermentation begins before the manioc is processed, it cannot be used, so DADTCO uses a ticket system, handing out tickets to every farmer with dates on them, providing them with a three-day window to deliver their manioc to the MPU. Once the starch (*massa*) is processed into starch blocks, it will last for months with little care required, so the crucial time period is the first twenty-four hours after harvest.

And this is where the difficulties begin. Based on interviews with two different manioc grower associations in Nampula, DADTCO representatives, and IFDC scientists, as well as a Director of Sales for Impala in Nampula, I make three arguments: first, IFDC and DADTCO worked hard to distinguish the manioc they wanted for the market from subsistence manioc; second, this meant that they applied these new techniques to the former, but the farmers struggled because these new planting techniques differed so dramatically from the way they traditionally planted (and thought of) manioc; third, the farmers rebelled against DADTCO because the company took the market logic too far, failing to provide subsidiary benefits such as schools or wells (to which the communities were accustomed, as per most development efforts in the region) and pricing the product according to the demand from CdM. In what follows, I briefly flesh out these arguments.

IFDC and DADTCO favored bitter manioc varieties and encouraged the farmers to plant sweet varieties for their own consumption and bitter varieties for the market. There was a brief media scandal when it was widely reported that the new initiative was stealing manioc from impoverished households, pushing farmers to sell their crop instead of eating it, but both IFDC and DADTCO insisted publicly that this was inaccurate. The organizations insisted that farmers should separate their land into easily distinguishable plots: one for the market and one for subsistence. The market-oriented advice was to plant the bitter varieties because they produced more per plant and the cyanide was easily removed during processing.

The new methods that IFDC promoted were disseminated through small workshops—one association I spoke with had attended a three-day workshop at a local hotel, which they liked because they got to "focus on manioc [. . .]

without any distractions." The President of the Farmers' Association suggested that, although the farmers had heard the same advice before the workshop, the repetition in a formal setting helped it to stick. IFDC technicians argued that these new methods were challenging to teach because they represented a "transformation," in large part because "people here never used to see manioc as a commercial crop; it was just a subsistence crop."

At the workshop and also in other one-day trainings at nearby experiment stations and experiment fields, the farmers learned how to plant in lines (*alinhamento*) and to space the plants closer together. They use a rope to help measure out straight lines, and so planting is usually done in a group. They have to measure the distance between the lines of manioc, which is supposed to be exactly one meter. This gives the manioc room to grow and provides space for other crops, such as beans or corn, to be intercropped between the rows of manioc. IFDC extensionists spend a lot of time working on *alinhamento* and tend to focus these efforts on the men because—as the men in the association I interviewed said, laughingly—"the women don't like to plant in rows because it's 'too difficult.'" One of the older women in the group laughed and said she planted half of her field in lines and then "gave up and planted the rest randomly." IFDC also teaches the farmers to cut the manioc stalks into shorter lengths for propagation so that they can plant a larger field with the plant material they have. The farmers also learned to mulch, but IFDC does not recommend mulching manioc fields because the plants "don't really need it, so they're not likely to waste [the mulch]."

In general, these new techniques are not difficult; they are just different. Planting manioc according to these specifications requires considerably more labor than planting for subsistence. This is much more likely to be the reason why women—who are juggling many jobs—do not take to planting in lines. In order to satisfy the higher labor demand, the associations and the farmers who have more land or who have managed to secure more manioc plants (whether because they are better connected, had leadership positions, or became familiar with IFDC or DADTCO early), *hire* laborers to clean their land, plant, weed, and harvest.

Although the relationship between the farmers and IFDC/DADTCO was very promising in the first year, by the second year, the market price for manioc had dropped by half, and there were strenuous complaints from the farmers. DADTCO established a floor price, but at 2.5 meticais per kilo, this was considered too low to warrant production.[12] DADTCO insisted that they could pay better only if they could be guaranteed a sufficient supply. Otherwise, the beer company would not increase its beer production, and there were few other market possibilities.

The farmers I spoke with conveyed their bitterness at DADTCO for not delivering what they considered to be a fair price, but they were also upset at not receiving what they saw as appropriate "help" from the company for things like new wells or a school building. DADTCO representatives shook their heads in dismay at this request for help, arguing that the local people were trained to ask for things instead of working. But asking for help is part of the history; it is the way people do business. As the president of the association I spoke with said: "We are asking for any project to help, any visitor that appears, we ask for help." He complained that "the company asks me for everything, and they don't do anything for us. We just think they should help us."

When I asked one of the DADTCO representatives about the things that the company had supposedly promised, he became agitated and said the company was doing "corporate social responsibility" just by operating its MPUs, "but we never promised anything—you can get water right on the DADTCO site—they have tons of water and the community already had four or five wells, why would they want another water source? And they ask for a hospital, but there's a hospital right there—it's less than 500 meters away! They just want things just for the association. It's not the company's responsibility to do something about social responsibility."

That sentiment illustrated the problem with the new initiative for manioc production. Manioc was the crop the colonial government and landowners used to maintain a labor force for their plantations. As such, manioc was the glue that allowed communities to survive harsh labor conditions. Under the new system, however, manioc was stripped of its social meaning and recast as the new plantation crop for which the farmers were to provide labor. That this labor was separated from social reproduction was evident in the fact that none of the farmers I interviewed had ever even tasted Impala beer—it sold for fifty meticais per bottle (roughly seventy-five cents today) in the local bars, well above what they could afford and well above the 2.5 meticais per kilo they received for the raw material.

Ultimately, although the players had changed and the targets were different, an analysis of manioc production suggests that rural producers in Mozambique today are treated much as they were under colonization. They are expected to assume responsibility for both their own survival and for the survival of the market, with no one caring for the needs of the community. This is a plant both sweet and bitter: a miracle crop that provides relief in times of famine and drought but does not nourish those who labor in its fields. Far from the diversified fields in which manioc once grew, the very nature of the plant has been manipulated to serve the needs of empire and market.

This chapter presents a brief history of a crop that rarely merits much attention. It is one of the most ubiquitous plants in Mozambique, but even local residents are embarrassed when asked about how they prepare and eat manioc. It is "poor people's food" and has long been neglected by colonial and postcolonial authorities in the country. The Portuguese saw the tuber as a local crop, one that illustrated how naturally unfit local inhabitants were for civilized agriculture. Their descriptions of the tuber echoed their descriptions of the local residents themselves, disdainful of their shifting agriculture and lack of European institutions. And yet, as they bent local labor to the colonial enterprise, they relied on manioc as a means of subsistence: a food that would keep the indigenous alive enough to carry out plantation work, even if it did not nourish them.

The transition to Independence in 1975 did little to change official attitudes toward manioc: first the socialist state and then the capitalist state (post-1987) envisioned a landscape that would be transformed by large-scale export agriculture. Manioc had no place in that except as food in times of famine. When that famine indeed struck, funds and scientific research were mobilized to study the crop, but even then, colonial attitudes about the inability of local residents to farm were evident. Scientists downplayed the ability of local farmers to control manioc viruses by planting their fields differently or better, and so they focused on breeding to combat diseases such as CBSD and the mosaic virus. The breeding program has been highly successful, generating new varieties that are highly resistant to disease, but it has been difficult for local farmers to access the new stalks.

One of the means for access to the new, disease-resistant varieties has been to participate in a creative program to turn manioc into a market commodity: the new beer Impala, made from cassava starch. Farmers are enrolled into a multiactor program to plant manioc for the beer, bringing regular bundles on predetermined days to the MPU run by the Dutch company DADTCO. But the project requires that the residents farm manioc in a way they are not used to doing: using relatively rigid market-oriented techniques of spacing, organizing the plant in rows, and harvesting on preset days. Farmers struggle with the new, time-intensive methods, and they protest the cold new culture of the market, where the company no longer provides social benefits for its workers.

Manioc beer may end up being successful, but the workers themselves have traded one naturalization (that of the Native) for another (that of the market). They have little reassurance that this new form of production will support them any better than the Portuguese did once the bottles are counted up and the Dutch go home.

NOTES

1. Not his real name. All names have been changed to protect anonymity, as per the agreement I had with all research interviewees even though, in most cases, interviewees were not sharing confidential or even highly personal information.

2. Poorly named because IFDC's work is not just fertilizer-related but deals with agricultural techniques and trainings more broadly.

3. See the *Boletim da Reparticao de Agricultura de Moçambique* (1908, no. 1) for articles by O. W. Barrett, F. T. Nicholson, and T. R. Sim.

4. Surveys and official records under the Portuguese tended to divide agriculture into two categories: civilized and Indigenous. See the famous Ecological-Agricultural Survey of Centro de Investigação Científica Algodeira (1955).

5. In Mozambique, I was affiliated with the Rural Observatory, and in Portugal, I was affiliated with the University of Lisbon. I thank the National Science Foundation (grant SES-1331265), the Fulbright Program, and Cornell University for the sponsoring that made this research possible. This chapter is part of a larger research project on the politics of land, agricultural research, and the state in Brazil and Mozambique.

6. The Portuguese brought manioc from Brazil to West Africa (as well as tobacco, corn, and groundnuts) sometime in the 1500s, probably to the Upper Guinea Coast and to the kingdom of Kngo in northern Angola (Karasch 2008, 183). It is likely that the former governor and Captain-General of Mozambique, Manuel Baltasar Pereira Lago (1765–1779), brought manioc to Mozambique along with coffee. This information comes from the survey of coffee and rubber undertaken in Mozambique in 1913 (99). It is not clear whether Pereira Lago went to Brazil and brought the seeds or plants back himself or whether he ordered them to be brought back by others.

7. See, for example, the comprehensive study of *Mozambican Agriculture* from 1973, which lists the various crops grown and land ceded for such purposes but suggests that the figures given do not include fallow land for traditional agriculture, which represented upwards of 2 million hectares when total land occupied was approximately 10 million hectares (5).

8. A compendium of "native customs" described the local residents as having no meaningful conception of property, in part because of "the facility with which the native cultivates the free land he inhabits" (ANTT-FCM 1907).

9. Manioc was also planted in military command sites. As one agronomist, Francisco de Mayrelles, says of the military command of Massinga, in southeastern Mozambique, "There was a beautiful planting of manioc there, which the commander had had done to feed the locals. I told the commander to get me a pan to roast the flour but he couldn't because they do not do that here" (Mayrelles 1909).

10. One article in the *Gazeta do Agricultor* (the Farmer's Gazette, published by the National Agricultural Services) expressed surprise that in Costa Rica "there exist references to the use of the plant's [manioc] leaves for human consumption" (*Gazeta do Agricultor*, March 1951, 75). Given that the plant's leaves are widely used in stews today, it is hard to believe that inhabitants were not preparing them in this way in the early 1900s when interest in Mozambique as a farming territory really developed.

11. The focus of research, almost entirely funded by external aid, tends to be on commercial crops. The largest single funder of agricultural research, USAID, is indicative: USAID will not fund manioc research as the "Feed the Future" crops of interest in Mozambique are soy, cowpea, pigeon pea, groundnuts, beans, and sesame.

12. Roughly 4 cents today, minus transportation costs from field to MPU, if required.

REFERENCES

Adam, Y., R. Goodyear, M. Greeley, M. Moore, J. Munguambe, M. Neves, P. Roberts, G. Taju, and S. Vieira. 1991. *Aid Under Fire: An Evaluation of the Mozambique-Nordic Agricultural Programme (MONAP)*. SIDA Evaluation Report, no. 1, Agriculture, Mozambique.

Albuquerque, J. A. M. de (1913). *Moçambique: 1896–1898*. Ministério da Colônias: Sociedade de Geografia de Lisboa.

ANTT-FCM. 1907. *Alguns usos e costumes indigenas da circunscrição de Sofala*. No. de ordem 2193, RA23.

Barradas, L. 1962. Esboço agrológico do sul de Moçambique II plano de fomento. Lourenço Marques (Maputo): Instituto de Investigação Científica de Moçambique.

Beckert, S. 2015. *Empire of Cotton: A Global History*. New York: Penguin.

Bowen, M. 2000. *The State against the Peasantry: Rural Struggles in Colonial and Postcolonial Mozambique*. Charlottesville: University of Virginia Press.

Centro de Investigação Cientifica Algodeira. *Esboço do Reconhecimento Ecológico-Agrícola de Moçambique*. Vol 1. Memorias e Trabalhos no. 23. Lourenço Marques (Maputo): Imprensa Nacional de Moçambique, 1955.

Costa, C. M. S. da, and H. M. Ferrinho. 1964. *Moçambique: Agricultura. Silvicultura. Piscicultura. Apicultura*. Maputo, Mozambique: Editora Lourenço Marques.

Delêtre, M., D. B. McKey, and T. R. Hodkinson. 2011. "Marriage Exchanges, Seed Exchanges, and the Dynamics of Manioc Diversity." *Proceedings of the National Academy of Sciences* 108 (45): 18249–18254.

Esteves, J. D. *A agricultura não-indígena de Moçambique—vista através da estatística (1941/2 a 1951/52)*. Serie B: Divulgação no. 3. Lourenço Marques (Maputo): Edição da Gazeta do Agricultor, 1957.

Geffray, C. 1991. *A Causa das Armas: Antropologia da Guerra Contemporânea de Moçambique*. Maputo, Mozambique: Edições Afrontamento.

Gengenbach, H. 2019. "From Cradle to Chain? Gendered Struggles for Cassava Commercialisation in Mozambique." *Canadian Journal of Development Studies*. https://doi.org/10.1080/02255189.2019.1570088.

Gengenbach, H., R. A. Schurman, T. J. Bassett, W. A. Munro, and W. G. Moseley. 2018. "Limits of the New Green Revolution for Africa: Reconceptualising Gendered Agricultural Value Chains." *The Geographical Journal* 184 (2): 208–214.

Heckler, S. L. 2004. "Tedium and Creativity: The Valorization of Manioc Cultivation and Piaroa Women." *Journal of the Royal Anthropological Institute* 10 (2): 241–259.

Heckler, S. L., and S. Zent. 2008. "Piaroa Manioc Varietals: Hyperdiversity or Social Currency?" *Human Ecology* 36 (5): 679–697.

Hillocks, R. J. 2003. *Research Protocols for Cassava Brown Streak Disease*. Chatham, UK: Natural Resources Institute, University of Greenwich.

Isaacman, A. F. 1996. *Cotton Is the Mother of Poverty: Peasants, Work, and Rural Struggle in Colonial Mozambique, 1938–1961*. Portsmouth: Heinemann.

Isaacman, A. F. and B. Isaacman. 1983. *Mozambique: From Colonialism to Revolution, 1900–1982*. Boulder: Westview Press.

Jones, W. O. 1959. *Manioc in Africa*. Stanford, CA: Stanford University Press.

Karasch, M. 2008. "Manioc." In *Cambridge World History of Food*. Edited by K. F. Kiple and K. C. Ornelas, 181–187. Cambridge, UK: Cambridge University Press.

Leitão, A. B. *Ensaios Realizados e em curso sobre a cultura da mandioca*. Informação Técnica no. 20. Lourenço Marques (Maputo): Instituto de Investigação Agronómica de Moçambique, 1971.

Lyne, R. N. 1913. *Mozambique, Its Agricultural Development*. London: T. Fisher Unwin.

Manual de iniciação ao conhecimento económico, agrícola, florestal e pecuário de Moçambique (mimeograph). 1962. Lourenço Marques: Serviços de Economia e Estatística Geral.

Martins Santareno, J. A. L. 1973. *Agricultura moçambicana, mimeo.* Lourenço Marques (Maputo): Imprensa Nacional de Moçambique.

Maugham, R.C.F. 1906. *Portuguese East Africa: History, Scenery, and Great Game of Manica and Sofala.* London: John Murray.

Mayrelles, F. de. 1909. *Relatórios e informações: Anexo ao boletim oficial.* 307–320. Lourenço Marques (Maputo): LM Imprensa Nacional.

Mintz, S. W. 1986. *Sweetness and Power: The Place of Sugar in Modern History.* New York: Penguin.

Moore, J. 2000. "Sugar and the Expansion of the Early Modern World-Economy: Commodity Frontiers, Ecological Transformation, and Industrialization." *Review (Fernand Braudel Center)* 23 (3): 409–433.

Moore, J. 2010. "This Lofty Mountain of Silver Could Conquer the Whole World": Potosí and the Political Ecology of Underdevelopment, 1545–1800." *The Journal of Philosophical Economics* 4 (1): 58–103.

Mota, T. P. 1970. "Características quimico-analiticas de algumas mandiocas em ensaio: Contribuição para o estudo." *Agron. Mocamb. Lourenço Marques* 4 (1): 21–29.

Newitt, M. 1995. *A History of Mozambique.* Bloomington: Indiana University Press.

Nunes, S. A. R. 1964. *Contribuição para o estudo da qualidade das mandiocas em ensaio no posto agricola da Mahalamba.* Lourenço Marques: Sociedade de Estudos de Moçambique.

O'Connor, K. 2013. "Beyond 'Exotic Groceries': Tapioca/Cassava/Manioc, a Hidden Commodity of Empires and Globalisation." In *Global Histories, Imperial Commodities, Local Interactions.* Edited by J. Curry-Machado. Cambridge Imperial and Post-Colonial Studies Series. London: Palgrave Macmillan.

O'Laughlin, B. 2002. "Proletarianisation, Agency, and Changing Rural Livelihoods." *Journal of Southern African Studies* 28 (3): 511–530.

Rodrigues, A. L. 1960. "A produção no setor indígena de Moçambique." Dissertation, Instituto Superior de Estudos Ultramarinos, Lisboa, Portuagal.

Saraiva, T. 2009. "Laboratories and Landscapes: the Fascist New State and the Colonization of Portugal and Mozambique." *Journal of History of Science and Technology.* 3 (Fall): 35–61.

Scott, J. C. 2009. *The Art of Not Being Governed: An Anarchist History of Upland Southeast Asia.* New Haven: Yale University Press.

Shankland, A., and E. Gonçalves. 2016. "Imagining Agricultural Development in South-South Cooperation: The Contestation and Transformation of ProSA-VANA." *World Development* 81: 35–46.

Vilhena, E. J. de. 1910. *A Mão de obra agrícola em Moçambique.* Presented at the International Congress of Colonial Agronomy, Brussels. Lisboa: A Editora, Ministério da Marinha e Ultramar.

Warman, A. 2003. *Corn and Capitalism: How a Botanical Bastard Grew to Global Dominance.* Chapel Hill: University of North Carolina Press.

Wolford, W. 2015. "From Pangaea to Partnership." *Sociology of Development* 1 (2): 210–232.

Wolford, W. 2019. "The Colonial Roots of Agricultural Modernization in Mozambique: The Role of Research from Portugal to ProSavana." *Journal of Peasant Studies* 48 (2): 254–273. https://doi.org/10.1080/03066150.2019.1680541.

Wolford, W., and R. Nehring. 2015. "Constructing Parallels: Brazilian Expertise and the Commodification of Land, Labour and Money in Mozambique." *Canadian Journal of Development* 36 (2): 208–223. https://doi.org/10.1080/02255189.2015.1036010.

"SITTING ON OLD MATS TO PLAIT NEW"

The Gendered Struggle over Land and Livelihood in Liberia

Gregg Mitman and Emmanuel King Urey Yarkpawolo

"We are sitting here naked," reflect a group of women in Dwindewea, a small rural village in the southwestern part of Liberia.[1] Dwindewea is one of eighteen communities that lost their customary land rights to Sime Darby, a Malaysian oil palm company that, in 2009, secured from the Liberian government a sixty-three-year lease for more than 500,000 acres of land, including 34,590 acres of monoculture rubber that was planted in the 1950s by American tire and rubber manufacturing company B. F. Goodrich.[2] Dwindewea is an island in a vast sea of oil palm that is transforming the landscape and livelihoods of people in rural Liberia. "'Sime Damage' has destroyed all our land and water," the women claim.[3] "We no longer have land to make farms," they continue. Without access to land on which to grow cash crops integral to the informal economy that sustains livelihoods in Liberia, rural people are forced into a wage economy that benefits only a few. To sit naked means to be left without access to resources vital to ways of living and being through which rural women, in particular, have relied upon the land and harvested and cultivated its bounties for greater freedom, independence, and security over their lives.

Nearby, in Senii Town, a small village isolated within a vast checkerboard expanse of newly planted oil palm extending as far as the eye can see, a middle-aged man angrily recounts how everything is gone now that Sime Darby has arrived. The swamps where his grandmother fished, the land upon which women made farms to send children to school, all had been taken. But Sime Darby was not a new story to Liberia. "We sit on old mats to plait new ones," the man reminded those gathered around. It is a Liberian turn of phrase, gesturing to the layers of past and present interlaced together, to the ways new ideas are built out of old ones. A mat woven out of raffia palm becomes the ground upon which one sits to braid a new mat for the future. "Firestone is the old mat here," the man argues. "The way the old mat was badly plaited is the same way the new ones are being plaited today."[4]

In southeastern Liberia, in the village of Queezahn, people are still awaiting a promise of resettlement benefits that the Firestone Plantations Company promised to their ancestors in 1926, when the Liberian government granted the American company a ninety-nine-year lease for up to one million acres of land to grow rubber (Mitman 2021). Queezahn literally means the "White or Civilized people took us from there." This Bassa place name memorializes the displacement of rural people that occurred in Liberia's first major land concession, which paved the way for the current wave of concessions that, in 2018, claimed approximately 50 percent of land in Liberia (Keyser 2013; Lowenstein 2017; Urey 2018).

In Queezahn, the memory of displacement in the making of a plantation world haunts the stories told about the past. When a Queezahn elder remarks that the community is still waiting for Firestone to rebuild their village, more than ninety years after the company took their land and destroyed their ancestor's homes, the large group, young and old, gathered together on a rainy afternoon, erupts in laughter. It is a joke that touches on the pain of past deeds that destroyed intimate relationships with the land and a recognition that the Liberian state will never afford a means through which to seek reparations and justice.

Unlike Queezahn, with its memories of loss, transformational change in Dwindewea and Senii Town is ongoing, remaking land, labor, and livelihoods to build and sustain an industrial plantation that was sold on a promise to benefit people and a nation struggling to recover economically after fourteen years of brutal civil war.

Liberia's story is not unique. Today, a massive wave of industrial plantation agriculture washes over the world in a rush for land. It is not unlike the late nineteenth and early twentieth centuries, when American and European firms grabbed lands in Latin America, the Pacific Islands, Southeast Asia, and Africa to grow tropical fruits, rubber, and oil palm to meet growing consumer demand for pineapples, bananas, automobile tires, and more. Estimates suggest that, globally, seventy-five million acres have been sold or leased in the past decade to foreign investors for large-scale oil palm, rubber, and other agricultural concessions (GRAIN 2016). The deeply layered history of Liberia's plantation economy—touched on in the stories of Dwindewea, Senii Town, and Queezahn—makes Liberia a particularly rich place for interrogating the changing and contested relationships, meanings, and values that constitute the social life of land. As Sharlene Mollett argues, "land-grabbing is far from novel. It is, instead, a routine and old phenomenon" (Mollett 2016, 413). The recurring stories of land dispossession, agriculture concessions, foreign direct investment, and failed promises of development intermingle and layer upon each other in Liberia. They represent a palimpsest of power relations, governing practices, and cumulative violence inflicted upon people and the land in the changing political economy of global agricultural commodities. Concession agreements accrue one on top of another in Liberia. They are like sitting on old mats to plait new. Scratch its surface, look beneath that which is visible in a concession agreement, and the whole layered history of Liberia's plantation economy is revealed.

One cannot, we argue in this chapter, comprehend the history of Liberia without an understanding of how land and the continuities and ruptures in human-land relationships have shaped the lives and livelihoods of Indigenous inhabitants and settlers alike. For Liberia is a settler colonial nation, whereby land dispossession, achieved through acts of violence, as well as legal and physical erasure of customary claims to land, was critical to the formation of a nation-state (Wolfe 2006). The paired narratives of civilization and savagery, critical to the ideologies of settler colonialism in its quest for territory, were certainly integral to the logic and discourse that shaped the "pacification" of Liberia's hinterland and alienation of land by the Liberian government and its ruling elite in the early twentieth century, paving the way for multinational concessions. But the need for territory was itself a condition of survival imposed upon Liberia by Western imperial nations that threatened its borders and economic independence (Liberty 2002). "Capitalism requires inequality and racism enshrines it," writes the geographer Ruth Wilson Gilmore (Gilmore 2017, 240). In a world where racial capitalism structured the flow of global finance, land and labor became the resources upon which a struggling Black republic, saddled with foreign debt, sought to maintain its sovereignty, as European nations in a scramble for Africa carved up the continent.

Settler colonialism and racial capitalism worked hand-in-hand in Liberia to shape how land, in the words of Donald Moore, came to be "inhabited, labored on, idiomatically expressed, and suffered for" (Moore 2005, 2). Throughout Liberia's history, land concessions have favored settler and Indigenous elites. Such concessions have reinforced autocratic and patriarchal structures of power that have most affected the livelihoods and rights of Indigenous women, who for generations have been cultivators and stewards of the land. A fourteen-year-long civil war, ignited in part by settler-Indigenous conflicts over huge wealth inequalities spawned by the country's patchwork of land concessions, turned Liberian society upside down. The war's aftermath left a chaos of land claims in its wake, and from this, a new opening has appeared. Rural women, empowered by helping to bring about peace and emboldened by Liberia's election of Africa's first female president, have become a powerful force in the passage of legislation that, for the first time since the founding of Liberia as a sovereign nation in 1847, grants legal recognition to customary land and equal rights of women to "own" land.

In Liberia, land is a repository of memory (Moore 2005; Richter and Yaalon 2011; Yusoff 2018). In it dwell layered stories of concession agreements and debt servitude, of commodity crops and widespread displacement, and of labor recruitment and changing livelihoods. Interviews, oral histories, company records, government documents, and photographs and films, among other sources, informed by theories and methods drawn from environmental history and political ecology, are the means through which we uncover these layers. In Liberia, land is also life. It is an active site of contestation where new relationships and alternative futures are being forged out of the ashes of war.

Land for Debt

The name Harbel is a contraction of the first names of Harvey Firestone Sr. and his wife Idabelle. It is a name the rubber baron used for all of his prized possessions: his hundred-acre Akron estate with its 118-room mansion; his fifteen-bedroom winter getaway on Miami Beach's Millionaire's Row; his prized Kentucky thoroughbred, which he gifted to President Warren Harding; and the ground central of his rubber plantation in Liberia (Firestone 1926; Lief 1951). Situated forty miles southeast of the capital city of Monrovia, in an area encircled by the Du, Junk, and Farmington rivers, Harbel was once an enclave of transplanted white American managers overseeing a sprawling industrial plantation that now extends over nearly 200 square miles.[5] It was also home to the Bassa people, whose customary lands were claimed as public land by the Liberian government and ceded to a foreign company in the hopes of securing desperately needed capital for the struggling Black Republic. Motion picture footage taken in 1926 of cultural dances performed by Bassa and Grebo peoples in an area just a few miles from Harbel's present location elicits a powerful response from Queezahn elders today. Harbel, they tell us, is *the* place from which their ancestors were removed. Elders also tell of the promises Firestone failed to keep. Payment for cash crops was lost, and the rebuilding of destroyed homes never materialized, they claim. Memories in Queezahn and the very place name of the town speak to the unhealed wounds of land rupture and displacement (Siegel and Mitman 2016).

The layers of land ruptures and dispossession in Liberia's history run deep. The Firestone concession was, in fact, built upon an old concession: the

1300-acre Mount Barclay Plantation, owned by the Liberian Rubber Corporation, a British syndicate. Between the years 1908 and 1911, at the very moment plantation rubber was displacing wild rubber in the global marketplace, the Liberian Rubber Corporation, led by the British naturalist and explorer Sir Harry Johnston, imported more than 200,000 seedlings of the species *Hevea brasiliensis* to Liberia from Ceylon by way of England. Unknown to Africa, native to Brazil, and domesticated in the Malay Archipelago, *Hevea brasiliensis* took well to the laterite soils and the heat and humidity of the Liberian climate. Falling rubber prices, export taxes, but mostly mismanagement, had led to the British plantation's demise (Johnston 1906; McIndoe 1968).

In 1924, the Firestone Tire and Rubber Company secured a lease for the rights to the Mount Barclay Plantation and took over its operation before a lease for an additional one million acres of land was granted. W. E. B. Du Bois, who had visited Mount Barclay on his first trip to Africa, initially threw his weight behind the Firestone agreements. "Liberia must have capital for her development," Du Bois urged in a July 29, 1924, letter to Liberian President Charles Dunbar Burgess King. Faced with a choice among England, France, and America, Liberia would be wise, Du Bois advised King, to choose white American investment, which he believed posed the least threat to the country's sovereignty and self-determination (Du Bois 1877–1965). Du Bois had cautiously held hope that white American capital working in partnership with "Black educated men, both African and American," might, he advised Harvey Firestone in a letter dated October 26, 1925, create an industrial plantation of "mutual dependence and prosperity" like none yet seen (Du Bois 1877–1965). Almost a decade later, when Du Bois became one of Firestone's most vocal critics, he looked back with regret on his advice. "I had not then lost faith in the capitalistic system," he admitted (Du Bois 1933, 684).

In a 1933 piece in *Foreign Affairs*, where Du Bois expressed his change of heart, the skilled economic historian brought historical and economic analysis to bear in mustering a brilliant defense of Liberia and its sovereignty at a time when Firestone eagerly sought to turn it into an American protectorate. Liberia's "chief crime," Du Bois wrote, was "to be black and poor in a rich, white world; and in precisely that portion of the world where color is ruthlessly exploited as a foundation for American and European wealth" (Du Bois 1933, 695). By the early 1900s, the collapse of Liberia's sugar cane and coffee economies had forced the Liberian government into a vicious cycle of debt upon debt, financially beholden to Great Britain, and forced to trade concessions for land and labor in exchange for capital needed to pay off foreign loans and protect its status as one of only two independent sovereign nations governed by Black people on a vast continent of nearly 12 million square miles. The Mount Barclay Plantation concession

Johnston secured was itself wrapped up in a 1906 loan in the amount of $500,000 at an interest rate of 6 percent granted to the Liberian government by Johnston's British syndicate on condition of British oversight of the country's custom revenues and access to its natural resources (Kilroy 1995).

Firestone followed a similar strategy of debt servitude to ensure a firm economic grip on the nation. Without a commitment from the US State Department guaranteeing military protection should political agitation send his plantation and investment up in flames, as it had in Chiapas, Mexico, Firestone sought other means to gain political control and ensure adequate protection of a "large capital investment" in a "far-off country" (US Congress 1926, 254). To the initial planting agreements granting Firestone land and labor in exchange for a tax rate of six cents per acre on leased land payable to the Liberian government, Firestone added a provision requiring the West African nation to accept a $5 million loan from the Finance Corporation of America (which Du Bois disclosed to be Firestone) at an interest rate of 7 percent, to be paid annually over forty years. Liberian officials entered the negotiations with Firestone, knowing full well, as statesman C. L. Simpson observed, that the loan was a form of "economic domination by a company belonging to a traditionally friendly country" (Simpson 1961, 141). But there were "selfish reasons for accepting the loan," noted Plenyono Gbe Wolo, the son of a Kru Paramount Chief, who, while studying at Harvard, became a strong voice in America for the rights of Liberia's Indigenous people (Wolo October 14, 1928). American investment would help stave off the very real threat to Liberia from encroaching European countries, notably France and Great Britain.

But whose land was it to lease, and whose labor was it to trade? That was a question in negotiating the Firestone agreement that went to the heart of the founding of the West African republic. Known as the Grain Coast among British, Dutch, French, American, and Portuguese traders, the stretch of coastline that became Liberia was dotted with provisioning grounds and ports of call for ships trafficking in goods and enslaved peoples in the latter years of the Atlantic slave trade. Many of the peoples these traders encountered—Bassa, Dei, Gola, Dan, Kpelle, Kru, Mano, and Vai, among others—had migrated to the area hundreds of years earlier along trade routes crossing savanna and rainforest, moving salt, kola nuts, and other goods between the African interior and the sea (Burrowes 2016). Then, in 1820, a frigate—the *Elizabeth*—accompanied by a US Navy sloop—the USS *Cyane*—arrived on the West coast of Africa with eighty-six free Black people from America destined for a new home.

The journey of the *Elizabeth* was sponsored by the American Colonization Society, a national group of prominent white politicians, religious leaders, and businessmen—many of whom were slaveholders. The project was undertaken as a solution to the perceived threat free Black people posed to a young nation whose economic fortunes were rising on the toil, sweat, and suffering of enslaved people of African descent. White colonizationists believed that through the gradual emancipation of enslaved Americans, on condition of their emigration from America to Africa, the United States could be cleansed of the troubling elements and problems that they believed jeopardized the future of a white settler nation. After living almost two years at a waystation on the British colony of Sierra Leone, the surviving passengers of the *Elizabeth* and additional settlers who came on a second ship from America established a permanent settlement on Cape Mesurado, a rocky promontory surrounded by mangrove swamps on the Grain Coast. In honor of US President James Monroe, who pledged federal support to the colony's establishment, the settlers named the coastal town Monrovia. Twenty-five years later, in 1847, this fragile settler society would declare independence from the United States to become the free Republic of Liberia (Bronwen 2013).

The area these Black settlers claimed was hardly unoccupied land. To the region's Indigenous inhabitants, these strangers from America were guests— sometimes tolerated, sometimes not—on lands to which chiefs granted access. The newly arrived settlers may have returned to a land from where their ancestors were born, but they brought with them a Western system of private property ownership alien to the customary practices and cultural beliefs of their West African forefathers. Different meanings, values, and relationships to land collided in these initial encounters. "To sell" or "buy" land was not a widely held West African concept. Chiefs were the custodians, not the owners, of the land. Among Liberia's Indigenous communities, conflicts over land, particularly territorial borders, were not uncommon. At the same time, communities considered land to be held in common; it belonged to the living, to ancestors long since dead, and to those yet to be born.

The arrival and settlement of free Black emigrants from America and later the Caribbean, who had come to carve out a place of freedom and a newfound home on the African continent, marked the first major rupture in the meaning and custodianship of land in Liberia. Settlers, who became the country's ruling elite, designated customary land as public land through acts of enclosure. Ownership, either through settler allotments or direct purchase, was restricted to Liberian citizens—namely, settler immigrants and Indigenous people—who, through assimilation, were recognized by settler elites as "civilized." Lands ceded by Indigenous groups to the Liberian government by treaty and/or force became recognized and protected as private land. By the time Firestone arrived in 1926, the last of the Indigenous conflicts with the settler government had been subdued, and the many chiefdoms and inhabitants of the hinterland were brought into the fold of the nation-state through indirect rule. Liberia's interior was open for business (Gershoni 1985; Mark-Thiesen and Mihatsch 2019).

The seizure of land by a settler colonial society marked the first land rupture in Liberia. The granting of the Firestone concession and the violence that accompanied the removal of people and the clearcutting of land marked the second. Liberia's ruling elite gave Firestone the land it desired with carte blanche. Technically, the Firestone agreements excluded "tribal reserves of land set aside for the communal use of any tribe within the Republic of Liberia" (Brown 1941, 275). But the government ran roughshod over customary land claims, rendering such a clause meaningless. Stories of Firestone's initial dispossession abound. A spry, old man from Sua Koko, who worked on and off the plantations dating back to when Edwin Barclay, president from 1930 to 1944, "was in the chair," told how he and other Kpelle men would tease Bassa workers for trading their land to Firestone for salt and fish (Na-Fallon, pers. comm, February 12, 2018).[6] But Kpelle people also suffered from acts of dispossession and enclosure that followed with the introduction of rubber to Liberia's economy. As one Kpelle elder, referring to rubber, remarked: "It came from the hands of the *kwii* people. They brought it here. It is what has broken our land" (quoted in Gay 1989, 37).

The violence of land seizure is remembered in tales told to us on a number of occasions regarding Firestone's clearing of the land that became Division 22. "They call the place *wolowoennie*, baboon burning," one man said in recounting a story passed on from his father, who, the man claimed, came in 1926 as a "slave" to work on the Firestone plantation. "People refused to move, so the whole area got burned, so the people that got burned they name them *wolo* (baboon)," he recalled (Will-ta D., pers. comm., February 1, 2018). Human inhabitants, burned intentionally or not in the massive fires set by Firestone in the dry season to clear the land, are memorialized in the place name.

Violence endured by local people extended beyond the immediate loss of land and life. The making of the Firestone plantations also cut ancestral ties to the land. Esther Warner, an American artist and novelist whose husband headed the botanical research division of the Firestone plantations, told the story of a Bassa chief, Kondea, with whom she studied West African wood-carving traditions. His village was marked for demolition. First, the village coffee trees, which signified a customary claim to the land, were mysteriously felled. It was a sign "the plantation people" would soon come, "break his roots, and force him to go across the river," Warner learned. Kondea did not want to leave his father, long since dead, who moved among the forest trees encircling the village. But the Frontier Force soldiers came, destroyed the village, and Kondea soon died (Warner 1948, 134).

The planting of tree crops is recognized among Liberia's rural people as a means to secure land tenure. The destruction of these crops by multinationals is a practice repeated up to the present day in Liberia. Tree crops—including cacao, kola, orange, and rubber, along with the majestic and sacred Ceiba, or cotton tree—physically substantiate in the land both the memory of ancestral occupation and the powers and benefits associated with land held in common (Ribot and Peluso 2003). Their physical destruction is an important act in land dispossession and constitutes a form of ecological violence, one that erases past relationships to the land and accompanying lifeways (Whyte 2018).

Acquiring land and removing its former occupants was the first step in the building of a modern industrial plantation. Securing labor was the second, now that local people had been removed. The Liberian government prevented the importation of unskilled labor in the making of the Firestone plantation. In contrast, the labor regimes that structured the majority of rubber plantations in the British Malay and Dutch East Indies relied upon indentured laborers drawn largely from India and Java. In early years, the Firestone plantations were "a veritable tower of 'Babel-babble,'" observed Plenyono Wolo, as more than 15,000 men, recruited largely from the Central and Western districts of Liberia, gathered together, speaking many different languages and dialects (Wolo January 9, 1927). They came for different reasons. Some saw plantation work—in the 1930s, a tapper could earn one shilling a day—as an escape from forced labor, as the Liberian government conscripted young men to build roads by hand without pay or contracted them out to the Spanish government to work the cacao plantations of Fernando Po, a small island off the west coast of Africa in the Gulf of Guinea. Wages earned at Firestone allowed young men to help their villages pay hut taxes, enacted in 1910 by the Liberian legislature as a means to bind the hinterland to Monrovia and generate needed revenue (Konneh 1996; Na-Fallon, pers. comm., February 12, 2018). But some retired Firestone workers say their parents were recruited to the plantations by force. Worried about securing a large enough labor supply, Firestone worked with the Liberian government to put in place a quota system in which each district was responsible for supplying thousands of men. In return, each chief would be compensated by the company: one shilling for each worker serving three months and twelve shillings for every laborer working one year on the plantations by the company. Chiefs were also obligated to return "runaway laborers" or supply Firestone with "fresh ones to serve out the term" of those who fled. Although workers were paid, it was a system prone to corruption and abuse (Circular no. 7, *Liberian Government Archives*, June 17, 1927; Knoll 1991; Sundiata 2003).

In more recent decades, dating back to the 1960s, some women have also found plantation work planting and caring for an estimated ten million rubber trees. They were attracted, not necessarily by wages, but by the opportunity to obtain access to education for their children and medical treatment for themselves and their family members available through the schooling and health care systems the company put in place during and after the Second World War. The postwar economic boom that came to Liberia, precipitated in part by the demand for rubber in a world at war, yielded great profits for Firestone, revenues for the Liberian government, and growing class consciousness among workers on the plantation. Conditions of life on the plantations were changing, even as wage rates remained low. As one woman remarked, "The little money we were making was big in our eyes because Firestone was taking care of us and our children even during illness. Those of us that were having children, once our time reached, we used to deliver at the Firestone hospital. We never used to pay money. So the little money was big in our eyes because goods were not expensive" (Siawa-Geh, pers. comm., January 30, 2018).

The modern plantation form, as Sarah Besky notes, differs from the industrial farm in its mix of both wage labor and elements of "peasant" agriculture (Besky 2014). Wages paid by Firestone were minimal. A group of Northwestern economists in the early 1960s calculated that the average wage of forty-five cents per day for unskilled labor at Firestone would need to double to equal the material benefits realized by making a rice farm during the growing season at a time when rice sold for approximately eight cents per pound. Such economic calculation did not account for the added benefit of a rice farm as a means to secure and retain customary land rights. Firestone workers did and still do depend upon nonmonetary forms of compensation to meet their basic survival needs. Free housing, medical care, and education, along with monthly rations of rice and palm oil, paid for at a subsidized rate and deducted from wages, were furnished by Firestone. The compensation structured a set of moral obligations and relations among the company, laborers, and the land and its crop. But workers were denied access to resources the land could provide. Firestone prevented workers from growing rice and cassava on concession land, which was not the case for independent rubber farms owned and operated by Liberian elites. Consequently, workers came and went on the Firestone plantations, moving in and out of a wage economy and a subsistence agricultural existence that shaped rural life in Liberia (Clower et al. 1966).

Under Liberian President William Tubman's administration, from 1944 to 1971, life and work on the plantations were highly segregated in space and time by both race and gender. The racial geographies visible on the 200-square-mile enclave and embedded in the structure of who managed labor and who worked the land were greatly shaped by the racial attitudes of an American company and town. Akron—the center of American rubber manufacturing—was home to one of the largest centers of the Ku Klux Klan north of the Mason-Dixon line. It was not until 1955 that Firestone, Goodyear, and Goodrich gave African Americans the right to be trained and employed as tire builders, one of the higher-paying factory jobs in the rubber industry. On the Firestone plantations, minstrel shows were performed in blackface at the Firestone Staff Club in Harbel, health care for white management and Black laborers was segregated, and the medical surveillance of and drug testing on workers' bodies was routine. Such conditions reinforced the impressions of African American diplomat Edward Dudley in 1951 that Firestone was "transferring US Jim Crow policies to Liberia" ("Secret, Memorandum of Conversation," November 29, 1951, Records of the Office of African Affairs). "Our Firestone House was in Liberia," Warner wrote in the 1940s, "but was not of it. It was an island of a transplanted America" (Warner 1948, 20). Well into the 1960s, not a single Black executive held a position in the company's Liberia operation.

But when it came to working the land, Firestone relied upon Indigenous knowledge and gendered divisions of labor embodied in swidden agricultural practices throughout Liberia. Among the Kpelle people, the ethnic group employed in the largest numbers on the Firestone plantation, Liberia's dry and wet seasons defined the rhythm of life in making farms and livelihoods in the country's interior. During the dry season, from mid-December to mid-April, men cleared the forest, felled the trees, burned the farm, and cleared debris. These were the months when worker shortages were greatest on the plantations. The need for male labor making farms far outweighed whatever monetary benefits accrued from tapping rubber. With the land cleared, women planted upland rice, usually from May to June, the beginning of the rainy season. The weeding, care, and harvesting of rice were traditionally done by women, as was the growing of cassava, swamp rice, peppers, okra, and other crops. Cash crops grown by women and sold at the market were one means of empowerment for women in a patrilineal society where access to land is still controlled largely by men today.

Firestone adopted the same swidden agriculture methods in transforming the rainforest into a profit-yielding, monoculture rubber plantation. Men were contracted to fell by axe giant trees—some up to four feet in diameter—burn the massive dry forests, and clear the land. Tapping, which Firestone considered unskilled labor but which, in fact, depended on craft knowledge to prevent damage to the tree, was also reserved for men. As women came to be employed on the plantations, they first found employment in the nursery farms, bringing their skills in cultivating crops to bear in the germination and nurturing of rubber seedlings. The planting of bud-grafted trees also became part of women's work on the plantations. The rainy season was planting time on the plantations, as it was up the country. Each day, a group of women working under a headman would be given from four to six bundles, twenty-five rubber stumps in a bundle, and assigned a cleared area to plant. It was laborious and careful work, supervised by white managers, who would suspend or fire someone if their rows were not straight or the tree was planted too loosely. Bonds were forged among women work crews who worked under group contracts for Firestone. Fast planters came to the aid of slower ones. "If you are strong," one retired worker recalled, "you will leave your friends behind and finish soon. If you are slow, your friends will help you to plant your remaining stumps before you can go home" (Lomalon, pers. comm., February 1, 2018). Mutual aid among women laborers ensured the contract was met and helped to nurture tree crops. Such forms of cooperation were reflective of *ku*, or communal farming practices back home, driven not by group contracts but by the social interactions arising among people holding land in common. Other women expressed pride in the nurturing and care of seedlings now matured into productive trees, much like they would speak of the cash crops they grew on their individual farms back home. "Most of the rubber trees you see, my hand work is on many," one retired woman proudly exclaimed (Lomalon, pers. comm., February 1, 2018).

Stop-work actions on the plantations in the Tubman years increased solidarity among Firestone laborers as the inequalities between the haves and have-nots escalated. Firestone had cultivated a symbiotic relationship with Liberian elites in its promotion of independent rubber farms, distributing free rubber seedlings and purchasing rubber from these estates. Such a policy heightened land alienation and suppressed worker's wages. The executive branch of the Liberian government had the power of enclosure. Customary land was converted into private property with legal title and granted to Liberian elites by President Tubman in exchange for political patronage. Land solidified his patrimonial rule. Ownership of independent rubber farms that encircled the Firestone plantations mapped closely onto family names who commanded power within the Liberian government. Of the seventy-eight plantation owners who made up the Rubber Planters Association of Liberia, created in 1967, Tubman operated the largest independent rubber farm in the country. To ensure that rubber worker wage rates remained low, to maximize profits on his farm and on those of his political patrons, Tubman had little qualms about using the Liberian military and police to violently squelch strikes on the Firestone plantations (Sawyer 1992; Munive 2011).

The accumulating tinder of inequality, oppression, and resentment sustained by Liberia's plantation economy only needed a spark to ignite conflict. That spark came in 1980 when a bloody *coup d'état* deposed Tubman's anointed successor, William Tolbert. The leader of the revolt, Samuel Kanyon Doe, appointed himself military head of state. Of Krahn heritage, he was the first Indigenous person to rule the country. Within weeks of the coup that saw the long reign of Liberia's settler elite come to a bloody end, Doe, the former sergeant of the Armed Forces of Liberia, declared in "A Message to the Nation": "For too long did the masses of our people live in their own country, only to be treated like slaves on a plantation [. . .]. A handful of families who ruled our nation for 133 years built up their heaven on Earth, while the masses of our people continued to live in a hell on Earth." The revolutionary song by Nigerian musical icon Sonny Okosun, "Papa's Land," blasted over the airwaves (quoted in Munive 2011, 367). It was a reminder of how deeply land and its contested meanings are woven into the multilayered structures and processes of settler colonialism and racial capitalism that helped give rise to and continue to perpetuate Liberia's plantation economy.

Sime Damage

On an August day in 2016, a group of aggrieved farmers, mostly women, gathered in Gon-Town in Grand Cape Mount County. They have come, willing to put their physical bodies on the line to block all roads leading into the Sime Darby Plantation. No vehicle is allowed entrance. The action is reminiscent of "no work day" stoppages in the 1950s and 1960s that brought the operations of the Firestone Plantations Company to a grinding halt (Mayson and Sawyer 1979). But these women are not Sime Darby workers; they are farmers who lost their land and farms in the wake of the Sime Darby concession and are demanding payment for their crops that the company destroyed between 2010 and 2013 without compensation. "Sime Damage needs to pay for our crops," the inscription on a poster held by two women reads. "We are suffering," declares another.

As the sun rises, a few junior Liberian managers employed by Sime Darby arrive. They try to convince the calm but resolved women seated in chairs at the main entrance of the Sime Darby production plant to give up their strike action. One speaks, in a barely veiled threat: "You know, some of your children work for Sime Darby, and the company can issue them rice. Today, the rice is supposed to be arriving, and we are begging you to please allow cars to go in." A tall, middle-aged woman interrupts: "We had our rice farm, our cassava farm, our gardens, but you people destroyed everything and did not pay for it. We will not move until Sime Darby pays our crop money" (demonstration spokesperson, pers. comm., August 22, 2018).

Just as Firestone was built on the remains of a previous concession agreement, one that ignored and erased the claims of rural people to customary land in a desperate effort to preserve Liberia's sovereignty as a nation, so too is the Sime Darby Plantation erected upon a layered history of land grabs, racial capitalism, corporate greed, corruption, and civil war that shapes who has access, and who does not, to land and the wage sector of Liberia's plantation economy. The land granted to Sime Darby included part of a 1954 concession granted to the American tire and rubber manufacturing firm B. F. Goodrich. It was one among many granted by Liberian President William Tubman under his Open Door Policy, which created lucrative financial incentives for foreign investors.

By the late 1950s, Liberia was a patchwork of agricultural, mining, and timber concessions that brought great profits to American companies like Firestone, Republic Steel, and B. F. Goodrich. The milky white sap collected from rubber trees planted as a vast monoculture by Liberian workers on more than 100,000 acres of Liberian land earned Firestone alone nearly $400 million in profits during the Tubman era (Kraaij 1983; Dunn 2009). In 1958, the American ambassador to Liberia confidentially noted that "a handful of American-owned companies and about 1,000 Americans working in Liberia make more money in Liberia than all Liberians put together" (quoted in Dunn 2009, 45). But concessions also helped to line the pockets of Liberian government officials and elites. In 1966, a team of Northwestern University economists published a study highly critical of the power structure in Liberia, one that concentrated political control in the hands of a small group of settler-descended families who profited most from the country's natural wealth. The Liberian government promptly banned the book *Growth without Development* (Clower et al. 1966) in Liberia.

Tubman used strong-arm tactics to secure 600,000 acres of land for B. F. Goodrich in Cape Mount County. Some Liberian government officials objected to the secretive nature of the negotiations that took place behind closed doors and opposed the awarding of customary land to the American firm, which gave B. F. Goodrich broad mining, forestry, and agricultural rights at a tax rate of six cents per acre per year (Kraaij 1983). Tubman invited the local chiefs to his home and forced them under oath to accept the terms of the concession agreement (Urey 2018).

Despite its ambition, B. F. Goodrich only planted 14,013 acres in rubber of the 600,000 acres leased in the years from 1954 to 1985. It did, however, survey the entire land area granted to it under the terms of the 1954 agreement. Cornerstones were placed by the company to mark the boundaries of its concession lands. The laid cornerstones imposed formidable power over land use in the region and altered people's relationships to customary land and the meanings and value it held for their future. The placement of cornerstones heightened land insecurity and troubled the decisions made by local farmers for decades to come, particularly with respect to planting long-term cash crops. To plant tree crops, such as rubber or oil palm, which took years to yield a source of livelihood, was risky business in the face of the concession, even if the land lay fallow. "We have been live here. Our people were born here, but each time we want to plant trees, some people say the land is for B. F. Goodrich because they have their cornerstones there," a local elder recalled (Jiahea elder, pers. comm., February 8, 2016). The laying of cornerstones also elicited resistance among local villagers, who did not bend easily to the surveys that staked out the taking of their surrounding lands by B. F. Goodrich. "Our people told us that they refused one cornerstone that B. F. Goodrich planted near our town across the creek," a local chief insisted (Jiahea town chief, pers. comm., February 8, 2016). Nevertheless, villages whose lands were appropriated faced relocation and resettlement. The company rebuilt structures found in former villages and resettled their inhabitants in nearby lands.

After thirty-one years in operation, B. F. Goodrich sold its concession rights to Guthrie, a British company. Prior to the sale, B. F. Goodrich renegotiated the terms of the 1954 concession agreement, giving the company additional incentives on the promise of expansion. A 2008 Government of Liberia audit report later concluded that the renegotiation that B. F. Goodrich reached five years before its sale was done in bad faith. The renegotiated terms were meant to enhance the concession's assets, making it easier for B. F. Goodrich to sell at a profit (Morlu 2011). Guthrie operated and expanded the former B. F. Goodrich plantation until civil war hit Liberia in 1989. The company continued to run the plantation during the war years with intermittent closures until October 2001, when Guthrie officially closed its operation. Two years later, forces of the Liberians United for Reconciliation and Development (LURD), a rebel opposition group against Charles Taylor, seized the Guthrie plantation. The rebels set up their own management team, which they named the High-Power Ruling Council, and forcibly recruited experienced tappers to work the former B. F. Goodrich holding. Profits made by the sale of rubber to Firestone, which the Akron rubber giant negotiated illegally with LURD rebels between 2003 and 2006, solidified the resistance group's hold over the plantation (Lidow 2011). When peace came, few LURD members occupying the plantation agreed willingly to the disarmament, demobilization, reintegration, and repatriation process. It took considerable efforts on the part of the United Nations Mission in Liberia and the Liberia National Police (LNP) to evict rebels from the plantation. Almost two decades after the war ended, however, the former rebel presence on the former Guthrie plantation, now a part of Sime Darby, played a determining role in who initially obtained jobs on the newly negotiated oil palm concession, further sedimenting the layers of violence that have been endured by rural people in this region with social ties to the land that extend deep into the past.

These layers of violence are what have brought the aggrieved women blocking the road to Gon-Town on that August day. "I had just gone to visit my mother in a nearby town when I heard that Sime Darby was destroying our crops," one woman shouted angrily. "We were sitting when we saw some people with yellow machines destroying our farms. They said that the government has given the land to Sime Darby," another lady lamented (focus group discussion, July 15, 2016). Such violent acts of erasure have been a staple of multinationals operating in Liberia to further private interests and the government's development policy operating in the country for almost one hundred years (Wily 2007; Lanier, Mukpo, and Wilhelmsen 2012).

As the women narrated the hardships accompanying land loss, three pickup trucks full of men dressed in the military-style blue uniforms of the Police Support Unit (PSU), a paramilitary unit of the LNP, arrive. The pickups pull over by the main road and stop. A muscular fellow, probably in his early thirties, leaps out of the truck and asks: "Who is the leader of this demonstration?" The attention of the group sways from the junior managers of Sime Darby to the PSU boss. A brave young man emerges from the crowd: "I am one of the leaders and one of the organizers of this peaceful sit-in action," he declares (pers. comm., August 22, 2016). "After exerting all efforts for Sime Darby to pay for our crops with no result, we have decided that this company will not work until our money is paid," he emphasizes. The commanding PSU officer reassures the crowd that his men were there simply to protect lives and property, and he encourages the demonstrators to remain peaceful.

On day two of the peaceful sit-in, an official of Sime Darby takes to the local radio airwaves and discounts the farmers' account. "Sime Darby owes farmers not a single dime," he announces (*Dao Metzger*, August 22, 2016). The Sime Darby manager accuses the farmers of making demands for payments already made. The dispute revolves around what price list was used to compensate farmers for lost crops. A 2009 price list, which had been used by Sime Darby to pay off farmers, was considerably less than the approved price list that came out in 2013. In 2009, the price for a mature rubber tree was $6; in 2013, the same remuneration was listed as $97. Farmers demand the difference. But it is not only the difference in price the protesters insist upon. They also take issue with the way such crops were inventoried. "How can one count crops in the absence of the crop owner?" an outspoken young man questions the police (pers. comm., August 22, 2016).

As the sit-in action moves to day three, company officials grow more concerned. They request government intervention. The government obliges, and the farmers, some of whom had never been to Monrovia, are transported to the Ministry of Internal Affairs, the governing authority over issues pertaining to rural Liberia. The investigation that unfolds leaves much to be desired. Sime Darby officials persuade the government's chief investigator that the company will consent to pay additional money, but the farmers need to first admit that the company has paid them fairly. The message is conveyed to farmers, who act in good faith, assuming the company will abide by its word. "Sime Darby paid for my crops, but the land they took is too big, so I want the company to pay me additional money," one farmer tells investigators (pers. comm.). Some refuse to play along, but many aggrieved farmers fall in line following the company script.

The investigation and assenting testimonies, documented on film, are later used by Sime Darby to exonerate the company of any wrongdoing.

The protest actions described here are recurring stories playing out across the land of present-day Liberia. Much like the residents of Queezahn, still awaiting compensation for crops destroyed by Firestone almost a century ago, the aggrieved farmers of Dwindewea, Senii Town, and other villages engulfed by Sime Darby await just compensation. They are, as the women of Dwindewea declared, sitting "naked," left without their traditional means of livelihood and social reproduction, stranded on an island in an ocean of oil palm. Women are particularly vulnerable in the ever-expanding patchwork of concessions that dominate the Liberian landscape. The predominance of men in the plantation workforce and their traditional control of customary lands for rice farming and the harvesting of naturally grown oil palms, two main sources of food and income for rural people, have marginalized women to the edges of Liberia's formal and informal economy.

In the face of such challenges, women have innovated production systems that suit their needs. One such response has been the cultivation of swampland (wetland) rice fields. Because wetlands lack the large secondary forest cover characteristic of upland slash-and-burn agriculture, women who cultivate wetlands are not reliant upon male labor to clear the land before planting crops. Before the arrival of Sime Darby, many women in the area maintained their own livelihoods by planting subsistence and cash crops in these low-lying areas. "We used to make our own swampland farms, laid baskets, and sell fish in the market," a woman maintained (pers. comm., May 10, 2016). "We were not depending on our men; we earned our own money," another woman said. The loss of access to swampland habitats that resulted when Sime Darby took over and expanded the former Guthrie and B. F. Goodrich concessions undercut the means of production that rural women use to make farms and realize economic independence. "Today, if your husband does not give you money, you will not have it," the women lamented (focus group discussion, May 5, 2016). Like other development projects in West Africa, ignorant of the gendered divisions of labor and complex tenure systems that shape resource access and use among agricultural peoples, industrial plantations in Liberia exacerbate land alienation for women and erode their economic and food security (Carney 1998).

The promise of jobs, infrastructure development, and tax revenues are common selling points that foreign investors have made repeatedly in the establishment and proliferation of Liberia's plantation economy dating back to Firestone's arrival. In the case of Sime Darby, such jobs have not benefitted those whose land and livelihoods have been most greatly impacted by the concession. By 2013, the company had appropriated 25,966 acres of land belonging to eighteen villages.

People from these eighteen villages, dubbed "Project Affected Communities" (PAC), initially had no employment with the company. Instead, the company first employed former rebels who had occupied the Guthrie plantation during the years of the civil war and were still living there. Sime Darby also began recruiting mostly men from the northern, central, and western districts of Liberia. As the suffering of those living in the PACs grew worse, young men from the affected communities sought out work with Sime Darby. Eventually, the company, under pressure from civil society, agreed to employ "one person from each house." House and household, however, mean different things in Liberia. A household refers to a group of people eating from the same pot. A house can consist of many households. As one Sime Darby employee living in a PAC explained: "This house has six families, but I am the only one working for Sime Darby" (pers. comm., May 17, 2016). For women living in PACs cut off from wetlands that furnished their means of subsistence and ability to engage in a petty cash economy and dependent on men who face little prospects working for Sime Darby, the future appears bleak. To them, reparations are a matter of survival, and claiming customary rights to land is the only avenue of recourse to plait the mat anew.

Seeking Reparations and Justice

On a May day, at the start of the rainy season in 2018, when low-lying clouds bring daily moisture to newly planted crops, women gathered at the Liberian Capitol building in Monrovia to protest the continued delay of the passage of a Land Rights Act, which was first drafted in 2014 but had lingered in the corridors of the legislature for more than four years. Their placards and banners spelled out the stakes of the land issue for rural women. "Women should have rights to own land individually and collectively," one read. "Women should have equal rights to land and equal participation in governance," read another. A third offered, "40,000 people signed for a pro-poor community land rights bill." Inside, at a hearing of the Senate Committee on Land and Natural Resources, a young woman stood to read a petition signed by more than 70,000 people from all fifteen counties of Liberia and from other parts of the world, demanding passage of the Land Rights Act.

Debates over the passage of the Land Rights Act in Liberia are indicative of the entrenched interests of Liberian elites who have profited from concessions for land and labor that have shaped the livelihoods and landscapes of rural people in Liberia for over a century. While such concession agreements have benefitted some, they have increasingly left the majority of Liberia's population landless and poor. A report issued by the Truth and Reconciliation Commission in 2008 identified inequality in land rights and land access as a major factor that contributed to the country's civil war (1989–2003) (Liberian Truth and Reconciliation Commission 2008). A 2008 report by the Governance Commission similarly concluded that land insecurity in Liberia was a time bomb waiting to explode and, if unresolved, threatened a relapse into another civil war (Topka, Saryee, and Asunka 2009, 6).

To address Liberia's land problem, the government started a land reform process in 2009 with the establishment of a Land Commission (LC). In May of 2013, the LC presented a draft Land Rights Policy (LRP) to the president that was officially adopted by a diverse sector of Liberians: government officials, traditional chiefs, community members, and civil society organizations, including women groups. Following the validation of the LRP in 2013, the LC drafted a Land Rights Bill that provided a legal framework to implement the LRP. The Land Rights Law recognizes four categories of land rights: Private Land, Customary Land, Government Land, and Public Land.[7]

For the most part, delineating the status of customary land and accompanying rights was the main focus of the law. Previously, customary land was designated public land and administered by the government (Stevens 2014). This was the category of land rights that the government gave to Firestone (1926), B. F. Goodrich (1954), and Sime Darby (2009). The new law specifically recognizes the full bundle of land rights of rural communities (Bruce et al. 2006). It devolves land use and administration decisions to community members through decentralized Land Management and Development Committees.[8] If the new law becomes operationalized, the Liberian government would no longer sit in Monrovia and grant large land concessions as it had done in the past.

Recognizing customary land rights of rural people proved to be the most contentious and time-consuming issue that occupied the majority of discussions during the Land Rights Act debate. Some Liberian elites felt that the Liberian government would be undermining its territorial integrity by recognizing the land rights of rural Liberians (Cecil T. O. Brandy, pers. comm., January 23, 2016). Others felt that such recognition would undermine or slow down economic development since investors would be forced to negotiate directly with community stakeholders rather than just securing agreements with the executive branch of government. Others, mainly from civil society, pushed back, arguing that Liberia is a signatory to many international protocols that recognize the rights of rural people and that contract negotiations and overall operation costs may prove lower when customary communities are given full land rights (Civil Society Working Group Presentation, June 19, 2018).

Women have been the most prominent members of Liberian civil society speaking out in favor of the passage of the Land Rights Act. Their involvement stems from the fact that women have been the most marginalized and vulnerable group when it comes to the land business in Liberia. Historically, they have represented only a small fraction of workers employed in the rubber sector in Liberia, and they are largely excluded from the labor market in the oil palm industry that is once again transforming the landscape of Liberia. Furthermore, in the traditional patrilineal system that governed customary land rights in Liberia, the lack of access women have to the full bundle of land rights undermines their productive capacity. For instance, unmarried young women have land-use rights on their father's land. Once they are married, their land-use rights become embodied in those of their husbands'. Such a land-tenure arrangement poses serious problems for widows and women in general. "My husband and I had two girls and one boy, but my son and his father were killed during the war," an elderly woman narrated (Kouwah Massaquoi, pers. comm., December 2, 2018). "Today, I do not have man, and my late husband's brothers have taken the land from us. If we want to make farm, we have to borrow land from different people," the daughter of the elderly woman explained (Ma-Gorpu, pers. comm, December 2, 2018). Consequently, many women are unable to make long-term investment decisions in how to cultivate the land.

Realizing these problems, rural women in Liberia have used the new land rights legislation as a vehicle to correct long-standing traditions that have excluded them from equal access to land. Their advocacy has led to significant improvements for women in the final version of the Land Rights Act passed in the fall of 2018. For example, the law defines a community member as someone who was born in the community, whose parent(s) were born in the community, who married and moved into the community, or who has resided in the community for a continuous period of seven years. This definition is important because community members have land ownership rights to agriculture, forestry, and commercial and residential land. Since the passage of the Land Rights Act into law, women now have the legal right to access or own land as community members, independent of their husbands or male relatives in the community. Like other community members under the new law, women have the right to residential plots, which they can hold in fee simple.[9] In addition, women are to form part of the Community Land Management and Development Committee, a body responsible for managing the community land.

The Land Rights Law is progressive. It seeks to correct the wrongs of the "old mats" and set the stage to plait the mat anew. The principles of the new mat, as set out in the Land Rights Law, are based on the principle of equal opportunity to own and access land by all Liberians. When fully implemented, rural Liberians, particularly women, stand to benefit. But as with other laws, implementation of the Land Rights Law is becoming a challenge barely four months after the law was passed. Under the new law, the Government of Liberia is forbidden to sign any mineral development agreement without first obtaining the Free, Prior, and Informed Consent (FPIC) of communities who would be affected by such agreements. Recently, the Liberian Senate and House of Representatives hurriedly ratified a 1,768,039-acre mineral development concession agreement that spans six counties (including Sinoe, Maryland, River Gee, Grand Kru, Nimba, and Bong) between the Government of Liberia and Hummingbird Resources, a London-based company. No FPICs were obtained. The ratification of the Hummingbird agreement is reminiscent of the passage of the B. F. Goodrich concession agreement some sixty-five years ago, when Liberian government officials complained that they were not given sufficient time to review and debate the agreement's contents. Four Senators staged a walkout in protest of the government's confirmation of the Hummingbird agreement. One Senator stated that the bill was presented to them while they were conducting impeachment proceedings for an Associate Justice of the Supreme Court. They never had time to read the bill before their colleagues in the majority passed it. Another Senator remarked: "I'm worried that the country is going to suffer because passing laws of such is worrisome. We can see people are now in the street demonstrating. We should be making laws to stop all these" (*Front Page Africa* 2019). The irony, of course, is that the Liberian Legislature had just four months earlier passed a law to do just that. The Hummingbird agreement was in clear violation of the terms laid out in the Land Rights Law for FPIC. Thus, the question remains: Will the Land Rights Law really plait the mat anew?

In a 2013 report published by the US National Academy of Sciences, the authors describe the wave of transnational land acquisitions over the last decade by foreign investors in sub-Saharan Africa and other regions across the globe as "a new form of colonialism" (Rulli, Saviori, and d'Odorico 2013). The case of land grabs in Liberia raises the question, what is new? As Mollett argues, "Land grabbing can only be conceptualized as new or novel if scholars continue to ignore enduring racial logics and accompanying racial discourses embedded in natural resource conflicts" (Mollett 2016, 416). The racial logics of capital, whereby the making of racial differences in land and labor justified Western exploitation and economic domination of regions like Liberia, reveal themselves time and again in the sedimentary histories of land concessions brokered by corporate empires like Firestone and settler elites in need of capital and territory to protect Liberia's sovereignty as a nation from the imposing imperial powers of Great Britain and France, whose colonies bordered Liberia.[10] Such agreements have been transformative of relationships, meanings, and values that comprise the social life of land in Liberia. They concentrated power in an oligarchy, exacerbated inequality, and planted the seeds of discontent and revolution among the country's plantation laborers and subsistence farmers, increasingly dispossessed of land upon which livelihoods were and still are being made. As farmers, rural women have most endured the layers of dispossession and violence that have accumulated over a century of Liberia's plantation economy. Limited by employment opportunities on rubber and oil palm plantations and denied access to customary land through which they have secured food security and economic independence, women have had the most to gain in advocating for land reforms in Liberia that grant them equal access and rights to land.

The land and surrounding infrastructure of the Firestone plantation complex bear witness to storied layers of dispossession and destruction, promises made and broken, growth without development, and the extractive nature of plantation economies. But as you drive along the forty-mile stretch of highway from Harbel to Monrovia, you will see plots everywhere: of half-built cinder block homes, of gardens with peppers, pineapples, or potato greens, and of planted tree crops, such as palm, papaya, banana, and coconut. Such plots stand in contrast to the plantation (Wynter 1971). These are plantings in keeping with customary rights to land, use rights that secure tenure, however ephemeral, in defiance of legal definitions of private property that settler elites and multinationals in the past have sought to impose. Whether Liberian law will now stand behind such acts of cultivation remains to be seen. Regardless, the planting and cultivation of subsistence and cash crops on whatever small plots of land can be claimed will continue, with or without the backing of the state. Of this, one can be sure. Land is life in Liberia. Access to it will not be, nor has it ever been, surrendered easily.

NOTES

1. Urey worked in the Sime Darby Concession area for ten months in 2016 conducting dissertation field research work on the impacts of large-scale land concession agreements on the lives of rural Liberians. Parts of this chapter appeared in *Empire of Rubber: Firestone's Scramble for Land and Power in Liberia* (Mitman 2021).

2. Following the example of Firestone, B. F. Goodrich Rubber Company was granted a broad land concession in 1954. A brief history of the B. F. Goodrich company can be found at http://www.referenceforbusiness.com/history2/31/The-BFGoodrich-Company.html.. Guthrie, a British company later bought B. F. Goodrich plantation in 1985.

3. The locals invented the name "Sime Damage" in place of the company name "Sime Darby" to describe the level of destruction the company carried out during the initial land appropriation.

4. Interview with James Bafalie, July 4, 2013.

5. On enclaves and extraction, see Appel (2012).

6. We have used fictitious Kpelle names as pseudonyms to protect the identities of Firestone workers we interviewed.

7. Article two of the *Land Rights Act of 2018* defines Private Land Rights as land that is owned or otherwise held by private persons. Customary Land Rights is a land owned by a "Community" and used or managed in accordance with customary practices and norms. Government land means land owned by the Government, including land used for government buildings, projects, universities, and similar government infrastructures. If a land does not fall in any of the first three categories of land rights, then it is considered a Public Land. The most contentious category of land rights is customary land.

8. Community Land Management and Development (CLMDC) is a leadership structure that would govern customary land. Articles 35 and 36 of the *Land Rights Act of 2018* describe processes of establishing the CLMDC. Each stakeholder group (women, men, and youth) in the community after selecting their representatives in a democratic process will form part of the CLMDC. The CLMDC will be responsible for community land administration and management.

9. Being a community member under the new *Land Rights Act of 2018* embodies the entitlement of land rights.

10. We are gesturing here to the rich literature on racial capitalism, from *The World and Africa* (Du Bois [1946] 1965) to Cedric Robinson's *Black Marxism: The Making of the Black Radical Tradition* (1983). See also Johnson et al. (2017).

REFERENCES

Appel, H. C. 2012. "Walls and White Elephants: Oil Extraction, Responsibility, and Infrastructural Violence in Equatorial Guinea." *Ethnography* 13: 439–465.

Besky, S. 2014. *The Darjeeling Distinction: Labor and Justice on Fair-Trade Tea Plantations in India.* Berkeley: University of California Press.

Bronwen, E. 2013. *Abolition and Empire in Sierra Leone and Liberia.* London: Palgrave Macmillan.

Brown, G. 1941. *The Economic History of Liberia.* Washington, DC: The Associated Publishers Inc.

Bruce, J. W., R. Giovarelli, L. Rolfes Jr., D. Bledsoe, and R. Mitchell. 2006. *Land Law Reform: Achieving Development Policy Objectives.* Washington, DC: World Bank

Burrowes, C. P. 2016. *Between the Kola Forest and the Salty Sea: A History of the Liberian People Before 1800.* Bomi County, Liberia: Know Your Self Press.

Carney, J. 1998. "Women's Land Rights in Gambian Irrigated Rice Schemes: Constraints and Opportunities." *Agriculture and Human Values* 15: 325–336.

Circular no. 7, Holsoe Collection. *Liberian Government Archives II, 1911–1968.* June 17, 1927. Bloomington, IN: Liberian Collections, Indiana University Libraries, 2008.

Clower, R. W., G. Dalton, M. Harwitz, and A. A. Walters. 1966. *Growth without Development: An Economic Survey of Liberia.* Evanston: Northwestern University Press.

Du Bois, W. E. B. *W. E. B. Du Bois Papers.* Special Collections and University Archives. Amherst: University of Massachusetts Amherst Libraries, 1877–1965.

Du Bois, W. E. B. 1933. "Liberia, the League, and the United States." *Foreign Affairs* 11: 682–695.

Du Bois, W. E. B. (1946) 1965. *The World and Africa.* New York: International Publishers.

Dunn, E. 2009. *Liberia and the United States During the Cold War: Limits of Reciprocity.* New York: Palgrave Macmillan.

Firestone, H. S. 1926. *Men and Rubber: The Story of Business.* In collaboration with Samuel Crowther. Garden City: Doubleday, Page and Co.

Front Page Africa. 2019. "House 'Controversially' Concurs with Senate in Ratifying Hummingbird Deal." March 10, 2019. https://frontpageafricaonline.com /politics/house-controvrsially-concurs-with-senate-in-ratifying-hummingbird -deal/.

Gay, J. 1989. "Cognitive Aspects of Agriculture Among the Kpelle: Kpelle Farming Through Kpelle Eyes." *Liberian Studies Journal* 14: 23–43.

Gershoni, Y. 1985. *Black Colonialism: The Americo-Liberian Scramble for the Hinter-land.* Boulder, CO: Westview Press.

Gilmore, R. W. "Abolition Geography and the Problem of Innocence." In *Futures of Black Radicalism.* Edited by G. T. Johnson and A. Lubin, 225–240. New York: Verso Press.

GRAIN. 2016. "The Global Farmland Grab in 2016: How Big, How Bad?" June 14, 2016. https://www.grain.org/article/entries/5492-the-global-farmland-grab-in-2016 -how-big-how-bad.

Johnston, Sir H.. 1906. *Liberia.* London: Hutchison and Co.

Johnson, W. et al. 2017. "Race, Capitalism, Justice." *Boston Review* Forum 1.

Keyser, C. 2013. *Good Laws, Weak Implementation.* Policy Brief no. 1. Washington, DC: USAID. http://pdf.usaid.gov/pdf_docs/PA00M7RK.pdf.

Kilroy, D. "Extending the American Sphere to West Africa: Dollar Diplomacy in Liberia, 1908–1926." PhD diss., University of Iowa, 1995.

Knoll, A. 1991. "Firestone's Labor Policy, 1924–1939." *Liberian Studies Journal* 16 (2): 49–75.

Konneh, A. 1996. "The Hut Tax in Liberia: The High Costs of Integration" *Journal of the GAH* 16: 41–60.

Kraaij, F. van der. 1983. *The Open Door Policy of Liberia: An Economic History of Modern Liberia.* Bremen, Germany: Bremer Afrika Archiv.

Lanier, F., A. Mukpo, and F.Wilhelmsen. 2012. *Smell-No-Taste: The Social Impact of Foreign Direct Investment in Liberia.* Sustainable Development Institute Report. New York: Columbia University.

Leiseron, E., K. Munyan, A. Saad, and A. Yamamoto. 2017. *Governance of Agricultural Concession in Liberia: Analysis and Discussion of Possible Reforms.* March 13, 2017. *Allard K. Lowenstein* International Human Rights Clinic at Yale Law School. https://law.yale.edu/sites/default/files/area/center/schell/document /liberia_final_2017.pdf.

Liberian Truth and Reconciliation Commission. 2008. *Final Report of the Truth and Reconciliation Commission of Liberia (TRC).* Vol. 1 of *Preliminary Findings and Determinations.* Monrovia, Liberia: Truth and Reconciliation Commission.

Liberty, C. E. Z. 2002. *Growth of the Liberian State: An Analysis of Its Historiography.* Northridge, CA: New World African Press.

Lidow, N. H. 2011. *Violent Order: Rebel Organization and Liberia's Civil War.* Redwood City, CA: Stanford University Press

Lief, A. 1951. *Harvey Firestone: Free Man of Enterprise.* New York: McGraw Hill Book Co.

Mark-Thiesen, C., and M. A. Mihatsch. 2019. "Liberia an(d) Empire? Sovereignty, 'Civilization' and Commerce in Nineteenth-Century West Africa." *Journal of Imperial and Commonwealth History* 47 (5): 884–911.

Mayson, D. T.-W., and A. Sawyer. 1979. "Labour in Liberia." *Review of African Political Economy* 6 (14): 3–15.

McIndoe, K. G. 1968. *The Rubber Tree in Liberia.* New Zealand: Jon McIndoe Limited.

Mitman, G. 2021. *Empire of Rubber: Firestone's Scramble for Land and Power in Liberia.* New York: The New Press.

Mollett, S. 2016. "The Power to Plunder: Rethinking Land Grabbing in Latin America." *Antipode* 48: 412–432.

Moore, D. S. 2005. *Suffering for Territory: Race, Place, and Power in Zimbabwe.* Durham, NC: Duke University Press.

Morlu, J. 2011. *Report of the Auditor General on the Guthrie Rubber Plantation: For the Period 1 January 2006–31 December 2008.* April 20, 2011. General Auditing Commission.

Munive, J. 2011. "A Political Economic History of the Liberian State, Forced Labour and Armed Mobilization." *Journal of Agrarian Change* 11: 357–376.

Ribot, J. C., and N. L. Peluso. 2003. "A Theory of Access." *Rural Sociology* 68: 153–181.

Richter, D. B., and D. H. Yaalon. 2011. "The Changing Model of Soil Revisited." *Soil Science Society of America Journal* 76: 766–778.

Robinson, C. 1983. *Black Marxism: The Making of the Black Radical Tradition.* Chapel Hill: University of North Carolina Press.

Rulli, M. C., A. Saviori, and P. D'Odorico. 2013. "Global Land and Water Grabbing." *Proceedings of the National Academy of Sciences* 110: 892–897.

Sawyer, A. 1992. *The Emergence of Autocracy in Liberia: Tragedy and Challenge.* San Francisco: Institute for Contemporary Studies Press.

"Secret, Memorandum of Conversation." Participants: Byron H. Larabee, M. Firestone, M. Feld, and A. F. Farmer. November 29, 1951. Records of the Office of African Affairs, Folder 10, Box 1, RG 59. Lot 56D 418, US State Department, National Archives.

Siegel, S., and G. Mitman. 2016. *The Land Beneath Our Feet.* Warren, NJ: Passion River Films.

Simpson, C. L. 1961. *The Memoirs of C. L. Simpson: The Symbol of Liberia.* London: Diplomatic Press and Publishing Co.

Stevens, C. J. 2014. "The Legal History of Public Land in Liberia." *Journal of African Law* 58 (2): 250–265.

Sundiata, I. 2003. *Brothers and Strangers: Black Zion, Black Slavery, 1914–1940.* Durham, NC: Duke University Press.

Topka, A., D. Saryee, and J. Asunka. 2009. *Land Disputes in Liberia: Disputes from Below, 2008.* Afrobarometer Briefing Paper no. 72, October 2009.

Urey, E. "Political Ecology of Land and Agriculture Concessions in Liberia." PhD diss., University of Wisconsin-Madison, 2018.

US Congress. *Crude Rubber, Coffee, Etc.: Hearings Before the Committee on Interstate and Foreign Commerce, House of Representatives.* Sixty-Ninth Congress, First Session on H. R. 59. January 6–22, 1926. Washington, DC: US Government Printing Office, 1926.

Warner, E. 1948. *New Song in a Strange Land.* Boston: Houghton Mifflin Co.

Whyte, K. P. 2018. "Settler Colonialism, Ecology, and Environmental Injustice." *Environment and Society: Advances in Research* 9: 125–144.

Wily, L. 2007. *So Who Owns the Forest: An Investigation into Forest Ownership and Customary Land Rights in Liberia.* London: FERN Press.

Wolfe, P. 2006. "Settler Colonialism and the Elimination of the Native." *Journal of Genocide Research* 8: 387–409.

Wolo, P. G. Plenyono Gbe Wolo to Emeline Fletcher Dickerson. In *The Plenyono Gbe Wolo Personal Archive.* 1913–1941.

Wynter, S. 1971. "Novel and History, Plot and Plantation." *Savacou* 5: 95–102.

Yusoff, K. 2018. *A Billion Black Anthropocenes or None.* Minneapolis: University of Minnesota Press.

Part III
SPECULATIVE TRANSFORMATIONS

11

PRODUCING ASSETS

The Social Strife of Land

Erik Swyngedouw and Callum Ward

Nature, as Raymond Williams (1976) claimed, may be the most complicated word in the English language, but we would argue that *land* runs it close. Land embodies a wide range of often competing and contested symbolic meanings, social attachments, material uses, and economic significations (Li 2014a; Haila 2016). Land and its appurtenances (the edifices constructed on, materials embedded in, cultural inscriptions conveyed through, or services provided by land) are central to organizing life in any society, strongly articulating with relations of gender, class, and race (e.g., Safransky 2016). In this chapter, we use the lens of rent theory to focus on the way that land's complex status as a material, social relation intersects with its very particular but pivotal role in capital accumulation to argue that the social life of land under financialized capitalism is characterized by "asset-class struggle."

There is growing recognition that income and profit have become outweighed by wealth and rent in recent decades, meaning that societies' surplus is accruing to asset holders rather than wage earners (extensively evidenced in the work of Piketty 2014; see also Christophers 2019; Birch and Muniesa 2020). In the Global North, this has occurred primarily through residential land markets (Knoll, Schularick, and Steger 2017), leading to debates over how we conceptualize class in an asset economy where social reproduction is increasingly dependent on housing wealth (Adkins, Cooper, and Konings 2020, 2021). This turns on the treatment of land as a financial asset, meaning that land is being managed for its exchange value (as an investment) as opposed to its use value (e.g., in the case of residential land, as the site of a home). The mediation of fictitious capital is necessary for this because land values are based on rents, which are expected to accrue over a matter of decades, meaning that to hold land as an asset requires a combination of institutionalized enclosure (to capture rents) and capitalization (to realize them in the present) that has been termed "assetization" (Birch and Muniesa 2020).

This process of land assetization is central to all manner of social struggles beyond the distributional impact of the treatment of residential land as a financialised asset in the Global North, for example, through processes of land grabbing, resource extraction, or large-scale agricultural production. We are less concerned in this context with descriptive typologies of class as with the question of how this increasing centrality of land rent has transformed the terms of engagement of class struggle itself (see Kaika and Ruggiero 2015). Specifically, as value grabbing—the appropriation of (surplus) value—rather than accumulation (the creation of new value) is increasingly central to the reproduction of contemporary capitalism (Andreucci et al. 2017), social conflict unfolds over the distribution and appropriation of the flows of value that circulate in and through privatized assets. To unpack the particular class antagonisms produced by this institutionalized value grabbing, we trace out the contours of mobilizing land as a financial asset starting from the dynamics of land rent extraction.

The Vexed Question of Land Value

The social life of land cannot be reduced to economic (exchange) value: there are enduring noncapitalist land regimes and significant amounts of noncommodified land in liberal market economies (e.g., Whiteside 2017). Nonetheless, the capitalist valuation of land and its peculiar metrics permeate every nook and cranny of the Earth's surface, in conflict or direct competition with other, often localized, valuations and significations. It is precisely these competing significations that suggest understanding the dynamics of land-as-capital is pivotal for a multitude of social struggles and conflicts. In today's era of financial globalization, for instance, even land that is not currently subject to capitalistic ownership will likely have been valued by prospective land grabbers. Such planetary rent gaps (Slater 2017) demonstrate that the potential for noncommodified land's transformation into a financial asset is ever present.

Although land is intrinsically relational, it appears in market exchange as a straightforward commodity: thing-like and fungible. But this fetishization—transforming the multiple meanings and values of land into the singular objectified metric of exchange value—involves all sorts of "metaphysical subtleties and theological capers" (Marx [1894] 1981), infusing the modalities by which land becomes enrolled in the capitalist accumulation process. The formation of fictitious capital, in particular, depends on contested narratives as to the future (Swyngedouw and Ward 2018, 1080), mediated by performative and cultural practices, which are reified as fungible assets through a process of "real abstraction" (Mann 2018).

In *The Great Transformation*, Karl Polanyi ([1944] 2002) argued that land, labor, and money are "fictitious" or "pseudocommodities" in the sense that they are treated as market commodities but have no market-based production process. This echoes Marx's view that (virgin) land has both use value and exchange value but not the thing that makes them commensurable—value, understood as socially necessary labor time. Socially necessary labor time is the average time required to produce a given commodity under historically given sociotechnical conditions. Value in this sense permits a concrete articulation between the exchange value (the price) of a commodity, which renders it universally exchangeable with every other commodity on the one hand, and its particular use value (its specific and particular material, sensorial, symbolic, or utilitarian qualities) on the other. Yet if land is not produced through labor and so embodies no socially necessary labor time, how does it command value? Therein lie the theological capers Marx identified.

The vexatious question to answer from a political economy perspective, then, is how land's endless range of potential use values are rendered commensurable in exchange. It is only through social construction—real abstractions—that this can be achieved. Such abstractions occur whenever the incommensurable is made commensurable in the process of exchange—and this has occurred for many centuries but has been increasingly formalized and systematized over the last century as investors, international organizations like the IMF or World Bank, and economists (and even some sociologists and anthropologist) constantly attempt to devise common denominators, which render it possible to compare and contrast different use values along a generalized yardstick, as per the complex equations and pseudoempirics of economists' location theory (Alonso 1964; Muth 1969). Such perverse homogenizing calculative procedures became received wisdom following neoclassical economists' rejection of any tension between use and exchange values in the marginalist revolution (see Ward and Aalbers 2016), permitting the modeling of nonmonetized use values into a universal exchange equivalence. However, things are rather more complex than these reifications allow for.

Land, as property, entails exclusive control over access to specific portions of the globe (Marx [1894] 1967). Land values derive from the private enclosure (through parcelization into property) of land in which *collective* accumulation processes are territorially embedded. The landlord appropriates as rent a portion of the social product that flows through their parcel of land (Swynge-douw 1992). The generalization of market exchange as one of the central institutions through which everyday sociomaterial life is organized is now so complete that a price (an exchange value) can be assigned to practically every square inch of the Earth's surface. But the process through which land was alienated in this way entailed long, difficult, and frequently bloody enclosure movements, something that David Harvey (2003) redubbed "accumulation by dispossession." This ongoing enclosure (see Goldman, this book) is an arena of intense and often emotionally charged contestation. It invariably involves the mobilization of extraeconomic, political, and institutional processes through which private ownership is legitimized, legally codified, and policed by an authority—e.g., the state—considered to possess the legitimate monopoly on violence.

Once land is parcelized as private property, it must be mobilized as fictitious capital to enable a land market. Fictitious capital, distinct from Polanyi's concept of fictitious commodities, is a tradeable claim to future wealth—specifically, it pulls the expectation of the extraction of future value (as socially necessary labor time) and trades that expectation as present exchange value (see Harvey [1982] 2006). This capitalization of the socially necessary labor time, which will be captured through rents, is fundamental to the land market. The social life of land under capitalist market relations, then, consists in the first instance in the construction and maintenance of the institutional configurations necessary to perpetuate the fetishization of land as private property and sustain its mobilization as a financial asset.

As such, the exchange value of land is determined by a complex set of semi-autonomous but interdependent forces. These include the existence of generalized market exchange, the rendering of land as private property through institutionalized dispossession, the specific existing or potential use values of the land, past capital invested, the exchange value of commodities produced in or passing through the land and the corresponding anticipated future returns, credit conditions through which land can be capitalized, and so on. The practically infinite heterogeneity of potential use values constituting land is essential to its potential to acquire exchange value; yet the latter is predicated upon turning land into a commensurable and exclusive good. Through ongoing enclosure and abstraction into fictitious capital, the reductive universal equivalent of exchange value is inserted into the complex relational composition of land so that these complexities are synthesized as a price through class struggle in the form of landowners' imposition of access costs on land users. Yet if capitalized rent explains how land can command value without this value being necessarily produced through the mobilization of labor (in the sense of socially necessary labor time), it still remains to be explained how an unproductive agent such as a landowner can systemically capture value within a capitalist economy? It is upon this question that Marx's rent theory turned.

The Production of Rent

The starting point for Marx is that land is an entitlement to the landowner in return for surrendering the use of that land to someone else, much like interest on money is an entitlement to the lender. The basic insight is that the fundamental relationship through which rents arise is a social one determined by conflict between classes, that is, between landowners on the one hand and those who wish to make use of the land on the other (Ball 1977, 1985) and not directly from the use values that inhere in the land. Rent, therefore, is a transfer of value produced elsewhere to the landowner.

If the actual process of setting this rent is the outcome of institutionally mediated conflict, there must be some basis in value to the user if landlords are to systematically make a claim to surplus value. Marx developed four basic categories of rent describing how land can be value-enhancing for the user of the land and, therein, produce a share of surplus that can be claimed as rent. These categories are monopoly, absolute, differential rent I (DRI), and differential rent II (DRII) (Marx [1894] 1967; Harvey [1982] 2006; Ward and Aalbers 2016). These forms of rent, taken together, determine the magnitude of rent on a plot of land but are empirically indistinguishable as the rent is given in one payment as the result of negotiations that depend on many mediating factors (see Ball et al. 1985).

The first—monopoly rent—relates to the specific and unique characteristics of a particular piece of land. Consider, for example, how the ownership of a plot of land in the Bordeaux wine region, near the Niagara Falls, or ice cream stalls near a summer tourist attraction, generates surplus profit for the owner by virtue of the unique character of the land itself or its location. These unique characteristics create products that have few substitutable competitors, creating a condition in which effective demand (how much people are willing and able to pay) is the only upper limit on the exchange value that the plot can command.

The second—absolute rent—is the most complex and controversial category because it is not merely distributional but potentially affects the price of production. Absolute rent derives from the imperfect mobility of capital as a result of there being a class of landowners at all. For Marx, absolute rent in the agricultural context was the outcome of fragmented landownership and imperfect capital mobility through land that blocks competition in the sector so that products tend to trade above their cost of production (Fine 1979; see Purcell 2018).

This has also been used to explain why particular (very often racialized) housing submarkets have been subject to higher-than-average rates of exploitation (see the concept of Class Monopoly Rent per Harvey and Chatterjee 1974; Aalbers 2011; Anderson 2019). While many Marxists argued that absolute rent would gradually disappear as the law of value imposed its iron logic across the globe, recent observers argue that this form of rent is not only persistent but fundamental to an increasingly monopolistic capitalism (Amin 2018; Purcell, Loftus, and March 2019). For example, many speculative urban developments precisely bank on such forms of absolute rent (Anderson 2019; Revington 2021).

The third—DRI—is related to the qualities of land as a means of production or reproduction: it refers to the *different qualities* of land with *equal amounts of capital* invested in it. These differing qualities are the result of given but usually historically—and thus sociomaterially—produced, sociospatial differences between different plots of land with respect to their ability to sustain the production of value when mobilized in a specific capital circulation process or situated in more favorable locations. For example, more fertile land or construction sites in highly desirable locations. Indeed, land of different qualities and locational attributes requires different mobilizations of socially necessary labor time to produce a given commodity with a given magnitude of capital investment. Similarly, plots with different qualities for reproductive functions attract greater rents—consider, for example, the effect well-regarded schools can have on local house prices. DRI, therefore, refers to the position of a particular plot of land in relation to all other possible positions and/or to its position within a larger geographical configuration (Swyngedouw 1992).

The three forms of rent discussed so far can be defined as ground rent proper. The full land rent also includes the fourth type of rent, DRII. DRII also derives from different qualities of land but is generated by *differential capital investments* in pieces of land of *equal quality*. In other words, the qualities of land can be enhanced (and over time greatly so) by capital investment (e.g., engineering, infrastructural improvements, new or upgraded buildings, ground improvement, soil engineering, state regulation, new investments for new functions in the built environment). This form of investment is comparable to capital investment in technological or organizational improvements in the production process. To the extent that this capital investment reduces the socially necessary labor time required for production on that plot, extra surplus value is generated. Marx defines this surplus, made possible by the sinking of capital into land, as DRII. DRII plays an important legitimizing ideological function for the land market as the value of appurtenances and improvements appear to the lay-person to account for the price paid, but, in fact, additions to the land, such as buildings, are not the primary factor accounting for the final price and do little to account for long-term secular trends toward rising prices—this, as Knoll, Schularick, and Steger (2017) demonstrate in their empirical analysis of house prices across OECD countries in the last century, is attributable to the price of land itself. In sum, while rent accrues to the landowner by virtue of the monopoly ownership of land, the magnitude of land rent (and hence the price of land) is composed of four distinct components: monopoly and absolute rent, and DRI and DRII.

Rent is the crucial variable through which sociospatial and socioecological differentiation in the capitalist landscape is triaged. In a market system, access to land is structured by rent as the process through which specific qualities or use values embodied in place are transformed into the concrete abstraction of exchange value and appropriated by landowners. The production of rent and its appropriation by landowners (themselves increasingly embroiled with financial capital) animates all manner of conflicts in the social life of land as the spatial unfolding of capital operates through and actively produces a complex rent map, which directs the distribution of sociospatial and socioecological functions. As such, it plays a unique, often under-appreciated role in capitalism.

The Role of Land Rent in Capitalism: Feudalistic Drain or the Motor of Competition?

The early stages of capitalism in Europe were marked by conflict between tradi-tional aristocratic land-owning classes and the ascendance of industrialists. Re-strictive landownership obstructs the maximization of surplus value production, so the assumption of many twentieth-century observers was that rent was an archaic feudal remnant. In this, rent was seen as a parasitic drain on profits that would be swept aside with the full development of capitalism (Haila 1990). Yet as the twentieth century progressed, it became increasingly clear that the historic defeat of the landed classes entailed not the abolition of land rent but its full integration into the dynamics and circulation of capital-ism, specifically that of finance (Ball et al. 1985).

While value is generated through the labor process, rent constitutes a drain on capital accumulation in that it is appropriated by the landowner purely by virtue of their ownership of the land. This pits landed capital against both pro-ductive and financial capital, as well as those who wish to make use of the land for reproduction (like housing or gardening) (Kaika and Ruggiero 2013). The cat-egories of rent can be understood as identifying the sociospatial relations upon which the landowners systemically succeed in capturing some of that value—through monopolistic means (monopoly/absolute rent) or the relatively enhanced position of the land (differential rent). Yet while the former, in particular, is often seen as a feudalistic drain on capital accumulation, both are pivotal to the everyday functioning of a capitalist economy.

First, the historic enclosure and privatization of agricultural land were central processes through which a "free" and landless labor reserve army was produced as the separation of workers from their means of subsistence underpinned processes of proletarianization and the making of a "free" working class that had no other choice than to sell their own bodily labor force as a commodity on the labor market (Marx [1894] 1981). This form of accumulation by dispossession is an ongoing process that, in part, accounts for the accelerating migration of landless workers to the megacities of the Global South and North. Consider, for example, the extraordinary privatization and accumulation by dispossession that has taken place in postsocialist states like Russia or China, where millions of people lost their attachment to land, and billions of dollars were extracted as a market was created out of socialized land. Large-scale land grabbing in Asia and Africa in recent years is also indicative of this still ongoing process of mass proletarianization. These are examples of landowners asserting their exclusive hold over land as private property, the most fundamental form of absolute rent in that they impose a price below which they will not release the land.

Second, the fact that the landowner takes the relative advantages of a plot of land as rent means that the capitalists cannot rely on spatial advantage. By ensuring that capitalists cannot live off monopolistic or differential advantages of location, they ensure competitive dynamism for the capitalist system as entrepreneurs must thus rely on technological innovation or intensified labor exploitation for profits (Harvey [1982] 2006). That is, they ensure the equalization of the rate of profit in the context of uneven geographical development, flattening the differential profit rates that would otherwise accrue to businesses as the result of spatial advantage. The very existence of a generalized land market ensures this is the case even where the capitalist owns the land: if they have bought the land in the market, then this means bidding against others at a price determined by the profitable use they could put it to (with the successful bidder likely to have to pay commensurate mortgage payments). If the land is owned outright by the capitalist, the existence of a land market simply means that the conflict between the roles of landowner and capitalist is internalized because by putting the land to less profitable use, they are effectively losing what they could receive by renting the land out or selling it.

Third, not only does land rent mitigate the effects of uneven spatial development on capitalist competition, but it also actively remakes space to facilitate capital accumulation. As differential rent depends on enhanced relative advantage, profit-oriented landowners/developers seek to create such enhancements.

DR1, recall, derives from the accrued locational advantages that have been produced over time as the collective outcome of many successive rounds of capital investments in space and its associated uneven development. The urbanization process is an excellent illustration of this process. Or they are the result of specific collective processes that assign specific and valued significations to a place, such as historical value, specific design qualities, and particular produced effects (truffle-rich areas, for example). These collectively or socially produced "locational" effects have a great (and, over time, increasing) effect on land rents that the landowner can cash in irrespective of his or her own capital investment in the land. It follows that all manner of individual investments, collective interventions, changing sociocultural significations, or state policies affect the magnitude of DR1 directly.

Through these functions, land rent acts as an essential mechanism regulating the application of flows of capital and labor to land. The rent relation orders the uses of land and organizes the spatial division of labor through its influence in allocating different moments, activities, and sociotechnical forms of production to different places and, as such, land rent organizes and regulates, in close articulation with the embodied specific use values, the landscapes of production and consumption. This allocation mechanism helps coordinate capital investment by assigning different forms of capital to distinct locations and activities, producing an unequal and uneven spatial division of labor and a highly variegated and socially triaged geographical landscape (Harvey [1982] 2006), whereby the power of money secures access to the most highly valued locations.

Here, as Harvey ([1982] 2006) argued, the treatment of land as capital whereby use follows exchange value is an essential mechanism for the operation of capitalism: it reshapes sociospatial processes according to the requirements of capitalism, ensures the equalization of profit among capitalists is possible within a context of uneven development, and provides an important means of capital absorption during periods of industrial stagnation through speculation on the built environment. This is not to say that rentiership has shed its "bad" parasitical character in favor of "good" entrepreneurial ones but that this is one of the great contradictions of capitalism: competition and freedom in exchange rely on monopoly and the social and political violence of enclosure. The contradictory, conflictual nature of the production and appropriation of rent is a constant tension within capitalism as the rentier does not altruistically seek to ensure capitalism's efficient functioning but simply seeks to maximize their own revenue. The extent to which they succeed or not depends on the conditions of class struggle, and the rentier class may always simply undermine their own basis in accumulation by squeezing users too much. This dialectical tension between the inherently monopolistic nature of property and competition as the engine of capitalism is complicated further today by a condition of economic stagnation and financialization wherein the profitability of the capitalist system itself appears to have come to rely on monopolistic rents extracted through financial channels (Amin 2018).

Putting aside wider questions of an emerging "rentier capitalism" (Standing 2016), these functions demonstrate that land rent is one of the most powerful and contradictory drivers of the geographical political economy of capitalism. Not only does it pit landed against industrial and interest-bearing capital, but it is also a determining factor in conflicts over competing uses of the land, such as for reproduction (housing, for example), resource exploitation (e.g., an ecological reserve or mine), particular cultural or symbolic values, or as a form of capital investment or factor of production. The nature and form of this constant struggle to appropriate value as rent characterizes the social life of land under capitalism. Insofar as land is mobilized as a financial asset and therein its use decided by exchange value, landowners have a powerful structural incentive to engage in sociopolitical struggle in order to remake space according to the incentives of capital accumulation.

The Liquefaction of Land: Assetization and Financial Circulation

In recent years, attention has focused on what Kaika and Ruggiero (2013, 2015) characterize as "the mobilization of land as a financial asset." Land grabs by institutional investors have become a central theme in the Global South (Ouma 2018), while a global housing affordability crisis driven by housing financialization has dominated discourse and practice in the Global North (Wijburg, Aalbers, and Heeg 2018). As we argued above, land markets, in general, are predicated on the capitalization of rent through fictitious capital, but in recent decades, this has intensified so that titles to land function and circulate increasingly as pure interest-bearing capital comparable to other financial assets. This occurs both as investors select land investments based only on the risk-return profile required for their portfolio and as real estate investments are bundled on secondary markets and sold as a despatialized income stream. In this, land markets increasingly function as markets in (paper) titles to future returns and have become an integral part of often speculative, fictitious capital circulation and accumulation (Andreucci et al. 2017). Blackstone or Macquarie Group, for example, are among the biggest international players in the field. The bundling and financial packaging of mortgages is another example. This is the fully developed capitalist form of the treatment of land as an exchange value, whereby an immobile good is rendered a liquid, footloose financial asset.

This process of assetization, that is, the socially contested and institutionally complex process of creating capitalized property, is the process by which exchange value is created from things that would otherwise not be exchangeable. As Birch (2015, 122) put it, assetization is "the transformation of things into resources which generate income without a sale," drawing in capital markets through "the production of a specific form of financial knowledge [. . .] through which the social, material, and temporal aspects [. . .] are aligned with the money management industry" (Ouma 2018, 3). It is the making of a real abstraction (see Toscano 2008; Mann 2018; Ward 2021), in which the concrete, varied, and qualitatively specific values present in land are stripped down to quantitative market metrics, rendering land commensurable with the universalizing logic of exchange and its monetary basis. This process of abstraction is "real" in the sense that it emerges through concrete sociotechnical practices and in that the emergent abstraction has its own material effects, actually performing (per Callon 1998) the process of realizing exchange values as it enters financial circulation. Land value today increasingly circulates as real abstractions in the form of financial assets. The social life of land, therefore, is increasingly to function as an asset base for nurturing the circulation of capital, something that articulates in conflicting manners with other real or potential uses of land.

The creation of an asset entails the manifold social and institutional practices required to produce a liquid investment product, such as the imposition of regulatory frameworks, institutionalization of particular calculative models (Mann 2008), massaging of cultural norms (Goede 2005), enrolment of sociotechnical expertise, and other legitimation procedures. The effective functioning of this market construction depends on appearing objective but is inherently objectionable and contestable: operations, in the first instance, of routinized and ritually codified power. The socially embedded and embodied nature of this process opens up a range of class and other struggles fought around the process of abstraction itself: who will be in a position to cash in on the generated exchange value stream and who will have access (or not) to the consequent distribution of goods/bads still inscribed in the fixed "thing." These are the key contours of what we dub as asset class war. Producing assets is a power-laden, strategic, and complex procedure whereby landowners have to engage with a variety of extraeconomic actors, most notably with the state at a variety of scales (Swyngedouw and Ward 2018) and confront competing and contested social, cultural, or ecological mobilizations of land. Because the sociolegal embedding of the "thing" is a necessary corollary for it to function as circulating fictitious capital, the process of making an asset is intrinsically political. Assetization cannot operate without the "Other of Exchange Value," that is, the crystallized socioinstitutional configurations that permit it to flow.

Recall that the exchange value of land is itself a legal fiction, a pseudocommodity created by state enforcement of the excludability of a plot of land as private property, a parcelization of territorially embedded activity, which allows its owner to claim a portion of surplus flowing through it. In the process of assetization, this pseudocommodity is reified as another money capital, becoming swept up in the dynamics of credit booms quite separate from any underlying activity in the process—as we saw in the 2007–2009 subprime mortgage crisis. Yet these assets still depend on a flow of underlying income, and this is profoundly shaped by the particularities of the legal geography of landed property (Blomley 2003).

Indeed, of all the diverse means of production and reproduction, land is among the most tightly regulated and intensely contested. An important reason for this is that the imposition of the rent relation introduces the fundamental contradiction of exchange value, undermining existing use values while producing new ones. The maelstrom of changing uses of land that is intrinsic to the social life of land under capitalism stands in direct opposition to historically produced long-term uses of land and the range of emotive, social, or material attachments to it. Sustaining the basis of accumulation within this complex panoply of contradictions requires the state (or another extraeconomic configuration) to regulate, manage, and coordinate the allocation and uses of land and, thereby, facilitate land markets as well as mitigating the inevitable conflicts both between competing interests for the land as between competing use values.

As such, not only is landownership (i.e., what one can do with one's land) often strictly regulated by the state through zoning, building codes, and planning (among others), but the state itself is an active agent in land markets (particularly through infrastructure planning and construction, public investment in urban development, eminent domain laws, and the like). Small changes in the rules governing land can have an extraordinary impact on the level of rent and, consequently, on profits generated through landownership. Consider, for example, how the state's mobilization of "eminent domain" has been systematically used to dispossess some landowners and transfer the lands to fractions of capital, guaranteeing a higher rent and return (e.g., in the construction of railroads, airports, seaports, large industrial estates, plantation economies in postcolonial states [Li 2014b], and the like). Needless to say, an intense, simultaneously inter- and intraclass struggle unfolds over land use, land rights, and access to land.

Asset Class War: Rent As Accumulation Frontier

We have traced out at length how land's use values are repackaged into exchangeable abstractions. This process of real abstraction transforms them into pseudocommodities, which permits the appropriation and redistribution of value while imposing the logic of self-expanding capital circulation on land's manifold use values. This not only pertains to land but also to a proliferating number of other "things" that are turned into assets that can subsequently circulate as fictitious financialized capital (Purcell, Loftus, and March 2019; Birch and Muniesa 2020). This process has become a pivotal terrain through which the circulation of capital articulates today. The analysis of the (exchange) value of land, therefore, permits casting new light on some of the most intricate and forceful, yet little understood, dynamics of contemporary capital accumulation.

The analysis of "assets" and "assetization" can, and indeed should, be extended to the proliferating set of social, natural, or socioecological constellations that characterize the contemporary economy. Key examples are water (Swyngedouw 2005), carbon dioxide (Felli 2014), patents on GMOs (Prudham 2007), wind (Serna 2021), ecosystem services (Hernandez 2019), superior urban locations or designated monopoly land (Champagne, Buffalo mozzarella), and may even include "organic" labeling for food (Guthman 2002), social networks (Rigi and Prey 2015), branded goods, and culture (Harvey 2012). Some of these assets contain value as socially necessary labor time—in the sense that they are created through a production process—but a significant part of their exchange value is determined by the property regime and rent entitlements. Indeed, increasingly, productive sectors are transformed into arenas of rent extraction through (public or private) reregulation; for example, in the construction of artificial exclusivity in platforms such as the shift of jet engine manufacturers from selling engines themselves to selling exclusive subscription-based maintenance services (Srnicek 2016).

In this way, a class of rentiers are increasingly "profiting without producing" (Lapavistas 2013, 793). Arguably, therefore, *value grabbing*—the appropriation of (surplus) value—rather than accumulation (the creation of new value) is increasingly central to the reproduction of contemporary capitalism (Andreucci et al. 2017). We maintain that such a perspective has far-reaching consequences for situating a wide range of new socioecological movements, tensions, and class conflicts as they unfold not only over institutionalized property regimes and entitlements but also over the distribution and appropriation of the flows of value that circulate in and through privatized assets. While the social relations of capital valorization in production unfold through the capital-labor relation, the rent-based social relation unfolds through class struggles over ownership of assets and the payment for the rights and modalities of their use. Tensions and conflicts increasingly emerge not only between classically productive and new forms of rentier capital but also over property rights and regimes and the institutionalized redistribution of value through rent and interest payments. Moreover, such entitlements are easily monetized, and this can, in turn, lay the foundation for their abstraction into fictitious capital formation and circulation. Securitized mortgages on land and housing are, of course, a case in point, but similar arrangements are in place for, among others, carbon credits, mineral resources, water, wind, or ecoservice payments.

We are now in a position to return to the vexed question of land rent and its materiality in the present conjuncture. Unpacking the rent relation opens up a vast new terrain of class struggle that we must understand to grasp the social life of land and contemporary capitalism, more generally. In particular, conflicts and struggles arise over the modalities of property formation, the configuration of use values, and the intense struggle over the distribution and appropriation of the subsequent rents. Rent, understood as a social relation (Haila 1990), unleashes an intense inter- and intraclass war, which mobilizes a range of social actors, institutional configurations, and state strategies. The social life of land around the world today is, precisely, that it is caught up in the multiple tensions, contradictions, and conflicts that animate the uneven and combined development of financialized capitalism.

The proliferation of private property under neoliberalization relations significantly expands the terrain for rent extraction and related struggles. The very possibility of rent relations and its associated struggles is predicated upon the deepening and further generalization of capitalist social relations of ownership and dispossession that remain the basis for surplus value production. At the same time, establishing private property rights is not just a basis for the self-expansion of capital but a central nexus in the struggle over the appropriation of rents. Escalating socioecological and political conflict around property regimes and private appropriation of a variety of "assets" shows clearly that new forms of social struggle and different layers of class conflict are unfolding over who captures rent and who pays it. Whether we consider the quest for land for bioenergy sources like sugar cane or aeolian energy, capturing high-value mineral deposits, or prestige urban development projects, they all demonstrate the highly contested and conflict-ridden choreography unfolding over and through land.

These class conflicts unfold between different classes and through varied configurations of institutions and scales of the state. On the one hand, conflicts increasingly lead to intensifying intercapitalist struggles between owners of extractable rent and industrial capitalists (that is, the owners of the means of production mobilized for the expansion of value) (Kaika and Ruggiero 2015). On the other hand, popular struggles occasionally unfold in parallel but often in tension with more traditional working-class struggles that develop over the appropriation of surplus value as produced in the expanded reproduction of capital. Such popular struggles are not primarily located along the traditional workplace-based capital-labor relation but articulate and orchestrate around property regimes and asset ownership, the distributional dynamics of capital, and over different use values of land—reflected, for example, in the increasing mobilizations and struggles articulated around the commons emerging across the world or the proliferating conflicts over mining and resources extraction in Latin America or Africa (Arboleda 2020). They bring together apparently heterogeneous social identities—consumers, noncapitalist producers, workers, men, women, intellectuals, and others—whose politicization does not relate to their role within the relations of production but rather to their position with respect to the distribution of value, socioecological amenities, and relations of reproduction. These distributional forms of inter- and intraclass conflict are one of the central axes around which anticapitalist struggles coalesce today. Consider, for example, the militant mobilization against the Dakota Access Pipeline that broke out in 2016.

In relation to rent, socioecological conflicts unfold over the appropriation and distribution of value as well as contestation over the underlying property relations upon which the extraction of rent is predicated. First, struggles over value distribution enabled by the rent relation are, strictly speaking, class struggles over rent. While this has traditionally been considered an intraclass struggle between rentiers ("landlords") and industrial capitalists, popular classes can exploit this contradiction and the barrier to capital it creates in order to force a downward redistribution of value—by, for example, demanding public institutions to capture and redistribute a share of rent. While these struggles are often not consciously and explicitly articulated as being about rent per se, in essence, they deal with the redistribution of value that has been grabbed. Second, struggles over the creation of property rights are instances of struggles against pseudocommodification. As mentioned, these include the enclosure of land and resources, the patenting of genetic material, the private appropriation of knowledge, and the privatization of public housing or state-owned land. In short, they manifest themselves typically as struggles for and over "the commons" with respect to the extent to which they are appropriated (or not) as financial assets and to whose benefit.

The Social Strife of Land

In this chapter, we have teased out essential features of the social life of land under capitalism, the first being that land, in the general sense, *is* social life. Beyond what is not sea, there is no standardized object we could call land, and certainly, no commodity produced as such. Land embodies no value in the sense of socially necessary labor time but is the manifold spatially embedded, socially produced use values; the "universal means of production" (Marx [1894] 1981) and of social reproduction as the raw material of the production of space (Lefebvre [1974] 1991). Specific territorial configurations, in combination with technological innovation, determine the conditions of production, and land gains its exchange value as the private appropriation of these spatially embedded social flows of value (Swyngedouw 1992). The social life of land under capitalism, then, is a tension-laden one as the collective, relational good of space—literally the sum of material human metabolic interaction—is parcelized by private property relations and traded as a pseudocommodity.

Yet the brute force of enclosure alone cannot create value beyond one-shot primitive accumulation. How do we account for the persistence of a land market given that the commodity being traded does not embody value qua socially necessary labor time? The answer Marx came to, as we outlined, was the relations of rent in their differential, absolute, and monopoly forms, denoting the surplus value-enhancing features of a particular plot, which the landowner siphons off as an access charge. Social life, as materialized in land, is thus forced into the commodity form on the basis of rent appropriation. To the extent that land becomes treated as a financial asset and so exchange values dominate use, land then acts as a mechanism to ensure a laboring population through the dispossession of "commoners," ensuring capitalist competition by removing industry of profit from spatial advantages and, in this, incentivizing landlords to reshape space according to the requirements of capital accumulation. Marx's answer to this puzzle thus paints the broad contours of how the relations of rent shape the sociospatial process, but the specifics of how to extend this analysis to the present financialized conjuncture remain hotly contested. In this chapter, we have contributed to doing so through a Marxist interpretation of land assetization, which highlights the social strife it engenders.

We pointed to how the material flows of social life embedded within land become liquefied in the capital's drive for fungibility. Once enclosed as property and so imbued with exchange value, land is subject to "real abstraction" (see Toscano 2008; Mann 2018). Real abstraction entails the concrete sociotechnical process of transforming and creating quantified, exchangeable material representations. Under conditions of financialization, this transformation of things into assets (Birch and Muniesa 2020) can quickly become untethered from the underlying sociomaterial processes they represent (Ward 2021), becoming responsive primarily to the dynamics of fictitious capital and therein the calculative practices of the money management industry (Ouma 2018). Having been assetized, land tends to become less responsive to social use values as it becomes mobilized as a pure financial asset (Harvey [1982] 2006; cf. Haila 1990).

It is in this way that "pseudocommodities"—assets—have become central to the contemporary economy. Pseudocommodities appear like commodities in circulation but have no value proper in production; they are based on ongoing "value grabbing" through the rentier relation. This is an ongoing feature not only of the land market but of a number of critical growth sectors and contemporary innovations through which the frontiers of rentiership are being extended. Here if, as some have recently argued, we are entering a new era of "asset-manager capitalism" (Braun 2018), "rentier capitalism" (Lapavistas 2013; Standing 2016; Christophers 2019), or even an "asset condition" (Muniesa et al. 2019), then the way that the institutionalized value grabbing this entails produces particular class antagonisms is crucial to understanding social conflict today. This value grabbing necessarily embroils the state or other forms of regulation in the ongoing maintenance of numerous forms of appropriation that reach into every facet of social reproduction, entailing intense political struggle. The social life of land under capitalism, then, is characterized by asset class wars.

REFERENCES

Aalbers, M. B. 2011. *Place, Exclusion, and Mortgage Markets.* Hoboken: Wiley.

Adkins, L., M. Cooper, and M. Konings. 2020. *The Asset Economy.* Cambridge, UK: Polity Press.

Adkins, L., M. Cooper, and M. Konings. 2021. "Class in the 21st Century: Asset Inflation and the New Logic of Inequality." *Environment and Planning A: Economy and Space* 53 (3): 548–572.

Alonso, W. 1964. *Location and Land Use: Toward a General Theory of Land Rent.* Cambridge, MA: Harvard University Press.

Amin, S. 2018. *Modern Imperialism, Monopoly Finance Capital, and Marx's Law of Value.* New York: Monthly Review Press.

Anderson, M. B. 2019. "Class Monopoly Rent and the Redevelopment of Portland's Pearl District." *Antipode* 51 (4): 1035–1056.

Andreucci, A., M. Garcia-Lamarca, J. Wedekind, and E. Swyngedouw. 2017. "'Value Grabbing': A Political Ecology of Rent." *Capitalism, Nature, Socialism* 28 (3): 28–47.

Arboleda, M. 2020. *Planetary Mine—Territories of Extraction under Late Capitalism.* London: Verso.

Ball, M. 1977. "Differential Rent and the Role of Landed Property." *International Journal of Urban and Regional Research* 1: 380–403.

Ball, M. 1985. "The Urban Rent Question." *Environment and Planning A* 17: 503–525.

Ball, M., M. Edwards, V. Bentivegna, and M. Folin, eds. 1985. *Land Rent, Housing and Urban Planning: A European Perspective.* London: Routledge.

Bennett, J. 2010. *Vibrant Matter: A Political Ecology of Things.* Durham, NC: Duke University Press.

Birch, K. 2015. *We Have Never Been Neoliberal.* Winchester: Zero Books.

Birch, K., and F. Muniesa. 2020. *Turning Things into Assets.* Cambridge, MA: MIT Press.

Blomley, N. 2003. *Unsettling the City: Urban Land and the Politics of Property.* London: Routledge.

Braun, B. 2016. "From Performativity to Political Economy: Index Investing, ETFs and Asset Manager Capitalism." *New Political Economy* 21 (3): 257–273.Callon, M. 1998. *The Laws of the Markets.* Oxford: Blackwell.

Christophers, B. 2019. "The Rentierization of the United Kingdom Economy." *Environment and Planning A: Economy and Space.* https://doi.org/10 .1177%2F0308518X19873007.

Coronil, F. 1998. *The Magical State: Nature, Money, and Modernity in Venezuela.* Chicago: University of Chicago Press.

Felli, R. 2013. "Managing Climate Insecurity by Ensuring Continuous Capital Accumulation: 'Climate Refugees' and 'Climate Migrants.'" *New Political Economy* 18 (3): 337–363.

Felli, R. 2014. "On Climate Rent." *Historical Materialism* 22 (3–4): 251–280.

Fine, B. 1979. "On Marx's Theory of Agricultural Rent." *Economy and Society* 8 (3): 241–278.

Goede, M. de. 2005. *Virtue, Fortune and Faith: A Genealogy of Finance.* Minneapolis: University of Minnesota Press.

Gunnoe, A. 2014. "The Political Economy of Institutional Landownership: Neorentier Society and the Financialisation of Land." *Rural Sociology* 79 (4): 478–504.

Guthman, J. 2002. "Commodified Meanings, Meaningful Commodities: Re-thinking Production–Consumption Links through the Organic System of Provision." *Sociologia Ruralis* 42(4): 295–311.

Haila, A. 1990. "The Theory of Land Rent at the Crossroads." *Environment and Planning D: Society and Space* 8 (3): 275–296.

Haila, A. 2016. *Urban Land Rent: Singapore as a Property State.* Oxford: Wiley.

Harvey, D. 1974. "Class-Monopoly Rent, Finance Capital and Urban Revolution." *Regional Studies* 8 (3–4): 239–255.

Harvey, D. (1982) 2006. *The Limits to Capital.* Oxford: Basil Blackwell.

Harvey, D. 2003. *The New Imperialism.* Oxford: Oxford University Press.

Harvey, D. 2012. *Rebel Cities.* London: Verso.

Harvey, D., and L. Chatterjee. 1974. "Absolute Rent and the Structuring of Space by Governmental and Financial Institutions." *Antipode* 6: 22–36.

Hernandez Trejo, M. *Conservation and Land Rent in a Rural Landscape: Payments for Ecosystem Services in Southern Mexico.* PhD diss., University of Manchester, 2019.

Kaika, M., and L. Ruggiero. 2013. "Land Financialization As a 'Lived' Process: The Transformation of Milan's Bicocca by Pirelli." *European Urban and Regional Studies* 23 (1): 3–22.

Kaika, M., and L. Ruggiero. 2015. "Class Meets Land: The Social Mobilization of Land As Catalyst for Urban Change." *Antipode* 47 (3): 557–828.

Knoll, K., M. Schularick, and T. Steger. 2017. "No Price Like Home: Global House Prices, 1870–2012." *American Economic Review* 107 (2): 331–353.

Lapavistas, C. 2013. *Profiting without Producing: How Finance Exploits Us All.* London: Verso.

Lefebvre, H. (1974) 1991. *The Production of Space*. Translated by D. Nicholson-Smith. Oxford: Blackwell.

Li, T. M. 2014a. "What is Land? Assembling a Resource for Global Investment." *Transactions of the Institute of British Geographers* 39 (4): 589–602.

Li, T. M. 2014b. *Land's End: Capitalist Relations on an Indigenous Frontier*. Durham, NC: Duke University Press

Mann, G. 2018. "Equation and Adequation: The World Traced by the Phillips Curve. *Antipode* 50 (1):184–211.

Marx, K. (1894) 1967. *Capital, A Critique of Political Economy, Volume III*. Moscow: International Publishers Co.

Marx, K. (1894) 1981. *Capital, A Critique of Political Economy, Volume I*. London: Penguin Books.

Muniesa, F., L. Doganova, H. Ortiz, A. Pina-Stranger, A. Paterson, A. Bourgoin, V. Ehrenstein, D. Juven, D. Pontille, B. Sarac-Lesarve, and G. Yon. 2019. *Capitalization: A Cultural Guide*. Paris: Presse des Mines.

Muth, R. 1969. *Cities and Housing: The Spatial Pattern of Urban Residential Land Use*. Chicago: University of Chicago Press.

Ouma, S. 2018. "This Can('t) Be an Asset Class: The World of Money Management, 'Society,' and the Contested Morality of Farmland Investments." Environment and Planning A: *Economy and Space* 52 (1). https://doi.org/10.1177/0308518X18790051.

Parenti, M. 2015. *Profit Pathology and Other Indecencies*. London: Routledge.

Piketty, T. 2014. *Capital in the Twenty-First Century*. Cambridge, MA: Harvard University Press.

Polanyi, K. (1944) (2002) *The Great Transformation*. Boston: Beacon Press.

Prudham, S. 2007. "The Fictions of Autonomous Invention: Accumulation by Dispossession, Commodification and Life Patents in Canada." *Antipode* 39 (3): 406–429.

Purcell, T. 2018. "'Hot Chocolate': Financialized Global Value Chains and Cocoa Production in Ecuador." *The Journal of Peasant Studies* 45 (5–6): 904–926.

Purcell, T. F., A. Loftus, and H. March. 2019. "Value–Rent–Finance." *Progress in Human Geography* 44 (3). https://doi.org/10.1177/0309132519838064.

Rigi, J., and R. Prey. 2015. "Value, Rent, and the Political Economy of Social Media." *The Information Society* 31 (5): 392–406.

Safransky, S. 2017. "Rethinking Land Struggle in the Postindustrial City." *Antipode* 49 (4): 1079–1100.

Serna, L. A. 2021. "Land Grabbing or Value Grabbing? Land Rent and Wind Energy in the Isthmus of Tehuantepec, Oaxaca." *Competition & Change* 26 (3–4).

Slater, T. 2017. "Planetary Rent Gaps." *Antipode* 49 (1): 114–137.

Srnicek, N. 2016. *Platform Capitalism*. London: Polity Press.

Standing, G. 2016. *The Corruption of Capitalism: Why Rentiers Thrive and Work Does Not Pay*. London: Biteback Publishing.

Swyngedouw, E. 1992. "Territorial Organisation and the Space/Technology Nexus." *Transactions of the Institute of British Geographers* 17 (4): 417–433.

Swyngedouw, E. A. 2005. "Dispossessing H20: The Contested Terrain of Water Privatization." *Capitalism, Nature, Socialism* 16 (1): 81–98.

Toscano, A. 2008. "The Culture of Abstraction." *Theory, Culture, and Society* 25 (4): 57–75.

Tse-Tung, M. 1937. "On Practice: On the Relation between Knowledge and Practice, between Knowing and Doing." In *Selected Works of Mao Tse-Tung*. 9 vols. https://www.marxists.org/reference/archive/mao/selected-works/volume-1/mswv1_16.htm.

Turner, A. 2015. *Between Debt and the Devil: Money, Credit, and Fixing Global Finance* Princeton: Princeton University Press.

Ward, C. 2021. "Contradictions of Financial Capital Switching: Reading the Corporate Leverage Crisis through The Port of Liverpool's Whole Business Securitization." *International Journal of Urban and Regional Research* 45 (2): 249–265. https://doi.org/10.1111/1468-2427.12878.

Ward, C., and M. B. Aalbers. 2016. "Virtual Special Issue Editorial Essay: 'The Shitty Rent Business': What's the Point of Land Rent Theory?" *Urban Studies* 53 (9): 1760–1783.

Ward, C., and E. Swyngedouw. 2018. "Neoliberalisation from the Ground Up: Insurgent Capital, Regional Struggle, and the Assetisation of Land." *Antipode* 50 (4): 1077–1097.

Whiteside, H. 2017. "The State's Estate: Devaluing and Revaluing 'Surplus' Public Land in Canada." *Environment and Planning A: Economy and Space* 51 (2): 505–526.

Wijburg, G., M. Aalbers, and S. Heeg. 2018. "The Financialisation of Rental Housing 2.0: Releasing Housing into the Privatised Mainstream of Capital Accumulation." *Antipode* 50 (4): 1098–1119.

Williams, R. 1976. *Keywords: A Vocabulary of Culture and Society.* London: Fontana Press.

12

THE FINANCIALIZED AND DISPOSSESSED

Transforming Land and Lives
into Speculative Assets

Michael Goldman

> **By justifying a model of economic transformation that does not treat rural citizens as partners in the largest rural democracy in the world, may ultimately be a deeper challenge to a substantive notion of democracy than corruption.**
>
> —Kanchan Chandra

> **We can fight for the right to the *paisa* (money) but never for the right to land.**
>
> —Dalit farmer activist

> **The growing treatment of land as a form of financial asset is arguably one of the most economically and politically noteworthy trends of recent capitalist history.**
>
> —Brett Christophers, "The State and Financialization of Public Land in the United Kingdom"

On November 26, 2020, marking one of India's most prominent national holidays, Constitution Day and its commemoration of the 1949 signing of India's postcolonial constitution, the country's capitals were at a standstill under the miraculous weight of India's Great Strike, its greatest for more than a century. India's umbrella association of farmers' unions estimates that 250 million people closed down the country.[1] Although that sounds like an exaggeration, it no doubt was one of the world's largest protests. Millions of trucks jammed the corridors into Delhi. It capped off disruptive actions that started in September 2020 when the central government passed three farm bills to end the postindependence "*mandi* system" in which farmers sold to government markets and got a minimum price guarantee, one that offered some security for small farmers at planting time when they typically take out large loans, banking on those minimum price guarantees. The ruling national government replaced it without any public consultation or debate with a marketplace in which the "buyers"—large agribusiness firms—would determine the right price for farmers' products.[2]

These 2020 farm bills laid to rest any hope that the government would support small farmers through cyclical market volatilities, drought, and debt. And yet more than 60 percent of India's population—and 70 percent of working women—depend upon farm employment for their livelihoods. Of female workers in farming, most are ("untouchable") Dalits, and most do not own land.[3] As one prominent journalist noted, "India's suffering female farmers have most to lose" by these new farm bills, and "the country's Dalits are already exploited—and know it can get worse" (Dastidar 2021).

Less dramatic are the slogans from Dalit farmers who were displaced by the new international airport on the northern outskirts of Bengaluru (formerly Bangalore) declaring that "the planes land on the graveyard of the Dalits!" This chapter focuses on the common process by which a government agency acquires "low-value" farmland and converts it into "high-value" urban real estate. This conversion of rural-to-urban land is seen as a prerequisite for any large urban real estate or infrastructural project and is part of a larger governmental strategy to revitalize the national economy by "globalizing" its cities. While the current Modi government actively *deagrarianizes* the countryside and *deindustrializes* the city of its manufacturing base, it is also doggedly following a global imaginary that envisions wealth creation coming from large-scale "world-class" urban projects, which promise to stem rising social inequalities and tensions and catapult India into a dominant economic power.

As this chapter will show, these land transactions, almost by a "sublime trick of the imagination," do generate huge amounts of surplus value—they are created, extracted, and mostly exported. But much of the Dalit farming population has been left without land or just compensation, without the promised wealth from this rural-to-urban land conversion. It has also left local developers and investors, and the city itself, heavily in debt and under a more onerous business model of urban financialization, one not that different from the woes of cities elsewhere around the world. Moreover, much of the land acquired for "world-class" infrastructure remains vacant, and many thousands of small farmers remain without land, even while land prices have reached astronomical levels, in some places increasing in value by 1,000 percent over a decade. How and why there is such uneven and combined development are the questions pursued here.

Protesting farmers and their legal advocates explain that in India, a regime of caste power rules over land transactions (of mostly men in government and in land brokering), one that has always existed in some form, but today it has been invigorated by the huge sums of finance (and politics-related) capital flowing into Indian cities since the liberalization of the economy in the early 1990s. Although the official discourse from the national government on caste claims caste violence and discrimination eventually disappear as the "backward rural" transforms into the "modern urban," nothing could be further from the truth here. In the conversion of the rural periphery of the fast-growing city of Bengaluru, we see that a patrimonial regime of gendered caste power rules over land transactions, which, along with the demands of an increasingly global set of financial actors, exacerbates existing social inequalities and enables the extraction and circulation of "liquid" (i.e., easily circulating) capital from land. This chapter looks at the city from the perspective of these social lives of land: what is being acquired, converted, displaced, and negated in a once-thriving rural society as a condition for the creation of an urban real estate market and the basis for the financialized global city.

Bengaluru, once the beloved "garden city" and "pensioner's paradise" for retiring government officials, is one of the fastest growing cities in Asia (2.8 million in 1980, nearly 13.6 million in 2023), with its extended reach into the countryside as one of its most attractive features for investors. It has converted hundreds of thousands of acres of the rural landscape into expensive urban real estate, a small proportion of which houses some of the country's most prominent growth industries, such as IT, aerospace, and biotechnology. Before 2007, the city was smallish—226 square kilometers—but in 2007, it officially expanded fourfold through a major incorporation of 120 villages and seven towns, with ambitious plans in the next few decades to become one of the world's largest megalopolises, comparable to the Tokyo-Yokohama conglomeration.

The chapter traces an emblematic case of a new (since 2008) international airport complex encircled by aerospace industrial and biotech/IT campuses at the edge of Bengaluru as an anchor and gateway to south India's "global city." The project's aspirations were much more than aeronautic or to replace the old ex-military airport in the center of town with a state-of-the-art facility thirty-five kilometers to the city's north. Built in a green belt of farming villages, public forests, and watersheds covered with a century-old network of constructed reservoirs and water channels, the Kempegowda International Airport has backers investing to catalyze the transformation of India's garden city into a global attraction for the other type of "greening," of finance capital.

At the start, plans were ambitiously afoot to surround the modest-sized airport with a self-governed Airport City, IT, and Biotech Region with linked clusters of Aerospace, Electronic Hardware, Software Tech parks, and a Global Finance District, mimicking the best urban infrastructure of Shanghai,

Singapore, and Dubai. Alas, twenty-five years later, few of these speculative projects besides the airport have materialized. Nonetheless, tens of thousands of acres of land have been acquired, mostly in highly contentious ways.

As one Dalit farmer activist and legal advocate explained, "For the last twenty-five years, we've been fighting for the rights of farmers. But now, the entire structure has been dismantled, now everyone has either become a land broker or a victim. Women are fighting against alcoholism and fatalism. Once people lose their land, they lose their sense . . . This is the new Bangalore" (Siddhartha, Devanahalli, July 2016).

This chapter employs the concept of "speculative urbanism" as an explanatory tool to highlight the hard work that goes into mobilizing resources (capital, labor, state, and caste) to build the dream, create the parastatal entities and regulatory regimes, entice the capital, draw up the contracts, acquire, consolidate and police the land, broker the land deals, remake rural ecologies and societies, and produce the new urban/state spaces in which these new projects can thrive (Goldman 2011; Goldman and Narayan 2021). It takes a lot of muscle, as well as an aspirational drive, to mobilize an array of actors to produce a new urban landscape. Why the speculative urbanism project gets constituted with the help of financial tools and players and how it exacerbates existing social inequalities and power relations while generating new ones are the questions this chapter seeks to answer.

Land's Financialization

As the economic geographer Brett Christophers notes (2016), the financialization of land has become a formidable global trend in recent capitalist history. Although finance has always played a pivotal role in capitalist—and colonial—expansion (i.e., think of the major financiers and surplus-value extractors from imperial wars, as well as from colonial railways, shipping lanes, ports, and the slave trade), the 1990s marked a palpable resurgence of finance power in the accumulation process. As Krippner (2012) explains, a significant trend in the twenty-first century has been the rise and dominance of financial power within the economy, as more corporate profits "accrue primarily through financial channels rather than trade and commodity production" (Krippner 2005, 174; Moreno 2018).

What about land itself as a source of financialization? In *Fields of Gold*, Madeleine Fairbairn (2020) stresses both the rise and the obstacles to financializing land in the US heartland—skeptical of how farmland can produce high-growth wealth for investors from anything else besides its basic industrial and food crops. In China, Fulong Wu (2022) finds that land has recently become used as collateral by the state for land development for infrastructure and housing. Gavin

Shatkin (2017) discovers across many Asian cities that land's monetization has become a requirement for municipalities left with few sources of revenue generation since central governments liberalized (or shirked) their obligations to municipalities. Hence, the new business of city governments tends to be as a land broker in order to provide basic public services. Swyngedouw and Ward (2018) unearth a similar trend in England: the need to assetize land to raise much-needed capital to run the basics of city government. Kaika and Ruggiero (2013, 4) argue that scholars should expand their research to study "how the socially embedded mobilization of land as a financial asset act[s] as a catalyst for 'capital switching' process from the 'real' urban economy of goods and service production to a fully financialized form of global accumulation," a topic this chapter engages.

What is this link between the financialization of the land and the larger economy? Taking their cues from Marx, scholars such as Henri Lefebvre and David Harvey have argued that when a crisis hits the global economy, capital tends to flee the productive/manufacturing sectors (which become risky and tumultuous due to overaccumulation) and enter the urban real estate and construction sectors, where it could "find refuge," exploit, and prosper until the productive side of the economy settles (Aalbers 2019a, 2019b). When the city becomes a primary site of refuge or a spatial fix for fleeing productive capital, both the city and the global economy are deeply affected. Indeed, since the 2010s, after the global financial crisis did its damage, scholars found that the financialization of land and real estate has led to the transformation of the city. But what about the countryside and rural-urban social relations? What are the dynamics unfolding between finance and local developers, small farmers and land brokers, and the role of the state facilitating these changes in land acquisition and land *deruralization*?

Across the neoliberalizing world, the financialization of land has become a dominant strategy for governments to meet the speculative urban imaginaries of elites, much to the benefit of the footloose and rootless financial sector. In the following, we see how global private equity firms have jumped into the space that central governments have vacated, supplying capital for major infrastructure projects that are designed to require an excess of external financing from the world's leading and monopolistic firms.

Phase One: The Birth of a Speculative Land Market

At a closed conference of investors and national government officials in a five-star hotel in New Delhi in 2010, a senior government minister announced the official strategy to build $1 trillion of urban infrastructure in the next two decades, "the likes of which India has never seen before," exceeding China's announcement of building its $900 billion "Silk Road" of infrastructure and trade across Asia. The kicker, however, was that for India, more than half of the capital was expected to come from foreign capital markets, creating a highly leveraged and risky national agenda of economic growth. Without hesitation or a sense of decorum, foreign investors retorted back to the podium that there would be no foreign investment unless specific obstacles in doing business in India were removed; they would not invest without upfront guarantees that they could access land. "Your courts are backlogged for decades with court cases against land claims," noted one investor in the audience. "It could take us years to build at a scale large enough to be worth our while," said another. A manager of a major Canadian pension fund based in China remarked from the audience: "If we can get 15 percent profitable rates of return on safe investments in the US and Europe, we will need at least 25 percent rates of return to invest in 'risky' India." Later that same day, some foreign investors explained to me that they were avoiding new projects that were not "concrete-ready" and current projects that were not already built. The biggest risks, they suggested, were wrapped up in the challenge of gaining access to contiguous swathes of individually owned land. The question on the table was: Can the government expeditiously facilitate investor access to land?

A sequence of changes was critical for the real estate and finance sectors to pick up speed. Earlier, there was the official Press Note 4 2001 that permitted foreign direct investment (FDI) to invest in real estate as long as investors developed a minimum of 100 acres and "locked in" industry and manufacturing projects for a minimum period of three years. But unlike in China's special economic zones that produced "factories for the world," few investors in India found the idea of tax-free production areas as appealing (Levien 2012; Cross 2014). The second change occurred soon after with the Press Note 2 2005 and the 2005 SEZ Act. Both relaxed the land-size requirement and the rule that land be solely acquired for industrial purposes, giving investors what they wanted: not land for factories but land that could generate higher rates of profit on its own (Babar 2017). By as early as 2008, only a fifth of the FDI flowing into India went into manufacturing (much of which was intrafirm, like Toyota to its Indian plants), and less than 0.2 percent flowed into agriculture, the sector employing much of the Indian population (Chalapati Rao and Dhar 2011, 2018). The bulk of FDI streamed into those sectors that could convert land into a valuable asset, namely finance, construction, and real estate.

In Bengaluru, these investment strategies materialized through the siting of the international airport, a key anchor for the city's expansion northward onto thousands of acres of government/public, commons, and smallholder farmland. For many decades, government land and village commons were used as forest, pasture, and a complex water catchment and distribution system in the form of reservoirs and canals managed by villages (Mathur and da Cunha 2006; Nagendra 2016; Goldman and Narayan 2019). Since the region exists on a semiarid high plateau far from rivers, this system, which captures monsoon water, provides essential surface and subsurface water to villages, farmland, and, ultimately, the city. The three main districts or *"taluks"* sited for global-city projects—Devanahalli, Doddaballapura, and Bangalore North—were home to 341 farming villages. At the start, plans ambitiously included an Airport City, IT and Biotech Region, Aerospace Park, Electronic Hardware Park, Software Tech Park, and Global Finance District. Seven-hundred and ninety-two square kilometers were placed under the jurisdiction of a new parastatal agency, the Bengaluru International Airport Area Planning Agency (BIAAPA). By 2009, a ten-year Master Plan was designed to double the area to include a total of 564 villages and absorb yet another rural district—significantly comprising an area larger than the existing Bengaluru city itself. Today, however, due to a lack of interest by investors and industries, the area under BIAAPA's control has been reduced by 50 percent. Land acquisition, however, has not slowed.

The reason that officials could acquire much more land than needed, displacing anywhere from 230 to 560 villages (with villages averaging 1,000 people or so), is because much of the land was either owned by smallholders or owned by the government but used by smallholders, a sizeable percentage of which are from the lowest tiers of the social order, Adivasi (tribal communities), or Dalits ("untouchables"). Together, they possess relatively little political power. According to the most recent census, these oppressed communities comprise approximately 35 percent of the region's population and two-thirds of the population living at ground zero of the airport complex (State of Karnataka Census, 2011). Most of them worked the land under insecure land tenure (Benjamin 2008; Benjamin and Raman 2011; interviews with the author). For example, the district where the airport is located, Devanahalli, is a Dalit "reserved constituency," a district ordered by law to have a certain number of Dalit elected officials because of the substantial size of the Dalit population and their historic negligence by government and political parties. This land falls under different land tenure categories, including village commons, sacred forest, government forest, and pasture. Of the smallest land holdings, many were granted during the "land to the tiller" era of the 1970s and 1980s as part of the attenuated promise from independence to give land to farm laborers from oppressed Adivasi and Dalit communities.

Once the region was recommended for global-city projects, these insecure land-tenure conditions offered easy opportunities for people in government administration and politicians to grab land by working closely with land-revenue offices to realign public land boundaries and forge ownership documents (interviews with the author; Gupta 2012; Doshi and Ranganathan 2017). We know this because many of our interviewees, including high-level government officials (and a retired high court justice) and real estate brokers (who lament or mock the intrusion of politicians in their business), described specific cases in which land was illegally grabbed. Moreover, two influential Task Force reports commissioned by the legislature—one approximately 300 pages in length and the other 1,000 pages—offer a mountain of evidence (Ramaswamy 2007; Balasubramanian 2011). According to the 2009 Legislative Task Force on land encroachment, approximately 1.2 million acres had been stolen across the state of Karnataka, with the largest number of cases of land encroachment filed in Bangalore North close to the airport; there, they estimated 25,000 acres of land worth Rs. 25 crores ($3.5 million, in 2009) had been stolen. (The report identifies several senior government officers, Karnataka Industrial Area Development Board [KIADB] officers, and political leaders, including a former Chief Minister, as grabbing the largest parcels.) Because very few of the more than 6,000 cases of land encroachment move through the existing courts, a special court was set up in 2016 specifically to help handle these cases; only a handful are settled each year, however, due to "administrative foot-dragging."

This next section focuses on the financial dimension of the airport project, the subsequent process of land dispossession, and the mechanisms by which the project became a catalyst for land conversion and valorization, small farmer displacement, and the creation of a speculative land market and its financialization. These are the dynamics that characterize Phase One of Bengaluru's era of speculative urbanism.

Jump-Starting the Financialization Process

The logic of twenty-first-century urban financialization emerged in the region in the form of the contractual agreement between the Government of Karnataka and the firms investing in and building the Bangalore International Airport (BIAL) (Ministry of Civil Aviation 2004). Even though the city had outgrown its old central city airport, the cost of building a new international airport was prohibitively expensive for the under-resourced municipal government. The Karnataka government thus agreed to a public-private partnership in which it offered substantial land along with financial and tax incentives to its Thai, Swiss, and German investors. The plum character of the contract reflected the fact that investors expected profits from not only the provision of a new airport but also from land speculation. Although the public was not allowed to see the contract on the grounds that it was "proprietary," it did not take long before the details were leaked.[6]

The Bangalore International Airport first opened in March 2008 as a modest structure with one runway, one café, and a gift shop. It was India's first public-private partnership airport, built 35 kilometers north of the city in an area long designated as the "green belt" that could not be sold for non-agrarian economic purposes without government approval. But as part of the deal, extra obstacles for oppressed communities were put in place for them to gain full rights to land. While their location in the social hierarchy is often publicly defined as the result of religious and cultural norms, as Rupa Viswanath demonstrates for neighboring regions in southern India, their inability to access rights to land is the result of powerful and enduring institutional and social barriers built up in the name of caste (Viswanath 2014). The situation in this region reveals that while deprived communities have enjoyed access to land, especially government and village land on which they cultivated, grazed animals, raised silkworms, maintained water infrastructure and sacred groves, fished, grew flowers, and much more, they have been typically barred from land ownership (Nagendra 2016; Upadhya, Gidwani, and Goldman 2017).

The airport's corporate owners, BIAL, received 4,000 acres, of which 1,000 acres comprised the aforementioned gift. Approximately 2,000 acres of government land were leased to the corporate consortium at Rs. 1/acre per year (1.5 US cents per acre). Yet when the value of the government land contributed to the project was assessed, the land was assigned a market price of Rs. 200,000/acre (US$3,000/acre). Ten years later, an acre of land not far from the airport sold for close to a million dollars and was priced at least twice that in 2018, reflecting a substantial rate of appreciation and return on investment. A villa on one-sixteenth of an acre nearby sold for $850,000, and the sales staff explained to me that most of the villa buyers in this upscale, gated community were not end users but speculators (interviews with the author 2015, 2016). These huge profits—created "out of thin air"—triggered a land market gold rush.

Two thousand more acres were set aside for an Aerospace Special Economic Zone (SEZ), 10,000 to 20,000 acres were earmarked for an IT Industrial Region, and there were promises of a Financial City and a Science City, similar to the speculative urban projects encircling Shanghai, Dubai, Jakarta, and Abu Dhabi (Roy and Ong 2011; Shatkin 2017; Günel 2019). BIAAPA was put in charge of overseeing these development areas, and KIADB became the agency to notify and then acquire farmers' land, paying them a set "guidance price" as compensation. To the farmers' clear detriment, this price reflected the rural value of land during a time of government disinvestment from the agrarian economy; it did not reflect the future urban value, which became appreciably higher as soon as the land was sold. The pronounced fear by investors was that if the price for farmers' compensation was "too high," then few investors would have been interested in buying. According to the 16th Annual Report of BIAL (2017), the airport consortium paid only about 1 percent of its annual profits in taxes, reflecting yet another incentive that sweetened the deal for foreign investors.

Whereas the government's initial promise to the people of Bengaluru was to turn low-value agriculture and rural land into high-value productive sites, the terms of the original contract strongly suggest that the consortium invested in the project *only under the condition* that they would receive heavily discounted and free land from the state of Karnataka. Parcels of farmland have changed hands many times since the initial acquisition, and each time, the value of the converted land has increased substantially. To some observers, this signaled the project's definitive success: building an airport in an "economically stagnant" countryside triggered a high-value land market that enticed investors from all over the world. But the specifics of the contract also signaled the fact that the construction of a global-city airport would not necessarily be a catalyst for foreign capital infusions into job-creating industrial or social projects.

Mobilizing Caste Networks, Creating the Social Technology of Land Grabbing

Phase One developed in three steps: first, with key legal reform, then through this financialized contract to do business triggering the birth of a land market through displacement, and, finally, via the process of making land available to investors. While it was easy enough to sign away access to land in the contract, it was something else to be able to actually acquire the land for sale. What emerged from these efforts was a contentious process that can only be briefly summarized here. Simply put, freeing up land depended on upper-caste networks inside government agencies and within villages mobilizing to convert an entangled history of land use based on oral commitments, exchanges, and obligations into a straightforward property market.

According to a legal advocate, Leo Saldanha, a key turning point for land acquisition and commodification nationally and in the city came when the government changed the legal framework to accommodate foreign direct investment or FDI. In one of several interviews with me, Saldanha highlighted the irony of setting up market mechanisms based on state subsidies. In his view, this opened the door to land speculation without any guarantees that investors would put money down on the slower and riskier process of establishing factories for global supply chains. As he explains it: "The KIADB Act Amendment of 1998 redefined 'infrastructure' as 'industry' and allowed for land to be acquired not at the market rate but at a lower rate, through a new interpretation of the old British notion of 'eminent domain.' Before this amendment, land could only be acquired by the state through eminent domain if it was 'in the public interest,' but now, land can be acquired at below-market rates for private interest. This was the official start of this current period of intensified commodification of land in Bengaluru" (interview with the author, July 2015).

The KIADB Act allowed for large-scale rural land acquisition with little oversight. It did not take long before state actors within the system realized the lucrative nature of handling land for domestic and foreign investors and began to collect rents from the many unofficial transactions set up to convert rural land into urban real estate. Quickly, they earned big transactional rents (otherwise known as bribes). But KIADB could not do it on its own, and the land acquisition process required the mobilization of the social networks of the upper-caste members in and out of government to acquire land cheaply and efficaciously.[4]

At various times since independence, especially in the 1970s, Dalits north of the city had received government land to graze animals, farm, and build their homes; these acts were considered as *just* or *fair* compensation for the poorest, who also deserved to benefit from the expulsion of British rule and the turn to independence. At the same time, according to our interviews, the village power elites—whom local Dalits refer to as Gowdas and Patels—interpreted their "just compensation" for managing village well-being and land as taking the form of guaranteed access to Dalit labor in the village. As Dalits gradually received legal rights to own land, some of them were able to reclaim their labor power that was otherwise obligated to Gowda landlords and to farm their newly acquired land for themselves. The act of returning "land to the tiller" might have been necessary as a national political promise, but the effects were not taken lightly at the village and district levels by elites. The compensatory act of allowing the rural majority to possess and till their own soils aggravated upper-caste landlords and village leaders, some of whom violently reclaimed the land from Dalits even before the airport was sited (interviews with the author).

According to one Dalit legal advocate who represents Dalit villagers in court:

> For the airport and nearby aerospace SEZ, 75 percent of the acquired land was Dalit land, approximately 3,000 acres of the 4,000 acres. Of three villages acquired for the Aerospace SEZ nearby, 90 percent of the villagers are Dalits. In 1978, the government gave Dalits some land,

what was called 'wasteland' by the British, but it was land we used as grazing land—it was given as part of the national "land to the tillers" struggle. We were bonded laborers working for village leaders and land-lords, the [upper caste] Patels and Gowdas. [Receiving land] created a lot of tension once Dalits [. . .] were officially free from the Gowdas.

Many Dalits expressed their dismay with the whole discourse of just compen-sation used by the airport real estate project and were angry not only with the minuscule funds they received but with the fact they and their families had to give up their land. At best, their concerns were reduced to a calculation of a bet-ter or worse price. "We can fight for the right to the *paisa* (money) but never for the right to land," the legal advocate lamented (interview with the author, Ben-galuru Rural district, July 2016).

The form of Dalit dispossession described above did not only enable a new market for land to be created but also unleashed this machinery of disposses-sion and rent seeking. Once state officials realized the size of the gap between the price that farmers, especially Dalits, could be paid for their land and the phenomenal value that it could generate in a speculative real estate market, officials were quick to exploit these opportunities, pushing Dalits off land that might never be developed. They used the captured rents for personal gain and further speculation, for purchasing positions within the state bureaucracy, and to support political parties and elections. Because land is the most lucra-tive outlet for large amounts of cash, this money invariably found its way back into the land market, ensuring a steady rise in land prices. These prac-tices comprise different elements of rent seeking by state actors, in which we find a few common features. First, KIADB and BIAPPA chose the sites where Dalits were in the majority and where their land tenure was most insecure and could more easily be exploited by staff and brokers. Second, records within the land revenue offices were manipulated, and government land was often ac-quired "in the middle of the night" when documents were forged. Third, family members were pressured to sell their small plots so that they could be assembled into large contiguous plots for sale. Finally, the state did its part by disinvesting in rural infrastructure, such as schools, public bus routes, and electricity, which helped to make farming impossible to pursue (interviews with the author, 2012–2015).

According to farmers and their legal advocates, KIADB officials stayed out of the house-to-house negotiations; they never visited the villages to survey the land. Instead, officials hired local brokers to do their bidding, keeping at arm's length the series of small transactions. As one farmer explained:

When the government asked for documents, we had no idea how to assemble them, and KIADB officials said these middlemen would help collect the papers necessary to prove ownership, use of the land, and taxes paid. The brokers promised to get the land records from the Tahsildar office [district-level tax/revenue office]. These brokers knew the local officials well; they worked for them. Many of us had claims to land that the government refused to acknowledge, so the brokers said we needed lawyers to file the cases in court in order to get the compensation. In the end, the broker and lawyer worked together to collect half of the compensation money for themselves!

Dalit villagers from Anneshwara (now absorbed by the airport complex) had been farming *gomala* (pasture) land since the 1970s, and some had finally received the possession certificate from the government. Just before the airport came, they were told that the paperwork was being processed into property deeds. But once KIADB stepped into the role of land acquisition, the processing stopped, and a majority of the Dalit farmers in the region never received proof of possession, even though they had been paying property taxes and fees for years.

Of the 400 acres of Anneshwara taken by the airport, half were still under dispute as of 2017. KIADB staff said they put the compensation money in a bank account while lawyers and brokers represented farmers in the courts. But this process had taken years, and dispute resolution rarely resulted in Dalit farmers receiving current (and hence real) urban market prices for their acquired land. As time passes, with cases moving slowly through the courts, the compensation originally offered loses its worth on the market. When half of the court settlement money goes to brokers and lawyers and compensation fails to keep up with rapidly rising market prices, farmers with little political power lose.

What started out as a contractual obligation by government agencies to the airport investors—acquiring land from farmers and converting it into urban real estate—turned into a set of actions that has become institutionalized. Money is extracted from every transaction, and a robust revenue stream flows through low-level bureaucratic offices up the hierarchy. The money also pours into the political party structure to help finance political elections (Kapur and Vaishnav 2011). According to the Center for Media Studies (CMS) in New Delhi, more than Rs. 10,500 crores (US$1.5 billion) were spent on the relatively minor May 2018 Assembly election in the state of Karnataka (CMS 2019). This sum was twice what was spent in the previous election in 2013 and represented "the most expensive election ever" for a state in India, according to the Indian Express newspaper

(Press Trust of India 2018). Researchers argue that the money came largely from real estate transactions (op. cit.).

In an interview, a senior government official reported to us the depth of this "patrimonial regime" (Piketty 2014; Moreno 2018). Born a Dalit and one of the few to move up the ranks, he is well known as one of the "clean" senior officials in the Karnataka government. The first step in this patrimonial regime, he explained, involved the making of the city's "master plan," which the Chief Minister's office oversees. This involved the zoning of land—some areas are for "green belt," where land is protected as farm, forest, lakes, and commons land and cannot become real estate; other areas are designated "yellow" for residential use, "purple" for industrial, and so on. It is big business, he explained, as to how zones become delineated because it affects where investment and development can go. Consequently, sizable bribes are paid for rezoning formerly off-limit areas into new sites for investment (Kumar 2015). "The Master Plan has been changed umpteen times," he told me. "Preparing the Master Plan is itself a huge money maker: to first declare a green belt draws in everyone to the office bribing for access or rezoning [of particular plots] [. . .]. The government runs on the money politics of land. The economy [referring to 2017] is not doing well, so everyone wants to buy land, even foreign investors . . ." (interview with the author, July 2017).

His revelations are not unique (Piliavsky 2014). In September 2016, due to public outcry and pressure, two special courts were created exclusively to prosecute land encroachment cases, and the Karnataka government admitted that anywhere between 25,000 and 35,000 acres of government land in urban and rural Bengaluru districts, including the airport region, were stolen with little accountability or punishment (*Hindu* 2016). Even though these legislature-backed reports have led to few prosecutions, pressure from civil society groups has forced some private developers to return encroached land in and around public lakes and has resulted in new Acts, such as the Karnataka Land Grabbing Prohibition Act 2011/2014 (Ramaswamy 2007; Balasubramanian 2011; Urs 2018).

Since the money from these land-based transactions cannot be deposited into bank accounts (as it would be easily traced and taxed), the land market has become the most common site for money laundering. The persistent rise in land prices is thus not a simple supply-and-demand phenomenon; rather, it is largely a result of sales driven by the need to launder money and then pull it back out as "clean." It is a form of wealth accumulation unrelated to the utility value of land, fed by patrimonial capital and embedded in extractive caste, bureaucracy, and political technologies of power (Piketty 2014; Moreno 2018). As these bureaucratic tasks related to land notification, acquisition, conversion, and resale are so enriching for intermediaries, these government positions are also being purchased and traded on an open market with incredible price inflation (Searle 2018).

These are some of the key micromarket practices that undergird the land market and have contributed to the skyrocketing of land prices in Bengaluru. In and out of government, the social workings of caste power have become entangled with efforts of finance capital to assure that land prices would continue to rise even while real estate property prices have become extremely volatile.

Phase One's Climax: Private Equity Rushes In

As I have demonstrated above and highlighted in figure 12.1, Phase One contained the birth of a speculative land market with three main features: it was based on cheap access to rural land, the displacement of nonelite small farmers and producers, and the circulation of rents in and out of the land market. From this feverish activity, the land market got red hot, and the price of land soared. Aside from the airport, most of the area's construction focused on a handful of luxury gated communities. Because none of the industrial sites had broken ground for the first decade or more, home buyers did not buy to move into this

TABLE 12.1.   Two phases of financialization

MARKET MAKING - PHASE ONE (MID-1990S–2010)	MARKET CONSOLIDATING - PHASE TWO (2010–PRESENT)
Major reforms on land and finance	Major economic reforms: REITs, RERA, demonetization; NPA market creation
Promise of global-city projects, mobilization of endogenous caste networks within and outside of parastatal agencies	High rates of unsold inventory and unfinished projects; capital scarcity/higher costs of capital
Large-scale land acquisition, illegal/corrupt grabbing/dispossession, ill-compensated Dalits and lower caste communities, creating a lucrative land market and high demand	Land acquisition as collateral for structured debt agreements and as most valuable asset once other assets held by developers deflate in value
Foreign "capital dumping" (easy and cheap access) spurring new business models for speculative large-scale projects and land acquisition/banking	PE only offering high-interest structured debt to developers, producing a steady income for PE; Sharp declines in share price
PE entry via infrastructure contracts, developers' IPOs, oversubscribed high-priced shares, profitable quick exits	New financial tools: REITs and NPAs lead to record-setting PE exits
High investment in luxury housing	High investment in depressed share prices and assets, especially commercial/office real estate, but not in construction/expansion or future projects

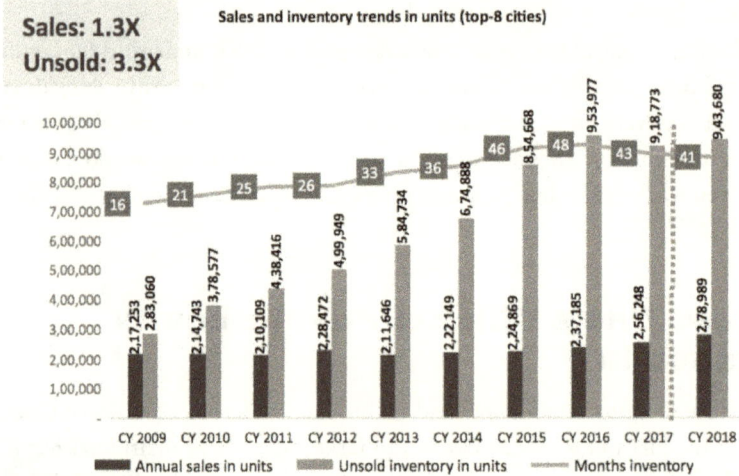

Sales and inventory trends in units (top-8 cities)

Sales: 1.3X
Unsold: 3.3X

	Annual sales in units	Unsold inventory in units	Months inventory
CY 2009	2,17,253	2,83,060	16
CY 2010	2,14,743	3,78,577	21
CY 2011	2,10,109	4,38,416	25
CY 2012	2,28,472	4,99,949	26
CY 2013	2,11,646	5,84,734	33
CY 2014	2,22,149	6,74,888	36
CY 2015	2,24,869	8,54,668	46
CY 2016	2,37,185	9,53,977	48
CY 2017	2,56,248	9,18,773	43
CY 2018	2,78,989	9,43,680	41

FIGURE 12.1. Developers' liabilities (low sales, high unsold inventory) in units over time.

Data from Liases Foras 2019.

vacant area but instead followed the urban craze and bought for speculation. This overheated market, however, soon collapsed, ultimately leading to Phase Two, when debt rather than equity took over (Goldman and Narayan 2021).

This process extended far beyond the airport area. Dispossession and land price spikes in the northern area of Bengaluru contributed to similar transformations occurring on the eastern and southern peripheries of the city and in the city core. Promises of the arrival of Google, Amazon, Walmart, and IBM created a mad rush for land in every direction. Although land acquisition surrounding the airport was managed by the state, elsewhere, it was developers who hired local land brokers to buy and aggregate rural land that could support new global-city projects such as multitowered gated communities. When global private equity first came to town, it introduced a completely different business model: rather than focusing on one project at a time, as local developers did, these private equity firms insisted developers take on ten to twenty projects at a time. It was a real game changer that shocked and inspired city planners, the aspiring new professional class, and the business elite alike. As one private equity consultant described it: "They came in saying we want to put in $50 or $100 million ... PE [private equity] funds started dumping their capital, buying 50 or 60 percent of stakes" (interview with the author, September 5, 2017). So, local developers changed their business model to accommodate the freshet of easy capital rushing in.

Private equity's largest imprint on the Indian economy occurred through its specialized financial tool, initial public offerings, which earned them high profits in the US and Europe up until the 2008 financial crisis. For Bengaluru's real estate firms, most of which were family owned, the decision to go public transformed developers from private small firms into foreign capital-flush public companies endowed with markedly different business logic and model. Developers were quick to use this capital to expand into new projects, acquire large land banks for future use, and pay down old debts (interviews with the author, 2018–2019). Yet doing so came at a price once the boom turned into a bust.

The cost of this strategy can be seen from the experience of one of Bengaluru's largest family-run firms, Top-Star (a pseudonym), which made its reputation in the 1990s as a premier builder, constructing luxury home (apartment) buildings one project at a time. Once the speculation wave hit, they chose to follow the trend to go public. Foreign investors pushed them to change their business model and erect more than twenty large-scale residential projects based on the 3,000-plus acres they acquired (annual reports, 2006–2018). They rode the boom and invested big, increasing their staff from a few hundred to 10,000 within a decade, but they incurred a significant amount of debt. By 2005, Top-Star's capacity was stretched too thin, with too many incomplete projects, too many angry subscribers demanding their homes, and investors calling for their payments (interviews with the author, 2016–2018). Private equity firms stepped in with an IPO, which many major firms were exploring across India. Its share price before the IPO was at approximately ten dollars, which doubled in price at the public offering of shares and then plummeted to a twentieth of that value within a year, with the largest equity investors having sold off at the peak. Thus, Top-Star's share value reached Rs. 6,000 crores ($844 million), then sunk to a dismal Rs. 1,500 to 2,000 crores, losing two-thirds of its value and remaining overleveraged with an expensive land bank. This financial experience was emblematic of the way foreign private equity would make its highest profits in this period, leaving its Indian partners in deep distress.

Phase Two: New Forms of Financialization and Dispossession

Foreign investors' exits in the mid-2000s helped to trigger a speculative crash that marked a rupture in Phase One and the rise of Phase Two. Unlike the

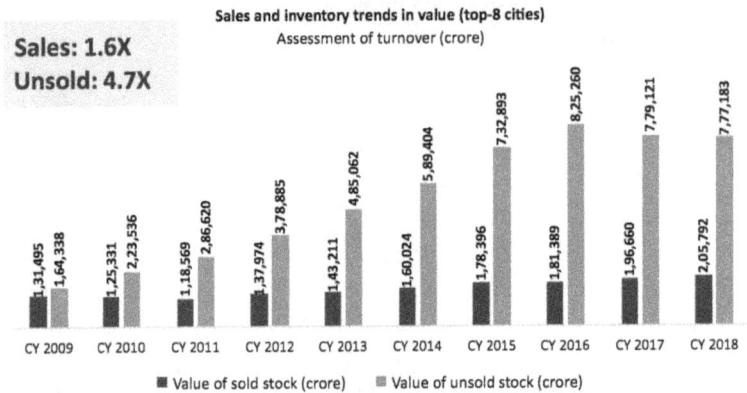

Sales and inventory trends in value (top-8 cities)
Assessment of turnover (crore)

Sales: 1.6X
Unsold: 4.7X

	CY 2009	CY 2010	CY 2011	CY 2012	CY 2013	CY 2014	CY 2015	CY 2016	CY 2017	CY 2018
Value of sold stock (crore)	1,31,495	1,25,331	1,18,569	1,37,974	1,43,211	1,60,024	1,78,396	1,81,389	1,96,660	2,05,792
Value of unsold stock (crore)	1,64,338	2,23,536	2,86,620	3,78,885	4,85,062	5,89,404	7,32,893	8,25,260	7,79,121	7,77,183

■ Value of sold stock (crore)   ■ Value of unsold stock (crore)

FIGURE 12.2. Developers' liabilities in rupee (crore) value over time.

From Liases Foras, February 2019.

preceding period, which had been characterized by the exuberance of limitless expansion and price hikes, the subsequent period has been shaped by a condition of being overleveraged with debt and unsold inventory, left with few options to access much-needed foreign and domestic capital.

Back in the airport region, such national and sectoral ripples doused investor enthusiasm. A study of land use changes in the airport area reveals what both the rise of speculative exuberance and the start of the downswing looked like on the ground. Mayur et al. (2013) analyzed satellite data of the region from 2002 and 2010 and identified some surprising trends. Before land acquisition and airport construction, almost half the land had been under agriculture, and much of the rest was covered with water bodies, forest, shrubbery, and pasture; only a few acres were "built up" in the form of village homes and a few public resources like schools. But by 2011, most agricultural practices had ceased, water bodies were reduced by 53 percent, and forests had shrunk by 37 percent, which included the replacement of actively managed biodiverse forests with commercial tree plantations of acacia and eucalyptus that require much less labor. Of the land under agriculture in the 1990s, only 16 percent by 2011 was "built up," while 48 percent was "excavated and kept as barren for further developmental buildups." That is, despite the clearing out of villages and the destruction of the agrarian economy, and even while land prices skyrocketed beyond anyone's wildest dreams, more than half the land that was to sport world-class infrastructure remained dug up but empty (Mayur et al. 2013).

Developers, too, were left barren as private equity was exiting the real estate market and selling off its shares in developers' projects. The era of easy capital was over, and debt pervaded the economic landscape. By 2018, media talk of the Biotech SEZ and the 10,000-acre IT Investment Region had vanished, and politicians no longer brimmed with news of the coming Finance City, Science City, or any major tenants filling the Aerospace or Biotech SEZs. Yet, despite the fact that many projects were put on hold, land acquisition continued. Our analysis of the annual reports and share-issue prospectuses of Bengaluru's major developers in the post-2010 period reveals that the principal objective remained the purchase of land, as land was the only arena of the regional economy that steadily rose in value. Although farmers' organizations, especially ones organized by Dalits, were up in arms, the commitment to acquire land was an important message and business strategy for investors to hear.

The following features characterize Phase Two, as highlighted in figure 12.1, with specifics on liabilities shown in figure 12.2. Nationally, FDI in real estate dropped from a high of almost $6 billion in 2008–2009 to $1.3 billion in 2012 and to a mere $113 million in 2015 (Aundhe 2019; Liases Foras 2019). This retreat only exacerbated developers' debt.

Total debt carried by India's major and midsized developers more than tripled from Rs. 120,000 crores in 2009 to Rs. 400,000 crores ($56.3 billion) in March 2019 (Chandrashekhar and Ghosh 2017). Their liabilities also rose due to the surfeit of unfinished projects and large land banks on their books. Worse still, their main source of loan capital, the Indian public banks, which had supplied more than 60 percent of developers' capital in Phase One, stopped lending because of the record-breaking size of the banks' nonperforming assets or "toxic" loans, much of which had been accrued since the mid-2000s. In 2017, India's public sector banks carried almost $20 billion worth of bad loans, and by early 2019, the size of its nonperforming assets had shot up to $60 billion (*Business Standard* 2018; interview with the author, July 2019). These nonperforming assets were a clear and measurable outcome of the heady days of the speculative urban craze that embroiled a full range of industries, from steel and cement firms to developers and the banks that lent to them.

Today, the real estate sector (nationally and in Bengaluru) suffers from a glut of homes, office space, and commercial/retail space on the supply side and from a deficit of buyers for the unsold inventory on the demand side. In the case of homes, developers overbuilt with a focus on luxury and speculative housing for private purchase rather than on building affordable housing for the vast majority of low-income Indians to rent. (More than 20 million Indians remain without adequate housing, according to a 2019 report, though housing rights activists say the number is much higher [Center for Sustainable Employment 2019]). By March 2019, India's top twenty-five developers were sitting on Rs. 780,000 crores

($110 billion) and nearly one million units' worth of unsold inventory (Liases Foras 2019; *Business Standard* 2019).

These liabilities—unsold inventory, depressed property assets, and nonperforming bank assets—have catalyzed global private equity to create a new business strategy. In Bengaluru, Phase Two took shape in these ways: First, private equity firms moved away from equity investment in the housing sector to "structured debt"—that is, no more equity capital for future projects but instead only loans with high interest and a regular repayment schedule to manage developers' liabilities. Second, private equity firms shifted into the commercial real estate market because of its potential for short-term gain. This strategy at first appeared counterintuitive since large developers, such as DLF in New Delhi and Embassy in Bengaluru, had office space that remained underutilized and unprofitable in a very down market. But with the speculative bubble bursting and FDI retreating from the sector, 50 percent of the developers in the nation's largest cities went bankrupt within the decade; of the largest cities, Bengaluru led the nation with more than 60 percent of its developers out of business by 2019 (propequity in Aundhe 2019). Analysts predict the public banking system will soon collapse and be reborn, with only a handful of extremely large banks thriving, much like what happened in Spain, the US, and many other countries after the 2008 financial crisis. In other words, these market downswings in the panic of an economic crisis are precisely what attracts private equity in Phase Two; they create exclusive opportunities for the few firms with unregulated monopoly access to capital and the power to make these markets work in their favor.

One investor explained to me how and why he and others shifted out of equity—real estate in Bengaluru—and into debt or "structured finance," using financial instruments to invest in project debt so as to avoid committing to the illiquid side of real estate projects:

> It became impossible to make money from real estate in the traditional way; too many ways in which projects would stall, government would step in the way, developers would be preoccupied with other dealings. So, finance people like me wanted to take a step away from investing in the assets and projects side of real estate and instead go into the realm of "safe finance," or structured finance. In real estate today, there are only two ways to make money: to buy shares in the stock market or to invest in debt. This is the strategy of most foreign investors: to stay liquid. We cannot make money from investing in projects, the equity of projects, but we can through raising money for debt [for stalled projects and indebted developers]. In this way, our money remains liquid and safe. There's no other way to make money in India.

We aren't betting on projects anymore but instead on three-year loans, for example. We don't care if the project is completed. Just look at Blackstone, they've invested billions in leased office buildings. But they put little of their own money down, their risk is low, and they plan to get out once the asset values increase. This is true across all of India. Low risk, high payoff (interview with the author, Mumbai, June 2013).

By 2018, distressed assets in India became foreign investors' biggest business. J. C. Flowers & Company partnered with an Indian firm to set up an "asset reconstruction company"—an arrangement that is being replicated by Apollo Global Management and India's ICICI Bank, Bain Capital and India's Piramal Enterprises, and Caisse de Dépôt du Quebec and Mumbai-based Edelweiss Group (with Carlyle Group as its minor owner). Together, these joint foreign-Indian ventures plan to invest up to $700 million in India's distressed assets in, among other sectors, commercial real estate, construction-related industries, and finance. The groundwork for such extractive profitability for private equity firms was laid with the Phase One promise of speculative urbanism and its land-based global-city projects. They set in motion the possibility of large-scale dispossession on the one hand and the monopolization of the financials on the other.

Critically, it is not just spectacular global city projects that have fallen deep into debt; municipal governments and agencies have become vulnerable clients as well. In 2014, a news headline announced, "Bangalore crumbles as civic body goes bankrupt" (Iyer 2014). The day after New Year's, Bengaluru's mayor declared he had mortgaged the city's classic-era Town Hall, six major public markets, two historic public buildings, a maternity hospital, a cemetery, and some slaughterhouses in order to pay off the city's largest debts (Chaturvedi 2014). Bankrupt and faced with the loss of revenue due to so many promises to developers of special "tax havens," the city faced little choice but to take many more pieces of its public infrastructure and offer them to investors as collateral. This shift in public management strategy enticed the largest private equity firms back to the city, as did the land, which state agencies continued to acquire through whatever means necessary.

In the city's northern region, the process of accumulation by dispossession was from the start a process of financialization, one that was heavily influenced by finance capital with its own situated and evolving logic and practices propelled by state guarantees, asset acquisition and liquidation, small farmer dispossession, and market monopolization—in India and abroad. The influx of finance capital, initiated by the original airport agreement, was catalyzed by the state's assurance that land would be accessible and cheap and could be used as collateral without little obligation to the majority of inhabitants. Although it seemed that every investor was playing and benefitting from the land game, soon, the smaller players buckled under the weight of their debt, and the larger ones—including developers and the municipal government—survived but became dependent upon transnational finance capital and its aggressive logic of expropriation and profit.

Financialization of distressed city assets, depreciated properties, and rural land banks have become the foundation of global city-making in Bengaluru and across India, creating a volatile urban landscape in which the most disruptive investors come from the world's largest private equity firms (Goldman and Narayan 2021). By 2018, the largest shareholder of BIAL, the airport complex, became Mauritius Investments Limited, a shell company based in "double-tax-free" haven Mauritius, owned largely by a Canadian private equity firm. The shift to rule by finance became complete.

India's era of speculative urbanism is manifested in two entangled practices. First is the imperative to move small farmers off land and acquire public lands to use as collateral for equity and debt. This process dispossessed many marginalized Dalit producers of the material basis of the agrarian economy. Second, for developers who once produced at medium and large scale, the housing stock in town became reliant on a financialized business model that alienated them from their original standards of producing homes or commercial structures for local clients; instead, they have adopted an incentive structure that pays premiums to offshore investors without the commitment or obligation to house the population or vitalize areas of the city or countryside. In this current Phase Two period, dispossession has spawned multiple manifestations across the region.

For example, even though India's real estate and banking sectors look their bleakest, one of the world's largest private equity firms, Blackstone, has put up more than $6.5 billion of its clients' capital into commercial real estate in the last five years (with $1 billion in just the first half of 2019) as a bet on the future of this depressed-asset market. One recent tie-up between Embassy and Blackstone illustrates the tactics. Embassy offered, at great discount, a sizeable portion of its flagging assets to Blackstone in 2018, including properties near the airport. Blackstone has used these assets to float India's first-ever REIT (real estate investment trusts). As soon as it hit the market in March 2019, the REIT raised $680 million in its first month, with much of its shares purchased by fifty-nine institutional investors from France, Wall Street, and shell holding firms based in double-tax-free Mauritius and Singapore. Individual Indians, too, bought, incentivized by the idea that though they cannot afford to buy a home, they can buy shares of Blackstone's real estate trust. Every dollar or rupee raised through the REIT's public offering (plus exorbitant management fees) has become money that Blackstone receives and pulls out of India's unsteady real estate market. The flagship Embassy-Blackstone project is a high-tech business park that leases office space to firms with an aggregate workforce of 100,000 people in east Bengaluru, and its asset value to Blackstone is a steady vehicle, like a giant ATM machine, for cash extraction from India.

By 2019, Blackstone owned 114 million square feet of India's office space; overnight, it became India's largest landlord, even though it only entered the real estate business in 2010 (Nandy 2018). This REIT, and the next set of REITs being planned, will open up the floodgates for Blackstone and others to exit Indian real estate profitably, leaving millions of small and large investors with the liability of owning office space (half empty and overleveraged). Blackstone has realized in its exits from India its highest global profit rates of 2018, higher than in the US or China (Alexander and Antony 2018). In 2019, India's business press celebrated that the distressed property assets market had become India's most profitable sector, selling the specious idea that all boats will rise in this financialized sea of speculation (Alexander and Antony 2018; Sarkar 2019). Instead, dispossession from land and public space has intensified in this period, as has growing social protest, such as in the form of the 2020 Great Strike.

The case of Indian cities reveals that not only does the state actively reform itself in order to facilitate and guarantee finance capital's fluid entrances and exits, but state actors within government offices create the conditions to enhance their own rent-seeking possibilities by promising support to "free up" land— public and private—for foreign investors and speculative urban projects. These projects require a dynamic and often violent engine of dispossession. As Dalit leaders and farmers explain, however violent the dispossession in Bengaluru's airport region has been, it is not their first experience, nor will it be their last, especially with the logic of finance, real estate, and urban expansion hinged on steady access to land and the patrimonial regime of caste power fully in charge. The speculative urban promise that this land-based rupture will lead to greater prosperity is based on the presumption that subaltern agrarian social structures and economies have little present or future value. That belief, and its material-discursive manifestations, is helping bring it to reality and defines the rapidly expanding contradiction of financialization by dispossession.

NOTES

1. This chapter is an edited and abridged version of Goldman 2020.

2. The research findings presented here come from interviews with more than 200 informants carried out over a ten-year period. These informants included farmers,

laborers, government officials at multiple levels, investors (local and international), activists, and scholars of the region's economy and ecology. Three research assistants conducted surveys and additional interviews in villages, in government offices with low-level staff doing the groundwork, with Dalit rights advocates and lawyers, and with high-caste farmers and officers in the districts of north Bengaluru. The research also benefitted from a multiyear National Science Foundation grant (# BCS-1636437) with four other co-Principal Investigators working in both Bengaluru and Jakarta on a comparative "Speculative Urbanism" project. These colleagues have deeply informed the analysis here. Thanks much to Rachel Schurman, Devika Narayan, Carol Upadhya, Vinay Gidwani, Eric Sheppard, Helga Leitner, Hemangini Gupta, Sanjiv Aundhe, Amay Narayan, Pierre Hauser, Manjunath, Vinay Baindur, P. Rajan, Karen Ho, Serra Hakyemez, and the scholars at NIAS-Bengaluru and ISEC-Bengaluru. Appreciation also goes to the insightful colleagues at the workshop on Dispossession in China and India at Singapore Management University organized by Michael Levien, Joel Andreas, and Qian Forrest Zhang.

3. As Viswanath's (2014) and others' studies of caste demonstrate, access and ownership to land and caste designations have been co-constitutive throughout history. The "pariah problem" in southern India reflects the obstacles for indigenous, low-caste and "untouchable" or Dalit communities to gain full rights to land; while their location in social hierarchy is discursively defined as religious and cultural, their inability to access rights to land is defined by powerful and enduring institutional and social barriers. Hence, the situation in this region reveals that, while communities were often barred from land ownership, many have enjoyed access to land, especially government and village land, on which they cultivated, grazed animals, raised silkworms, maintained water infrastructure and sacred groves, maintained fisheries, raised flowers, and much more. But once land has value in the marketplace, such "privileges" bestowed by elites can be withdrawn. Though of course, little of this sanctioned violence happens without a fight, as noted in this introduction and the interviews (Nagendra 2016; Upadhya, Gidwani, and Goldman 2017).

4. KIADB, or Karnataka Industrial Area Development Board (formed in 1966), is the largest parastatal organization in the state of Karnataka and is responsible for acquiring and assembling land to sell to the private sector, supplying basic infrastructure, such as roads, electricity, and basic drainage for industrial development. The land documents described are the farmers' and should not need a broker to retrieve them. KIADB has been well documented in the press and in court as the most corrupt parastatal agency in Karnataka, perhaps in South India. It is financed by external sources and loans, such as from the World Bank and Asian Development Bank—supposedly dogged anticorruption crusaders—and yet is only accountable to the Chief Minister of Karnataka and its own creditors and not to any democratic institutions such as the city council (called the city corporation) or state legislature.

REFERENCES

Aalbers, M. B. 2019a. *Financial Geographies of Real Estate and the City: A Literature Review*. Financial Geography Working Paper Series, no. 21. University of Leuven.

Aalbers, M. B. 2019b. "Financial Geography III: The Financialization of the City." *Progress in Human Geography* 44 (3).

Alexander, G., and A. Antony. 2018. "Blackstone India: How Blackstone Turned India into Its Most Profitable Market." *Economic Times*, March 12, 2018.

Aundhe, S. 2019. "Financialisation of Real Estate in Bangalore." NSF Speculative Urbanism Working Paper, Bengaluru, October 2019.

Babar, K. 2017. "Private Equity Now Funds 75% of Indian Property Market as Banks Pull Out." *Economic Times*, March 20, 2017.

Balasubramanian, V. 2011. "Task Force for Recovery of Public Land and Its Protection: Greed & Connivance." Task Force Report, Government of Karnataka.

Benjamin, S. 2008. "Occupancy Urbanism: Radicalizing Politics and Economy beyond Policy and Programs." *International Journal of Urban and Regional Research* 32 (3): 719–729.

Benjamin, S., and R. Bhuvana. 2011. "Illegible Claims, Legal Titles, and the Worlding of Bengaluru." *Revue Tiers Monde* 2 (206): 37–54.

BIAL. 2017. *16th Annual Report (2016–2017)*. Bangalore International Airport Limited.

Business Standard. 2018. "Year Ender 2018: NPAs of Indian Banks Surged Past Rs. 10 trillion." Dec 25, 2018.

Center for Sustainable Employment. 2019. *State of Working India*. Azim Premji University.

Chalapati Rao, K. S., and B. Dhar. 2011. "India's FDI Inflows: Trends and Concepts." *Social Science Research Network*, February.

Chalapati Rao, K. S., and B. Dhar. 2018. "India's Recent Inward Foreign Direct Investment: An Assessment." *Social Science Research Network*, July.

Chandra, K. 2015. "The New Indian State: The Relocation of Patronage in the Post-Liberalisation Economy." *Economic and Political Weekly* 50 (41): 46–58.

Chandrashekhar, C. P., and J. Ghosh. 2017. "Real Estate India Crisis Loan Default Developers." *Hindu*, September 25, 2017.

Chaturvedi, A. 2014. "Town Hall as Collateral." *Bangalore Mirror*, January 3, 2014.

Christophers, B. 2016. "The State and Financialization of Public Land in the United Kingdom." *Antipode* 49 (1): 62–85.

CMS (Center for Medical Studies). 2019. *Political Expenditures: The 2018 Elections*. New Delhi.

Cross, J. 2014. *Dream Zones: Capitalism and Development in India*. London: Pluto Press.

Dastidar, R. 2021. "India's Suffering Female Farmers Have Most to Lose by These Farm Bills: The Country's Dalits Are Already Exploited—and Know It Can Get Worse." *Foreign Policy*, April 13, 2021.

Doshi, S., and M. Ranganathan. 2017. "Contesting the Unethical City: Land Dispossession and Corruption Narratives in Urban India." *Annals of the American Association of Geographers* 107 (1): 183–199.

Fairbairn, M. 2020. *Fields of Gold: Financing the Global Land Rush*. Cornell Series on Land. Ithaca: Cornell University Press.

Goldman, M. 2011. "Speculative Urbanism and the Making of the Next World City." *International Journal of Urban and Regional Research* 35 (3): 555–581.

Goldman, M. 2020. "Dispossession by Financialization: The End(s) of Rurality in the Making of a Speculative Land Market." *Journal of Peasant Studies* 47 (6): 1251–1277.

Goldman, M., and D. Narayan. 2019. "Water Crisis through the Analytic of Urban Transformation: An Analysis of Bangalore's Hydrosocial Regimes." *Water International* 44 (2): 95–114.

Goldman, M., and D. Narayan. 2021. "Through the Optics of Finance: Speculative Urbanism and the Transformation of Markets." *International Journal of Urban and Regional Research* 45 (2):209–231.

Gupta, A. 2012. *Red Tape: Bureaucracy, Structural Violence, and Poverty in India.* Durham, NC: Duke University Press.

Günel, G. 2019. *Spaceship in the Desert: Energy, Climate Change, and New Urban Design in Abu Dhabi.* Durham, NC: Duke University Press.

Hindu. 2016. "Special Courts to Try Land-Grab Cases Inaugurated." September 1, 2016.

Iyer, R. 2014. "Bangalore Crumbles as Civic Body Goes Bankrupt." *NDTV,* February 25, 2014.

Kaika, M., and L. Ruggiero. 2013. "Financialization as a "Lived" Process: The Transformation of Milan's Bicocca by Pirelli." *European Journal of Urban and Regional Studies* 23 (1): 3–22.

Kapur, D., and M. Vaishnav. 2011. "Quid Pro Quo: Builders, Politicians, and Election Finance in India." *Center for Global Development Working Paper No.276.* http://dx.doi.org/10.2139/ssrn.1972987.

Krippner, G. 2005. "The Financialization of the American Economy." *Socio-Economic Review* 3:173–208.

Kumar, S. 2015. "List of 56 Encroachments Released." *Hindu,* May 16, 2015.

Levien, M. 2012. "The Land Question: Special Economic Zones and the Political Economy of Dispossession in India." *Journal of Peasant Studies* 39: 933–969.

Liases Foras. 2019. *Developers Need to Scale up Sales by 2.5X to Stay Afloat.* White Paper, Vol. 15, February 2019, Mumbai.

Mathur, A., and D. da Cunha. 2006. *Deccan Traverses: The Making of Bengaluru's Terrain.* New Delhi: Rupa.

Mayur, A. M., S. Hattapa, M. Mahadevamurthy, and A. K. Chakravarthy. 2013. "The Land Use Pattern Changes Due to Establishment of Bangalore International Airport." *Global Journal of Biology, Agriculture & Health Sciences* 2 (2): 34–37.

Ministry of Civil Aviation. 2004. *Concession Agreement for the Development, Construction, Operation and Maintenance of the Bangalore International Airport between Ministry of Civil Aviation, Government of India and Bangalore International Airport Limited.* July 5, 2004.

Moreno, L. 2018. "Always Crashing in the Same City." *City* 22 (1): 152–68.

Nagendra, H. 2016. *Nature in the City: Bengaluru in the Past, Present, and Future.* New Delhi: Oxford University Press.

Nandy, M. 2018. "The Rise and Rise of Blackstone in India." *Mint,* March 26, 2018.

Piketty, T. 2014. *Capital in the Twenty-First Century.* Cambridge, MA: Harvard University Press.

Piliavsky, A., ed. *Patronage as Politics in South Asia.* Cambridge, UK: Cambridge University Press, 2014.

Press Trust of India. 2018. "Karnataka Elections Most Expensive Ever in Terms of Expenditure by Parties, Candidates: Survey." *Indian Express,* May 14, 2018.

Raman, B. *"Reading into the Politics of Land:* Real Estate Markets in the South-west Peri-urban Area of Chennai." *Economic and Political Weekly* 51 (17): 76–84.

Ramaswamy, A. T. 2007. *Joint Legislature Committee on Encroachments in Bengaluru Urban District: Interim Report Part II.* Karnataka Legislature, July 2007.

Roy, A, and A. Ong. 2011. *Worlding Cities: Asian Experiments and the Art of being Global.* Malden, MA: Wiley-Blackwell.

Sarkar, P. 2019. "How Blackstone Made India its Largest Market in Asia." *Forbes India,* June 7, 2019.

Searle, L. 2018. "The Contradictions of Mediation: Intermediaries and the Financialization of Urban Production." *Economy and Society* 47 (4).

Shatkin, G. 2017. *Cities for Profit: The Real Estate Turn in Asia's Urban Politics*. Ithaca: Cornell University Press.

Upadhya, C., V. Gidwani, and M. Goldman, eds. 2017. "Bangalore's 'Great Transformation': The Problem." *Seminar* 694: 12–16.

Urs, A. 2018. "Nearly One-Fifth of Lake Area in Bengaluru Encroached." *Hindu*, July 9, 2018.

Viswanath, R. 2014. *The Pariah Problem: Caste, Religion, and the Social in Modern India*. New York: Columbia University Press.

Ward, C., and E. Swyngedouw. 2018. "Neoliberalisation from the Ground Up: Insurgent Capital, Regional Struggle, and the Assetisation of Land." *Antipode* 50 (4).

Wu, F. 2022. "Land Financialization and the Financing of Urban Development in China." *Land Use Policy* 112 (January).

13

PEOPLE, LIVELIHOODS, AND CONTESTED MEANINGS OF LAND IN TANZANIA

Emmanuel Sulle and Richard Mbunda

Land is the basis of human life and all Tanzanians should use it as a valuable investment for future development. Because the land belongs to the nation, the government has to see to it that it is used for the benefit of the whole nation and not for the benefit of one individual or just a few people.

—Mwalimu Nyerere

There is no doubt that Tanzanian policies, laws, and programs to date have been shaped by Mwalimu Nyerere's visions and his intellectual contributions. As the Founding Father of the Nation, Nyerere considered land as the primary asset for development for present and future generations. He strongly rejected ideas that land can be privately owned and traded (Shivji 1996; Rwegasira 2012). Nyerere's vision was guided by the *Ujamaa* policies—an ideology that emphasized equality among people, who should live together in peace and in the absence of exploitation (Nyerere 1968). In the context of the *Ujamaa* policy, land as a major means of production was an important determinant of wealth creation, which should not have been left in the hands of a few people. According to Mwalimu Nyerere, Ujamaa was premised on precolonial African societies whose main feature was the absence of classes (Rodney 1972). Tanzania is an important case to explore and expand on evolving debates about the meanings of land beyond the view that land is capital, ignoring other aspects, such as historical, political, cultural, and social values. This is because Tanzania's land laws allow the coexistence and interaction of different legal regimes—the customary laws and statutory laws, a situation often referred to as legal pluralism.[1] Also, since the global food, finance, and fuel crises of 2007–2009, Tanzania has attracted significant large-scale land-based investments (Locher and Sulle 2014), and it has recently embarked on a land policy reform, which is likely going to trigger further reforms to the land and land-related laws. Given these ongoing reforms in the country, it is critical to understand how the meanings and views of different peoples and groups on land are reflected in these reforms.

While Nyerere's successors maintained some elements of his policies, they embraced various reforms championed by the World Bank and International Monetary Fund, including the privatization of state assets, such as industries and plantations. President Benjamin Mkapa, the third president of Tanzania, considered the formalization of land and other informal businesses as the gateway to development by allowing people to access credit using their formalized land and businesses as collateral. Mkapa is a proponent of Hernando de Soto, who, like many other mainstream economists, considered land as a mere productive resource and the core source of rent for the state and landlords. This perception allows the government to confiscate land that is deemed unused and/or underdeveloped (Sulle 2017), and the Tanzanian government is still guided by this view today. However, the government is also touted to be implementing progressive land laws by recognizing and respecting the land rights held under customary tenure and acknowledging that any transfer of these rights requires the consent of local people (Locher 2016). The Tanzania government has the power to compulsorily acquire local peoples' land for national interests, which includes investments in agriculture, mining, and tourism (Chachage and Baha 2010; Jacob et al. 2016).

The contrasting view is that land for people is not only a capital and/or about its use. This is the central argument of this chapter. As Colin Murray and Gavin Williams (1994, 320) argued, when it comes to land, people "do not generally like to be told what to use it for or how to use it." Along the lines of Nyerere view, land is life because it is what provides not only habitat but also all types of foods and other amenities needed for the survival of flora and fauna (Martin et al. 1961). These two contrasting views of land as a capital and land as life are strongly held by various senior policy makers in Tanzania today. For example, addressing the Annual Meeting of the Tanzania Network for Smallholders (commonly known as MVIWATA) in Morogoro in 2008, then-ruling party's Secretary General Bashiru Ally was quoted saying: "You have heard the Commissioner for Land saying land is a capital. But, for us, 'land is life' . . . it is not a capital." The secretary general's statement was not unexpected since the ruling party, instituted by Mwalimu Julius Nyerere—Tanzania's founding father—is built around the Ujamaa Policy (African Socialism). In Bashiru's quote, we confirm the two important aspects that form the fundamental parts of the arguments this chapter seeks to make. One is the view, which Tanzanians and others around the world need to recognize, that land is a capital and needs to be secured through a piece of paper—"the title deed"—for easy recognition and transaction. The second view reaffirms Nyerere's vision that land is a life and an important asset for present and future generations.

This chapter draws from existing literature review and authors' previous work on land and land-based investments in the country (Chachage and Mbunda 2009; Sulle and Nelson 2009, 2013; Locher and Sulle 2013, 2014; Sulle 2016). It focuses on three existing categories of land: general land, village land, and reserved land. In the first two categories of land, individuals and groups of villagers, domestic and foreign investors, and different arms of the government are competing for land rights related to large-scale investment projects. However, contestations also exist over the use of reserved lands, particularly in the Wildlife Management Areas (WMA), which are village land set aside for conservation purposes but governed by wildlife laws. The legislation on reserved land undermines the powers of village authorities who use the Village Land Act. We argue that the recent efforts, which reduce land reforms to individual land titling, have lost sight of the holistic land reform informed by local contexts, which represents the true meaning of land use among diverse groups of people in Tanzania. We confirm that when it comes to the meanings of land, the government bureaucrats hold a position quite different from diverse groups of communities in Tanzania.

The next section historicizes land tenure in Tanzania from colonial to contemporary times. Thereafter, we analyze various meanings of land in Tanzania and then discuss the contrasting views on the use of land among rural people and state bureaucrats. The chapter then explores land conflicts and investments as political hotspots and the government's attempts to advocate and advance land formalization as a solution for the rural poor to secure credit. In conclusion, the chapter illuminates our understanding of various views of land and the implications such view has on land and resource access and rights of diverse groups of people in the country and elsewhere.

Historicizing Land Tenure in Tanzania

Historically, the term *tenure* originated from the Latin word *tenere*, which translates as "hold" (Rwegasira 2012, 45). In this chapter, we use *land tenure* to refer to the "kind of a system of land ownership or control patterns" (45). This section thus examines land ownership from the precolonial era to independent Tanzania and from Ujamaa policies to the adoption of neoliberal policies.

During the precolonial era, land was governed by the customary law of different families, clans, or tribes. Importantly, land was communally owned, but it was administered by headmen, elders, or chiefs depending on the sociopolitical setup of the society (Aberg 2005). Tanzania's colonial rule was under two masters. The first colonizers of Tanzania (then Tanganyika) were Germans, who ruled from 1893–1916. This was a short colonial stint, but it left important marks in the land tenure system of Tanzania. In 1895, the German colonial rule passed the Imperial Decree, which declared all land to be "Crown land," vested in the empire (Aberg 2005). Under the Imperial Decree, the settlers were offered Title Deeds to assert their occupation and ownership of land, while the local people, that is, Tanzanians, had no claims of land ownership through titles and, thus, had only permissive rights of occupancy (Rwegasira 2012).

After the First World War, Germany lost all its colonies, including Tanganyika, which was formerly under the German East African territory. Tanganyika was designated Trust Territory and was placed under British Administration in 1917. The major legal changes effected by the British were introduced through the Land Ordinance of 1923, which declared all lands as public land under the control of the governor. Unlike the Germans, the British introduced a tenure system, namely the right of occupancy. While on the one hand, the Land Ordinance of 1923 provided for the Granted Right of Occupancy (GRO) as a statutory tenure security document, on the other hand, the Ordinance provided for a deemed right of occupancy, which was based on native law and custom (Aberg 2005; Sylivester 2013). The natives (Tanzanians) under the deemed right of occupancy did not enjoy the same tenure security as that provided under the GRO. Notably, under both the German and British colonial administrations, Indigenous peoples lost their land, which was alienated in favor of settlers' plantations and farms. When Tanganyika got her independence in 1961, not much was changed from the inherited Land Ordinance Cap 113, except the authority in which land is vested. According to Haki Ardhi (2005), at best, a legal framework that governed land replaced the governor as the custodian of the public land with the president. The legal system regulating the administration of land in Tanzania came with the enactment of the 1999 Land Law and the 1999 Village Land Act. These acts are discussed in the later sections.

We, therefore, argue that Tanzania's current land policy, laws, tenure regimes, and ongoing reforms need to be reviewed in order to resolve existing tensions against the backdrop of colonial rules and efforts to maintain elements from the past while embracing new visions. A review is necessary because, to date, key colonial legal provisions, such as the Land Ordinance Act 1923, still form the basis of the current land laws. For example, under British rule, land administration was centralized in the Ministry of Lands, which allowed the land commissioner to limit customary rights for local communities, especially villagers. Unfortunately, this provision remains and is the source of contestation between the village and central authorities.

Influenced by the colonial laws, all land legislation maintains that all land is a public property. Ownership is vested in the president, who holds the radical title over land and is treated as the trustee on behalf of all citizens of the country. In practice, this means that Tanzanian citizens do not own land in a formal sense, but they have customary rights to use the land they occupy. Holders of these user rights can sell and/or pass on such rights to their children on an inheritance basis (Shivji 1998; Locher 2016). This radical title also means that there is no freehold in Tanzania since it was abolished in the country. Rather, there is a leasehold system, where few estates that were not nationalized after independence remained with leasehold titles.

Although the reforms implemented by the independent government under Mwalimu Nyerere, such as the Ujamaa Villagization Program, tried to dismantle the colonial land rules, customary rules that revolve around tribal and religious practices remain influential. As a result, to date, Tanzania's constitution and land legislation recognize two land tenure regimes: land governed by formal legislation and land under customary rules. The customary tenure is further subdivided into tribal rules, religious laws (mainly Christian and Muslim), and German and British Colonial laws (Locher 2016).

Other notable land reforms were carried out in the 1990s based on the recommendations of the Presidential Commission of Inquiry on Land Matters, famously known as the Shivji Commission. The commission's report led to the formulation of the 1995 National Land Policy and the 1999 Land Acts. The current (1995) National Land Policy (now under review) explicitly recognizes growing social conflict, environmental concerns, and land use conflicts due to haphazard alienation of rangelands for large-scale agriculture. It advanced the issuance of Certificates of Village Land to protect common property regimes for special groups, such as pastoralists.

Securing the land rights of rural populations is critical to ensuring their capabilities and assets because these rights determine their daily strategies to increase agricultural productivity and improve food security (FAO 2002). Further, understanding land rights and the ways in which conflicting interests in land are reconciled is also important because it relates to how each party with a stake in land is formally given certain rights, as well as how such rights are recognized and protected by both formal and informal institutions. Although Tanzania has a single National Land Policy, dating from 1995 (currently under review), each of the three land categories—general land, village land, and reserved land—is governed by several different pieces of legislation. These include the Land Act 1999, which governs general land, and the Village Land Act 1999, which governs village land. Reserved land is governed by a variety of statutes, such as the Wildlife Conservation Act 2009 for wildlife resources and the Forest Act 2002 for forestry.

The 1999 Land Act, which supersedes the 1999 Village Land Act, identifies the Commissioner for Lands as the "principal administrative and professional officer of, and adviser to, the Government on all matters connected with the administration of land [who] shall be responsible to the Minister for the administration of this Act and the matters contained in it." Appointed by the president and based at the Ministry of Lands, Housing, and Human Settlement Development (hereafter Ministry of Lands), the commissioner thus oversees all categories of land, although some of his or her powers have been decentralized to local authorities, including district councils, village councils, and village assemblies.[2]

However, as in many other African countries (Peters 2013, 2016), the land rights and tenure security of many villagers in Tanzania, who inherited their land under customary law, remain at risk because of the state's de facto failure to recognize or weak recognition of their customary tenure rights, especially when large-scale land appropriations have occurred (Kamanga 2008; Sulle and Nelson 2009; 2013; Chachage and Baha 2010). According to Ringo Tenga (2013, 121), this contradiction arises because the real problem in Tanzania is the enactment of laws that "focus partly on the protection of the citizen's right to land, and partly allow the erosion of the same protection in favor of foreign investment." As elaborated below, this situation leads to the infringement of people's rights to access, control, and own land, as well as their future rights to other resources attached to land, such as water, forests, and wildlife, to mention just a few.

Contested Meanings of Land in Tanzania

In Tanzania, land is defined differently, as shown in the section above. The official definition of land presents the geographical and geological components of the Earth's surface, with a great emphasis on what components cannot be owned by an individual. For example, although lakes, seas, rivers, gas, petroleum, gemstones, and minerals are all found on land, they are not regarded as part of land that can be owned by an individual. These land components are regulated by other laws. However, the meaning of land currently being held by the government resonates with neoliberal ideals, motivated by Hernando de Soto's (2000) concept of dead capital, which claims that land is dead capital until its value can be (financially) exploited. As such, this conception encourages individualization, registration, and titling of the land. The ultimate goal of the process is to have marketable titles and access to credit (Sundet 2006). This line of thinking has pushed the government to undertake legal reforms in order to consistently foster that vision. The government has undertaken land reforms in, notably, three pieces of legislation with the aim of commoditization and marketization of land.

For instance, the Land Act No. 4 of 1999 had initially restricted the value of land to only exhaustive developments, but in 2004, this Act was amended to give value to any bare land. This particular reform was engineered in order to allow the use of land as collateral in commercial banks (Shivji 2008).

Moreover, the Urban Land Planning Act No. 8 of 2007 followed suit by opening up land in urban areas to the market. Later on, the Mortgage Financing Act 2008 was formulated to legalize the use of land as collateral. Our scrutiny shows that the government's perception of the value of land and its meaning does not necessarily reflect the views of Tanzania communities from different backgrounds and contexts. For many rural communities, with the exception of disruptions caused by the villagization program in some areas, their land has often been inherited from generation to generation. Land is part of their culture and source of livelihood because they have been farming in some parcels to get food, and they hunt wild animals and gather fruits from forests in the land that is considered common property. But they also have designated areas for burials and land that are used for rituals connecting them with their ancestors.

Statements that "land must be developed" often do not resonate with the people on the ground because, for them, land is not only a resource for production. Therefore, unlike the common people in Tanzania, bureaucrats and investors have a rather simplistic view of land. To most of them, land is capital that needs to be put to good use to generate rent for the state and the landlord. This is precisely why different interpretations of land exist, even in the Land Act No.4 of 1999 and the Village Land Act No. 5 of 1999. The current definition of general land includes "all public land that is not village land or reserved land and includes unoccupied or unused village land" (URT 1999). Based on this definition, general land could be any land that is not cultivated or built on, even if it is used for seasonal grazing, spiritual activities, and other communal purposes. Based on this interpretation, it is likely that the government will transfer what it perceives to be unused village land to general land as part of its effort to increase land in its land bank. As we illustrate in the next section, this will help the government secure land for large-scale land-based investments in mining and agriculture.

Rural People versus Bureaucrats: Contrasting Views over Land Use

In contemporary Tanzania, significant contestation is apparent between rural people and government bureaucrats about the use of land and the type of agriculture to be practiced in the country. In Tanzania, there is currently a significant focus on large-scale farming as a means to modernize and commercialize agriculture (Sulle 2015, 2020). In this chapter, we use the development of the Southern Agriculture Growth Corridor of Tanzania (SAGCOT), which focuses on integrating smallholders in large-scale investments to examine the extent to which it undermines land use and ownership by rural people—the smallholders in their diverse categories of crop producers, pastoralists, beekeepers, and hunter-gatherers.[3] The SAGCOT aims to create an environment in which agribusiness will operate alongside smallholders to improve food security and environmental sustainability while reducing rural poverty (SAGCOT 2012).

To date, however, there is not much progress in implementing this corridor, which was initially mapped as occupying one-third of the country (see fig. 14.1). The corridor's development is hampered by the difficulties in securing land for large-scale investments (Mwami and Kamata 2011), change in government position on the terms of agreement with key financier the World Bank, and the delay in getting the project implementation on the ground (Sulle 2020). Initial proponents of the corridor, who were mainly government bureaucrats, development partners, and investors, thought they could change most of the land used by rural people into general land that could be easily granted to investors and converted into investment land. But, as recent research into agricultural corridors has shown, this was not immediately possible as local politics of land and resource ownership unraveled the top-down plans (Ngala et al. 2020).

Tanzania's existing land legislation, such as the 1967 Land Acquisition Act, 1999 Land Act, and 1999 Village Land Act, all provide a legal and procedural framework for transactions to acquire and dispose of land. The laws also provide some protection of existing rights to land; however, the framework has some ambiguities in terms of how these rights are protected during investment processes (Makwarimba and Ngowi 2012; Sulle and Nelson 2013). The different categories of tenure described above and the different rules create different dynamics but also share some commonalities. A long-established tradition of compulsorily acquiring land for "public" investment purposes under the Land Acquisition Act, which may also include a wide range of private investments, has contributed to administrative practices for land grabbing and disregard of the local rights to land (Kamanga 2008; Chachage and Baha 2010).

Also, the differentiated legal and administrative frameworks for domestic and foreign investors in terms of access to use, control, and own land complicates the land definition and use matters. For example, foreign investors are not allowed to own land, but they can secure derivative rights to land held by a Tanzanian citizen and/or company, typically through the Tanzanian Investments Center. The challenge presented by these dual procedures for both domestic and foreign investors is that procedures are not always clear, and deviations are common. Many commentators have expressed concern that the current challenges witnessed in the land sector, including land grabbing, are due to the fact that the country is not fully prepared to handle foreign direct investment in land (Kamanga 2008; Makwarimba and Ngowi 2012; Tenga 2013; Sulle and Nelson 2013; Sulle 2017).

Under the current administrative settings, the Ministry of Lands oversees all general land, which often includes all surveyed urban land and those under granted rights of occupancy for thirty-three, sixty-six, or ninety-nine years. Under the Land Act 1999, any holder of the granted right may sell it to any willing buyer, but any action to transfer a right over the land is subject to the commissioner's approval (Sundet 2006). General land is, in theory, easier for investors to access than village land since it has already been transferred de jure and is outside of village control. Village land requires the consent of rural people, including village bodies, especially the village council and village assemblies (SAGCOT n.d.). In practice, however, given the differentiated view of land use among the rural people, bureaucrats, and investors, general land is often occupied by people who believe they are the rightful owners because they were either evicted from such lands or occupied them for years when they were left idle (Chachage and Baha 2010; Mwani and Kamata 2011; Sulle 2017).

Communities' occupation of unused or underdeveloped lands is currently rampant in Tanzania, mainly because those who have occupied such land are not necessarily in need of the big chunk of it, while a majority of the rural peasants remain in significant shortages. Some of the current conflicts are pitting individuals against companies that have secured their title deeds (GROs) for estates and plantations on general land since colonial days. However, since some of these estates have either been abandoned and/or underdeveloped, the government has decided to privatize them under the state parastatals, and for those under private leasehold, the government has revoked such titles (Chachage and Mbunda 2009).

While many bureaucrats speak of possibilities for large-scale land-based investments in Tanzania as specified in initiatives like SAGCOT, the problem is that the category of general land currently accounts for a relatively small proportion of total land in the country. Conservative estimates indicate that village land and reserve land represent 70 percent (Hayuma and Conning 2006) of all Tanzanian land.[4] This means that only 2 percent of the total land is general land. Given this situation, bureaucrats and investors are targeting village lands for large-scale investments.

But the Village Land Act 1999 somehow shields villagers' land from improper procedural acquisitions. The law states that "any rule of customary land and any decision taken in respect of land held under customary tenure, whether in respect of land held individually or communally, shall have regard to the customs, traditions, and practices of the community concerned" (URT 1999, sec. 20, 2). Therefore, it is difficult for investors to acquire these lands. The Village Land Act empowers village councils and village assemblies to deal with administrative and management issues regarding village land. Upon the approval of the village assembly, the village council has the mandate to allocate land to villagers and enter into joint ventures with investors through leases, using a type of lease called a "customary lease," the "mode of creation and incidents of which including its termination are governed by customary law" (URT 1999, sec. 7–21). In the next section, we expand on land-based conflicts.

Land Conflicts Induced Reforms

Partly because of the economic, social, cultural, and spiritual values attached to land, there have been land-related disputes in several places in the country. In 2015, the Parliamentary Probe Team investigating conflicts between pastoralists and farmers in Tanzania established that there were high rates of conflicts in a number of districts in different regions.[5] For example, Kilosa and Kilombero districts in the Morogoro Region, where the highest production of cash crops like sugarcane and rice is taking place, are also the areas with the highest number of deaths, injuries, and loss of property resulting from persistent fighting between pastoralists and farmers (Mwamfupe 2015). The available evidence shows that in 2015, land-based disputes constituted about 46 percent of all the cases of clients being assisted by the Tanzanian Legal and Human Rights Center (LHRC 2016, 131). While some argue that there is abundant land in Tanzania, this overlooks the fact that most users are competing for a limited quantity of highly fertile land with access to water and infrastructure. The land targeted by investors is often the same prime land that farmers and pastoralists depend on for their livelihoods. In the absence of strong dispute resolution mechanisms, conflicts often escalate into violence, costing the lives of rural farmers and/or pastoralists (Benjaminsen et al. 2009).

As part of the solution to curb land-based conflicts, the fifth phase of government under the late President Magufuli carried out what can be regarded as "mini reforms." According to Nyamsenda (2018), the mini reforms, which involve revoking land titles owned by investors who have abandoned land, were carried out partly in response to the outcry in rural areas of existing absentee landlord farms. Villagers had wanted such titles to be revoked so that they could use the land for agricultural activities. The mini reforms were also intended to lessen tensions and conflicts in the countryside. In an attempt to avoid further conflicts between the owners of "idle estates" and invading villagers, President

Magufuli, who took office on November 5, 2015, used his powers to revoke numerous title deeds. On January 12, 2016, in the coastal Pwani Region, the title deeds of seventeen farms, mostly owned by ordinary villagers (not heavyweight politicians or businessmen), were revoked. Again, on January 17, 2016, it was reported in the media that the president had revoked the title deeds of five estates in the Tanga Region alone. In addition, according to the Ministry of Agriculture, the title deeds of at least seven farms with a total of 1,880.6 hectares have been revoked in the Morogoro Region, which has the highest number of conflicts between pastoralists and farmers. According to the Deputy Minister of Agriculture, these farms will be redistributed to citizens in an attempt to tackle land-based conflicts, particularly conflicts between farmers and pastoralists. In addition, local government authorities have reportedly received and submitted to the Ministry of Lands for revocation the title deeds for farms with a total area of 549,000 hectares in the Morogoro Region (Mkama 2016; Sulle 2017).

Further, in a politically controversial move, the president revoked the ownership of a thirteen-hectare (thirty-two acre) farm owned by the former prime minister Frederick Sumaye, who in 2015 decamped from the ruling party and joined the opposition Chama Cha Demokrasia na Maendeleo (Makoye 2016). Indeed, it seems that President Magufuli's attempts to protect the rights of ordinary citizens go beyond abandoned or not fully utilized farms. In December, the president ordered a stop to a plan to evict artisanal miners in the Shinyanga Region who were claimed to have invaded an area allocated to a Canadian Mining Company called Acacia (formally known as Barrick Gold) (*Ippmedia* 2016). However, the reform was carried out to the displeasure of the rural population inasmuch as most of the revoked land titles remain with the state, and the state holds such land in land banks for anticipated investment. To date, these emerging and increasing land use conflicts and competition among various actors to access, use, and control land are used by state bureaucrats to justify the neoliberal agenda of land formalization, as illustrated below.

Land Formalization in the Neoliberal Era

This section shows how land formalization is framed around a narrow view of individual land titling, especially to enable people to secure loans from commercial banks using their land as collateral. We further show why land formalization is against the needed holistic land reform and how it suffocates the need to implement and or maintain other alternative approaches to secure land rights. We assess land formalization programs and their impacts on land ownership by diverse groups of people in Tanzania.

In Tanzania, different procedures govern the formalization of individual, community, and company land, but the focus has been on individual titling. In his speech to officiate the result of the study on the rights and security of land ownership and settlement in 2017/18, the Ministry of Lands, Housing, and Human Settlement Development (hereafter Ministry of Land) identified land as the main resource for implementing the ruling party's election manifesto of 2015–2020 (URT 2018, 4). The minister specifically stressed that in order for Tanzania to achieve its middle-income status by 2025 (of which the country attained the lower middle-income status in 2020), his ministry has huge responsibility of preparing and supervising strategic land use plans, especially in urban and rural areas (URT 2018, 4). Formalizing land is advanced on the basis that although the protection of customary rights is provided for in the country's land laws, there continues to be weak recognition of customary and communal land rights in practice. Therefore, as the country's population grows, the demand for land also expands, not least for large-scale land-based investments by local and foreign companies, and it is critical to secure local people's rights to access, control, and own land.

Inspired by Soto's infamous book *The Mystery of Capital: Why Capitalism Triumphs in the West and Fails Everywhere Else* (2000), in 2004, then-President Benjamin Mkapa launched and installed in his office the Property and Business Formalization Program, locally known as *Mpango wa Kurasimisha Rasilimali na Biashara za Wanyonge Tanzania* (Mkurabita). This program had one fundamental goal: to register and thereby formalize land owned under customary laws, sometimes called land owned informally and by informal businesses—that is, unregistered businesses. Since its establishment, Mkurabita has received both donor and government funds to commission and facilitate land-use planning, land demarcation, the creation of land registries, and the issuance and registration of Certificates of Customary Rights of Occupancy (CCROs) at the village and national levels.

As studies show, land formalization in Tanzania tends to be a bureaucratically slow and expensive process for individuals, communities, villages, and companies (Stein et al. 2016; Notes et al. 2018). Therefore, by November 2017, it was reported that of about 12,545 Tanzanian villages, about 10,690 have had their boundaries surveyed, mapped, and issued with a Certificate of Village Land. Once a village's land has been demarcated and a land use plan has been drawn up, villagers may apply for CCROs for their parcels. Although villagers are not required to apply, proponents of formalization argue that the formal documentation of rights may provide a greater sense of security. This documentation may provide villagers with a stronger basis on which to enter negotiations with the state and/or investors when land is transferred from the category of village to general land. Recent statistics show that only about 13 percent of villages have moved to the next step by conducting land use plans, which were later approved by the Commissioner of Survey and Maps at the Ministry of Lands (URT 2015; *Citizen* 2015).

The main challenge in implementing land formalization projects is funding and poor responses from people who are not willing to finance the process yet. As such, the government has mainly relied on donor funds to implement land formalization initiatives. On this basis, currently, the large land formalization programs in the country are donor financed and donor led. For example, the Ministry of Lands implemented the Land Tenure Support Programme (LTSP) in three districts—Kilombero, Malinyi, and Ulanga, in the Morogoro Region. Mainly funded by three development partners—the United Kingdom's Department for International Development (DFID), the Swedish International Development Cooperation Agency, and the Danish International Development Agency (British High Commission 2016), LTSP is the largest land formalization project ever to be implemented in Tanzania. LTSP focused on land-use planning and titling; it also aimed to improve transparency and benefits of large land deals by establishing a national database for land-based investments and registration in the country. Anecdotal evidence, however, shows that while the project has managed to demarcate and adjudicate 174,606 parcels of land in the three districts (iLand 2018), it is yet to establish a database on large-scale land-based investments as one of its initial core objectives. The evaluation of the LTSP noted concerns about the progress of the project, especially on the completion rate of adjudication and issuance of CCROs. The report strongly recommended that the surveying team of the project should not start in any village if they are not sure they can complete it. The report further cautioned about the need to ensure people are aware of what they can do with the CCROs, including meeting villagers' expectations on the use of CCROs (iLand 2018).

A controversial but also important aspect of land formalization is its impact on women's access to use, control, own, and dispose of land. While formalization is considered a possibility to strengthen women's land rights, the same process is shown to cause women to lose out their land. Based on her intensive field research in the southern highlands of Tanzania, Rie Odgaard (2005) has shown that titling, registration, and individualization of land, all carried out as the means to secure legitimate rights coupled with a growing shortage of land, largely concentrate land in the hands of men. In addition, despite the provisions of modern laws, which are nondiscriminatory, in practice, land is inherited based on inheritance laws and customary laws. The existing inheritance law favors male siblings in matters relating to inheritance, and many customary laws remain problematic, with gender discriminatory impacts at the household and community levels, mainly because these laws remain unchanged despite the progressive reforms in land laws in the 1990s (Dancer 2015; Dancer and Sulle 2015).

Therefore, we need to ask: Do land titling efforts address the requirement for tenure security and the needs of the rural poor more generally? A recent systematic review of property rights interventions across the three continents of Africa, Asia, and Latin America, published in 2014, found that secure tenure is not by itself a sufficient condition for improving farmers' incomes: the "context matters" (Lawry et al. 2014, 6). The review further establishes that, while there has been almost zero success in titling in Africa in terms of promoting economic growth, the associated success of land titling in Latin America was the result of direct state investments in public infrastructure, all of which is lacking in the African context (Lawry et al. 2014).

Despite the reality that land titling is not a panacea for land tenure security or for productive use of land, the new draft of Tanzania's National Land policy proposes the need to roll out land titling throughout mainland Tanzania. This ambitious policy proposal is embedded in regional and international donor-driven initiatives rather than locally articulated programs. The current "land titles," especially CCROs, are promoted as a way for rural communities to secure collateral to access commercial bank credits for improving land productivity and income. However, research shows that such titles do not necessarily enable people to secure loans because having a creditworthy business is more important for securing loans (Stein et al. 2016). Furthermore, several existing land formalization initiatives do not raise awareness about the danger of losing their land if they fail to repay loans and have used their land as collateral. People need to adequately understand this new environment of land rights; otherwise, the risk of disenfranchisement is very high (Sulle 2017).

In addition, the focus on individual land titling ignores existing innovative approaches to secure communal lands that have been implemented by a few stakeholders in the country, such as nongovernmental organizations and the Ministry of Livestock and Fisheries Development, who have recently implemented the joint village land use planning to secure rangelands among the pastoral communities (Flintan 2012). Under joint village land use planning, villagers designate their land for various uses: homesteads, grazing areas, spiritual areas, and farming areas, to mention just a few. Therefore, the focus on individual titling leaves little room to research and adopt more innovative approaches to secure, govern, and manage communal land or collective land rights, such as rangelands or group customary rights of occupancy. Indeed, as Cousins (2019) has shown in the case of South Africa, reliance on one approach, such as "individual titling" alone, will not solve land reform issues because this process is costly and is avoided by individuals because of other risks and compliances that may be attached to land title.

In this chapter, we showed that, in Tanzania, land remains a crucial asset not only for individual development but also for the nation at large. From the founding father of the Nation, Mwalimu Nyerere, to current leaders, land has remained a central economic asset, which they have banked on. We have shown how different meanings and views on land use have differed between the Founding Father and his successors and between the common people and contemporary government bureaucrats. The current land formalization program, although being implemented, is hampered by inadequate resources, and it misses the focus on what type of tenure security fits diverse groups of land users. We argue that the state needs to understand and respect peoples' perception of the meanings of land, land use, and other cultural and spiritual values attached to land if it has to implement people-driven land reforms in the country.

We argue that the recent efforts, which reduce land reforms to individual land titling, have lost sight of the holistic land reform informed by local contexts, the true meaning, and land use among the diverse groups of people in Tanzania. We confirm that when it comes to the true meanings of land, the government bureaucrats have their own position that is quite different from those of diverse groups of communities. Our findings are in line with the common view held by scholars, such as Colin Murray and Gavin Williams (1994) and Ruth Hall and Tembeka Kepe (2017), who have argued that any land reform effort that attempts to reduce land to a productive resource is misguided and doomed to fail, while, in reality, people hold land as their cultural identity and political and social resource. Indeed, as the initial findings about ongoing land formalization initiatives have shown in Tanzania, without further articulation of the approaches to recognize and secure land rights in the country, individual land titling is likely to face backlash, and it may have significant ramifications for communities that are much more used to communal use of land resource, such as pastoralists and hunter-gatherers.

NOTES

1. As Locher (2016) illustrates, Tanzania has the highest level of legal pluralism, whereby the land has both statutory and customary laws, which work in parallel and often in a contradictory manner. We elaborate more on this, too, in the later sections of this chapter.

2. The Village Assembly is a meeting of all villagers who are eighteen years of age and above, while the village council consists of fifteen to twenty-five elected village residents.

3. In this chapter, we are aware of the fact that the term smallholder is loaded, and they are differentiated (see Cousins 2010).

4. These figures are likely outdated given the recent expansion in urban and agricultural areas.

5. The Parliamentary Probe Team suggested that conflicts were rife in Kilosa, Mvomero, and Kilombero districts in Morogoro Region, Kilindi and Handeni districts in Tanga Region, Mbarali districts in Mbeya Region, Rorya and Tarime in Mara Region, Mwanza and Arumeru districts in Arusha Region, and Simanjiro, Kiteto, and Babati districts in Manyara Region (OSIEA and OSF 2013, 43, quoted in URT 2015).

REFERENCES

Aberg, E. "An Evaluation of Land Laws in Tanzania." Master's thesis, Lulea University of Technology, 2005.

Benjaminsen, T. A., F. P. Maganga, and J. M. Abdallah. 2009. "The Kilosa Killings: Political Ecology of a Farmer-Herder Conflict in Tanzania." *Development and Change* 40 (3): 423–445.

Bonnemaison, J. 1984. "Social and Cultural Aspects of Land Tenure." In *Land Tenure in Vanuatu*. Edited by H. Alatoa and P. Larmour. Suva, Fiji: Institute of Pacific Studies of the University of the South Pacific.

Brennan, J. 2014. "Julius Rex: Nyerere through the Eyes of His Critics 1953–2013." *Journal of East African Studies* 8 (3): 459–477.

British High Commission. 2016. "DFID Supports Tanzania Land Tenure Support Programme." Dar es Salaam. https://www.gov.uk/government/world-location -news/dfid-supports-tanzania-land-tenure-support-programme-ltsp.

Chachage, C., and B. Baha. 2010. *Accumulation by Land Dispossession and Labour Devaluation in Tanzania: The Case of Biofuel and Forestry Investments in Kilwa and Kilolo*. Dar es Salaam: Land Rights Research and Resources Institute and Oxfam.

Chachage, C., and R. Mbunda. 2009. *The State of the Then NAFCO, NARCO and Absentee Landlords' Farms/Ranches in Tanzania*. Dar es Salaam: Land Rights Research and Resource Institute.

Citizen. 2015. "Ownership of 1,870 ha of Rice Fields Revoked." September 26, 2015. http://www.thecitizen.co.tz/News/Ownership-of-1-870ha-of-rice-fields-revoked /1840340-2886448-10c9eo9z/index.html.

Cousins, B. 2010. "What Is a 'Smallholder'? Class Analytic Perspective on Small-scale Farming and Agrarian Reform in South Africa." In *Reforming Land and Resource Use in South Africa: Inpact and Livelihoods*. Edited by P. Hebinck, and C. Shackleton, 86–111. New York: Routledge.

Cousins, B. 2019. "Land Reform, Accumulation and Social Reproduction: The South African Experience in Global and Historical Perspective. *Inkanyiso: Journal of Humanities and Social Sciences* 11 (1): 1–12.

Dancer, H. 2015. *Women, Land and Justice in Tanzania*. Woodbridge: James Currey.

Dancer, H., and E. Sulle. 2015. *Gender Implications of Agricultural Commercialisation: The Case of Sugarcane Production in Kilombero District, Tanzania*. Working Paper. Brighton: Future Agricultures.

DFID (Department for International Development). 2013. *The New Alliance for Food Security and Nutrition: Progress Report Summary*. Policy Paper. https://www.gov .uk/government/publications/the-new-alliance-for-food-security-and-nutrition -progress-report-summary.

FAO. 2002. *Land Tenure and Rural Development*. FAO Land Tenure Studies. Rome: FAO.

Flintan, F. E. 2012. *Participatory Rangeland Resource Mapping as a Valuable Tool for Village Land Use Planning in Tanzania: A Report for International Land Coalition*. Rangelands 2. Rome, Italy: International Land Coalition.

Hall, H., and T. Kepe. 2017. "Elite Capture and State Neglect: New Evidence on South Africa's Land Reform." *Review of African Political Economy* 44 (151): 122–130. https://doi.org/10.1080/03056244.2017.1288615.

Hayuma, M. and J. Conning. 2006. "Tanzania Land Policy and Genesis of Land Reform Subcomponent of Private Sector Competitiveness Project. In *Land Policies and Legal Empowerment of the Poor*, 2–3. Washington, DC.

IFAD (International Fund for Agriculture Development). 2015. *United Republic of Tanzania: Bagamoyo Sugar Infrastructure and Sustainable Community Development Programme (BASIC)*. Final Project Design Report. Rome, Italy: IFAD.

iLand. 2018. *Annual Technical Review of the Land Tenure Support Programme*. United Kingdom: iLand Consulting Ltd.

Ippmedia. 2016. "Magufuli Orders Removal of Top Mining from Gold Field." December 7, 2016. http://m.ippmedia.com/en/news/magufuli-orders-removal-top-mining-gold-field.

Jacob, T., R. H. Pedersen, F. Maganga, and O. Kweka. 2016. *Rights to Land and Extractive Resources in Tanzania (2/2): The Return of the State*. Working Paper. DIIS.

Kamanga, K. C. 2008. *The Agrofuel Industry in Tanzania: A Critical Enquiry into Challenges and Opportunities*. Research Report. Dar es Salaam: Land Rights Research and Resources Institute.

Kimaro, D., A. Munga, A. Mollel, A. Maganya, and G. Walalaze. 2014. Proceedings for Conference on Land Justice for Sustainable Peace in Tanzania held at the Bank of Tanzania, September 9–13, 2013.

Kulindwa, K. 2008. "Feasibility of Large-Scale Biofuel Production in Tanzania: Introduction." Presented at the Biofuels Conference, Dar es Salaam, December 1, 2008.

Lawry, S., C. Samii, R. Hall, A. Leopold, D. Hornby, F. Mtero. 2014. "The Impact of Land Property Rights Interventions on Investment and Agricultural Productivity in Developing Countries: A Systematic Review. *Campbell Systematic Reviews* 10 (1): 1–104.

LHRC. 2016. *Tanzania 2015 Human Rights Report*. Dar es Salaam: LHRC.

Locher, M. 2016. "How Come Others are Selling Our Land?' Local Land Rights and the Complex Process of Land Acquisition by a UK-Based Forestry Company in Tanzania." *Journal of East African Studies* 10 (3): 393–412.

Locher, M., and E. Sulle. 2013. *Foreign Land Deals in Tanzania: An Update and a Critical View on the Challenges of Data (Re)Production*. Working Paper No. 31. Bellville, South Africa: Land Deal Politics Initiative.

Locher, M., and E. Sulle. 2014. "Challenges and Methodological Flaws in Reporting the Global Land Rush: Observations from Tanzania." *Journal of Peasant Studies* 41 (4): 569–592.

Maganga, F., K. Askew, R. Odgaard, and H. Stein. 2016. "Dispossession through Formalization: Tanzania and the G8 Land Agenda in Africa." *Asian Journal of African Studies* 40: 4–49.

Makoye, K. 2016. "Tanzanian Ex-PM Loses Farm, Accused by Government of Leaving Land 'Idle.'" Thomson Reuters Foundation News. http://news.trust.org/item/20161129181235-bo9qd.

Makwarimba, M., and P. Ngowi. 2012. *Making Land Investment Work for Tanzania: Scoping Assessment for Multi-Stakeholder Dialogue Initiative*. Final Report. Natural Resources Forum. http://www.tnrf.org/LBI-report.pdf.

Martin, A. C., H. S. Zim, and A. L. Nelson. 1961. *American Wildlife and Plants: A Guide to Wildlife Food Habits: The Use of Trees, Shrubs, Weeds, and Herbs by Birds and Mammals of the United States*. New York: Dover Publications.

Mkama A. 2016. "Tanzania: Investors Lose Seven Farms in Morogoro." *Tanzania Daily News*, April 26, 2016. http://allafrica.com/stories/201604270311.html.

Mkapa, B. 2013. Remarks at the Conference on Land Justice for Sustainable Peace in Tanzania, Dar es Salaam, September 9–11. Bank of Tanzania.

Mkurabita. 2008. *Mpango wa kurasimisha rasilimali na biashara za wanyonge Tanzania*. Reform Proposal, Vol. 1. Dar es Salaam: Property and Business Formalization Programme Management Unit.

Murray, C., and G. Williams. 1994. "Land and Freedom in South Africa." *Review of African Political Economy* 21 (61): 315–324.

Mwamfupe, D. 2015. "Persistence of Farmer-Herder Conflicts in Tanzania." *International Journal of Scientific and Research Publications* 5 (2).

Mwami, A. and N. Kamata. 2011. *Land Grabbing in the Post Investment Period and Popular Reactions in Rufiji River Basin*. Dar es Salaam: Hakiardhi.

Myenzi, Y. 2005. *Implication of the Recent Land Reforms in Tanzania on the Land Rights of Small Producers*. Paper prepared for internal reflections at the Land Right Research Resources Institute.

Nelson, F., E. Sulle, and E. Lekaita. 2012. *Land Grabbing and Political Transformation in Tanzania*. Paper presented at the International Conference on Global Land Grabbing II, Ithaca, NY, October 17–19.

Ngala, C., E. Ngonzales, I. Scoones, and E. Sulle. 2020. "'Demonstration Fields,' Anticipation, and Contestation: Agrarian Change and the Political Economy of Development Corridors in Eastern Africa." *Journal of East African Studies* 14 (2): 291–309.

Notess, L., P. Veit, I. Monterroso, E. Andiko, E. Sulle, A. Larson, A. Gindroz, J. Quaedvlieg, and A. Williams. 2021. "Community Land Formalization and Company Land Acquisition Procedures: A Review of 33 Procedures in 15 Countries." *Land Use Policy*, Vol. 110, 104461. doi.org/10.1016/j.landusepol.2020.104461.

Nyamsenda, S. 2018. "Bulldozing Like a fascist? Authoritarian Populism and Rural Activism in Tanzania." In *Authoritarian Populism and the Rural World*, Conference Paper 78, The Hague, March 17–18. The Hague: ERPI.

Nyerere, J. K. 1968. "Freedom and Socialism.: In *Uhuru na Ujamaa: a selection from writings and speeches, 1965–1967*. Oxford, UK: Oxford University Press.

Odgaard, R. 2005. "The Struggle for Land Rights in the Context of Multiple Normative Orders in Tanzania." In *Competing Jurisdictions: Settling Land Claims in Africa*. Edited by S. Evers, M. Spierenburg, and H. Wels. Leiden: Brill Publishers.

Peters, P. 2013. "Conflicts over Land and Threats to Customary Tenure in Africa." *African Affairs* 112 (449): 543–562.

Peters, P. 2016. "The Role of the Land Policies, Land Laws and Agricultural Development in Challenges to Rural Livelihoods in Africa." *Afriche e Orienti* 17 (3): 25–45.

Rodney, W. 1972. "Tanzanian *Ujamaa* and Scientific Socialism." *African Review* 1 (4): 61–76.

Rwegasira, A. 2012. *Land as a human right: A history of land law and practice in Tanzania*. African Books Collective. Dar-es-Salaam: Mkuka Na Nyota.

Sachedina, H. *Wildlife Is Our Oil: Conservation, Livelihoods and NGOs in the Taran-
gire Ecosystem, in Tanzania.* PhD diss., University of Oxford, 2008.

SAGCOT (Southern Agriculture Growth Corridor of Tanzania). 2012. *SAGCOT
Investment Partnership Program: Opportunities for Investors in the Sugar Sector.*
www.sagcot.com.

SAGCOT (Southern Agriculture Growth Corridor of Tanzania). n.d. Appendix III:
Land Development. http://www.sagcot.com/uploads/media/Appendix_III
_Land_Development_04.pdf.

Salcedo-La Viña, C. 2015. *An Assessment of Community Participation in Land
Acquisitions in Mozambique and Tanzania.* World Resources Institute. African
Biodiversity Collaborative Group. http://www.abcg.org/document_details
?document_id=720.

Shivji, I.G.. 1996. "Land Tenure Problems and Reforms in Tanzania." In *Sub-regional
Workshop on Land Tenure Issues in Natural Resource Management in the
Anglophone East Africa with a Focus on the IGAD Region, Addis Ababa,
Ethiopia,* 11–15. Paris: OSS.

Shivji, I. G. 1999. "The Land Acts 1999: A Cause for Celebration or a Celebration of a
Cause?" Keynote Address to the Workshop on Land, Morogoro, Tanzania,
February 19–20. https://mokoro.co.uk/wp-content/uploads/land_acts_1999
_cause_for_celebration.pdf.

Shivji, I. G. 2009. *Accumulation in an African Periphery: A Theoretical Framework.* Dar
es Salaam: Mkuki na Nyota Publishers Ltd.

Soto, H. de. 2001. *The Mystery of Capital: Why Capitalism Triumphs in the West and
Fails Everywhere Else.* London: Bantam Press.

Stein, H., F. Maganga, R. Odgaard, K. Askew, and S. Cunningham. 2016. "The Formal
Divide: Customary Rights and the Allocation of Credit to Agriculture in
Tanzania." *The Journal of Development Studies* 52 (9): 1306–1319. https://doi.org
/10.1080/00220388.2016.1146701.

Sulle, E. 2015. "Land Grabbing and Commercialization Duality: Insights from Tanzania's Agricultural Transformation Agenda." *Afriche e Orienti* 17 (3): 109–128.

Sulle, E., 2017. *Of Local People and Investors: The Dynamics of Land Rights Configuration in Tanzania.* DIIS Working Paper, No. 2017: 10.

Sulle, E. 2020. "Bureaucrats, Investors and Smallholders: Contesting Land Rights and
Agro-Commercialisation in the Southern Agricultural Growth Corridor of
Tanzania. *Journal of Eastern African Studies* 14 (2): 332–353.

Sulle, E., E. Lekaita, G. Massay, A. Ndiko, B. Baha, P. Kitua, and O. Minani. 2016.
"Making Tanzania's National Land Policy Inclusive and People-Centred."
PLAAS blog, Bellville, South Africa.

Sulle, E., and F. Nelson. 2009. *Biofuels, Land Access and Rural Livelihoods in Tanzania.*
London: International Institute for Environment and Development.

Sulle, E., and F. Nelson. 2013. *Biofuels Investment and Community Land Tenure in
Tanzania: The Case of Bioshape, Kilwa District.* Future Agricultures Consortium
Working Paper 73, Brighton, Future Agricultures Consortium.

Sundet, G. 2006. *The Formalisation Process in Tanzania: Is It Empowering the Poor?*
Consultancy Report Prepared for the Norwegian Embassy in Tanzania.

Sylivester, S. "Land Tenure Reforms and Investments in Tanzania." Master's thesis,
University of Dar es Salaam, 2013.

Tenga, R. 2013. "Opening up Tanzania's Land to Foreign Investors: The Legal Constraints." Presented at the Conference on Land Justice for Sustainable Peace in
Tanzania, Dar es Salaam, October 2013. Bank of Tanzania.

URT (United Republic of Tanzania). 1967. *The Land Acquisition Act.* Dar es Salaam: URT.

URT. 1997a. *Tanzania Investment Act.* Dar es Salaam: URT.

URT. 1997b. *The National Land Policy.* Dar es Salaam: URT.

URT. 1999. *Land Act 1999.* Dar es Salaam: URT.

URT. 2010. *Guidelines for Sustainable Liquid Biofuels Investments and Development in Tanzania.* Ministry of Energy and Minerals.

URT. 2015. A Report of Select Parliamentary Committee Formed to Investigate the Reasons for Conflicts Between Farmers, Pastoralists, Investors and Other Land Users in the Country. Select Parliamentary Committee, 2013. Dodoma, Parliament of Tanzania.

14

DANCES WITH LAIRDS

Lessons from Scottish Land Reform

Kirsteen Shields

**Waves wash in, out, in,
menhirs incline to each other:
farmers grumbling.**

—Kathleen Jamie, "Orkney Haiku," *The Way We Live*

In 2013, the then First Minister of Scotland, Alex Salmond, took to a podium at the Community Land Scotland Conference at the Gaelic college Sabhal Mor Ostaig on Skye Island to announce a commitment to transfer one million acres of land into community ownership by 2020.[1] He envisaged "a radical reshaping of the right to buy landscape that has the potential to transform the fortunes of communities across the country" in order to "achieve our own shared aspirations: new jobs and new amenities in areas that long denied them, and the regeneration and repopulation of communities across Scotland" (Salmond 2013). The community land vision is part of a wider governmental commitment to "radical and ambitious" land reform in Scotland. Notwithstanding much chagrin from dominant landowners (the lairds) and their representatives, this commitment led to significant changes in land governance in Scotland, including the creation of a new set of rights to enable communities to buy land in Scotland. Community rights to buy land and obligations to consult local communities in planning decisions are embedded in legislation passed by the Scottish Parliament: the Land Reform (Scotland) Act 2003, the Community Empowerment (Scotland) Act 2015, and the Land Reform (Scotland) Act 2016. This legislation creates new community rights to own land and other assets in Scotland. With some optimism, this may be viewed as part of an upward curve toward legal protection of community rights globally.

More than 50 percent of the world's land is community land, and as many as 2.5 billion people depend heavily on these lands for their livelihood (RRI 2017). Estimates from 2015 suggest that only just over 10 percent of collectively owned land was estimated to be formally recognized (RRI 2015). More up-to-date information is not available, and the precise amount of collectively owned land may be much larger. Further, not all legally recognized community land is registered and documented, and in many countries, national laws do not recognize collectively held land, hold an accurate land register, or establish a formalization procedure (Alden Wily 2018).

Collectively owned lands (including community and customary lands) have historically been vulnerable to acquisition by powerful political and economic elites. Since the 2007–2008 financial crash, a new rise in community land acquisitions has been reported (World Bank 2017). Land for agriculture and food production has been widely recognized as a key driver, creating a scramble for the acquisition of farmland, particularly where land suitable for cultivation and water is abundant, labor is cheap, and access to the global markets is relatively easy (De Schutter 2011). The financial crash of 2007–2008 and the consequent worldwide food price spike aided the acceleration of the "global farm race" as both farming and land investment rose in value in the post-2008 changed global economic forecasts and outlook (Cotula 2013).

Edelman, Oya, and Borras Jr. (2015) make the case that drivers are more complex than "farming" and include various related dimensions, including "green grabbing," "water grabbing," biofuels and biomass, the financialization of agriculture, and the seizing of land for industrial, mining, and urbanization projects (citing Fairhead, Leach, and Scoones 2012; Mehta, Veldwisch, and Franco 2012; Borras Jr., McMichael, and Scoones 2010; Ghosh 2010; and Levien 2013, respectively). It should also be noted that some report instances of counterclaims on land rights or "grabbing back" (Ross 2014), and more research is needed to understand the impact and role of smallholders in new land ownership patterns (Hall et al. 2015). Scoones et al. (2019) make the case that the narratives of this trend have been dominated by concerns over resource "scarcity." They argue that "notions of scarcity are presented as a deliberate political strategy, justifying resource control, appropriation, dispossession, population restrictions, and the securing of exclusionary property rights" and make the case for an alternative framing that integrates politics and political scarcity (Scoones et al. 2019).

The post-2008 drive for agricultural land is the latest installment in a historical trend spanning centuries. As Robert Nichols notes in his analysis (this book), Adam Smith acknowledged that agriculture is more productive than other forms of capitalism, such as manufacturing or trade and finance, and has historically been at the "pinnacle" of relative capital return. Nichols writes that the effect of the economic thinking around the time of Smith, David Ricardo, Thomas Malthus, John Stuart Mill, and others (which coincides with the Scottish Enlightenment period) was to generate "a renewed sense that colonization and capitalism were commensurable and that it was the task of the political econ-omy to unite them." It is posited here that law acted as the servant of the political economy on this quest, and in many respects, it continues to do so. In the tran-sition from republicanism to the commodification of land that Nichols describes, we can observe that law has played an essential role in the coding and recoding of land value and meaning, particularly in relation to laws around rent, succes-sion, and the establishment of property rights, long before and well in advance of the development of human rights as we know them today.

Although law has evolved since the period described by Nichols (ca. 1776–1873), the foundations that were laid in law at this time (the legal norms and constructs) assisted the configuration of land and labor as commodities (Polanyi 1944), which are central to many of the exploitative deals that surround land ac-quisition today (Cotula 2013). As Lorenzo Cotula's empirical research on land acquisitions in Africa highlights, this ideology plays out in land deals today that prioritize trade and investment over the treatment of local inhabitants, work-ers, and the environment.

Meanwhile, other branches of law have grown, in particular human rights and environmental law, that have strengthened support for the protection of In-digenous, customary, and community lands. Liz Alden Wily identifies the fol-lowing trends globally from the late 1980s onward: (1) declining attempts to deny that community lands are property on the grounds that they may not be sold or are owned collectively; (2) increased provision for communities to be registered owners to the same degree as individual and corporate persons; (3) a rise in the number of laws catering specifically to the identification, registration, and gov-ernance of community property; and (4) a rise in the number of laws that ac-knowledge that community property may exist whether or not it has been registered, and that registration formalizes rather than creates property in these cases (Alden Wily 2018).

Yet more recently, law has been used to secure community and customary tenure directly through the passing of new legal provisions at the country level. Notable legislative developments at the country level include the 2015 Zambia Forest Act n°4 that formally recognizes collective ownership rights of commu-nity forests; the 2016 Colombian Peace Accord that enables local communities and rural women to receive collective land titles to help rehabilitate the peasant economy; the 2016 Myanmar Community Forestry Instructions that strength-ens management, exclusion, due process, and compensation rights of rural com-munities; the 2016 Kenya Community Land Act that formally recognizes community ownership rights to registered and unregistered lands, including the tenure rights of women and other vulnerable persons; and the 2017 Mali Agri-cultural Land Law that provides communities authority to resolve land disputes through local commissions and strengthens customary land rights and mechanisms to secure these (RRI 2017).

Despite these successes in passing and codifying laws, there are still many challenges to overcome with respect to the implementation and enforcement of the new laws. Notess et al. (2020) review thirty-three procedures to protect community lands in fifteen countries. The research highlights significant procedural challenges, encoded in the law and realized in practice, to communities obtaining formal land rights. It also highlights inequalities in how regulatory frameworks and implementing actors treat community procedures as compared to company land acquisition procedures. Redress remains out of reach for many: "Geographic barriers, power imbalances, and constrained information stand in the way—as does limited finance for legal support" (Columbia Center on Sustainable Investment 2019). Global Witness reports (2018) that harassment and assassinations of land rights defenders are on the rise.

At the international level, legally binding commitments have been yet more difficult to codify and cement. Of the nine core international human rights treaties, land is only mentioned once in relation to the rights of rural women to have equal access (United Nations, CEDAW, Article 14; Gilbert 2013). The recently ratified United Nations Declaration on the Rights of Peasants and other people working in rural areas (United Nations 2018) recognizes the dignity of the world's rural populations, their contributions to global food production, and the "special relationship" they have to land, water, and nature, as well as their vulnerabilities to eviction, hazardous working conditions, and political repression (Claeys and Edelman 2020). The draft UN Committee on Economic, Social, and Cultural Rights General Comment n°26 (United Nations 2021) promises to be a major breakthrough with regard to identifying provisions in ICESCR relevant to land and asserting obligations of state parties at home and abroad. At the international level, political developments take the form of growing networks of Indigenous and community leaders and rights defenders who are lobbying for rights, including NGO alliances, such as The Global Call to Action on Indigenous and Community Land Rights (and accompanying Land Rights Now campaign) (RRI 2017).

Against this ever-changing global landscape, here I focus on new legal provisions facilitating transition to community ownership in Scotland as a possible pathway out of the steel grip of markets that prioritize property rights over human rights and the environment. Although aspects of this pathway are specific to Scotland, every state and constitution is unique. Scotland is no more unique than any other territory in this regard; that is, it should not be viewed as an outlier or a one-off. That said, the provisions do not provide a blueprint but rather some hope that the primacy of individual property rights within legal systems can be challenged and reordered where democracy and the rule of law prevail.

In what follows, I consider how and why new community land laws came into effect by analyzing the defining sociopolitical and governance features in the Scottish land reform process. In other words, I seek to explain how and why it was possible to challenge consolidated land ownership in a region where extreme inequality in land ownership has long prevailed. The "success" of the legal provisions to date in effecting transfers of land into community ownership is described in numbers in a few examples, and more work is underway to measure their success qualitatively, but the focus here is on the process rather than the outcomes for establishing new legal norms in land rights and property rights.

The study draws on a wide range of primary and secondary resources, including legislation, jurisprudence, parliamentary reports, government reports, legal opinion, news reports, land surveys, ethnographic literature, and poetry. In so doing, I seek to unearth some of the cultural, constitutional, and institutional factors that have fueled land politics and assisted their conversion into *law*. Some of those roots are also entwined with the development of human rights law at the Scottish Parliament, and the Scottish land reform story is presented as part of a broader process of institutional and constitutional change that sees the Scottish Government legislate to align ever more closely with the UN human rights framework.*

To assess the cultural, constitutional, and institutional factors that help convert land *politics* into land *law*, I take a constructivist approach to law—more frequently used in international law—and apply it to national lawmaking in the Scottish context. This approach runs counter to the more dominant approach in legal practice and in property law—i.e., legal positivism—the approach that asserts that *law* is a matter of what has been posited (ordered, decided, practiced, tolerated). All of this draws back to an understanding that law is neither objective nor neutral and that, in order to truly effect change, we must understand not only how laws are made but also *why* they are passed, accepted, legitimized, and upheld.

---

* This chapter draws on earlier work by the author bridging land reform and human rights, see Shields (2015, 2017a, 2017b, 2017c, 2018, 2022); Calo et al. (2021), Calo, Shields, Iles (2022). For historical and sociological grounding, it draws on the work of Jim Hunter (1976, 1994, 1995, 2013, 2015) and Andy Wightman (1996, 1999, 2010); for critical approaches to law the work of Priscilla Claeys (2012, 2015, 2019, 2020), Jennifer Franco (2008, 2018), and Susan Marks (2000, 2005, 2008, 2020) are key; for scrutiny of property law in respect of justice and human rights, Eduardo Peñalver (2004, 2009, 2010, 2011), Jeremy Waldron (1988, 2000, 2009, 2011, 2012), and Lorenzo Cotula (2013, 2015, 2021). Inspiration also comes from contemporaries researching diverse aspects of land reform in the Scottish context, Calum McLeod, Malcolm Combe, Chris Dalglish, Bobby Macauley, Megan MacInnes, Annie McKee, Frankie McCarthy, Calum McLeod, Adam Calo, and Annie Tindley—some of whom have provided helpful comments on this chapter.

Although the specifics of the sociopolitical context and institutional land-scape are unique to Scotland, the cultivation of these contexts is not necessarily exceptional to Scotland. I focus on the following three key aspects of the Scotland case as key to the success of land reform legislative change: (1) the sociopolitical context, in particular the memory and legacy of land loss that helped legitimize the case for land reform and its conceptualization as a just reform; (2) the legal strategy, notably the Scottish Parliament's reconceptualization of the relationship between land, property, and human right; and (3) the outward significance of the Scottish case study for the evolution of human rights and land movements globally.

The Story So Far

While the recent land reform legislation and vision may be exceptional in transferring private land into community land, from a wider lens, Scotland is somewhat behind the curve. Scotland has the most concentrated pattern of ownership in Europe (Hunter 2013; Hindle et al. 2014; Glass, McMorran, and Thomson 2019). In 2010, Wightman's landmark book *The Poor Had No Lawyers* gave the staggering statistic that 50 percent of privately owned rural land in Scotland is owned by 432 landowners (Wightman 2010, 148). This statistic traveled far and wide, and the book achieved cult status in the process.

A research review published alongside the Land Commission's most recent investigation provides more texture to Wightman's statistic: In 2014, 1,125 estates were estimated to control about 70 percent (4.1 million hectares) of privately owned rural land; 667 of these estates were between 1,000 and 10,000 hectares in size, and 87 were larger than 10,000 hectares (Glass, McMorran, and Thomson 2019). There is a strong preference among the owners of large estates to pass them on to heirs. Succession law in Scotland has generally allowed estates to stay intact, suggesting that the long-term pattern of low turnover in estates is unlikely to change in the foreseeable future. In this way, Scotland differs markedly from other European countries where, typically, the bulk of a country's land is owned by very large numbers of people and where extensive estates of the Scottish sort are few or nonexistent.

Against this backdrop of entrenched land ownership consolidation, Salmond's speech on Skye (2013) and the effective revision of property rights thereafter is all the more significant. What follows explains the mechanics of new community rights to buy and own land, which the Scottish Government introduced to facilitate the transition to community ownership.

New Community Rights

In 1998, the UK Parliament passed the Scotland Act 1998, which created a devolved administration in Scotland consisting of a legislature (the Scottish Parliament) and an executive (latterly known as the Scottish Government). The Scotland Act serves to relinquish power from the UK Parliament to the Scottish administration to govern and legislate on areas that are not "reserved" to the UK Parliament (specified in Schedule 5, Scotland Act 1998, as amended by subsequent revisions to the devolution settlement in the Scotland Act 2012 and Scotland Act 2016). Devolved matters include land use planning, housing, and justice.

To facilitate the transfer of land into community ownership, the Scottish Government proposed new land legislation containing a set of community rights to buy, which was passed into law by the Scottish Parliament. The Land Reform (Scotland) Act 2003 introduced "a *community right to buy* land when it comes on the market" and "an absolute *crofting community right to buy* land." The 2003 community rights to buy only apply if there is a willing seller, in which case the community right is one of first refusal. The next wave of rights from the Community Empowerment (Scotland) Act 2015 and the Land Reform (Scotland) Act 2016 create community rights to buy land even where there is not a willing seller, that is, against the present owner's wishes.

The Community Empowerment (Scotland) Act 2015 introduced a "community right to buy abandoned, neglected, or detrimental land." This was done through amending Part 3A of the LRS Act 2003—effectively extending the preexisting right. This creates a community's right to purchase land deemed to be "abandoned or neglected" by Ministers from an "unwilling seller" (sometimes referred to as the "Part 3A CRtB"). It also extended the scope of the 2003 Right to Buy to include urban communities—as the original provision only applied to areas with a population of less than 10,000, it had generally only covered rural and village areas (see Reid 2019). It also extended the crofting right to buy to a crofting community right to buy.

The LR(S) Act 2016 introduced a new "community right to buy land to further sustainable development" (sometimes referred to as the "Part 5 CRtB"). The provision came into force as of April 26, 2020. Where it is successfully invoked, the Part 5 Right to Buy will lead to community ownership of land irrespective of whether the owner is willing to sell. In other words, a community body that successfully exercises its Part 5 Right to Buy will have an absolute right to buy the land if it can demonstrate that the community acquisition will help achieve "sustainable development" on the land. The LR(S) Act does not include a definition of sustainable development but states: "[T]he sustainable development conditions are met if—(a) the transfer of land is likely to further the achievement of sustainable development in relation to the land, (b) the transfer of land is in the public interest, (c) the transfer of land—(i) is likely to result in significant benefit to the relevant community to which the application relates, and (ii) is the only practicable, or most practicable, way of achieving that significant benefit—and (d) not granting consent to the transfer of land is likely to result in harm to that community."

For the exercise of these community rights to buy, there must be an eligible community incorporated into a "community body." For the purposes of the legislation, *community* is defined on a geographical basis, which can be defined by postcode units and/or a prescribed area. This definition of *community* has been chosen to reflect the importance of place, reflected within current Scottish Government policy and current legislation, as well as the implicit objectives of the one million acres target. The legislation states that a relevant "community body" must have a number of essential characteristics, which collectively ensure that community-owned assets are used for the benefit of the wider community rather than one particular interest group. The community body should

- have a clear definition of the geographical community to which the body relates;
- have a membership open to any member of that community;
- be locally led and controlled;
- have as its main purpose the furthering of sustainable development in the local area;
- be nonprofit distributing; and
- have evidence to demonstrate a sufficient level of support/community buy-in.

Ownership is defined in the legal sense as "a legal title coupled with exclusive legal right to possession." While communities can lease (i.e., from the Forestry Commission Scotland) or manage and jointly own (i.e., equity stake) assets, it was agreed that for the purposes of achieving the target, the definition should be restricted to outright ownership (Scottish Government 2015, 2017a).

In addition to defining the land in question and demonstrating the community's connection to the land, the proposed use, development, and management of the land, and the existence of community support, the community body must explain the reasons why it considers that the land is either wholly or mainly neglected or abandoned or how it is causing harm. To benefit from Part 5 CRtB, the community must outline how they propose to use the land for sustainable development. A copy of the application must be sent to the landowner and other relevant parties as defined in the Act (Community Land Scotland 2016.).

The Rising Tide of Community Ownership

Seven years after Salmond's speech at Sabhal Mor Ostaig on Skye (2013), the headline-grabbing "one million acres" target remains elusive, but a steady increase in community ownership is palpable. A wave of community ownership has swept from the Highlands, where it was historically concentrated, through the Central Belt to the Lowlands and from rural to urban areas. The latest statistics at the time of writing suggest that the area of land in community ownership in 2018 was 209,810 hectares. The area of land in community ownership has increased by 170,154 hectares compared to 1990 (see fig. 14.1) (Scottish Government 2018).

Community ownership is now widespread across Scotland. However, there is a large difference in the concentration of community assets and a very large difference in the scale and size of assets between the Highlands and elsewhere. For example, 38 percent of assets and 39 percent of community groups are located in two highland local authorities: Highland and Argyll and Bute. Yet in terms of land area of community-owned assets, Na h-Eileanan Siar and Highland together contain 96.4 percent (202,174 hectares) of the land area in community ownership in Scotland. This reflects the purchase of a small number of very large estates in the Na h-Eileanan Siar and Highland regions. It also reflects the difference in size and scale between rural and urban assets.

Consequently, the method of measuring land ownership has been revised to reflect this reality. In 2018, the Scottish Land Commission (SLC) recommended that the Scottish Government develop a new suite of indicators to replace the "one million acres" target (considered to be a headline-grabbing magic number) with targets and indicators that reflect the outcomes sought from community ownership and that are relevant to both rural and urban contexts. The SLC advised that the target to achieve one million acres of land in community ownership by 2020 provided a clear statement of ambition but did not reflect the nature and public value of community ownership in an urban context, nor necessarily the value of targeted asset acquisition in rural communities (SLC 2018).

Recast in these terms, community groups who own land parcels/assets are widespread across Scotland. As of December 2018, there were 593 assets in community ownership owned by 429 community groups, amounting to 209,810 hectares, or 2.7 percent of the total area of Scotland. In 2018, thirty-seven assets came into community ownership, an increase of 7 percent from 556 in 2017, contributing an additional 3,223 hectares. That year, twenty-seven community groups took ownership of assets for the first time. The Scottish Land Fund has awarded over £4 million to support sixty community initiatives and has a renewed annual budget of £10 million for 2016–2020 community buyouts over the coming years (Scottish Government 2019). Types of land acquired by community bodies include whole

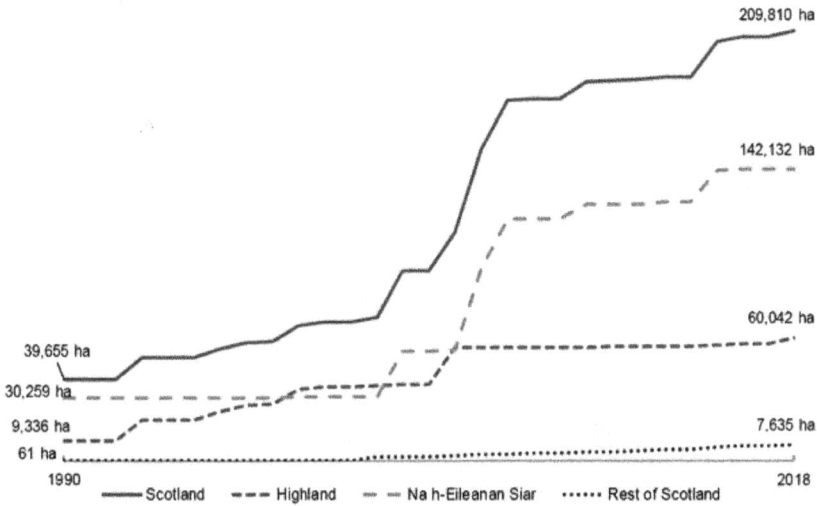

FIGURE 14.1.   Area of land in Scotland under community ownership from 1990 to 2018.

Graph from Scottish Government 2019.

estates, crofting estates, woodland, land, amenity, farm/crofts, and building development plots.

The process for determining the price of the assets for sale is set out in various provisions of the 2003 and 2016 legislations (Part 2 A, s. 38G, 59–60, 62, and s. 88 and 92 with respect to the right to buy croft land of the Land Reform Scotland Act 2003; s. 65 and 70 of the Land Reform Scotland Act 2016). The process is as follows: Ministers appoint a suitably qualified, experienced, and independent valuer. The valuer shall invite the owner of the land and the community body, which is exercising its right to buy the land, to make written representations about the value of the land and any moveable property being bought with the land and shall consider any representations made accordingly. If one or both of the parties do not agree with the valuation, they may appeal to the Land Court to challenge the valuation. In short, the seller cannot easily refute the valuation.

Examples of Community Acquisitions

Examples of community acquisitions include:

- Ardnamurchan Lighthouse. A local group entitled the Ardnamurchan Lighthouse Trust was awarded £224,900 from the Scottish Land Fund to buy a lighthouse building from the Highland Council in 2019 (*Oban Times* 2019).

- The island of Ulva, a small island (1990 ha) on the Inner Hebrides on the west coast of Scotland. A local group, the North West Mull Community Woodland Company, received an unprecedented award of £4.4 million to buy the island from the previous private owner, Jamie Howard, in 2018 (*Press & Journal* 2018).
- Portobello Old Parish Church in Edinburgh. A local group, Action Porty, was awarded £647,500 from the Scottish Land Fund to buy a church and halls from the Church of Scotland in 2017. It was heralded as the first urban community buyout (Scottish Government Newsroom 2017).

Not all acquisitions are transfers from private owners; sometimes, they are from public bodies, such as councils, while some are from quasi-public bodies, such as churches. Importantly, most community acquisitions to date have relied on the 2003 CRtB—i.e., the original community right-to-buy provision where there is a willing seller.

It is too early to know the uptake and long-term impacts of the 2015 and 2016 rights. However, as John Lovett writes, these new rights mean that "[communities can now bring property owners, whether owners of large rural estates or even an entity as historically powerful as the Church of Scotland, to the bargaining table to discuss the transfer of property either in the shadows of the new legislation or under the formal auspices of that legislation" (Lovett and Combe 2019, 222). Data gaps around the value of land that has been transferred into community land ownership and the reasons and rationales why sellers are selling land present opportunities for future research (see also the work of Annie McKee).

Why Now?

Beyond the more exciting aspects of these developments, there are the questions of why and why now. Previous attempts at land reform in Scotland were often piecemeal or thwarted. Real change only began once the Scottish Parliament engaged with emerging political demand by creating new community rights to buy. Even earlier significant developments embodied in the 2003 Act stopped short of challenging landowners' rights. How and why have attitudes toward private property rights shifted? To identify and trace this shift, I look at the cultural context and institutional landscape that enabled this change, in particular, the creation of the Scottish Parliament as a human rights-orientated institution.

It would be wrong to suggest that the new legal provisions occurred in isolation or were legal breakthroughs only. Instead, the process of legislative review of the proposed new laws ran in parallel with building political momentum and citizen engagement in land reform. The Scottish case thus highlights the relationship between the perceived legitimacy of the law and societal acceptance and compliance with it. The process of consultation on land reform led to a reflection on the role and power of property rights, which was not confined to Parliamentary chambers or courtrooms but poured out into mainstream media and debate. This chapter speaks to Peter Houtzager's research questions on the struggle for land waged by the Movement of Landless Workers (MST) in Brazil: "What forms of legal change can social movements set in motion to diminish systemic and durable forms of social exclusion? And when are movements successful at doing so?" (Houtzager 2005). The following sections consider key aspects of Scotland's new land laws as the sociopolitical context and the legal strategy before considering the significance of this legislative development on land struggles and the international human rights movement beyond these.

The Sociopolitical Context: The Memory of Loss (and Its Power)

Sociocultural narratives and memories can generate demands to dismantle or disrupt the law of property. In his beautifully evocative essay *Property's Memories*, Peñalver explains, "Where memory of property departs from the present distributive reality, it can delegitimize the present reality or provide a source of utopian inspiration" (Peñalver 2011, 1075).

The history of land struggles in Scotland runs deep and wide. In contemporary times, these struggles are relatively subdued compared to their predecessors in Scotland and counterparts in other parts of the world. Much of the subaltern peasant movement discourse that surrounds land reform elsewhere in the world does not translate easily to the Scottish context. Yet there are synergies regarding collective memory of land loss.

Scotland does not have a "peasant class" identity like other countries do, and, to a certain extent, this avoids some of the problematic conceptions of peasant life, which have been well documented elsewhere (Wolford 2010). The majority of rural dwellers and agricultural workers—the quintessential "peasant class"— were dispossessed and dislocated to make way for sheep. The Highland Clearances in the 1700s depleted the agricultural underclass, and they were dispersed to the coast, the city, or "set adrift upon the world" to New Zealand, Australia, the United States, and Canada or the great unknown (Hunter 2015). Remnants and fragments of those communities remain within the modern-day crofting tradition. Yet the modern crofting identity is detached from the historic communities; it is often made up of newcomers, and for the most part, associations with "indigeneity" are avoided as a divisive and unhelpful term.

A collective memory of this loss permeates Scottish culture, heritage, and politics. The sharp rise in support for the Scottish National Party (SNP) over the past two decades suggests that for some, the SNP's particular brew of civic nationalism and self-governance appeals to that narrative of collective loss embodied in the country's history, some might say imaginary. That narrative is otherwise known as "The Highland Clearances" (Prebble 1963), since broadened to "The Clearances" (McGrath 1981) and recently redefined as "The Scottish Clearances" (Devine 2018). Anyone who would like the express "cut" of this history is encouraged to read the short article by poet Kathleen Jamie, *Uncovering the Facts of the Scottish Clearances*, in the *New Statesman* (Jamie 2019). Reviewing Tom Devine's book, she writes: "Prior to 1750, the vast majority of Scots had some small stake in the land. But by the early eighteenth century, landowners in the Borders were already planning the removal of their poorest subsistence tenants to create large sheep holdings, so beginning an Enlightenment-approved, landlord-driven march of "improvement" and profit (Jamie 2019).

For those who know the history of the "Clearances," it is a phony romanticism of Scotland that is immortalized in the ubiquitous portraits of a solitary brazen stag on a barren hill, the "Monarch of the Glen," and his many reincarnations as beer mat, tea cozy, and other objects. As ethnographer Mairi McFadyen writes, such romantic representations of Scotland have provided "not only a psychological escape from contemporary reality but also an escape from the history of Scotland itself." She identifies the harm of such misrepresentations as having "wreaked havoc on the public's ability to not only know the story of their own place—through no fault of their own—but also on their ability to imagine progressive and democratic alternatives" (McFadyen 2014). Since the Clearances, the big estates are a "classic," fetishized fixture of the Scottish landscape. The stag represents the cultivation of "estates" in the Scottish Highlands, which cleared people and vegetation from the land to make way for large sporting estates. The estates are privately owned and stocked with live game for shooting, such as pheasants and deer, and "do a roaring trade with visiting aristocracy" (Henderson 2018). They are often misunderstood to be places of wilderness, and their pinch on national resources and the deep structural inequalities that reach into every crevice of Scotland are hidden from view.

In the 2000s, an emerging popular demand for land reform was fueled by this backstory and propelled by the possibility of change. A greater understanding of the relationship between the extreme wealth of the estates and extreme poverty elsewhere in Scotland, which had been seeded through Wightman's work in 2000, became tinder to renewed activism for Scottish independence in 2014. The Scottish Independence Referendum was an exercise not only in civic engagement but also in "public law for the masses." Televised debates and social media commentary would tell and retell the knowns, unknowns, and half knowns of the new constitutional arrangements of independence. The finer details of the Scotland Act 1998 became general knowledge and pub quiz fodder.

To return to Houtzager's questions: "What forms of legal change can social movements set in motion to diminish systemic and durable forms of social exclusion?" This intensified popular interest in law, particularly public law, and no doubt had an impact on the land reform movement's ability to demand legal change—because it was possible to present and explain the demand as legitimate. "And when are movements successful at doing so?" In the Scottish context, claims for land reform were mobilized due to attachment to a wider moral framework (human rights law) within a human rights-orientated and democratic institution (the Scottish Parliament).

Quantifying Poverty and Loss in Human Rights Terms

Recognition of the connection between ownership of large swathes of land in rural Scotland and community degeneration, inequality, poverty, and homelessness have become more widespread in recent years, partly through the writings of Wightman, among others. Connections between ecological crises and large estate ownership have also become more explicit in popular accounts of environmental degradation in the UK (Monbiot 2013). For a long time, it was unclear how to package this poverty and degradation in a way that empowered places and communities to demand change.

In parliamentary and media debates surrounding the new land reform laws, the human rights framework, particularly the economic, social, and cultural (ESC) rights branch, and also emerging environmental rights (such as the right to clean air and water and to a healthy environment) became a useful tool for identifying and labeling harms caused by centuries of exclusion and marginalization from the land.

To give an example of how human rights are used to identify harms or losses, on the Isle of Harris, the viability of the community was threatened by a declining population and the seasonal, unsustainable nature of housing and employment on the island. The situation began to reverse when the West Harris Trust bought over 17,000 acres of land from the Scottish Government in January 2010. In partnership with the Hebridean Housing Partnership, the Trust built six affordable homes and has plans to build more. By providing access to decent, affordable housing, the community ownership initiative had a positive impact on the *right to housing*. The creation of a mixed business tourism development in a former school building created several new full-time jobs, thus meeting the right to employment. This regeneration may enable the key public services on the island to reopen and, therefore, may have knock-on effects on the right to education or the right to cultural life, among others. There is also potential for community ownership initiatives to support the right to health and the right to food through enabling access to green spaces and supporting food-growing projects (Shields 2018). Peter Peacock, Policy Director for Community Land Scotland, said at the time, "The integration of economic, social, and cultural rights to the land agenda changed everything. Suddenly there was a vocabulary and a structure to balance the interests involved" (interview with the author, October 10, 2016).

The potential for community ownership to empower communities is central to the Scottish Government's rationale for intervention in the new community rights. In the guidance on the right to buy land for sustainable development, the Scottish Government states under the heading "Rationale for Government Intervention": "Ministers consider that community ownership has a transformational impact on communities, increasing community confidence and developing vibrant and flourishing communities. It can also allow more people and communities in Scotland to make use of land as a resource, which can provide economic, social, and environmental benefits and, in general, support sustainable development" (Scottish Government 2020, 4).

Democracy by Design: The Creation of the Scottish Parliament as a "Human Rights-Orientated Institution"

A key enabling factor to the land reform movement's ability to effect legal change was the existence of a functioning democratic institution in the shape of the Scottish Parliament in Edinburgh. The Scottish Parliament building was designed by Catalan architect Enric Miralles to represent a modern European democracy that emerged organically from the land. The physical architecture is distinct from Westminster in that it facilitates consensual politics rather than the adversarial and confrontational design found in the House of Commons at Westminster (Brown 2000, 543).[2] The chamber is set in concentric circles, as opposed to benches separated by the length of two swords (the House of Commons design). The viewing gallery above the chamber is a sweeping, elliptical expanse intended to recreate a metaphorical hillside gathering. Described as a "building of pure poetry" (Kay 2016), Miralles's architectural designs stipulated that the Parliament "should originate from the sloping base of Arthur's Seat and arrive into the city almost out of the rock."[3]

Human rights are central to the constitution of the Scottish Parliament. The Scotland Act 1998, the constitutional document for the Scottish Parliament, contains commitments to respect the UK Human Rights Act 1998 and the

European and international human rights obligations.[4] These obligations are embedded into the Scottish Parliament's constitutional document. The UK Parliament has not embedded these commitments to the same extent as it does not have a single constitutional document; instead, these documents form part of the UK's living constitution. The creation of the Scottish Parliament also opened the door to the promise of land reform. As the inaugural First Minister of Scotland, Donald Dewar, declared: "There is undoubtedly a powerful symbolism—which attracts me greatly—of land reform being amongst the first actions of our new Scottish Parliament" (Dewar 1998).

Yet despite this founding ethos, in much of this earlier phase of land reform at the Scottish Parliament, the European Convention on Human Rights (ECHR) right to property was the main human rights concern. This is largely because early clashes with the ECHR had left the Scottish Parliament with "something of a bloody nose" (Drane and Tainsh 2015; McCarthy 2020). For example, the ECHR's right to property was the only right given detailed consideration in the Scottish Law Commission reports (McCarthy 2020). However, these traditional perspectives and priorities were able to evolve in line with progressive democratic developments elsewhere. This is in no small part due to the Scottish Parliament's power, independence, and capacity to connect with the international human rights movement and operate within a wider framework of legal, cultural, and moral norms. This enables land questions to be disentangled from the property rights concerns that had historically engulfed them, though they have not quite escaped the property rights web altogether.

The Legal Strategy: Land, Property, and Human Rights

In the law, land quickly becomes treated as "property" and increasingly as "private property." Therefore, in order to achieve land reform or land justice, there has to be significant engagement with or disruption of property law. Private property regimes are considered immutable; as a result, land rights movements often operate in the margins of private property regimes. Yet, in order to be successful, land rights movements must engage with private property structures. This is a necessary strategy that most land struggles to, does not, or cannot find, partly due to institutional and legal silos. In this section, I look at these silos and the efforts of ESC lawyers and land activists to create a bridge between their domains, as seen in a growing number of successful invocations of human rights to justify land reform.

Property and Land

The ideological differences between "property" and "land" play out in legal scholarship and are generally transposed to the distinction between property lawyers (private lawyers) and human rights lawyers (public lawyers). Traditionally, property lawyers deal in contracts that leave little room to read between the lines or reflect on the wider social, political, and cultural effect of the application of the law. Human rights lawyers, on the other hand, work on documenting injustice and advocating for legal reforms that respond to contemporary needs and challenges.

These two types of legal approaches treat land in different ways. For example, land scholarship and activism in the Global North often focus on diversifying the use and consolidation of already publicly owned land through "community land trusts," such as in the US, Europe, Australia, and (other parts of) the UK (Housing Europe 2012; Thompson 2018; Crabtree et al. 2019; Hobson et al. 2019; Shrubshole 2019). This focus serves to mitigate rather than reverse land consolidation and ignores the power asymmetries embedded in land distribution. Consequently, embedded legal attitudes, approaches, and practices on property can escape scrutiny and even deepen the legitimacy of dominant property logic (Morris 2008; Van der Ploeg 2009, 266).

This clash of ideologies—between private and communal property, between individual and collective goods—is also present in human rights law. Civil and political (CP) rights are generally treated as individual rights, while ESC rights are understood as collective rights. ESC rights have historically been secondary both in evolution and in status to CP rights. When the UN International Covenant on Economic, Social, and Cultural Rights was drafted, the doctrines of "progressive realization" and, consequently, "non-justiciability" were attached to ESC rights. This meant that ESC rights were to be implemented progressively, subject to the state's resources, and, as a result, they could not be upheld in court as entitlements against the state (see Nolan 2007; Young 2008).

This legacy has had a significant impact on structures and patterns of land ownership.

Lengthy jurisprudence on CP rights, such as free speech and the right to a fair trial, in the Global North, have traditionally been created and developed by the propertied, that is, those who can afford to go to court. In other words, if a person cannot afford housing, he or she may not be able to afford to prosecute the state for violating their right to housing (and ESC right). Resource constraints of potential litigants are compounded by a general reluctance on the part of the justiciary to tackle questions of state resource allocation. These embedded legal attitudes, whether intentionally or not, have, over several decades, contributed to the subordination of ESC rights as a set of "second class" rights. Within human rights scholarship, a core contingent actively challenges these attitudes on the grounds that universality and human dignity (or core values of the international human rights movement) require that certain minimum core obligations be met (see the works of Waldron and Shields).

Land activists and ESC rights lawyers are, therefore, natural allies in the struggle to topple property and rights hierarchies. Social movements protesting for control over natural resources are strategically engaging in human rights discourse to advance collective demands, sometimes through ESC rights, sometimes through demanding that new rights be created (Claeys 2012, 851). For example, La Via Campesina (the international movement that represents peasant organizations and Indigenous communities) advocated for peasants' rights and a new right to food sovereignty (Via Campesina 2009), helping lead to the adoption of the United Nations Declaration on the Rights of Peasants and Other People Working in Rural Areas by the Human Rights Council on September 28, 2018, which includes the right to land (UN 2018).[5] The turn toward collectivism in human rights, embodied in the call for a right to food sovereignty, is also found in demands for the right to land to be recognized by the UN (De Schutter 2010; Gilbert 2013).

Arguably, land lawyers and scholars have been most effective in challenging the logic of private property rights in Latin America, where challenges to the financialization of land have come in various forms, often relying on human rights. For example, in Nicaragua, an Indigenous group living in the rainforest was successful in winning recognition of its collective right to land at the Inter-American Commission on Human Rights (IACHR) in the celebrated *Awas Tingni* judgment of August 31, 2001 (IACHR 2001; Anaya and Grossman 2002). In Brazil, the MST succeeded in making access to land more equitable in parts of Brazil by redefining how property rights operate in practice (Houtzager 2005). In Colombia, two legal reforms—the 2011 Land Restitution Law and the Comprehensive Rural Reform contained in the Agrarian Chapter of the Peace Agreement between the national government and the FARC-EP in 2016—integrated alternative criteria for granting property rights over rural lands based on processes of restitution and redistribution (Coronado 2019).[6] These outcomes are historical achievements at a time when the most powerful international institutions, like the World Bank, are committed to globalizing a new interpretation of liberal property rights. They have been brought about by political movements engaged in legal strategy, who have developed a concern for human rights sometimes, as Houtzager puts it, "out of necessity" (Houtzager 2005, 234).

The shared struggle for both land and rights activists is, therefore, the struggle of collectivism over individualism. The defense of collectivism—still vigorous in Latin America—is harder to grasp in the West, where engaging in land means engaging with the politics and law of private property—"a historically daunting prospect" (Williams and Gimenez 2017, 3). Renewed legal and political interest in community land in Scotland is thus of relevance for land struggles globally.

Creating a Community Right to Buy

In 2015, the Scottish Parliament undertook a public consultation as part of the legislative process. Opponents argued that the community right to buy without a willing seller would violate the right to property—and that this right was "fundamental" or "absolute."[7] Their comments included "Landowners' human rights must not be infringed" (Big Lottery Fund) and "Potential investors and developers making a crucial contribution to the Scottish economy need certainty and would be deterred from investing in Scotland if there was potential for their land to be purchased compulsorily by or at the direction of the state. The mere existence of a state power to do that could deter investment and development, and such a power would be a further interference with the fundamental right to private property" (Pinsent Masons LLP).

Around thirty people expressed concern that attempts to deploy new purchase powers over private landowners might lead to costly legal challenges, delays, and costs to the public purse (Scottish Government 2015, 55).

The Scottish Parliament Committee on Rural Affairs and Climate Change and the Environment (RACCE) was responsible for undertaking the process of public consultation around the proposed land reform legislation. In response to such comments, the Committee on RACCE chose to review the human rights aspects of the bill. The Committee heard evidence that the right to property is not absolute and may be legitimately curtailed under the ECHR. People are entitled to the peaceful enjoyment of their property and should not be deprived of their property—unless it is in the public interest and follows a specified legal procedure (RACCE, Scottish Parliament 2015).[8] The Committee noted that in deciding whether a measure taken by Scottish Ministers is genuinely in pursuit of the public interest, the ECHR is inclined to defer to the government in question to decide on what constitutes the public interest (McHarg 1999; *Handyside v. United Kingdom 1976*; *Silver and others v. United Kingdom 1983*; *Lingens v. Austria* 1986). It was, therefore, for the Scottish Parliament to set the criteria for defining the public interest in creating a community right to buy.

The Committee also heard that the state is obliged to use natural resources to their maximum availability in order to support ESC rights in accordance with the UN ICESCR (RACCE, Scottish Parliament 2015). Under current arrangements, land has been underutilized as a means to support the population's ESC rights. The right to property has been disproportionately protected at the expense of ESC rights (Shields 2015). Rather than thwart the community ownership agenda through right to property claims, human rights were used to legitimize and give structure to long-awaited changes in land ownership.

Consequently, in the development of the land reform legislation at the Scottish Parliament, ESC rights were used to represent the public interest—and to be an effective way of measuring and balancing competing claims on the public interest. This was expressed throughout evidence sessions, and in the final debate (Scottish Parliament 2016, 49–52), the LR(S) Act 2016 expressly refers to the ICESCR, as well as the UK Human Rights Act 1998, for definitions of human rights. The ICESCR is also embedded in the Land Rights and Responsibilities Statement (Scottish Government 2017b), which informs the work of the SLC in implementing the community right to buy. In this way, ESC rights emerged as a new rationale for land use, necessitating land ownership reform.

The Global Significance of Reordering Property Rights

Besides demonstrating how key social and cultural aspects can make land movements "legitimate" and thus successful in securing legal change, what is the broader significance of the Scottish land reform movement? I argue that Scotland offers important insights for both land struggles and the international human rights movement. By placing "human rights" and, more recently, "community rights" at its core rather than private property rights, Scotland's recent land legislation can inspire similar efforts elsewhere in the world. It can help land reform movements confront the myth of property regimes as unmoveable apex norms within Western legal regimes.

In particular, the Scottish example demonstrates that to change land patterns, it is necessary to change property law and that this can be done. As has been widely established, interventions in property rights are within the remit of the state; however, they rarely occur beyond the realm of taxation. That the government has the power to intervene in property distribution is overlooked within land debates to such an extent that it is sometimes assumed that the state does not hold that power, let alone have a responsibility to use it to intervene and prevent human rights violations. The 2014–2016 land reform discussion at the Scottish Parliament established that the government *can* intervene in property rights and defined the grounds for such interventions. In so doing, the Scottish Parliament invited, encouraged, and enabled scrutiny of the role of private property rights within the wider schema of resource governance and within a wider system of justice.

In his ground-breaking study on the justifications of private property in 1988, Waldron is scathing in his criticism of the blanket application of private property rights. He foresaw a need for limitations on private property rights globally: "[P]roperty rights are going to have to be constrained by a general background right to subsistence [. . .]. Under serious scrutiny, there is no right-based argument to be found which provides an adequate justification for a society in which some people have lots of property and many have next to none" (Waldron 1988, 5). A general background right to subsistence exists in the ICESCR right to an adequate standard of living, including food, water, and housing (Article 11), but it relies on empowered local governance to find creative and effective ways of enforcing it. Regarding proponents of property rights, Waldron noted: "The slogan that property is a human right can be deployed only disingenuously to legitimize the massive inequality that we find in modern capitalist countries" (Waldron 1988, 5). The Scottish case shows that property rights can indeed be limited and that human rights arguments to protect individual property, which in reality uphold a lopsided distribution of land, can be effectively opposed in favor of more socially based property rights.

More broadly, the Scottish case breathes new life into the international human rights movement as a means of legitimizing the redistribution of resources. The Scottish land reform movement addressed the following key critiques, which have impeded the development of the international human rights framework:

- The "nonjusticiability" critique—that ESC rights are not justiciable and therefore not to be counted. By placing the ICESCR as a key consideration in laws relating to land, the LR(S) Act 2016 and the LRRS 2016 moved the contestation of rights upstream of courts to the Parliament and parliamentary bodies. Courts do not have to play a decisive role.
- The individualization critique—the UN human rights framework is essentially "individualizing" and "Western" and risks alienating activists from their "own local cultural understandings" (Merry 1997, 32). By presenting the ICESCR as a framework for identifying and labeling existing collective needs and interests, the LR(S) Act 2016 demonstrates the scope for a rebalancing of rights toward the collective rather than the individual.
- The state-centricity critique—that reliance on the state to protect rights is overstated and unachievable, and that in light of the vastly different capacities of states, this leads to the nonuniversality of rights in practice (Elias 2010, 44). By redirecting focus from state accountability

to resources for rights realization, the land reform agenda presents a realistic approach to rights realization that connects with sovereignty movements globally and counters the contradictions inherent in the state-centricity argument.

- The liberalism critique—that the UN human rights framework prioritizes civil and political rights and relatedly economic liberty—understood as individual appropriation of, access to, and control over economic resources at the expense of equality of outcome and welfarism (Charvet and Kaczynska-Nay 2008, 11–12; Claeys 2012, 847). Using ESC rights to effectively "offset" and place limits on unrestricted property rights facilitates a rebalancing of the asymmetry between ESC rights and property rights, welfarism and liberalism, which may lead to a real impact.

By engaging and countering these critiques, the Scottish land reform movement supports the continued evolution of the international human rights movement.

The approach to human rights integration within Scottish land legislation, in particular the focus on ESC rights, represents a rebalancing of rights relationships. The Scottish Government's approach to ESC rights treats these commitments with rigor, which belies a seriousness about these much-neglected human rights obligations.[6] These norms are often badged as important governmental objectives but are rarely treated as constitutional priorities or established norms. By placing "human rights" and "community rights" at its core, Scotland's land law offers a paradigm shift in legal hierarchies. Land reform is often promoted as a vehicle for ESC rights; in the Scottish example, ESC rights served as a vehicle for land reform.

The developments in the Scottish context are not a silver bullet, and land use decisions remain problematic—with new clashes between rewilding and repopulating, between land for carbon restoration and land for homes, coming into focus.[7] The ideological debates that prevented the UN from codifying the right to property as a legally binding entitlement continue today, yet these can no longer be accurately attached to East/West geographical divides. New alliances between land activists and human rights activists and advocates and growing recognition of the relationship between land rights and human rights have brought strength to alternatives to prevailing systems of private property rights, both within and across countries. Those alternatives have long been established in the Global South, particularly in South America, and now cracks in property rights dominance are emerging in the Global North. The Scotland story is not necessarily a template that can be easily replicated, but it does speak to new possibilities.

NOTES

1. Continues, "A lift from a lobster fisherman! With red hands. Driving slowly up and down farm tracks, life on the sea bed."

2. See further: "The arguments for a new parliament were based on a critique of the centralisation of power into the hands of the Westminster government, a voting system which favoured the two main political parties in British politics, giving power to a government with only minority support in Scotland, and a political system that was seen as increasingly unrepresentative, indeed alien to the lives of most people." (Brown 2000, 543.)

3. Miralles's original design proposals for the Scottish Parliament can be viewed here: https://archive2021.parliament.scot/visitandlearn/15914.aspx.

4. According to the Scotland Act 1998 s. 29 (2) (d). and s. 58, in conjunction with Schedule 5, para. 7 (2), Scotland is obliged to respect "international obligations," including the UN international human rights treaties.

5. United Nations Declaration on the Rights of Peasants and Other People Working in Rural Areas, a resolution adopted by the Human Rights Council on September 28, 2018. The Declaration reaffirms existing human rights, including the right to food, and recognizes that peasants have the right to land (Article 17), the right to seeds (Article 19), the right to biodiversity (Article 20), the right to sustainable use of natural resources, and the right to participate in the management of these resources (Article 5). There are several other rights advocated by La Via Campesina that do not feature in the Declaration, including the "right not to disappear," "the right to produce," the "right to be a peasant," and the "right to the protection of agriculture values."

6. Ley 1448 de 2011 (Decree from the Congress of Colombia), "Por la cual se dictan medidas de atención, asistencia y reparación integral a las víctimas del conflicto armado interno y se dictan otras disposiciones" (http://wp.presidencia.gov.co/sitios/normativa/leyes/Documents/Juridica/LEY%201448%20DE%202011.pdf). "Final Agreement for Ending the Conflict and Building a Stable and Lasting Peace," signed on November 24, 2016, between the Government of Colombia and the Revolutionary Armed Forces of Colombia-People's Army (FARC-EP): https://colombia.unmissions.org/sites/default/files/s-2017-272_e.pdf.

7. See, for example: *Scotsman* 2013, *Telegraph* 2015; and *Telegraph* 2015a.

8. See Council of Europe (1950), European Convention on Human Rights, Protocol 1, Article 1. ¶1: "Every natural or legal person is entitled to the peaceful enjoyment of his possessions. No one shall be deprived of his possessions except in the public interest and subject to the conditions provided for by law and by the general principles of international law."

¶2: "The preceding provisions shall not, however, in any way impair the right of a State to enforce such laws as it deems necessary to control the use of property in accordance with the general interest or to secure the payment of taxes or other contributions or penalties."

REFERENCES

Alden Wily, L. 2018. "Collective Land Ownership in the 21st Century: Overview of Global Trends." *Land* 7 (2): 68.

Alexander, G. S. 1998. "Critical Land Law." In *Land Law: Themes and Perspectives*. Edited by S. Bright and J. Dewar, 52–78. Oxford: Oxford University Press.

Alvarez, J. E. 2018. "The Human Right of Property." *University of Miami Law Review* 72 (3): 580.

Anaya, S. J., and C. Grossman. 2002. "The Case of Awas Tingni v. Nicaragua: A New Step in the International Law of Indigenous Peoples." *Arizona Journal of International & Comparative Law* 19 (1).

Blandy, S., S. J. Bright, and S. Nield. 2018. "The Dynamics of Enduring Property Relationships in Land." *Modern Law Review* 81 (1): 85–113.

Borras Jr., S. M., P. McMichael, and I. Scoones. 2010. *Biofuels, Land and Agrarian Change*. London: Routledge.

Brown, A. 2000. "Designing the Scottish Parliament." *Parliamentary Affairs* 53 (3): 542–556.

Calo, A. et al. 2021. "Achieving Food System Resilience Requires Challenging Dominant Land Property Regimes." *Frontiers in Sustainable Food Systems* 5: 683544.

Calo, A., K. Shields, and A. Iles. 2022. "Using Property Law to Expand Agroecology: Scotland's Land Reforms Based on Human Rights." *The Journal of Peasant Studies* 50 (5): 1–37.

Charvet, J., and E. Kaczynska-Nay. 2008. *The Liberal Project and Human Rights: The Theory and Practice of a New World Order*. Cambridge: Cambridge University Press.

Claeys, P. 2012. "The Creation of New Rights by the Food Sovereignty Movement: The Challenge of Institutionalizing Subversion." *Sociology* 46 (5): 844–860. https://doi.org/10.1177/0038038512451534.

Claeys, P. 2015. *Human Rights and the Food Sovereignty Movement: Reclaiming Control / Priscilla Claeys*. London: Routledge.

Claeys, P., and M. Edelman. 2020. "The United Nations Declaration on the Rights of Peasants and Other People Working in Rural Areas." *The Journal of Peasant Studies* 47 (1): 1–68. https://doi.org/10.1080/03066150.2019.1672665.

Columbia Center on Sustainable Investment. 2019. *Innovative Financing Solutions for Legal and Technical Support to Communities*. Research Project. Columbia Climate School. Climate, Earth, and Society. https://people.climate.columbia.edu/projects/view/1011.

Combe, M. M. 2018. "Community Rights in Scots Property Law." In *Legal Strategies for the Development and Protection of Communal Property*. Edited by T. Xu and A. Clarke, 79–101. Oxford: Oxford University Press.

Community Land Scotland. 2016. *Summary of Community Rights in Law to Seek to Purchase Land*.

Coronado, S. 2019. "Rights in the Time of Populism: Land and Institutional Change Amid the Reemergence of Right-Wing Authoritarianism in Colombia." *Land* 8: 119.

Cotula, L. 2013. *The Great African Land Grab? Agricultural Investments and the Global Food System*. London: Zed Books.

Cotula, L. 2015. *Land Rights and Investment Treaties: Exploring the Interface*. London: International Institute for Environment and Development.

Cotula, L. 2021. "Towards a Political Economy of the COVID-19 Crisis: Reflections on an Agenda for Research and Action." *World Development* 138: 105235–105235. https://doi.org/10.1016/j.worlddev.2020.105235.

Council of Europe. 1950. "Article 1 of Protocol to the Convention for the Protection of Human Rights and Fundamental Freedoms." *European Convention on Human Rights*.

Crabtree, L., C. Sappideen, S. Lawler, R. Conroy, and J. McNeill. 2019. *Enabling Community Land Trusts in Australia*. Melbourne: ARENA Publications.

De Schutter, O. 2010. "The Emerging Human Right to Land." *International Community Law Review* 12 (3): 303–334.

De Schutter, O. 2011. "The Green Rush: The Global Race for Farmland and the Rights of Land Users." *Harvard International Law Journal* 52 (2): 503–559.

Devine, T. M. 2018. *The Scottish Clearances: A History of the Dispossessed, 1600–1900.* London: Allen Lane - Penguin Books.

Dewar, D. 1998. *Land Reform for the 21st Century.* The 1998 McEwen Lecture. http://www.caledonia.org.uk/land/dewar.htm.

Drane, A., and L. Tainsh. 2015. "Scottish Government Agricultural Holdings Review—Final Report 2015." *Davidson Chalmers: News and Insight,* January 28, 2015. https://www.dcslegal.com/news-and-insights/scottish-government-agricultural-holdings-review-%E2%80%93-final-report-2015.

Edelman, M., C. Oya, S. M. Borras Jr. 2015. *Global Land Grabs: History, Theory, and Method.* London: Routledge.

Fairhead, J., M. Leach, and I. Scoones. 2012. "Green Grabbing: A New Appropriation of Nature?" *Journal of Peasant Studies* 39 (2): 237–261, https://doi.org/10.1080/03066150.2012.671770.

Franco, J. C. 2008. "Making Land Rights Accessible: Social Movements and Political-Legal Innovation in the Rural Philippines." *The Journal of Development Studies* 44 (7): 991–1022. https://doi.org/10.1080/00220380802150763.

Franco, J. C., and S. M. Suárez. 2018. "Why Wait for the State? Using the CFS Tenure Guidelines to Recalibrate Political-Legal Struggles for Democratic Land Control." *Third World Quarterly* 39 (7): 1386–1402. https://doi.org/10.1080/01436597.2017.1374835.

Frison, C., and P. Claeys. 2019. "Right to Food in International Law." *Encyclopedia of Food and Agricultural Ethics* (January): 2163–2169. https://doi.org/10.1007/978-94-024-1179-9_323.

Ghosh, J. 2010. "The Unnatural Coupling: Food and Global Finance." *Journal of Agrarian Change* 10 (1): 72–86.

Gilbert, J. 2013. "Land Rights as Human Rights: The Case for a Specific Right to Land." *SUR International Journal on Human Rights* 10 (18): 115–136.

Glass, J., R. McMorran, and S. Thomson. 2019. *The Effects Associated with Concentrated and Large-Scale Land Ownership in Scotland: A Research Review.* Report prepared for the Scottish Land Commission. Scotland's Rural College.

Global Witness. 2018. *At What Cost?: Irresponsible Business and the Murder of Land and Environmental Defenders in 2017.* Report. http://bit.ly/2SLxy4k/.

Golay, C. 2013. *Legal Reflections on the Rights of Peasants and Other People Working in Rural Areas.* Paper presented at the First Session of the Working Group on the Rights of Peasants and Other People Working in Rural Areas, July 15–19, 2013.

Hall, R., M. Edelman, S. M. Borras Jr., I. Scoones, B. White, and W. Wolford. 2015. "Resistance, Acquiescence or Incorporation? An Introduction to Land Grabbing and Political Reactions 'from Below.'" *The Journal of Peasant Studies* 42 (3–4): 467–488.

Henderson, A. 2018. "Changing Mood Increases Sales of Private Estates." *Scotsman,* April 24, 2018.

Hindle, R., S. Thomson, S. Skerratt, R. McMorran, and P. Onea. 2014. *Economic Contribution of Estates in Scotland: An Economic Assessment for Scottish Land & Estates.* Final report for Scottish Land and Estates.

Hobson, J., K. Lynch, H. Roberts, and B. Payne. 2019. "Community Ownership of Local Assets: Conditions for Sustainable Success." *Journal of Rural Studies* 65 (January): 116–125.

Housing Europe. 2012. *Profiles of a Movement: Co-operative Housing Around the World.* http://www.housingeurope.eu/resource-115/profiles-of-a-movement.

Houtzager, P. P. 2005. "The Movement of the Landless (MST), Juridical Field, and Legal Change in Brazil." In *Law and Globalization from Below: Towards a Cosmopolitan Legality*. Edited by B. De Sousa Santos and C. Rodríguez-Garavito, 218–240. Cambridge, UK: Cambridge University Press.

Hunter, J. 1976. *The Making of the Crofting Community*. Edinburgh: Birlinn.

Hunter, J. 1994. *A Dance called America: The Scottish Highlands, the United States and Canada*. Edinburgh: Mainstream.

Hunter, J. 1995. *On the Other Side of Sorrow: Nature and People in the Scottish Highlands*. Edinburgh: Mainstream.

Hunter, J. 2013. *Scottish Land Reform to Date: By European Standards, A Pretty Dismal Record*. Community Land Scotland. http://www.andywightman.com/docs/jim_hunter_20130603.pdf

Hunter, J. 2015. *Set Adrift Upon the World: The Sutherland Clearances*. Edinburgh: Birlinn.

Jamie, K. 2012. "The Stags." In *The Overhaul*. London: Picador Poetry.

Jamie, K. 2019. "Uncovering the Facts of the Scottish Clearances." *The New Statesman*, January 16, 2019. https://www.newstatesman.com/culture/books/2019/01/Scottish-Clearances-TM-Devine-review.

Kay, J. 2016. "Threshold." *Oral presentation to the Scottish Parliament*. Republished online, https://www.scottishpoetrylibrary.org.uk/poem/threshold/.

Levien, M. 2013. "Regimes of Dispossession: From Steel Towns to Special Economic Zones." *Development and Change* 44: 381–407. https://doi.org/10.1111/dech.12012.

Lovett, J. A. 2011. "Progressive Property in Action: The Land Reform (Scotland) Act 2003." *Nebraska Law Review* 89 (4): 739–818.

Lovett, J. A., and M. M. Combe. 2019. "The Parable of Portobello: Lessons and Questions from the First Urban Acquisition Under the Scottish Community Right-to-Buy Regime." *Montana Law Review* 80 (2): 211–228.

Marks, S. 2000. *The Riddle of All Constitutions: International Law, Democracy, and the Critique of Ideology*. Oxford: Oxford University Press.

Marks, S. 2008. *International Law on the Left: Re-examining Marxist Legacies*. Cambridge, UK: Cambridge University Press.

Marks, S. 2020. *A False Tree of Liberty: Human Rights in Radical Thought*. Oxford: Oxford University Press.

Marks, S. R., and A. Clapham. 2005. *International Human Rights Lexicon*. Oxford: Oxford University Press.

McCarthy, F. 2020. "Property Rights and Human Rights in Scottish Land Reform." In *Land Reform in Scotland: History, Law and Policy*. Edited by M. Combe, J. Glass, J., and A. Tindley, 213–235. Edinburgh: Edinburgh University Press.

McFadyen, M. 2014. "Scotland the Brand." *The National Collective*. July 29, 2014.

McGrath, J. 1981. *The Cheviot, the Stag and the Black, Black Oil*. London: Bloomsbury.

McHarg, A. 1999. "Reconciling Human Rights and the Public Interest: Conceptual Problems and Doctrinal Uncertainty in the Jurisprudence of the European Court of Human Rights." *The Modern Law Review* 62 (5): 671–696.

Mehta, L., G. J. Veldwisch, and J. Franco. 2012. "Introduction to the Special Issue: Water Grabbing? Focus on the (Re)Appropriation of Finite Water Resources." *Water Alternatives* 5 (2): 193–207.

Monbiot, G. 2013. *Feral: Searching for Enchantment on the Frontiers of Rewilding*. London: Penguin Books.

Morris, A. W. 2008. "Easing Conservation? Conservation Easements, Public Accountability, and Neoliberalism." *Geoforum* 39 (3): 1215–1227.

Nolan, A., B. Porter, and M. Langford. 2007. "The Justiciability of Social and Economic Rights: An Updated Appraisal." *CHRGJ Working Paper No. 15.*

Notess, L., P. Veit, I. Monterroso, Andiko, E. Sulle, A. M. Larson, A.-S. Gindroz, J. Quaedvlieg, and A. Williams. 2020. "Community Land Formalization and Company Land Acquisition Procedures: A Review of Thirty-Three Procedures in Fifteen Countries." *Land Use Policy* 110 (November). https://doi.org/10.1016/j .landusepol.2020.104461.

Peñalver, E. M. 2004. "Is Land Special? The Unjustified Preference for Landownership in Regulatory Takings Law." *Ecology Law Quarterly* 31 (2): 227–287.

Peñalver, E. M. 2009. "Land Virtues." *Cornell Law Review* 94 (4): 821–888.

Peñalver, E. M. 2010. "The Illusory Right to Abandon." *Michigan Law Review* 109 (2: 191–219.

Peñalver, E. M. 2011. "Property's Memories (The Social Function of Property: A Comparative Perspective)." *Fordham Law Review* 80 (3): 1071–1088.

Polanyi, K. 1944. *The Great Transformation.* London: Routledge.

Prebble, J. 1963. *The Highland Clearances.* London: Secker and Warburg.

Reid, A. 2019. "Land Reform at 20: What Does a Post-Feudal Era Look Like?" SPICe Spotlight, December 20, 2019. https://spice-spotlight.scot/2019/12/20/land -reform-at-20-what-does-a-post-feudal-era-look-like/.

Ross, A. R. 2014. *Grabbing Back: Essays against the Global Land Grab.* Oakland, CA: AK Press.

RRI (Rights and Resources Initiative). 2015. *Who Owns the World's Land?: A Global Baseline of Formally Recognized Indigenous and Community Land Rights.* Washington, DC: RRI. https://rightsandresources.org/wp-content/uploads /GlobalBaseline_web.pdf.

RRI. 2017. *Securing Community Land Rights: Priorities and Opportunities to Advance Climate and Sustainable Development Goals.* Washington, DC: RRI. https:// rightsandresources.org/wp-content/uploads/2017/09/Stockholm-Prorities-and -Opportunities-Brief.pdf

Salmond, A. 2013. *Keynote Address at the Community Land Scotland Annual Conference 2013.* Sabhal Mor Orstaig, Skye, June 7, 2013. http://www.andywightman .com/docs/Alex_Salmond_20130607.pdf.

Schabas, W. A. 1991. "The Omission of the Right to Property in the International Covenants." *Hague Yearbook of International Law* 4: 135–170.

Scoones, I., R. Smalley, R. Hall, D. Tsikita. 2019. "Narratives of Scarcity: Framing the Global Land Rush." *Geoforum* 101 (May): 231–241. https://doi.org/10.1016/j .geoforum.2018.06.006.

Scotsman. 2013. "Lairds Warn Holyrood Over New Land Buyout Powers." August 1, 2013. https://www.scotsman.com/news/politics/lairds-warn-holyrood-over-new -land-buy-out-powers-1566014.

Scottish Constitutional Convention. 1995. *Scotland's Parliament: Scotland's Right.* Edinburgh: Convention of Scottish Local Authorities.

Scottish Government. 2015. *One Million Acres by 2020: Strategy Report and Recommendations.* https://www.gov.scot/publications/one-million-acres-2020-strategy -report-recommendations-1-million-acre/.

Scottish Government. 2017a. *Estimate of Community Owned Land in Scotland 2017.* Community Ownership in Scotland. https://www.gov.scot/publications /estimate-community-owned-land-scotland-2017/.

Scottish Government. 2017b. *Scottish Land Rights and Responsibilities Statement.* September 28, 2017.

Scottish Government. 2019. *Community Ownership in Scotland: 2018: An Official Statistics Publication for Scotland.* Community Ownership in Scotland. https://www.gov.scot/publications/community-ownership-scotland-2018/.

Scottish Government. 2020. *The Right to Buy Land to Further Sustainable Development: BRIA.* Final Business and Regulatory Impact Assessment. https://www.gov.scot/publications/business-regulatory-impact-assessment-secondary-legislation-part-5-land-reform-scotland-act-2016-right-buy-land-further-sustainable-development/.

Scottish Government Newsroom. 2017. "Scotland's First Urban Right to Buy." May 9, 2017. https://news.gov.scot/news/scotlands-first-urban-right-to-buy.

Scottish Law Commission. 1999. *Report on Abolition of the Feudal System.* Edinburgh: HMSO.

Scottish Law Commission. 2000. *Report on Real Burdens.* Edinburgh: HMSO.

Scottish Law Commission. 2003. *Report on Law of the Foreshore and Seabed.* Edinburgh: HMSO.

Scottish Law Commission. 2006. *Report on Conversion of Long Leases.* Edinburgh: HMSO.

Scottish Parliament. 2001. *Policy Memorandum on the Land Reform (Scotland) Bill (SP Bill 44).* Edinburgh.

Scottish Parliament 2015. *Official Report of the Rural Affairs, Climate Change and Environment Committee.* Land Reform (Scotland) Bill, Evidence Session, October 7, 2015. http://www.parliament.scot/parliamentarybusiness/report.aspx?r=10140.

Scottish Parliament 2016. *Official Report: Meeting of the Parliament.* March 16, 2016, Session 4. http://www.parliament.scot/parliamentarybusiness/report.aspx?r=10440&mode=pdf.

Shields, K. 2015. "Tackling the Misuse of Rights Rhetoric in Land Reform Debate." *Scottish Human Rights Journal* 68: 1–4.

Shields, K. 2018. *Human Rights and the Work of the Scottish Land Commission: A Discussion Paper.* Scottish Land Commission. https://landcommission.gov.scot/downloads/5dd6a5d2e58f3_Land-Lines-Human-Rights-Kirsten-Shields-May-20182.pdf

Shields, K. 2022. *A Review of Evidence on Land Acquisition Powers and Land Ownership Restrictions in European Countries.* Scottish Government.

Shrubsole, G. 2019. *Who Owns England?: How We Lost Our Green and Pleasant Land, and How to Take It Back.* Glasgow: William Collins Pub.

SLC (Scottish Land Commission). 2018. *Programme of Work 2018–2021.* Scottish Land Commission. https://landcommission.gov.scot/about-us.

Sprankling, J. G. 2014. "The Global Right to Property." 52 *Columbia Journal of Transnational Law* 52 (April).

Oban Times. 2019. "Ardnamurchan Trust Wins Bid to Buy Lighthouse." September 26, 2019. https://www.pressreader.com/uk/the-oban-times/20190926/282926682117834.

Press & Journal. 2018. "Ulva Buyout Plan Receives £4.4M Boost from Scottish Land Fund." March 19, 2018. https://www.pressandjournal.co.uk/fp/news/highlands/1436600/ulva-buyout-plan-receives-4-4m-boost-from-scottish-land-fund/.

Telegraph. 2015a. "SNP to Target Landowners' Property Rights 'for Public Good.'" May 20, 2015.

Telegraph. 2015b. "SNP's Four Tests to Strip Lairds of Their Land." June 24, 2015. https://www.telegraph.co.uk/news/earth/countryside/11616876/SNP-to-target-landowners-property-rights-for-public-good.html.

Thompson, M. 2018. "From Co-Ops to Community Land Trusts: Tracing the Histori-cal Evolution and Policy Mobilities of Collaborative Housing Movements." *Housing, Theory and Society* 37 (1): 82–100.

United Nations. 1979. *Convention on the Elimination of All Forms of Discrimination against Women*. United Nations General Assembly. https://www.ohchr.org/en/professionalinterest/pages/cedaw.aspx.

United Nations. 2018. *United Nations Declaration on the Rights of Peasants and Other People Working in Rural Areas*. United Nations General Assembly. Session73. https://www.geneva-academy.ch/joomlatools-files/docman-files/UN%20 Declaration%20on%20the%20rights%20of%20peasants.pdf.

United Nations. 2021. *Call for Written Contributions to the Draft General Comment (No. 26) on Land and Economic, Social, and Cultural Rights*. Treaty Bodies. https://www.ohchr.org/EN/HRBodies/CESCR/Pages/CESCR-draft-GC-land .aspx.

Van Der Ploeg, J. D. 2009. *The New Peasantries: Struggles for Autonomy and Sustain-ability in an Era of Empire and Globalization*. London: Earthscan.

Via Campesina. 2009. *Declaration of Rights of Peasants, Women and Men*. https:// viacampesina.org/en/declaration-of-rights-of-peasants-women-and-men/

Waldron, J. 1988. *The Right to Private Property*. Oxford: Clarendon Press.

Waldron, J. 2000. "Homelessness and Community." *The University of Toronto Law Journal* 50 (4): 371–406.

Waldron, J. 2009. "Community and Property for Those Who Have Neither." *Theoreti-cal Inquiries in Law* 10 (1).

Waldron, J. 2011. "Socioeconomic Rights and Theories of Justice." *San Diego Law Review* 48 (3).

Waldron, J. 2012. *The Rule of Law and the Measure of Property*. Cambridge, UK: Cambridge University Press.

Wightman, A. 1996. *Who Owns Scotland*. Edinburgh: Canongate.

Wightman, A. 1999. *Scotland: Land and Power. An Agenda for Land Reform*. Edin-burgh: Luath.

Wightman, A. 2010. *The Poor Had No Lawyers*. Edinburgh: Birlinn.

Williams, J. M., and E. H. Gimenez. 2017. *Land Justice: Re-imagining Land, Food, and the Commons*. Berkeley: FoodFirst Books.

Wolford, W. 2010. *This Land Is Ours Now: Social Mobilization and the Meanings of Land in Brazil*. Durham, NC: Duke University Press.

World Bank. 2017. "Enabling the Business of Agriculture 2017." Washington, DC: World Bank.

Young, K. G. 2008. "The Minimum Core of Economic and Social Rights: A Concept in Search of Content." *Yale Journal of International Law* 33 (1): 113–174.

List of Contributors

Kati Álvarez is a professor of social work and jurisprudence at the Universidad Central del Ecuador in Quito, Ecuador.

Clint Carroll is an associate professor and associate chair of graduate studies in Native American and Indigenous studies at the University of Colorado at Boulder.

Michael Goldman is an associate professor of sociology and global studies at the University of Minnesota, Twin Cities.

Flora Lu is a professor of environmental studies at the University of California, Santa Cruz.

Richard Mbunda is a lecturer and doctoral student at the University of Dar es Salaam, Tanzania.

Gregg Mitman is the Vilas Research and William Coleman Professor of History of Science, Medical History, and Environmental Studies at the University of Wisconsin, Madison.

Paul Nadasdy is a professor of anthropology and American Indian and Indigenous studies at Cornell University.

Robert Nichols is a professor of history of consciousness at University of California, Santa Cruz.

Andrew Ofstehage is a postdoctoral associate at Cornell University.

Nancy Lee Peluso is the Henry J. Vaux Distinguished Professor of Forest Policy at the University of California, Berkeley.

Laura Schoenberger is an assistant professor at Durham University.

Kirsteen Shields is a lecturer in international law and food security at the University of Edinburgh.

Emmanuel Sulle is a researcher at the institute for poverty, land and agrarian studies.

Erik Swyngedouw is a professor of human geography at The University of Manchester.

Gabriela Valdivia is a professor of geography and chair of Latin American studies at the University of North Carolina at Chapel Hill.

Katherine Verdery is the Julien J. Studley Faculty Scholar and Distinguished Professor of Anthropology at CUNY, The Graduate Center.

Callum Ward is a post-doctoral fellow in human geography at Uppsala University, Sweden.

Ciara Wirth works at the Tiputini Biodiversity Station, Colegio de Ciencias Biológicas y Ambientales, Universidad San Francisco de Quito, Ecuador.

Wendy Wolford is the Robert A. and Ruth E. Polson Professor of Global Development at Cornell University.

Emmanuel King Urey Yarkpawolo is the founder of One Life Liberia and former country director of Liberia for Landesa.

Index

Page references to figures, illustrations, maps, and tables are italicized.

www.ingramcontent.com/pod-product-compliance
Lightning Source LLC
Chambersburg PA
CBHW030900270326
41929CB00008B/505